Catherine the Great and the Culture of Celebrity in the Eighteenth Century

Cultures of Early Modern Europe

Series Editors: Beat Kümin, Professor of Early Modern European History, University of Warwick, and Brian Cowan, Associate Professor and Canada Research Chair in Early Modern British History, McGill University

Editorial Board:

Adam Fox, University of Edinburgh, UK
Robert Frost, University of Aberdeen, UK
Molly Greene, University of Princeton, USA
Ben Schmidt, University of Washington, USA
Gerd Schwerhoff, University of Dresden, Germany
Francsesca Trivellato, University of Yale, USA
Francisca Loetz, University of Zurich, Switzerland

The "cultural turn" in the humanities has generated a wealth of new research topics and approaches. Focusing on the ways in which representations, perceptions and negotiations shaped people's lived experiences, the books in this series provide fascinating insights into the past. The series covers early modern culture in its broadest sense, inclusive of (but not restricted to) themes such as gender, identity, communities, mentalities, emotions, communication, ritual, space, food and drink, and material culture.

Published:

Food and Identity in England, 1540-1640, Paul S. Lloyd (2014)
The Birth of the English Kitchen, 1600-1850, Sara Pennell (2016)
Vagrancy in English Culture and Society, 1650-1750, David Hitchcock (2016)
Angelica's Book and the World of Reading in Late Renaissance Italy, Brendan Dooley (2016)
Gender, Culture and Politics in England, 1560-1640, Susan D. Amussen and David E. Underdown (2017)
Food, Religion, and Communities in Early Modern Europe, Christopher Kissane (2018)
Religion and Society at the Dawn of Modern Europe, Rudolf Schlögl (2020)
Power and Ceremony in European History: Rituals, Practices and Representative Bodies since the Late Middle Ages, Anna Kalinowska and Jonathan Spangler (eds.) with Pawel Tyszka
Private/Public in 18th-Century Scandinavia, Sari Nauman and Helle Vogt (eds.)
Catherine the Great and Celebrity Culture in the Eighteenth Century, Ruth Pritchard Dawson

Catherine the Great and the Culture of Celebrity in the Eighteenth Century

Ruth Pritchard Dawson

BLOOMSBURY ACADEMIC
LONDON • NEW YORK • OXFORD • NEW DELHI • SYDNEY

BLOOMSBURY ACADEMIC

Bloomsbury Publishing Plc

50 Bedford Square, London, WC1B 3DP, UK
1385 Broadway, New York, NY 10018, USA
29 Earlsfort Terrace, Dublin 2, Ireland

BLOOMSBURY, BLOOMSBURY ACADEMIC and the Diana logo are trademarks of
Bloomsbury Publishing Plc

First published in Great Britain 2021
Paperback edition first published 2024

Copyright © Ruth Pritchard Dawson, 2021

Ruth Pritchard Dawson has asserted their right under the Copyright, Designs and
Patents Act, 1988, to be identified as Author of this work.

Cover image: La Mascarade Belongs to: [Collection. Collection of Vinck. A century
of French history through print, 1770-1870. Vol. 26 (parts 4348-4477),
Ancien Régime and Revolution]

(Bibliothèque nationale de France)

All rights reserved. No part of this publication may be reproduced or transmitted
in any form or by any means, electronic or mechanical, including photocopying,
recording, or any information storage or retrieval system, without prior
permission in writing from the publishers.

Bloomsbury Publishing Plc does not have any control over, or responsibility for, any
third-party websites referred to or in this book. All internet addresses given in this
book were correct at the time of going to press. The author and publisher regret
any inconvenience caused if addresses have changed or sites have ceased
to exist, but can accept no responsibility for any such changes.

Every effort has been made to trace copyright holders and to obtain their
permissions for the use of copyright material. The publisher apologizes for any
errors or omissions and would be grateful if notified of any corrections that
should be incorporated in future reprints or editions of this book.

A catalogue record for this book is available from the British Library.

A catalog record for this book is available from the Library of Congress.

ISBN: HB: 978-1-3502-4462-7
PB: 978-1-3502-4466-5
ePDF: 978-1-3502-4463-4
eBook: 978-1-3502-4464-1

Typeset by Deanta Global Publishing Services, Chennai, India

To find out more about our authors and books visit www.bloomsbury.com
and sign up for our newsletters.

This book is joyfully dedicated to my patient, inspiring, and cherished husband Steve and to the beloved foursome, Robin, Adam, Iris, and Ian, who are always there to help.

Contents

List of Illustrations	x
Acknowledgments	xiv
Note on Translations	xvi
Note on Spelling	xvii
Introduction	1

I Celebrity Ingredients

1	Celebrity-Making Coup of 1762: The Crucial Role of Story	17
	Signs of Celebrity Emerging	19
	Catherine's Efforts to Control the Narrative: Her Manifestos and Their Reception	21
	The Matrix of Celebrity and Story	24
	New Accounts and Their Spread	25
2	Scandal and Engrossing Coup Backstories, until 1765	28
	The Tsar's Scandalous Death and the Tsarina's Alluringly Uncertain Future	28
	Reaching the Least Privileged Audiences with Words and Pictures	30
	Celebrity Tropes of Marital and Sexual Squabbles	34
	Challenges to Peter's Masculinity	37
3	Media Workers and Their Commodities in Word and Image	41
	Representing the Empress	41
	Making Visual Images	42
	Commodifying Further: Eighteenth-Century Celebrity Endorsements	57
4	Fans and Anti-Fans for a Commodity Empress	60
	Fan Access to Celebrity Discourse	62
	What Celebrity Offered Fans: From Entertainment and Identification to Fantasies of Social Mobility	66
	Ambivalence and Rejection: Criticism, Anger, and Anti-Fans	69
	"Europe's Tsarina"	72
5	The Star as Contributing Subject and Living Object	74
	Where Regal *Gloire* Meets Popular Celebrity	76

	Court Rituals of Seeing and Being Seen	78
	Impolitic but Indispensable Body and Mostly Male Watchers	80
	Shape, Appearance, and Decorum of the Visible Body and Face	81
	The Rude Body Visualized	82
	Aging	84
II	Engaging Themes, Sustaining Celebrity	
6	Woman Philosopher on the Throne	91
	Boundary Breaking Relationships	93
	Redemptive Early Projects	95
	Mid-Reign Cracks in Catherine's Enlightened Image, 1773–89	100
	Further Intellectual Engagements	102
7	Consuming Catherine II: Gender and Wealth	104
	The Complex Mix of Wealth and Gender	106
	Glamour	107
	Extravagant Display	109
	Art, Literature, Learning, and Patronage	110
8	Disconcerting Mother of Her Country: Gender and Power Again	116
	Russia's "Petticoat Government"	118
	Debut in Satires, Both Textual and Visual: Poland 1772–3	121
	"Astonisher of All Regions," from Constantinople to Amsterdam and Antwerp	125
	Outbreak of the Second Russo-Turkish War: More Political Cartoons	127
9	Empress of the Other	132
	Russia—Exotic or Barbaric?	132
	Pugachev Rebellion, 1773–5	136
	Others Who Spoke for Themselves: Catherine and Her Jewish Subjects	141
	1787: Crimea Trip and the Staged Exotic	143
III	Transgressions Accruing and Secrets Revealed	
10	Final Eight Years: Reassessment and Satirical Critique	151
	Metaphors of Gender and Sexuality and the Dominance of *An Imperial Stride!*	152
	Force Unsettling Gender: The Indeterminate-Androgynous Woman Ruler	155
	Ridiculous Heroine	157
	Lascivious Libertine	158
	Indecorous and Abject Being	162
	Monstrous-Feminine Body	164

11	Still Relishing the Failed Marriage, the Coup, and Its Deadly Aftermath	169
	The Dribble and Then Flood of Curiosity-Stoking Texts	170
	Skillful Narratives	174
	Unhappiness, Weakness, and Discord	177
	Sexual Difficulties	179
	Peter III's Mysterious Demise	181
12	The Lovers: Dabs of Fiction, Grains of Truth, Gobs of Scandal	186
	Phases of Lover Publicity	186
	Lovers Slipping into Print in Catherine's Last Decade	188
	Celebrity Appeal of Sexuality Reports	189
	Love Affair Trajectories	190
	The Gush of "Revelations" Posthumously	192
	Completing the Record of Catherine's Intimate Life	193
	Venomous Poetry and Further Fiction	196
13	Celebrity after Death	199
	Accounts and Images of Catherine II's Demise for All	199
	Further Accusations and Complex Response	203
	Criminality	206
	And Yet Ambivalence	207
	Invented Libertine Death as Crime and Punishment	208
	Becoming an Icon: Afterlife	210

Notes	213
Bibliography	256
Index	278

Illustrations

Frontispiece	Catharine, the present Empress of Russia	xviii
0.1	Catherine, riding astride, her hair flowing loosely down her back, leads the coup that puts her on the Russian throne	7
0.2	The empress visits the school for girls that she founded	8
0.3	Catherine II's commission of a statue of Peter the Great became one of the most noted sculptures of the eighteenth century	9
0.4	Catherine posts captured Turkish military banners to the grave of Peter the Great	10
0.5	Setting out in winter for her grand inspection tour to newly acquired territories on the Black Sea, Catherine rides in an open sleigh here, not in the roomy enclosed sledge of contemporary descriptions	11
0.6	Potemkin kneels at the feet of his former lover as she arrives at an extravagant party he gave for her	12
2.1	Johann Martin Will retold the coup in six scenes of action, the top row about Catherine II and the bottom about Peter III	32
3.1	To take advantage promptly of public attention to the new Russian empress, Pierre Adrien LeBeau (1744/8–1817) revised an earlier image of Catherine as grand duchess and enriched the grandeur of the print with an elaborate frame	43
3.2	Daniel Berger (1744–1824), in Berlin, relied on the same source image as LeBeau but depicted Catherine II wearing the insignia—sash, star, crown, and ermine cloak—that marked her new status as empress	44
3.3	Georg Siegmund Facius rests his profile-in-braids image of Catherine II on palm leaves and a branch of laurel	45
3.4	An anonymous engraver in Paris provided an unusual printed cursive statement about his source being a print—he mangles the engraver's name, Radigues—of a painting by Erichsen	46
3.5	On this woven commemorative cloth celebrating the Peace of Hubertusburg Catherine is depicted second from right; how such textiles were used is unknown	47
3.6	Charles Mosley, who worked mostly for booksellers in London, designed and engraved this postcard-sized print as a fashion picture of Catharine II wearing military "habit"	48
3.7	The popular terracotta specialist Nini made plaques in several designs showing Catherine II in profile	50
3.8	A well-made version of the profile-in-braids type has a caption intended to reach an audience in Spain but anomalies in word choice and spelling suggest the caption writer was not fully literate in Spanish	52

3.9	The publisher Duflos sold his fashion images in sets and offered them both plain and meticulously painted	53
3.10	An exquisite (now disassembled) miniature book depicted Catherine II among eight other, mostly German, rulers	54
3.11	A card for the shop "At the Russian Empress" in Vienna advertised in German and French the wonderful goods that could be purchased there	58
4.1	This clumsy invented image of Catherine II holding a huge scepter suggests an appeal to fans unfamiliar with state portraiture	62
4.2	This crudely made woodcut, on a page labeled *Depiction of Russian Empress Catherine II*, appeared in a Swiss Limping Messenger almanac for 1773	65
4.3	Puzzle prints such as this invited viewers to find silhouettes hidden in the scene and connect them with famous personalities, including the empress of Russia	67
5.1	Charles Turner Warren projected the braids print to full length to invent a luxurious and exotically Russian fashion—and a stiff pose—for the empress in 1789	77
5.2	Unlike the anonymous French head-and-shoulders excerpt of Eriksen's grand portrait of Catherine II standing before a mirror (Figure 3.4), Cornelis van Noorde added a sumptuous backdrop to his Dutch-captioned image	82
5.3	Augustin de Saint-Aubin's print, made in Paris between 1784 and 1790, classicizes Catherine II and faintly suggests her aging	85
5.4	Neatly capturing the anti-monarchical spirit of the French Revolution, *Jeu de quilles républicain* uses a bowling game to satirize Catherine II as an ugly hag in an old-fashioned court dress and standing in the absurd and offensive colossus pose from an earlier satire, *An Imperial Stride!* (Figure 10.1)	86
5.5	The details in *Jeu de quills républicain* invite the viewer to look closely and see Catherine II depicted as a hideous and aged empress with a mask-like face and clawed hands	87
6.1	A Russian medal that signaled Catherine's dedication to both learning and war by depicting her as Minerva was copied on a complex plate	93
7.1	Catherine's costly chains of office and other jewels are shown in a print made by Caroline Watson in 1787	108
7.2	Catherine II used commemorative medals as a form of publicity within and beyond her domains, in this case, celebrating her famous statue of Peter I	113
8.1, 8.2	Printmakers such as Johann Friedrich Bause used standard monarchical portraiture to depict both Peter III and Catherine II, but with subtle gendered differences beyond dress and hairstyle	119
8.3	Lavater, in his *Physiognomy*, illustrated his claims about Catherine II's "manly spirit" with a profile portrait that gave her a close physical resemblance to both Frederick II of Prussia and, below him, Voltaire	121

8.4	"Le Gateau des Rois/The Troelfth Cake," in its several versions, showed a mocking representation of Catherine II and the kings of Austria and Prussia planning to seize territory from Poland, to the shock of the Polish king, who grabs for his slipping crown as Catherine looks on	123
8.5	*Vorstellung und Abbildung* (Presentation and Illustration) is a woodcut broadsheet printed in Copenhagen by Johan Rudolph Thiele and partly painted	126
8.6	In belligerent German verses below their images, Catherine II and Joseph II speak with each other about their eagerness to attack the sultan, who stands apart, proclaiming his own military might and asserting in his verses that Mohamed is on his side	128
8.7	In *Kriegs Theater*, the possible meanings of "theater of war" suggest more than merely an elegantly dressed woman in a fine private room	129
8.8	The anonymous *Christian Amazon* of 1787 shows the threesome of Joseph, Catherine, and the Ottoman sultan again	130
9.1	An allegorical print about Voltaire's death used Catherine II to represent Asia, although her clinging gown was more reminiscent of classical Greece	133
9.2	One of the few attempts to depict the Crimea trip, a hand-colored print by Johann Hieronymus Löschenkohl, shows Joseph II and Catherine II meeting together, with members of their entourage, in an empty landscape	145
9.3	A few years before the empress set out for Kiev on the way to the Crimea, a print dated 1784 depicted her comfortable means of riding along bonfire-lit tracks in winter	146
9.4	An undated allegorical print of Joseph II, the sultan, and Catherine II depicts the three rulers together	148
10.1	*An Imperial Stride!* satirizes Catherine II's aggression against the Ottomans as a giant step she is taking over the heads of amazed monarchs from St. Petersburg to Constantinople	153
10.2	*L'Enjambee Imperiale* is the French version of *An Imperial Stride*, but whether it came first is unclear. Both satires, but especially this bare-breasted French one, became immensely well known and were repeatedly cited by French and English visual caricaturists	154
10.3	In *The Prussian Prizefighter*, though the half-naked Russian empress looks powerful, her sex is indeterminate	156
10.4	In the anonymous *La Mascarade* (1791), Catherine II, receives dwarfish émigrés from revolutionary France	157
10.5	*Tous mes beaux Pays-bas* (All my beautiful Low Countries) uses a pornographic image of Catherine II to depict the Austrian emperor's helpless inability to counter Belgian independence	159
10.6	*An Amusing State of Uncertainty*, citing the head and bare breasts of *L'Enjambee Imperiale*, shows Catherine with two competing illicit suitors, the British politicians William Pitt "the Younger" and Charles James Fox	160

10.7	Politics is represented as sexual activity in an anonymous British satirical print, *Saint Catharine and St. George,* with a whorish Catherine in charge	161
10.8	Cruikshank's *Bobadil Disgraced or Kate in a Rage* depicts a fierce and determined Catherine mistreating two military officers and transgressing the strictures on upper-class feminine decorum	163
10.9	Catherine II, her upper body again echoing *L'Enjambee Imperiale*, is inserted here into a whole scene of abject revolutionary bodies raining excrement down on the rulers and leaders of Europe, who are only partially protected by a black imperial eagle and crown	164
10.10	*The Northen Bugga Bo*, addressing Catherine's second war with the Ottomans, depicts her as a penis-equipped, gigantic, crowned figure wearing the empress's iconic dress and a peculiar, canon-like undergarment (the reverse of the canon in Figure 10.9)	165
10.11	Late in Catherine II's reign, Isaac Cruikshank's *Royal Recreation* satirized her repulsively celebrating the slaughter of Polish women and children	166
11.1	The stipled illustration in one of the numerous biographies of the empress brings Peter and Catherine together again and notes that, while he was emperor for six months, she reigned for thirty-five years	172
11.2	The volume of Voltaire's correspondence with Catherine II included the first print, by Jean Baptiste Fosseyeux, that showed a small excerpt of Erichsen's great equestrian painting of the empress conducting her coup against Peter III	179
12.1	Catherine's pursuit of Potemkin in his monastic cell is depicted in Laveaux's *Histoire secrète* and in its translations, such as here in the Dutch version	193
13.1	In *Representation of the Russian Empress Catherine II Surprised by Death*, the slender empress is elegantly gowned and wears a huge ring, but the imperial crown is already slipping from her head	200
13.2	An anonymous German artist imagined the Russian setting of Catherine II lying in state, with bearded priests and prostrating mourners	201
13.3	Cruikshank's furious etching of Catherine II's death, hand colored in this instance, is dated December 26, 1796, less than two weeks after news of her demise reached London	202
13.4	In a large foldout print, a beautiful young Catherine sits astride a festively accoutered white horse amid a crowd of glad courtiers and soldiers	209

Acknowledgments

During the two decades that I have worked on this book, I have been endlessly indebted to a large and diverse group of friends, scholars, and organizations. At the top of the organization list is the Institute of Modern Languages Research, which has undergone three name changes over the period. This unit of the School of Advanced Studies at the University of London has provided an inspiring scholarly home for me in Europe; Jane Lewin and Godela Weiss-Sussex in particular have been unwavering in their encouragement and help. The Women's Studies Department at the University of Hawaii at Mānoa, my wonderful home department, has been fundamental to my development as a feminist scholar and has given me multiple opportunities to present the various phases of my work. The Klassik Stiftung Weimar provided crucial assistance at the start with a stipend and residency in their haven of eighteenth-century culture. Print collections and libraries both there and from St. Petersburg to Honolulu have allowed me to use treasured sheets and volumes. I especially thank the Russian National Library, the Staatsbibliothek Berlin, the Kupferstichkabinet in Berlin, Herzogin Anna Amalia Bibliothek in Weimar, the Austrian National Library and its digital ANNO, the Bibliotheque Nationale de France, the British Museum (for prints), the British Library (for newspapers, books, and pamphlets), Senate House Library of the University of London, Hamilton Library at the University of Hawaii at Mānoa, and a host of other libraries as well; at each of these I was the beneficiary of knowledgeable librarians, to whom I am profoundly grateful. Meanwhile, I am also indebted to all the libraries participating in the amazing projects of Google Books and the Hatha Trust. They have sometimes revealed gems I had missed and often allowed me to double-check my records, especially the handwritten notes I scribbled years ago when my laptop's batteries failed after long hours of typing.

Two nineteenth-century Russian men and one British woman were my most constant guides. B. von Bilbassoff (1838–1904), as his name appears on the title page of his book, ran into problems with the censor in Russia and so published in German his massive bibliography of every separate publication he could find about Catherine II that had appeared in print outside of Russia. (Careful bibliographers today use the transliteration V. A. Bil'basov.) For the years of interest to me, between 1762, when Catherine came to the throne, and 1810, he provided me with an annotated baseline list of 890 items to look for—biographies, polemical pamphlets, novels, poems, travel books, and even operas in which she was allegorized.

D. A. (Dmitriĭ Aleksandrovich) Rovinskiĭ (1824–95), another brilliant and diligent nineteenth-century Russian scholar, is Bilbassoff's counterpart for prints. His list of printed portraits of Catherine II is part of an astonishing work of erudition in which all such portraits of any historically specific Russian individual are listed. It was a happy day in the Kupferstichkabinet in Berlin when the Russian specialist there, Frau Jelena

Funck, told me about his hard-to-find catalog and very generously offered to xerox the crucial pages for me in which he identified over 450 different images on paper that had labels in one of the languages of Western Europe (and yet more with labels in Russian, of course); he complemented his description in Russian of each image with replication in the original language—French, Italian, English, German, Greek, Russian, and so on—of all of each print's text. Importantly for my purposes, he included every picture, not just the fine ones that meet high aesthetic criteria, and the organization of his work on Catherine gave me a usable way to categorize the images I was accumulating: Frontal images, profiles, scenes, caricatures. Also invaluable were the small reproductions, scattered through the pages of his book, of a sampling of the itemized images. These pictures helped to clarify the Russian text for me—I can decipher but not actually read Russian—but also meant that I could usually insert unlisted pictures into his system. With Rovinskii's irreplaceable aid, and again working in Britain, Germany, France, Austria, Hungary, Russia, the United States, and, eventually, online, I have found a wide further array of images of Catherine the Great.

As for the British woman, I owe several aspects of my theory and methodology to Princess Diana (1961–97), a modern royal celebrity, who, like Catherine, found herself in prolonged and distressing limbo seeking to be accepted at the palace, waiting for her husband to take the throne, and growing away from him emotionally. As she made her way through marriage and motherhood, through disaster and divorce, she awakened an abundance of fantasies in her audience, and elicited floods of text. Death was not the end, but rather, as with Catherine's death, a new opening of representations—particularly by survivors with varied stakes in her reputation. Diana pointed the way for me to see eighteenth-century public reception of Catherine II outside the northern parts of Europe in terms of celebrity.

Part of the work on this book that I especially treasure is the acquaintances it has enabled with distinguished scholars of Slavic studies, especially Simon Dixon, Roger Bartlett, and Anthony Cross. An afternoon in Highgate discussing my project with Professor Isabel de Madariaga was a special joy, but benefiting from the expertise of two American Slavicists, Erin McBurney and my colleague Lurana Donnels O'Malley, has also been immensely helpful. Consultation with art specialists—most memorably Elizaveta Renne at the Hermitage Museum—was indispensable for my analysis and understanding of the visual materials that are a crucial part of my argument. Experts, whose names I too often did not learn, in London at the Print Room of the British Museum, in the National Portrait Gallery, in the National Gallery, and, most recently, Rosie Razzall of the Royal Collection Trust, gave me invaluable insights about the engravings, paintings, and plaques that I have found representing Catherine. Then there are the many colleagues from near and far who challenged and encouraged me along the way, beginning with Cornelia Moore, Silke and Detlef Klotz, and Rüdiger Görner, and including Naomi Siegel, Heide Wunder, Falko Schnicke, Christian Klein, Peter Nusser, Meda Chesney-Lind, Kathy Ferguson, the late George Simson, and Craig Howes, to name only a few (and with apologies to the many, many others).

Finally, I cannot thank my writing group enough for their tolerance, patience, and thoughtful commentary over the years, particularly the indomitable and generous Kathy Phillips and the incisive, always helpful Deborah Ross.

Note on Translations

When eighteenth- or early nineteenth-century English translations of cited texts were available, I have used them (unless otherwise noted). For my own translations and for reassurance about my understanding of eighteenth-century expressions in a variety of languages, I received generous help from patient colleagues in London and Hawaii, but especially Cornelia Moore, Katia Pizzi, Jean Toyama, Marie-Jose Fassioto, and Jochem Kiesewetter.

Note on Spelling

Where available, I am following the transliteration of Slavic names from *Webster's New Biographical Dictionary*. For names that do not appear there, I adopt what appears to be the predominant current usage. For artists, I use the Union List of Artists Names Online.

CATHARINE, the present EMPRESS of RUSSIA.

Introduction

A swift coup that she launched against her husband, the tsar of Russia, made the newly minted Catherine II instantly famous in the Europe of her time. Information about the brash usurper, suddenly the richest and most powerful woman in the world but originally only a minor German princess, reached not just rulers and governments but also a distant populace in the west of Europe for whom accounts of her had no material utility. Their fascination, however, and their desire to acquire more particulars quickly turned Catherine II into a modern international celebrity and the first who was a woman. Her socially and economically most privileged contemporaries across Europe, the royalty and upper aristocracy who were her approximate international peers, were riveted too, but it was members of society from the lower aristocracy down to even the most disadvantaged urban and rural dwellers[1] whose curiosity generated the piles of print, heaps of pictures, and medleys of songs about the new empress that qualify her, this book argues, as an eighteenth-century celebrity. An immense gulf in daily life, education, wealth, manners, and, all-important at the time, rank separated both lower-level aristocrats and all commoners from the empress. Yet exactly the multiple conditions of separation that made accessibility to Catherine II and her world utterly impractical for distant viewers, readers, and listeners are typical of fandom; they invite engrossed observers to focus on the famous person's private life and persona, savoring gossip about her with others, testing the possibilities of identification, and sometimes practicing the scorn that shimmering celebrity discourse may also elicit.

Such discourse required mass media, or at least large-scale media, exactly as was developing in eighteenth-century towns and cities from Hamburg to Rome and from Vienna to Dublin. Writers and editors of newspapers and magazines, picture makers and printsellers constantly looked for new material and gladly commodified the interest of fans and potential fans by covering the faraway empress. Peddlers, itinerant singers and storytellers, and puppeteers pausing in marketplaces large and small across Europe played their part too. Often, over the thirty-four years of Catherine II's remarkable and sometimes shocking reign, such colporteurs accompanied their songs and rhymed news reports with strips of pictures painted on banners, similar in narrative quality, though not in elegance to a set of eight tiny pictures that the engraver Daniel Chodowiecki in Berlin published with bilingual captions. (Six are reproduced in this chapter; two that did not include the figure of the empress are omitted.) His meticulous scenes were included in a little book—a "calendar" or almanac—about the size of a deck of cards, that was meant to fit easily in an eighteenth-century pocket. Along with the pictures, in both the French and German editions of the *Historical-Genealogical Calendar* for the year 1797, was also an essay about the recently deceased tsarina and an array of further pictures of her and related to her.[2]

Celebrity, as it is understood today, occurs when an audience establishes an intense and un-pragmatic, parasocial relation to a famous contemporary based in large part on representations of that person that are mediated and widely commodified.[3] Is it anachronistic to read this form of celebrity into eighteenth-century evidence? As Robert Darnton has repeatedly argued regarding France in the ancien régime, the responses of audiences "took place in a mental world so different from our own that we cannot project our experience onto" them.[4] Still, recent scholarship has shown that the cultural, economic, and social conditions necessary for celebrity discourse had come into existence in much of eighteenth-century Europe. Though the very word "celebrity" in, for example, French, English, and German appeared mostly in its older usage as a synonym for celebration or to indicate well-deserved notability, it was also deployed, with hints of triviality, ambivalence, or worse, to indicate a new and different phenomenon of crowd-pleasing fame.[5] (What did not emerge until the nineteenth century was the use of the term to designate individual figures who had captured the public imagination.)[6] A stern letter to the editor of a London newspaper, for example, targeted what it calls the "sort of celebrity" enveloping Rear-Admiral Samuel Hood in 1784. Dismissing the naval officer's alleged heroism and complaining of "the manufacture" of his "popularity," the letter notes the thrilled crowds greeting Hood, vast newspaper coverage of his every move, and countless printshop portraits of him, "at large or in miniature."[7] Hood was not alone. Certain locally and regionally renowned actors, dancers, musicians, and writers of the period, recent scholarship shows, were marked by similar avid but contested popular reception.[8] A few political figures too—from Henry Sacheverell and Benjamin Franklin to Mirabeau and Napoleon, for instance—acquired such celebrity, providing fodder for sociable interaction among observers and arousing ardent interest to the point of identification.[9]

But eighteenth-century monarchs? Could they be celebrities? It is the argument of this book that a member of royalty might occasionally become not just well known, influential, controversial, or famous, but renowned in the manner of celebrity among ordinary people. That eighteenth-century media workers far outside the domains of Catherine II designed, produced, and sold innumerable representations of her for non-elite customers shows the upstart empress as part of this contested phenomenon of popular culture, this "new market-oriented, media-driven concept of fame," as Heather McPherson calls it.[10] The location of the empress's non-elite audiences away from her power contributes to the argument for her celebrity, and this book also enlarges the geography of eighteenth-century celebrity culture to all of Central, Western, and Southern Europe, well beyond the areas addressed in current scholarship.[11] Popular attention to Catherine II, I argue, was based on her story of scandal and social mobility, her savvy patronage choices, her whiff of exoticism, her impolitic female body, and more. Despite her primary public status as unmistakably political—which classes her as a political celebrity—audiences outside her domains, protected from her by distance, could treat her as an almost imaginary figure, and for long periods they cared little or nothing about her imperial politics, either diplomatic or military. Catherine II became an international celebrity, probably the first modern woman in this category.

As the letter about Admiral Hood complained, celebrity often has and had negative connotations stemming, as Antoine Lilti notes, from its being "both sought after, as a modern form of social prestige, and decried as a media artifice,"[12] a "manufacture." On a deeper level, social critics charge celebrity discourse with using "spectatorial pleasure and identification" to lure fans into a "system of false promise" that leaves their lived conditions unchanged[13] and with giving credibility and rewards to questionable individuals who often display no significant skills, achievements, or socially approved qualities. In celebrity culture, as Ellis Cashmore writes, "fame and accomplishments are decoupled."[14] A hero can gain celebrity, but the moral and social aspects of heroism are supplementary, not essential for celebrity discourse. Rather, this form of popular adulation emphasizes notions of a private person who can be located beyond or behind the elevated figure's public façade.

Yet that façade is and was important, especially to rulers. Louis XIV of France, who died in 1714, fifteen years before Catherine II's birth, established a pattern of daunting majestic glory to control his court and country and to compete with rival monarchs. Following the same system, the Russian tsarina demonstrated awesome and ostentatiously magnificent imperial *gloire*. That such courtly representation and the official and unofficial publicity of it were apt for eliciting spectatorial pleasure from distant anonymous publics about whom Catherine cared (almost) nothing was entirely incidental to her, but precisely her efforts to attain *gloire* could mesh neatly with the urges of growing crowds of capitalist media makers, distributors, and venders hoping to sell accounts and images of renowned figures to non-elite buyers. Media workers living beyond Russian control could feed and foster the tsarina's popular fame by crafting abundant, affordable versions of her that were calculated to generate audience fantasies and desires. Non-elite potential buyers of such products in the center and west of Europe were evolving in ways that made them more receptive to such potential celebrity discourse. Their increasing secularism and changing reading habits produced the space and demand for new published materials and encouraged, as Chris Rojek argues, new feelings of parasocial relationship that celebrity discourse seemed to offer.[15] When gentry, burgers, shopkeepers, hired laborers, peasants, and more read or heard accounts of well-storied, distant Catherine II, many developed the interest and feelings—even if completely one-sided, unwarranted, and possibly ambivalent or even hostile—that made her a celebrity.[16] Their attention to her in the decades after the coup fluctuated irregularly, both as international relations changed and as seeming glimpses emerged of her life at court, her private concerns, and her engagement with scholars, artists, and potential colonists close to the audiences' homes.

Controversial Catherine II, admirable to some, villainous to others, with both fans and anti-fans, was not alone among eighteenth-century rulers who became celebrities, at least regionally. The popular fame of two German monarchs, Maria Theresa (1717–80) of the Habsburg Empire and her northern rival, Frederick II (1712–86) of Prussia, started in 1740, two decades earlier than Catherine's, and then, beginning in 1762, was nourished or neglected under the influence of many of the same events and conditions as hers—though often with radically different implications of politics, nation, and geography. The martial Frederick, who as of 1747 was already called "the Great" because of his military achievements, offered the eighteenth-century public a distinctly masculine version of celebrity, while Maria Theresa, as another unwelcome woman attempting to succeed a man to a mighty empire, offered a feminine version, resembling Catherine in this respect but not in others.

Maria Theresa, twenty-three years old in 1740 when she became the monarch in thriving and elegant Vienna, had a dynastic history that traced to the eleventh century. She was set to inherit vast territories along with a safe full of famous crowns. Her army, however, was a hodgepodge, the finances of her domains were disastrous, and the vast, but uneven, hereditary Habsburg territories that she ruled, including the whole southern half of Central Europe to the border of the Ottoman Empire plus pieces scattered from Naples in the south to most of present-day Belgium in the north, did not even have a unifying name. Also, as a woman, she was not able to gain the main traditional title of her dynasty, emperor of the Holy Roman Empire; that status required election by a select group of powerful princes not inclined to gender experiments. Her husband, whom she had chosen herself, could be of only limited help in her struggle to preserve her dynasty's power; he had the title of Duke of Lothringia but no longer ruled any territory.

When the 28-year-old Frederick II gained his throne a few months before Maria Theresa took hers, his capital, Berlin, was undistinguished and his kingdom little known. It had no glorious history and no significant political clout, though it could boast of its self-proclaimed status as a kingdom, its solid finances, and its large and well-trained (also unused) army, whose status the young king was eager to switch from display to deploy. Relishing the fragility of Maria Theresa's claim to power, a claim her just deceased father had worked feverishly for years to secure, Frederick invaded and seized one of her richest provinces, Silesia. A host of other princes and princelings, hungry for territories and titles, including that of emperor of the Holy Roman Empire, quickly joined in. The multiple wars that resulted lasted until 1748 and then resumed in 1756 as Maria Theresa repeatedly but vainly tried to recover her lost province from the Prussian king. Eventually, her husband was able to draw on his wife's dynastic credentials to obtain the coveted emperor title. Although Maria Theresa rejected the empty designation of empress, for which her husband's new rank qualified her, she was widely labeled the empress-queen.

Frederick's original invasion of Maria Theresa's domains and the Habsburg monarch's spirited and well-publicized resistance quickly made the two rulers famous within Germany, or rather within the extensive patchwork of principalities, baronies, duchies, ecclesiastical states, free imperial cities, and the like that were loosely knitted together under the ancient name and institutions of the Holy Roman Empire of the German Nation.[17] This is a now almost forgotten conglomeration that included part of the territories both of the king and of the empress-queen. Overtly, eighteenth-century monarchs cared little or nothing about what non-elite folk thought of them, but Frederick, whose overwhelming obsession was with the combined standing of himself and of previously lackluster Prussia, sometimes resorted to acts of popular publicity as a means of competing with other sovereigns,[18] and Maria Theresa, passionate about the past and future glory of her motley dynasty too, used a range of strategies that produced news extending beyond the most privileged few. To fulfill, for example, one of the traditional components of the Hungarian coronation ritual, she gained equestrian skills; to offset disadvantages that gender imposed on her, she held audiences in the rooms of her palace that were considered masculine; and to reassure both adversaries and supporters of the eventual return to traditional norms of male power, she brandished her baby son at key moments.[19] In short, the magnification of monarchical glory that Frederick and Maria Theresa practiced took many forms, some of which could lead to the kind of broad publicity conducive to celebrity. Their personal lives, as displayed in public words and images, contributed to their popular reception too, matching them well with their younger contemporary in Russia. Yet the magnitude of attention they received outside their own combined territories, especially the amount of commodified attention, as indicated by the abundance of celebrity products not made for their diverse subjects, dwindles in comparison with that of the captivating Empress Catherine II in St. Petersburg and gives Frederick and Maria Theresa no substantial claim to international celebrity. Still, both the king and the empress-queen provide valuable points of comparison in the chapters that follow.

Celebrity depends significantly on the lifetimes of stars and their fans overlapping. Antoine Lilti says celebrity's public "is defined not by rational arguments but by sharing the same curiosity and the same beliefs, by being interested in the same things at the same time and by being aware of this simultaneity."[20] When death interrupts the audience's experience of simultaneity and of ever unfolding story, a dead celebrity must either disappear or, after a few years, I argue, change into an icon, part of the society's cultural vocabulary.[21] Late in 1796, four years after the traumatic executions in France of Louis XVI and Marie Antoinette, at a time when revolution in France had abruptly affected public attitudes toward kings and empresses, Catherine II died. The new tsar, her son Paul (1754–1801), soon revealed his distaste for his mother, whereupon any previous wariness outside of Russia about criticizing the tsarina vanished. Now, attacks on her reputation appeared in newspapers and bookshops across Western Europe. Intrigued and sometimes horrified distant audiences of ordinary folk could read the accounts of favorites and lovers that were previously snickered over only by diplomats perusing secret dispatches. Yet suddenly, beginning in 1801, after the tyrannical Paul had been murdered in his bed and replaced by his son, one of Catherine's beloved grandsons, Alexander (1777–1825), representations of the great eighteenth-century empress changed again, shifted by new political tides, especially as chaotic relations between Russia and Napoleonic France washed back and forth and as propaganda correspondingly changed direction. Taking into account the gradual demise of aging fans who had outlived Catherine and the many changes in European society around 1810 that affected how a new public would respond to the discourse surrounding the eighteenth-century empress, the last phase of her celebrity, I argue, ended then; after 1810, her notorious fame as an icon would start.

I began seeing Catherine II, born as obscure Princess Sophie Friederike Auguste von Anhalt-Zerbst-Dornburg, as an eighteenth-century celebrity while I worked on a book about German women writers. I was intrigued to find that the empress was a playwright and that several of her comedies and dramas had been published in French and German as well as Russian during her lifetime. I was also struck that other women whom I was researching had mentioned her as though they were her fans. I saw that ordinary readers and listeners far from the empress's territories might have responded to Catherine II—she changed her name when she converted to the

Russian Orthodox Church before marrying the Russian heir to the throne—the way many of my contemporaries responded to Princess Diana. Both during her lifetime and, significantly for my analysis, after her death, superabundant representations of Diana evoked passionate attention and identification among ordinary people near and far.

Catherine's status as a celebrity in the west of Europe is not as instantly obvious as Diana's. Direct fan evidence of the kind I had noticed among a few German women is sparse.[22] Indirect evidence, however—representations in words and images that fit celebrity discourse by depicting Catherine II in private or personal terms or by touching themes that might elicit the daydreams of a general public outside her realms—is plentiful. When necessary, I use language to indicate a representation's intended readers or viewers. The fact that, for practical and political reasons, virtually all representations of the empress in Western European languages were produced outside Russia's borders, beyond Catherine's direct control, adds significantly to their variety and their importance for celebrity. Since the mid-eighteenth century is when large-scale journalistic media and extensive media distribution were underway, Catherine II could be followed approximately in "real time" by a substantial non-elite audience of fans far from St. Petersburg or Moscow.

Although responses to a celebrity may be locally inflected, my analysis mainly omits exploring how particular texts are imbricated in the specific national identities suggested by their writers or presumed audiences. I try, however, to point out the immediate political context when it is especially salient to a work. Most of all, as Toril Moi writes, even when we "use the same language," we "have different interests—. . . political and power-related interests which intersect in the sign. The meaning of the sign is thrown open—the sign becomes polysemic rather than univocal."[23] Some writers and artists chose genres that rely clearly on this openness—satires, for example—that repeatedly produced a different meaning from the official words or images to which they alluded. Other genres, such as newspaper items, usually seemed to aim for a single meaning but could not prevent the polysemic readings that their audiences produced and that give me pause as an interpreter of eighteenth-century texts today. The issue is especially important for celebrity: try as they might, the central figures in celebrity discourse do not control how they are represented or how their representations are read.

The little suite of scenes incised by Daniel Chodowiecki, each carefully labeled in German and French, can be used to preview the book sections and chapters that follow and to suggest their chronological flow. Part I, "Celebrity Ingredients," explores in five chapters the key components of Catherine II's popular reception. Chapter 1, showing her dramatic introduction to an astonished and fascinated foreign audience, traces the public communication of the coup as it moved to the capitols, cities, and towns of central and Western Europe and argues that the use specifically of story was crucial to the emergence of her celebrity. The first of the Chodowiecki images (Figure 0.1) depicts this scandalous debut, with Catherine in military uniform riding to compel her husband Peter III's abdication. Chapter 2 emphasizes the role of controversy in sustaining the first burst of publicity; as the miniature print of her cross-dressed figure hints, European observers had plenty of scandal to gobble up as they read the shocking and often contradictory accounts both by backers of the new empress and

Figure 0.1 Catherine, riding astride, her hair flowing loosely down her back, leads the coup that puts her on the Russian throne. Source: *Historisch-genealogischer Calender auf das Gemein-Jahr 1798*. Berlin: Unger, 1797. Public Domain.

by defenders of soon dead Peter, each attempting to make or unmake Catherine as empress. Transformed political considerations, as well as the celebrity discourse suddenly swirling around Catherine II, induced immediate lascivious speculation about her sexual body as well.

Chodowiecki's prints, both as the glorification of a ruler and as themselves commodities, exemplify the role of media workers in transmuting famous people into celebrities, the topic of Chapter 3. Outside of Russia, beyond the empress's direct control, rich opportunities arose for media workers of all kinds to commodify Catherine II, producing and selling words and images about her that both induced and fed on her celebrity. The particular technologies and genres on which artists, especially printmakers, had to rely require special consideration as they worked to produce (relatively) affordable representations of the empress. Over the years of her reign, the commercial exploitation of Catherine's name and title in the promotion of assorted merchandise from toothpaste to carriages further affirmed her celebrity.

Chapter 4 uses both the scattered direct evidence of fan enthusiasm and the rich record of indirect signs to show that for a growing potential audience of non-elite observers—many literate, but many not—in eighteenth-century Western Europe, fandom promised benefits ranging from entertainment and sociability to private fantasy and identification. It could supply imagined proximity to inaccessible and highly mediated famous individuals and so gave diverse audiences—from rich merchants and lesser gentry to the urban poor and even landless farmworkers—the chance both to admire and—as anti-fans—to condemn the celebrity tsarina's unattainable power, individual choices, and, on occasion, transgressive behavior.

Chapter 5 examines the dual role of the star in celebrity discourse as active subject and passive object, both shown in the Chodowiecki prints. The chapter considers too the attitudes of media workers (and, through them, of fans) toward the tsarina's physical body. I argue that when Catherine II participated in the standard, eighteenth-century, monarchical competition for *gloire*, and when she occasionally also directly addressed less-privileged distant contemporaries, she seemed to reveal a (much glamorized) self, and that, with this direct or indirect visibility to a non-elite public, she became an object of often fantasy-filled scrutiny. Though the Chodowiecki miniatures purportedly refer, for example, to events over the more than three decades of Catherine II's reign, the depicted empress remains slim, fashionable, graceful, elegant, and almost ageless in

Figure 0.2 The empress visits the school for girls that she founded. Source: *Historisch-genealogischer Calender auf das Gemein-Jahr 1798*. Berlin: Unger, 1797. Public Domain.

each. Other images over her reign and after her death showed her impolitic female body in many different ways, recording and arousing various gendered fantasies and fears.

Part II, "Engaging Themes, Sustaining Celebrity," explores particular elements of Catherine II's distant non-elite representation over the early and middle courses of her reign. Chapter 6 examines how, as a new empress, she undertook several well-publicized Enlightenment projects, such as the school for girls that Chodowiecki shows Catherine visiting (Figure 0.2), and argues that her reputation for Enlightenment enabled knowledgeable segments of her distant audience to overcome their revulsion at Peter III's overthrow and death and so helped to legitimize her on the throne. By the middle of her reign, however, cracks were developing in this image.

Chapter 7 addresses Catherine II's fantasy-inducing wealth and outsized expenditures, as hinted in Chodowiecki's picture of the immense and costly statue of Peter the Great that was one of her famous mid-reign arts project (Figure 0.3). Her name in minuscule letters and her precursor's are both legible on the pedestal in the print. The chapter argues that the extravagant displays of *gloire* among elites became celebrity-

Figure 0.3 Catherine II's commission of a statue of Peter the Great became one of the most noted sculptures of the eighteenth century. Source: *Historisch-genealogischer Calender auf das Gemein-Jahr 1798*. Berlin: Unger, 1797. Public Domain.

making glamor in the eyes of the middling classes. The chapter examines the public attention excited by Catherine's purchases of "positional goods" (status-signaling objects such as diamonds and artworks) and by her patronage of artists, art collectors, and writers outside Russia.

Chapter 8 explores the clash between prevailing gender expectations for women (especially motherhood and marriage or remarriage) and the immense power and authority of the autonomous Russian monarch. All this sparked exactly the kind of lively discourse that promoted and maintained celebrity, often converting even her political and military actions (partitioning Poland, protecting trade, warring with Turkey) into celebrity-ready materials. One of the vignettes, underscoring Catherine's claim to be the true successor to Peter the Great and thus transferring her gender-inappropriate territorial aggressions onto him, depicts her demurely posting beside his grave the standards of the Turks whom her troops defeated at a famous battle in 1770 (Figure 0.4).

Chapter 9 looks at notions of Catherine II as ruling over an exotic and sometimes also a barbaric empire peopled by unkempt serfs, Kyrgyz nomads, bearded priests, and

Figure 0.4 Catherine posts captured Turkish military banners to the grave of Peter the Great. Source: *Historisch-genealogischer Calender auf das Gemein-Jahr 1798*. Berlin: Unger, 1797. Public Domain.

jingling shamans. The major peasant and ethnic uprising that marred the second decade of her reign is obliquely acknowledged in a vignette (not included) depicting the exodus in 1771 of Kalmyk peoples from central Russia into China. Partly offsetting memories of the peasant revolt was the long journey, some of it by sleigh, commemorated in another tiny image that shows the empress in 1787 grandly processing to her exotic new territories along the Black Sea (Figure 0.5).

Part III, "Transgressions Accruing and Secrets Revealed," shows in four chapters how, during the final eight years of Catherine II's reign, 1789–96, and for almost fifteen thereafter, until 1810, perceptions of Catherine II's old and new transgressions were accumulating and the norms of her distant public, under pressure from the French Revolution's monumental interventions, were here hardening or there mutating.

Chapter 10 sketches the public reassessment of the Russian empress as ruler, especially her aggression against Poland and the Ottoman Empire. One of Chodowiecki's little images (omitted here) depicts one of her bloodiest generals sitting by a campfire on the night before a horrifying massacre outside Warsaw in 1794. By then, harsh criticism

Figure 0.5 Setting out in winter for her grand inspection tour to newly acquired territories on the Black Sea, Catherine rides in an open sleigh here, not in the roomy enclosed sledge of contemporary descriptions. Source: *Historisch-genealogischer Calender auf das Gemein-Jahr 1798*. Berlin: Unger, 1797. Public Domain.

of Catherine was already burgeoning in the new genre of political cartooning, which, blossoming at the time in England and beyond, produced ferocious depictions of Catherine variously as a loathsome despot, a creature of unsettled gender, an uncaring and lascivious libertine, or a horrifying example of the monstrous-feminine. Even when a repulsive empress could not offer the "spectatorial pleasure and identification" that celebrity discourse usually promises, images and accounts of her could claim to unveil her secret motives or make evident her atrociousness, and this could be the stuff of celebrity too.

Chapter 11 returns to the first little image, showing ways in which posthumous revelations about the marriage of Catherine and Peter fascinated audiences and maintained the empress's popular fame late in her reign and especially after her death. The chapter addresses the varied narrative techniques and new kinds of information that pervaded the late torrent of coup retellings.

Chapter 12 addresses celebrity discourse's engagement—both late in her reign and posthumously—with the mighty woman ruler's extramarital sexuality. The alleged libertine behavior that always underwrote her celebrity status lurks vaguely

Figure 0.6 Potemkin kneels at the feet of his former lover as she arrives at an extravagant party he gave for her. Source: *Historisch-genealogischer Calender auf das Gemein-Jahr 1798*. Berlin: Unger, 1797. Public Domain.

in Chodowiecki's suite of images, hinted at in the male figures around her, especially in the vignette of Potemkin at a fabulous party he gave in her honor (Figure 0.6). The chapter shows how her kingly sexual strategies were represented and received once the French Revolution ignited many changes in attitudes. Then, after her death in 1796, further pungent voyeuristic tales about the woman king roused more fantasies and anxieties about the supposedly voracious empress and her "favorites."

Chapter 13 briefly discusses the reporting of her demise. It summarizes the posthumous mix of praise and condemnation of Catherine II in Napoleonic Europe, especially the charge that she was misled by the fake villages that Potemkin organized along her journey to the Crimea, the new accusations of criminality that were brought against her, and the persisting ambiguity in many accounts of the empress before her fading relationship with the public changed Catherine the Great from a celebrity coexisting with her fans into an icon whose name is still remembered and whose alleged misbehavior is regularly revived.

Powerful woman, rich woman, female patron of the arts, independent woman, sexually self-defining woman—all this was the material for the earliest instance of modern international female celebrity. Considering the many studies of less-privileged women on whom feminist scholarship has long concentrated, the examination of a rich and powerful one adds nuance to feminist analyses of how dominant social categories operate. Examining how Catherine the Great was represented to her contemporary distant publics, those who did not live in palaces or hold high social rank, aids in better mapping the place of this important monarch in the cultural history of the eighteenth and early nineteenth centuries. Although the effects of her popular reputation among distant non-elite citizenries on her political options and her possibilities for alliances or cooperation are tangential to this study, celebrity, especially political celebrity such as Catherine's, had and has political dimensions concerning, for example, the legitimacy of powerful women and the intersection of sexuality with power. Most of all, seeing Catherine II as a celebrity, a woman celebrity, helps us better understand the European cultural and social history of her time and the role of celebrity discourse in it, gives meaning to many never scrutinized cultural artifacts, and adds depth to the analysis of gender.

I

Celebrity Ingredients

The discourse of celebrity around Catherine the Great of Russia was a remarkable and multifaceted phenomenon that lasted from 1762 until after her death. Launched by a shocking, globally publicized act of gendered political malfeasance, her further popular fame depended on the eighteenth century's means and practices of communication, on the unstable responses of non-elite European audiences outside the territories where she directly or indirectly held institutional power, and on the empress's own willingness to perform the emerging role of star. Riveting story, engaged media, intrigued public, and a central figure who was at least occasionally obliging to her audience—these, I will argue here, are the indispensable basic ingredients of international celebrity in its eighteenth-century form.

1

Celebrity-Making Coup of 1762

The Crucial Role of Story

She did what no one alive in the year 1762 could remember any woman doing: she deposed her husband from a powerful throne in a country where she was a foreigner. Of course, other women in history had usurped power, and some women were effectively in power behind the ostensible rule of their husbands or lovers, but the thirty-three-year-old princess from a miniature principality in Germany shoved from his throne the tsar of Russia, the grandson of Peter the Great. By doing that before astonished eyes across Europe, Catherine II (1729–96) inadvertently took a step that sped her toward popular celebrity, with its promise to entertain, to thrill, to reveal the secrets of apparently special people, and to make money for the many intermediaries between the empress and her emerging fans.

But first came shock, especially because of possible effects of the coup on the conflict now known as the Seven Years' War. It was a complex struggle that historians today often regard as two simultaneous wars, a global one between Britain and France fighting in North America and India as well as on the high seas, and a continental one with many combatants, but mostly between Prussia and Austria battling in central Europe.[1] Both sets of hostilities had already induced heightened public interest in contemporary affairs among ordinary Europeans. The resulting boost to the readership of newspapers inadvertently assisted in the establishment of an enlarged audience for international celebrity discourse. Then came the sensational coup. On July 24, 1762, the Prussian poet Anna Luisa Karsch wrote to a friend that the tsar, Prussia's friend Peter III, had been deposed and replaced by his wife;[2] the dangerous potential military consequence for Karsch's embattled country horrified the poet.[3]

Peter III had ascended the Russian throne only seven months earlier and had spellbound newspaper readers and listeners far from his territory by his abrupt decision to switch sides in the war, from alliance with Austria to armistice with Prussia. Peter's settlement with Prussia saved its ruler, Frederick II, "the Great," from looming defeat, giving him instead a heroic reputation[4] and establishing a bold image for the new Russian tsar as well. Then the coup that occurred over the two days of July 9 and 10, 1762, aroused new fears about Russia's stance in the war and added the massive misbehavior of a usurping woman to the tumult. If it turned out, Karsch prophesied, that this ungrateful wife had had the slightest part in the plot against Peter, she would arouse disgust forever.[5]

Of course, eighteenth-century newspaper readers did not learn of the stunning overthrow instantly. Couriers had first rushed word of it to Europe's governments. Maria Theresa's court in Vienna, roughly 2,000 kilometers from the Russian capital, got the message on July 21, twelve days after the events. Prussian Berlin, slightly closer and better positioned to benefit from summertime communications partly by sea, perhaps got the shock slightly sooner, and Karsch, writing her letter on July 24, had soon learned of it from her insider source. Within days, newspaper editors received the confounding information. On July 27, a paper in Brussels announced a "great revolution" in Russia; on July 30, several detailed, mostly accurate, versions were being printed in newspapers in The Hague; and on the same day, garbled, hesitant rumors were published in London.[6] Far to the south, readers of the *Gaceta de Madrid* received their first report on August 10.[7] Overall, within little more than a month of the event, European readers everywhere could devour the extraordinary story. Quickly, copies of British newspapers were in the holds of ships sailing across the Atlantic, to be copied weeks later into American broadsheets for the edification of the colonists, and a detailed Spanish pamphlet account was passing around Cape Horn to Peru, where it was reprinted the next year.[8]

It was not just distance that caused delays. The infrequency of a newspaper's publication could be an impediment too. The Vienna paper appeared twice weekly, the same as in Paris, where the *Gazette de France* first printed word of the coup on August 2. In England, the provincial *Northampton Mercury*, which appeared only on Mondays, told the tale on August 9. Like many gazettes in small and medium-sized towns across Europe,[9] the *Mercury* excerpted its content from multiple larger, better known papers elsewhere, a richness that at least partially offset the disadvantage of tardiness. In Bologna, part of a papal territory, the weekly gazette's August 3 edition contained both pre- and post-coup articles. An item from St. Petersburg on its second page gave prescient reasons why Peter's rash reforms might make Russians dangerously discontented, and on its final page, where the type was set last, the coup appeared. There, squeezed into small print, the "unanticipated news" of the dethroning appeared,[10] including the confident, but inaccurate, announcement that Catherine was to be the regent during the minority of her young son, Paul.[11]

Editorial choice could also retard the spread of information. In the small, central German town of Erlangen, editor J. G. Gross decided to await confirmation of the ridiculous Russian yarn before publishing it. He prided himself on keeping nonsense out of his supra-regional, large-circulation, thrice-weekly (Tuesday, Thursday, Saturday) *Auszug der neuesten Weltgeschichte* (Excerpts from the latest world history). Other observers too were perplexed and doubtful, confused by initial accounts "so contradictory that reasonable people laughed about the idea that they should persuade themselves the Russian emperor had been deposed [and] taken captive."[12] On August 3, a Tuesday, Gross decided to admit that the public had been buzzing for "several days" about the bewildering rumors, including that a new tsarina was restoring the rights of the Russian church to their properties, their black robes, and their "thick long beards," and that she had nullified the peace with "Russia's worst enemy," Prussia.[13] Peter's reign had been controversial, Gross admitted, but he nonetheless felt so confounded by "unclear, paradoxical, and incomprehensible" parts of the reports that he pronounced himself unable to either endorse or deny their truthfulness.[14] A postscript in his August 3 issue cited new messages "that the Russian tsar had been in great danger, was in fact wounded in the arm, but had fortunately pushed through, and was now already in Frankfurt an der Oder," a town belonging to Russia's Prussian ally. Neither the wound nor the escape turned out to be true.

On Thursday, August 5, Gross put his slightly belated coverage of the overthrow on the front page under the common heading, "Affairs of State" (headlines had not yet been invented, and items in newspapers were often organized by date or by location of source). Having seen numerous confirmations of the revolution, it could no longer be doubted, but Gross still wanted to know whether Peter had been "massacred" or jailed, "as some report." Had the tsar been deported to his paternal territories in Germany, or had he saved himself in some other way? Who had initiated the overthrow?[15] On August 10, Gross still attributed this "revolution . . . of a kind perhaps no nation has ever experienced before" to a group of men, "the executive senate of the empire." But it had been announced, he continued, that "there was no other tsar or ruler" of the Russian Empire than "Catherine Alekseevna."[16] Her new name, Gross did not yet realize, was Catherine II.

Signs of Celebrity Emerging

The sensational coup story was rich fodder for making the tsarina a figure of broad popular fascination. Celebrity is an iridescent kind of fame, changing colors from different angles with alternating instants of dark and bright. It is a large-scale discourse recognizing and engaging emotionally with the "star," often to the point of identification, through media products that emphasize both personal, trivial aspects of the figure, those that star and beholder are likely to have in common, and exceptional, unusual qualities, those that set them far apart.[17] Operationally, celebrity is a troika of interactions among a central persona, the media, and an audience. The central figure must be a "real" embodied being, one who might, even if fictively embroidered, be available for the scrutiny of fans. Additionally, the figure must be one who functions to seize the attention and rouse the fantasy of the audience, whether deliberately or not, and to maintain attention for more than a transitory moment.[18] Such a star—the very term, admittedly anachronistic, stresses visibility—must engage in self-display, and this requires assistance, which is what media workers provide. Their role is to prepare, distribute, and sell representations of the star. The third party in the troika, engaged beholders from ordinary circumstances, fans, whether positive or negative, buy the representations on which celebrity fundamentally depends and, with their purchases, encourage the star or the publicists, distributors, and sellers to produce ever more.

In 1762, items published beyond Russia's borders initially induced and gradually registered geographically diverse audiences receiving the new empress as a celebrity. Tracing them, especially the members of the lowest levels of society,[19] is difficult, but the sheer proliferation of coup materials in a wide price range demonstrates intense popular interest in towns and cities from the North Sea to the Mediterranean. Readers and listeners wanted to know whether Catherine's Russia would switch back to

Austria's side of the war (it did not) and were transfixed by the two principals' apparent gender role reversals, as well as by the galvanizing situation of the empress on her own. This chapter examines the first accounts of the overthrow, those published within approximately the first four weeks of the events, and explores how these accounts meshed with the phenomenon now called celebrity.

Before the news could resonate as the stuff of celebrity, however, it had to spread. A piece of doggerel about two men who deal in stocks, or "scrip," published in the London *Gazetteer* gives an example of informal diffusion of the coup story. One of the men says: "D'ye year the news which 'larms the town, / The Czaar is dead, and Scrip is down." The other man, labeled the Bull because he expects stocks to rise, hurries to Jonathon's, the coffeehouse that was gradually turning into London's stock exchange:

> He first accosts a noisy Bear
> And speaks aloud to gain his ear;
> Well, Tom, what news makes *Scrip* so low?
> Th' Emperor's had a fatal blow;
> Dethron'd, confin'd, some say he's dead;
> The Bull on this hangs down his head.

The hurrying man sells his scrip and proclaims himself undone.[20] The lines show coffeehouses as sites where news could move with extra speed, at least to groups such as the stock jobbers, for whom the effects of the overthrow could be financial. For most readers of the amusing rhyme, however, the coup, having no practical impact on them, monetary or military, could don an entertaining, even comic, aspect, thus edging toward celebrity discourse about the event's protagonists.

Early informational tidbits about the new tsarina—even the brief, seemingly dry outline of the male side of Catherine's family tree that several papers promptly offered[21]—invited readers to engage with her story of social mobility, common stuff of celebrity discourse.[22] Indications of a minor German princess leaping from the obscurity of tiny and insignificant Anhalt-Zerbst to wealth and immense privilege as wife of the Russian grand duke, the empire's crown prince, stirred discussion, ignited imaginations, and suggested wishful identification. Peter III's path to great riches and distinction, equally circuitous and improbable, started, like hers, in one of eighteenth-century Germany's pocket principalities, as readers had been reminded when he first took the imperial throne, almost seven months before he was overthrown. His mother was Peter the Great's illegitimate older daughter, who had married the ruler of an inconsequential state near the border of Denmark. She perished soon after giving birth, and the child's father died eleven years later. When the boy's aunt, Elizabeth, Peter the Great's other daughter, seized the Russian throne from one of her father's weakest successors and chose to stabilize her reign by identifying an heir, she selected her young nephew to be grand duke. Then, at the end of 1761, Elizabeth's death brought him to the throne as Tsar Peter III. Yet with the coup, the grandson of Russia's most famous ruler was overthrown by a dynastically unqualified foreign woman. When the highly respected gazette from Leiden printed a report of public fascination with the coup, the interest was attributed to the incongruities and improbabilities of Catherine's and Peter's paths to power.[23]

Catherine's Efforts to Control the Narrative: Her Manifestos and Their Reception

As cultural studies theories point out, dominant elites express their power by giving validity and exposure to their versions of events and to their sets of values. A Russian tsar's chief public relations tool was the manifesto, and Catherine II immediately published one to announce and defend the overthrow, then a second to counter and quash delegitimizing speculation, and, not much later, a third to announce a further shocking development, Peter's death. Each contributed dramatically to Catherine's sudden popular fame.

The first manifesto, written by Nikita Panin and Grigorii Teplov[24] and distributed on the day of the coup, provided a brief, partly coded justification for the takeover by citing religion, war, and social stability. It asserted that Peter III was endangering the Russian Orthodox Church by starting to introduce an unnamed foreign religion, an allusion to Lutheranism; that he was concluding a peace with Russia's "greatest enemy," meaning Prussia; and, in an oddly vague final charge, that he was overturning the internal domestic regulation of the empire.[25] With these accusations against the tsar, a new and possibly temporary dominant elite asserted its power by imposing as forcefully as possible its story of the disruptive events and by declaring which behaviors it condemned. Yet dominant elites never attain complete control over the narrative of events, and observers far from Catherine's power base, who could defy this hegemony more easily than those geographically and politically closer to her, were able to pose different narratives and show the gaps and inconsistencies in the narrative that the new empress and her gang offered. Celebrity discourse, furthermore, with its central figure, media workers, and fans, always involves a struggle for control of communications. For many readers, the manifestoes and discussion about them were immediately incorporated into Catherine II's new and contentious celebrity. Newspapers outside of Russia, for example, noted that the first proclamation's accusation of Peter colluding with the country's "worst enemy" was modified in reprinted copies of the manifesto to the far less specific "enemies." In fact, when a second manifesto about the coup appeared a few days later, the enemy reference had entirely disappeared.

The very existence of a second manifesto suggests Catherine's desire to control the story by providing a more thorough account of the events and what motivated them. When the monthly *Clef du Cabinet des Princes de l'Europe* (Key to the Cabinet of Europe's Princes) excitedly asserted that the second manifesto "says all, exposes all," it was pointing to a quality that is particularly sought after in celebrity discourse, as scholars of celebrity such as David Marshall, Antione Lilti, and Joshua Gamson emphasize:[26] revelations that ostensibly enable the audience to peer behind a star's public façade.[27] In the manifesto, conventional political reasoning merges with Catherine's personal grudges, large and small, and with assorted strategies for delegitimizing Peter and justifying herself. For distant readers agog in those first days over Catherine II as an intriguing and suddenly imposing personality, anything revealing her private life was worth close attention.[28]

The expectation that an official manifesto might make personal revelations resulted in part from the identity of its narrator. All three of the central coup manifestos were narrated, purportedly, by the empress herself. This was a conventional structure, yet the effect of the personal, "internal" narrator—"internal" because narrator-Catherine is an agent in the action the manifestos describe—gained special meaning: she was recounting a massively unconventional event in which she played a leading part. Narrator identities, however, are fraught; the closeness of this narrator's persona to the spirit, feelings, and motives of the "real" Catherine II was and is impossible to determine. In fact, scholars of narrative always distinguish between the narrator and the author, even if the two insist on their unity. The narrator may be a version of the author, but narrator and author are not the same. Nonetheless, the autobiographical representation of Catherine II speaking in the royal first-person-plural and claiming to be a reliable eyewitness added appeal to her government's official documents and contrasted with most newspaper accounts of the same events, with their "external" narrators, impersonal and dispassionate, with no clues to their individual identity and providing an omniscient or nearly omniscient perspective.

The second manifesto's narrator-Catherine begins immediately with a seemingly private matter, the death of "our most august and dear aunt, the empress Elizabeth Petrovna, of glorious memory." Russians, "groaning for the loss of so tender a mother," found "consolation in obeying her nephew," narrator-Catherine claimed. But when the "weakness" of the nephew's mind became evident, obeying Elizabeth was not enough to justify Peter's reign. Allegedly thinking the tsar would know "his own insufficiency," the narrator continued, loyal Russians "sought our maternal assistance in the affairs of government." The manifesto reworks gender so that a woman's position of power is normalized. With Elizabeth serving as the touchstone for dynastic respect and for Russianness, the manifesto overflows with lurid denunciations of Peter's alleged disrespect. When ceremony required that he approach the funeral bier, "he did it with his eyes manifestly replete with joy; even intimating his ingratitude by his words."[29] That an heir in waiting (and his wife) might well rejoice upon at last attaining the throne is disallowed in favor of a sentimentalized theater of grief.

The Elizabeth theme enables the manifesto to address one of the obvious objections against Catherine as tsarina, an objection that newspapers outside her domains had immediately mentioned: her German background. But here the fictive narrator declares Russia to be "our native country," insinuates herself into the dynasty of Peter the Great, calling him "our most dear predecessor," and clings to Elizabeth, claiming "ties of blood" to her. Feminizing the Russian throne by focusing on Elizabeth, the text makes Peter III's reign an aberration and Catherine II's a return to the customary. Elizabeth's rule was maternal; so would Catherine's be. Peter III's place in the family scheme remained merely "nephew." But worse even than his insolence toward Elizabeth was his disdain for Russia itself and his failure to "conduct himself as the heir of so great an empire." The manifesto then demands with a rhetorical flourish, "What were the consequences of all this?" and leaves the delegitimizing question hanging.[30]

One of the early British newspaper accounts of the new empress had included a moral commentary condemning ambition, a quality often considered dangerous by the subjects of male rulers, and especially anathematized for ruling women. "If she was engaged to take this extraordinary Step by any ambitious View, it is hardly possible that a Revolution so founded can long subsist,"[31] a safely distant British writer proclaimed, though a coup conducted without aspirations for power was unlikely. Catherine, of course, knew that eschewing unfeminine ambition was a wise strategy for her public image, and the second manifesto poses her in the ideologically infused roles of caring mother and patient wife, who suffered in private until "the endeavors he [Peter III] made to ruin us, rose to such a pitch, that they broke out in public, and then charging us with being the cause of the murmurs, which his own imprudent measures occasioned, his resolution to take away our life openly appeared." Despite Peter's purported threats to kill her, Catherine exhibited such correctly feminine submissiveness that her subjects were "astonished at our patience under these heavy persecutions." The manifesto construes the usurper as the aggrieved and vulnerable feminine party who was eventually prodded into action only by the desire to protect her son and to defend herself. At that point, both she and "some of our most trusty subjects ... resolved ... either to sacrifice our life for our country, or save it from bloodshed and calamity."[32] These generous sentiments are the manifesto's entire account of the conspiracy by a small group of Russian nobles that led to Peter's overthrow.

From there, the second manifesto's version of the coup jumps forward to the moment when Catherine rides at the head of her troops toward the palace where she expected to find her husband. Her purpose, she explained, was to prevent Peter from "placing his confidence in the imaginary power" of a small contingent of troops from his German territories, "for Whose sake he stayed at Oranienbaum, living in indolence, and abandoning the most pressing exigencies of the state." Catherine piously proclaims her desire to avoid carnage but declares her march "a necessary duty towards our subjects (to which we were immediately called by the voice of God)."[33] Not ambition but divine authority summoned her to this task. Before the manifesto appeared, the press outside of Russia had already made clear the masculinity of her behavior, emphasizing that she personally led troops to confront Peter, that she did so riding on horseback, and that she wore a man's military coat and pants and donned the blue cordon of the ruler. This was also the image of the coup that Catherine II later commissioned to be painted and recopied for distribution to other princely courts.[34] It was her most widely cited and most political performance of explicit masculinity—but she does not touch on those details in her narrative. Still, her striking self-display as a singular autonomous agent embodied a notion of individualism that meshed well with Enlightenment ideas current in the eighteenth century and that had the additional side effect of nourishing celebrity discourse, in which messages of personal uniqueness abound.[35]

Meanwhile, narrator-Catherine reported receiving letters from Peter asking for permission to return to his German estates in Holstein. But because "he had still resources left him" and "had also in his power several personages of distinction belonging to our court," the second manifesto avers, she left the letters unanswered. Continuing the march toward Oranienbaum, she decided her husband must make a "voluntary and formal renunciation of the throne, wrote by his own hand, for the public satisfaction."[36] In this version of events and motivations, the abdication was not a step that dressed up her seizure of power but rather a humane means of protecting eminent subjects and of meeting a supposed demand by an unidentified Russian public.

The rare procedure of renouncing the throne seemed to seal the accomplishment of a nonviolent coup. In what purports to be Peter's voice (but in weaker first-person-*singular* forms), the abdication document, embedded in the second manifesto, begins: "In the short time that I have ruled as head of the Russian Empire, I have learned that my powers are not sufficient for such a burden."[37] He asserts and pledges that he will never try to resume the throne (as he had supposedly already promised in a letter). Adding that he wrote the abdication with his own hand, Peter performs another act of submission in this text-laden coup. The key issue, the abdication affirms, was personal incompetence. Of course, if competence legitimized and dynasty did not, then Catherine, unmentioned in the abdication, could well be a legitimate ruler. The resigning tsar's statement contained nothing about being the grandson of Peter the Great, no allusion to having a son, for whom a regent might act temporarily, no reference at all to dynasty and its privileging of men. After Peter's abdication document was obtained, Catherine's public account of the coup was done. She added two paragraphs emphasizing that the change of rulers had happened "without spilling one drop of blood" and that she planned to rule "in such a manner as to comfort the discouraged hearts of all true patriots." With a reassurance of "our imperial favour" to her "loving subjects," her second manifesto was complete.

The Matrix of Celebrity and Story

To distant readers and listeners, however, the coup story continued to unfold, with writers, editors, printmakers, and distributors of all sorts producing a steady dribble of new materials that initiated Catherine II's popular fame and the production of her celebrity. Indeed, by the middle of August 1762, the new Russian empress was probably the best-known woman in all of Europe, eclipsing Maria Theresa, the "empress-queen," as she was often misleadingly called, who ruled the Austrian Habsburg dominions but not the ancient Holy Roman Empire of the German nation. For Catherine's reputation, coup texts that acquired respectability and urgency as news were also the stuff of celebrity discourse. Yet another key to this status was that the coup was a riveting story.

Celebrities are always wrapped in stories.[38] "Khloe breaks silence," "Justin storms off stage," "Amal's pals urge break up," early-twenty-first-century tabloids announce. Such accounts provide fans with entertainment and elicit the sense of connection and intelligibility that celebrity depends on. Without a story featuring the star, there is no celebrity. Telling stories, listening to them, remembering and discussing them, establishing identities through them: these activities are anchored in our humanity. Celebrity discourse gains much of its accessibility and effectiveness from the stories—the series of told events, factual, fictional, or both—that it provides. It is packaged, as analyzed by literary scholars, in a "narrative," a story told in a particular way, either in words or in images, with primary and often also secondary agents, entangled in primary and secondary plots that occur in settings of many possible kinds. In memorable and often intimate form, stories offer fans the feeling of insider knowledge that they yearn to attain and that enables them to believe they understand a remote star's public and private personality and world. Indeed, the wide dissemination of coup accounts might have been only a briefly significant news item except for the scandals and the fantasies that saturated the story. These shifted Catherine and her seizure of the throne into eighteenth-century celebrity and thus, importantly, almost always took the coup story and other tales about her out of her control. By furthering "informal talk between members of social groups"—the Erlangen editor Gross mentioned that effect[39]—and by serving "as a means to negotiate and maintain social norms and values," as today's scholars of celebrity indicate, celebrity journalism could provide entertainment, inspire fantasy, and help communities cohere.[40] Catherine's story did not just tell of astounding social mobility but anchored it in her childhood in Germany, in a cultural setting approximately familiar to an audience of ordinary Europeans; it then added the speculation-inducing appeal of exotic Russia. This was rich stuff for fans' imaginations, especially when an array of new, unofficial accounts offered additional details and raised fresh questions about Peter's actions as well as Catherine's.

New Accounts and Their Spread

Some of the supposed particulars that appeared in newspapers across Europe within days of publication of Catherine's second manifesto were relatively personal. *The London Evening Post*, for example, reported on August 3–5 that private letters from Petersburg quoted Catherine's blunt language to her spouse: "Come, Sir, will you sign this your abdication for the good of me and your son; if not, we must take another method with you!"[41] According to the report, he promptly complied. The *Courrier d'Avignon* for August 10 provided its readers a series of claims that historians today would consider erroneous or misleading: that Catherine had not plotted the overthrow; that Peter was informed of the danger, but his order to arrest six insurgents was not immediately carried out; that three of the six evaded capture and put the coup into effect; that when two of the highest-ranking conspirators led their troops to capture the tsar, Peter's German uncle was wounded and several of his soldiers were killed; and that he defended himself at first before giving up. Various enigmatic elements also helped keep readers enthralled. Why, for example, had Peter the Great's grandnephew Ivan, or John, as British newspapers called him, not succeeded Peter III to the throne? Ivan had reigned briefly as an infant before Elizabeth ousted and imprisoned him, and to many observers, especially those for whom deliberately selecting a woman to rule seemed unthinkable, the failure to choose Ivan, now almost twenty-one years old, was a mystery.[42]

Not long after Catherine's manifestos, two new accounts of the coup events appeared and were widely republished. One promised to reveal the "principal circumstances" of the "extraordinary revolution" and the other claimed to provide "some particulars." The first account, from The Hague, seemed to give Catherine complete and sole responsibility for the coup: she drove into Petersburg, asked the guards to assist her, gave orders, went to the principal church of the city, where she performed the ruler's role in the service, and then set out with her newly acquired troops to capture the emperor.[43] The second account, which began circulating a few days later, emphasized the coup as a conspiracy. This version, which appeared in the *Gazette de France* on August 6 and was then copied in British, German, Belgian, and other French-language papers and magazines, added a startling new actor to the cast, the previously unmentioned nineteen-year-old "Princess Datschkow, at whose house the conspirators met."[44] Taken together, the two accounts (omitting some errors) fit what historians accept today about the coup. On August 21, Gross published the account from The Hague, now squarely crediting Catherine with a decisive role in the overthrow.[45]

With these two versions, newspaper readers could learn that a critical incident occurred as both Peter and his wife were at separate palaces on the Gulf of Finland several hours from the capital: A member of the conspiracy was arrested. Catherine, informed at Peterhof palace in the middle of the night, realized the authorities could soon know everything from their detainee. She immediately rode into the city, arriving at the barracks of a guards' unit early in the morning. There she gave an inspiring speech (quite possibly reinforced by bribes, as later reports would claim) and induced the men to side with her. Then, with the guardsmen cheering and the populace shouting "Long live Catherine II," she proceeded to the Kazan Cathedral, where the highest members of the church hierarchy, including the archbishop of Novgorod, gave her their blessing.[46] Not long afterward, the empress, "dressed in the uniform of the guards, and wearing a blue ribbon, mounted her horse and put herself at the head of 9 or 10,000 men and marched toward Oranjebaum" to confront Peter.[47]

Meanwhile, readers were told, the tsar was surprised that same morning when he came to Peterhof and discovered his wife was missing and a coup was underway against him in the city. After hours of hectic consultations and vacillation, the distressed emperor boarded his yacht and headed for safety and assistance at the Cronstadt naval fortress in the middle of the Gulf of Finland. Hardly had he cast anchor there, however, when he learned that Catherine's emissary had already commandeered the garrison. In dismay, Peter retreated to the Oranienbaum palace. The next day, faced with the imminent arrival of Catherine, the other conspirators, and the troops, Peter "judged that all was lost" and, "laying aside his sword, stepped into a carriage, went to Peterhof, and surrendered himself" without a fight.[48]

In these accounts, the tsar of Russia, a man with great pretenses as a professional soldier and with excellent dynastic qualifications, never took up the arms available to him against his opponents and never activated the soldiers he could have led. Rather, a mere woman deploying beguiling oratory persuaded military forces, the church, and key members of the aristocracy to follow her as she toppled him. With his glaring failures of masculinity and her massive offenses against masculine prerogatives and feminine decorum, this "memorable revolution" fascinated distant observers of every rank.[49]

Then, suddenly, the announcement appeared—in some cases just a few lines down from details of coup events—that Peter III had died. His death had been rumored from the beginning; when London's *Gazetteer* first announced the coup, it mentioned reports that the emperor had been murdered or perhaps only "carried off," and the *St.*

James's Chronicle printed claims that Peter had been "surprised at Supper, wounded, and carried to a remote Part of his Empire" or perhaps "assassinated in the Night in the Streets, as he was going Home."[50] Now the Russian government announced the actual event as having occurred on July 17, eight days after his abdication. Hamburg's highly respected newspaper published the news on August 3,[51] though doubts continued even as late as August 12. In Gross's Erlangen publication on that day the thrilling news appeared from Leipzig that Peter had resumed the throne, thanks to the action of Count Münnich, an aged military leader whose pathos-filled speech had supposedly inspired the troops to liberate their tsar at the exact moment when he was supposed to be sent off to icy Archangel. A few lines later, however, Gross abruptly announced that Peter's hopes for freedom were in fact utterly ended, a violent illness having "finished him off."[52]

But the fact of Peter III's death, far from finishing the stories around the new empress, initiated fresh opportunities for writing, newspaper editing, picture-making, and pamphlet production outside of Russia. Squire's wives and washerwomen, councilmen and cobblers, across wide swathes of Europe, consumed the latest updates of Russia's woman-led coup, augmented frequently for almost three years by a scandalous marital-sexual backstory and by the strange official announcement of the deposed husband's demise. All this contributed further to Catherine II's early notoriety, her celebrity.

2

Scandal and Engrossing Coup Backstories, until 1765

On August 13, 1762, the *Gazette de France* joined a host of European newspapers by publishing the short Russian manifesto announcing the death of "the late emperor" and signed by Catherine II. It was soon followed by a statement from the Russian senate urging the empress not to risk the stress of attending Peter III's funeral. These were shocking new events and important ingredients in Catherine II's emerging celebrity. Like most scandals, including the coup that preceded it, outrage about Peter's precipitous demise depended on a series of unfolding, well-publicized revelations, explanations, disavowals, new disclosures, and revised explanations popping up in protracted disorder. Scandals, as moments of impending humiliation, occur "when private acts that disgrace or offend the idealized, dominant morality of a social community are made public and narrativized by the media," producing a range of effects. They amplify the transgressiveness that sometimes produces and often nurtures celebrity discourse. They "fascinate at the same time as they infuriate" and are often "essentially struggles of symbolic power," in which infractions against a society's moral standards are up for discussion.[1] In the process of such debates, as Antoine Lilti argues, the observing public "becomes aware of itself . . . as a group of curious spectators, excited or shocked, enthusiastic or reproving, adherents or skeptics, yet all interested in learning more,"[2] and in that sense observers are on their way to becoming fans (Chapter 5). In some cases, the symbolic struggle around the disgraceful behavior is accompanied by a rudely material event, such as death.

The Tsar's Scandalous Death and the Tsarina's Alluringly Uncertain Future

The political importance of Peter III's death was unmistakable. To Catherine II as a usurper, several newspaper writers promptly noted, her husband was a danger as long as he was available to return to power. Her grip on the Russian scepter, they argued, was necessarily weak because she, like Peter, was "German by Birth, and was bred either Lutheran or Calvinist," not in the orthodox state church of her populace, with the result that Russians cannot have "any more Love for her than for her Husband."[3] Speculation about the instability of the new empress's situation had almost instantly joined with the expectation that dethroned rulers are often killed to produce rumors of Peter's demise. English newspapers compared the overthrow of the tsar to that of a fourteenth-century English king, Edward

II, who was deposed by his wife and then maliciously murdered; when German papers printed the comparison too, they showed that news did not simply move from west to east but echoed back and forth among cities far from Catherine's new empire.

Political reasons required that the ex-tsar's demise become public knowledge, especially in Russia, and that a cause of it, preferably natural, be stated. Thus to achieve the finality of his departure and the firm establishment of his successor that the murder (as historians now classify Peter III's death[4]) was meant to accomplish, a "most *curious* and singular declaration," as *The Gentlemen's Magazine* for July 1762 called the new manifesto,[5] was published. It stated, according to London newspapers, that Peter III had suffered from "a most violent, griping cholick" caused by "a bloody accident in his hinder parts, commonly called Piles, to which he had been formerly subject," and though Catherine had ordered "that the said Peter should be furnished with every thing that might be judged necessary to prevent the dangerous consequences of that accident," nonetheless, "by the permission of the Almighty, the late emperor departed this life." Adding a formal hint of her interiority,[6] narrator-Catherine mentions her "great regret and affliction" at the news but continues: "[W]ith our imperial and motherly voice, we exhort our faithful subjects to forget and forgive what is past, to pay the last duties to his body, and to pray to God sincerely for the peace of his soul." Not omitting the political usefulness of the event, she also urged her subjects "to consider this unexpected and sudden death as a special effect of the divine providence."[7]

The manifesto, widely read but not widely believed, was the target of much commentary and derision, another indication that the celebrity tsarina could not control the stories from which her fame was made. An anonymous German poem addressing the tsar mildly affected to accept the disease claim:

> You weep, the long and worrisome ache
> Grinds and makes your dull heart break,
> And then the hemorrhoid,
> Accompanied by a colicky pain,
> Removes you from this world so vain
> To peace quite unalloyed. [8]

It was a clever bit of doggerel, amusing whether it reached only readers or also illiterate listeners. But to many Europeans outside of Russia, the announced cause of Peter's death was an invitation to sneers. A bon mot attributed to D'Alembert was "that he refused Catherine's invitation to become tutor to Paul lest his piles prove too dangerous in Russia," a riposte that Frederick the Great cited in 1768 in his Political Testament.[9] Publications in Britain noted that Peter's death from "a disorder in his Bowels" meant "the Parallel becomes still nearer" to Edward's murderous rape "by Means of a red hot Piece of Iron thrust up his Body."[10] With that, the empress's intended message of death by natural causes is overwritten by the parallel to Edward's killing,[11] and, at the same time, the intimately scatological notion of hemorrhoidal colic placed Peter III's fatal vulnerability in the genital area and so reinforced the perception of him as emasculated.[12] Indeed, protests and cynical commentary persisted for Catherine's whole life and long thereafter (Chapter 12).

Her reaction to Peter's death was also jubilantly doubted. A letter in the *London Chronicle* sarcastically noted "the high-wrought scene of tragical sorrow that appeared in the conduct of our magnanimous and tender-hearted Empress," claiming, "She tore her hair, she bedewed her serene and majestic countenance with the precious tears, that flow from heart-felt affliction."[13] Calling the death manifesto an effort "to do justice" to Peter III's memory, "and to apologize for her dethroning a consort, whom she loved so tenderly, and laments so sincerely," the letter satirizes Catherine's enumeration of Peter's "virtues":

> his ignorance, imbecillity, and impotence—to govern; his despotick and passionate temper, his shameful conduct, his sensibility to every dictate of honour, and every sentiment of decency, his heretical opinions, and . . . his trampling on all laws natural and divine so far, as to lay a scheme for excluding from the throne, his only son and heir Paul Petrowitz, and other things of an equally heinous and criminal nature.

Readers were invited to smirk at Peter III's vilification and to doubt the announced cause of death.

Reaching the Least Privileged Audiences with Words and Pictures

The engrossing story that first made Catherine II a celebrity was *la strepitosa notizia*[14] (the amazing news) of the coup. But the plot, the set of causal connections linking the story's events, was profoundly murky, with no sense of what instigated the strange happenings. Early news items alluded sketchily to discontented Russian clergy, insulted units of palace guards, and meddling foreign ambassadors, but they also mentioned the imperial couple's marriage as difficult. For celebrity discourse about Peter and Catherine, closer inquiries into their lives offered not only possible insight into the overthrow but also another quintessential element of celebrity discourse, a purported glimpse of the private sphere, what Joseph Roach calls "public intimacy."[15] To distant readers and listeners, tales of personal foibles and of intimate relationships augured familiarity and invited identification even while, in other respects, the central figures remained unreachably remote. Drawing on and reinforcing notions of individuality that were already circulating in the eighteenth century, celebrity discourse exhibited its "will to uncover a hidden truth, . . . to uncover the 'real' person behind the public persona."[16] This interest in the individual and intimate appeared in such scandal tropes as tumultuous relationships, sexual difficulties, and unexpected demonstrations of individual agency, often with a dose of transgression, all standard ingredients of celebrity discourse as it was emerging then and exists today, especially when wrapped in stories. The imperial coup provided an excellent pretext for delving into or inventing personal incidents, and the suspiciously convenient death of Peter III added to that impulse. Occurring at exactly the moment when Catherine II was gaining broad attention in the west of Europe, it undercut the admiration for her that the first steps of the overthrow had begun to evoke. It also generated more curiosity about who she was, who Peter had been, and what their marriage had been like. Writers and artists responded to this curiosity with an array of products, many intended for the least privileged audiences in their regions, the audiences that are fundamental to the non-elite phenomenon of celebrity.

The poem, for example, that recounted Peter III's removal "from this world so vain" uses the market news-ballad singer's colloquial, humorous, and folksy tone to narrate the deceased tsar's public and private biography. Published four years after Catherine seized power, though possibly written much closer to the events, the poem is addressed directly to the deceased Peter III. Beginning, "My dear Peter, good night!" it continues with a stanza stressing that even servants and peasants (those in "attic and field") had been amazed by Peter's various drastic policy changes and personal choices following the death of his aunt, the empress Elizabeth:

Attic and field meanwhile proclaim
To your quite well-deservéd fame,
That your two dozen weeks
Sufficed to make the world amazed
So it more at you than a hero gazed
And stunned about you speaks.

The verse suggests that even the least elite people, implicitly including those who were dependent on oral transmission of the news, avidly followed Peter's surprising story.[17]

As "My Dear Peter, Good Night" offers an auditory approximation of a market crier's news report, a narrative print illustrating the coup in a sequence of images resembles the pictorial banners that such criers used to elucidate their songs and stories (Figure 2.1). It consists of six detailed scenes, each about 11.5 centimeters high and 12 centimeters wide and six elaborately lettered inscriptions, arranged horizontally in two strips. A print this size, made, or perhaps commissioned, by the prolific Augsburg printer and engraver Johann Martin Will, would have been too expensive for many, but the folk tone of the rhymed labels and the choice of scenes meant the print could appeal to buyers in a mix of German-speaking states with diverse political affiliations, especially because the multipart composition omitted all the divisive military and political repercussions of the events.

The top row portrays Catherine being gladly accepted as new empress by key social groups while the bottom row, with only the vaguest hints at a conspiracy, acknowledges resistance to the coup and tells Peter's fate. The first scene in the upper strip, showing an elegant female figure in a fine horsedrawn coach, depicts the tsarina's acceptance by platoons of palace guards, as a rhymed couplet below the scene declares: "Sight of the empress so moved the guards crowd/ that they with joy their loyal oath avowed"; the date, July 9, is oddly placed at the end of the two lines. The second scene signals wide public approval by showing a swarm of ordinary men, women, and children venerating the new empress's portrait mounted on a steep pyramid; the caption explains that the assembled people are shouting "Long live Catherine the Second." In the third scene, Catherine under a palinquin follows priests carrying holy pictures to a church; in the right foreground a group of ladies in short capes, nuns perhaps, watches, and the caption jingle states that the clergy give her their sanction.

Only in the next row does it become evident that an existing ruler was being overthrown. The picture on the left shows Peter's uncle, the well-dressed Prince George of Holstein, handing over his sword to a man with a walking stick; the text specifies that the prince and "others who were found in some way suspect" were promptly arrested. Squeezed into this caption is the name of the engraver along with his claim,

Figure 2.1 Johann Martin Will retold the coup in six scenes of action, the top row about Catherine II and the bottom row about Peter III. Source: Johann Martin Will, *Der Czarin Anblick*. Courtesy of the Prints Department, National Library of Russia, St Petersburg.

in abbreviated Latin, as was standard, to have made the picture: "m. will escud av." In the middle image, a walled castle labeled Oranienbaum is approached by figures on horseback, though with no definite sign of Catherine: "So that the kaiser too in custody is placed, / the troops are swiftly sent and he is quickly traced."

Unlike the seemingly unmotivated coup in the print, the anonymous poem that bade good night to "my dear Peter" gave background political information about him. His change of alliance from Austria to Prussia is mentioned along with other policy alterations that could explain why he had so completely lost support at home. The thirteenth stanza offers a provisional summary, referring to frequent drunkenness and comparing Peter III with his famous grandfather, Peter the Great:

> You put on, as boys often do,
> Your grandpapa's great cozy shoes
> Then tripped and took an awful fall.
> His spirit was great, but yours is small.
> In liquor and in folly too
> Your flops just grew and grew and grew.

Several stanzas later, the poem repeats the dangers of Peter III's situation and adds another, his strained relations with Catherine.

> That's how Peter Three appeared
> Whose house afire was quickly seared
> Before he had a clue
> And that's because he lacked the wile
> To see the worst of any guile
> A woman's wile, tis true.

The notion of feminine wiles ironically poses the contest between Peter and Catherine as unfair, since men are implicitly not deceitful, but it also suggests the panicky anxiety in masculinist societies about women as power hungry.

The poem then deftly weaves in another scandalous item, the omission of their proclaimed son from Peter's earlier manifesto of accession. The implication that Paul was illegitimate is made explicit in the poem, as is the jeopardy that an infidelity charge imposed on Catherine. The lines allude as well to the practice of assigning sable-trapping duties to Siberian exiles:

> Catherine's son, Paul Petrovitz,
> You named not in your legal writs
> To follow you as czar.
> Paul, you said, was not your son;
> You wanted him to take his mum
> And go away quite far.

> But she was much too smart for you
> The lady whom the world loved true,
> Though you could not abide her.
> She thought for you it would be best

> In polar climes to find your rest
> And sable furs provide her.

The coup itself is then succinctly told, particularly the rumor that Peter's incautious reference to a conspirator's arrest had triggered action:

> One word you spoke and had not weighed,
> One word, you in your cups conveyed,
> Heard by some spy asnooping.
> Now or never! Vengeance thirsts,
> The fuse burns, the bomb bursts,
> And Peter in jail sits drooping.[18]

The poem concludes as it begins, by wishing good night to Peter, without specifically stating his death. Will's print, on the other hand, is unequivocal about the tsar's demise, though not about the manner in which it occurred. The last scene shows Peter lying on a plain bier while courtiers and soldiers in tall bearskin hats stand beside him. The laconic caption merely states: "Thus unexpected did the emp'ror die, / Once he the crown and throne to Catherine did supply." The date, July 18, the day after Peter's death, is squeezed in beneath the line in less skillful lettering.

"My Dear Peter, Good Night!" was composed sometime between 1762 and 1766, when it appeared in a German book. Will's undated print was probably manufactured very soon after news of the coup and of Peter's demise eight days later reached the west. Within their separate genres, the two accounts, one in words and one (mostly) in pictures, represent narratives intended for the undiscriminating and not particularly wealthy audiences that are necessary for the development of celebrity discourse. By enabling a broad public to savor the shocking misadventures of the distant imperial couple in Russia, the print and the poem contributed to the short-lived fame of Peter III and the long-lived celebrity of Catherine II, though the Augsburg engraver notably omitted their private misdemeanors. The poem, in contrast, with its colorful but dismissive account of Peter and with its implication of sexual improprieties by "the lady whom the world loved true," could provide especially delectable fare for its keen public in "attic and field." Along with newspapers that were read aloud to listeners in taverns and workshops, it was poems sung or declaimed in market squares or on street corners and pictures held up by the singing market criers that gave information about kings and queens to "the people without books," those who could not read,[19] and so helped store the tale of the coup in Europe's collective memory for years.

Celebrity Tropes of Marital and Sexual Squabbles

Many consumers of the early coup narratives probably suspected from the start that, like all royal marriages (and most others too) of the eighteenth century, it was not love that had brought Peter and Catherine together. Candidates to be a prince's wife had to be scouted, shortlisted, and interviewed before selection, and the final deals were concluded not by the couple but by power brokers, Peter's aunt and Catherine's mother in their case, performing a role common for older royal and aristocratic women.[20] With the main function of a royal wife being to have a male heir, a bride candidate needed to be not only reasonably healthy but also capable of maintaining the appearance, first, of a partnership with her husband (regardless of his behavior) and, second, of her own chastity so that her offspring would be accepted as his. Furthermore, the royal wife needed to play her part in adhering to court etiquette. Catherine as grand duchess had generally appeared to carry out this script correctly. At the start of 1762, when Peter at last came to the throne, one of the prayers printed for the new tsar contained the hope that God would give Catherine more children, a wish that fit the official account of a functioning, seventeen-year, marital relationship between Peter and Catherine.[21] Six months later, newspapers identified her children as "Paul Petrowitz, Great Prince of Russia, born Oct. 1, 1754, and Anna Petrowna, born Dec. 21, 1757."[22] (Anna had died in infancy.)

Almost at the moment of the coup, distant newspapers offered ironic warnings about descriptions of Peter and Catherine: "'Princes (says a French Writer) at their first ascending the Throne are possessed of the highest Accomplishments;' to this we think may be added, 'so are Princesses.' The Empress of Russia, since she mounted the Throne, has eclipsed all the rising perfections of the late poor unhappy emperor, who has even been loaded with opprobrious Epithets."[23] As another paper put it, Peter's descent from power "truly alarmed newspaper writers," and it added more generally, "an unexpected accident befell the attitude of outsiders who had only described and known Peter from the good side. He was thought of as a peacemaker and the father of his people; and suddenly he was felled by his wife."[24] Within a few months of Peter's overthrow, many papers reprinted a supposedly "intercepted" letter from the famously skeptical Frederick the Great of Prussia belittling Peter and sarcastically praising Catherine: "*Voila*, the poor Emperor of Russia is dethroned by his wife: this was expected. The Empress has a great deal of wit, no religion, and the disposition of the deceased Empress," perhaps a reference to Elizabeth's sexual promiscuity.[25]

From 1762 to about 1765, publications about the coup appeared almost continuously, luring ever more shillings from ordinary readers and viewers and constituting the emergence of Catherine II's celebrity. Late in Catherine's reign and after her death, fresh accounts were published, bursting with scandalous new details and intriguing the public all over again (see Chapter 12), still pursuing the original themes of Peter's suspiciously convenient and sudden death, and the backstories of the obviously problematic imperial marriage, the dubious status of Paul and its implications for Catherine, and certain inchoate doubts about Peter's masculinity.

From the start, tales of domestic discord in a world of privilege could kindle sociable discussion among people who had no practical stake in the affection or affliction of the imperial couple. In the initial iterations, Peter's overthrow, with all its complex political and military dimensions, became an easily recognizable tale of conjugal misery and betrayal, perfect material for celebrity discourse. The allegation was soon widely repeated that "there had not been any harmony" in their marriage "for a Year and a Half past,"[26] and it was confirmed by Catherine's second manifesto, which claimed "persons of probity" had warned her that Peter's plans endangered both Paul and herself.[27] Within a few weeks, in Spain, the *Mercurio Histórico y Político* added a new detail, the date when Peter had supposedly planned to marry "a young countess."[28]

A few papers had speculated that the deposed emperor must have been comforted "on finding his Son Paul not excluded from the Succession"[29] that Catherine announced, but that misreading of Peter's feelings did not last. Allegations that he doubted Paul's paternity were well publicized, as in a hastily written German chapbook entitled *Truthful News of the Revolution that happened in Petersburg on July 9, 1762*.[30] Indeed, some outsiders to the Russian court may have long heard rumors that Peter III denied fathering Paul.[31] This at least is the claim made in an obscure publication composed a few months after the coup by the entrepreneurial Friedrich Ludwig Anton Hörschelmann. Living in a village, he was part of the disbursed communication system that allowed Germany's patchwork of states to disseminate Catherine's celebrity widely, even without a dominant metropolis. Hörschelmann asserted that an infidelity accusation against Catherine had circulated ever since Paul's birth almost eight years earlier and that the rumors sprang from Peter's own comments. Hörschelmann's assertion was then repeated almost exactly in one of the first biographies of Peter III,[32] and the tsar's lack of circumspection on the matter recurs in a slightly later work of characteristic eighteenth-century hybridity, *Anecdotes russes, ou lettres d'un officier allemand à un gentilhomme livonien, écrites de Pétersbourg* "Russian anecdotes, or letters of a German officer to a Livonian gentleman, written in Petersburg." The book, written in French by a writer who had probably never been to Russia, was published several times, allegedly in London but more likely in The Hague;[33] it was immediately twice translated into German.[34] In one of its fictive letters, supposedly composed before the coup, the writer asserted of the illegitimacy charge:

> I cannot hide from you in the slightest that there is no one in Russia who approves of the prince speaking about that so boldly and often using expressions which are no honor to him. No one would ever have thought of such detestable things, if he had not himself offered the occasion. Is it not painful for this princess and for the whole nation that the only heir to the throne, who is beloved and valued by all his subjects, was declared a bastard by his own father?[35]

Of course, even while claiming not to believe the allegations, the author spread the zesty rumors of the dysfunctional imperial marriage, enabling readers to relish this sturdy ingredient of celebrity discourse.

For ordinary readers and listeners far from the events happening in St. Petersburg, such rumors became easy to believe, given the long tradition that instantly conjoined notions of a woman who seeks power with fantasy-inducing sagas of sexual misdeeds. Sexualized discourse of this kind cropped up already in the letter by Prussian poet Anna Luisa Karsch announcing Peter III's overthrow to her friend. There the prolific, self-taught protégée of the Berlin Enlightenment declared that an informal, but horrifying, biography of the new empress was immediately in circulation in the city deploying fearful references to Livia and Mary Stuart, two women who were emblems of power hunger and sexual voracity.[36] Strikingly, however, early documents, such as Karsch's letter, do not speculate about Catherine having a particular lover at the time of the coup. In these accounts, that actual paramour, Grigory Orlov, was repeatedly named as a conspirator but not as inamorato;[37] the general public would not see information in print about him in that role until late in Catherine's reign (Chapter 13).

Challenges to Peter's Masculinity

While charges against Catherine circulated, Peter could not march through the story of his marriage with his own sexual behavior unscathed. A week into the coup news, the Northampton paper's single hint of sexual scandal appeared in a report forwarded from Germany: "Advices of good Credit assure us, that the principal Motive for deposing the Emperor was the Disregard he shewed to the Empress, for whom he openly discovered an Aversion, and the Assiduities he had long paid to a Sultaness."[38] Events in Russia aroused exotic dreams; to imagine who might seduce a tsar, a sultaness is envisioned. Although original coup reports had omitted naming Countess Vorontsova as Peter's mistress, despite identifying her among those detained by Catherine's faction, other sources quickly (and accurately) labeled her as the woman whom Peter preferred to Catherine—after all, Catherine's second manifesto had stated that Peter wanted "Elizabeth Woronzoff" to go with him to Holstein.[39]

Some of the disparagement of Countess Vorontsova in print implied outsiders' disdain for Peter's sexuality. One early book about the coup described her as "of extraordinary fatness and as ugly as the night in the new moon. Her face is blackish brown, covered with fat flesh and full of pockmarks into which the makeup, which she uses to excess, is solidly packed." Her character and intellect were disparaged as well: "Much understanding is not to be sought in her, but she is filled all the more with great cunning and many intrigues."[40] Peter had a mistress who was degraded as ugly, unlikeable, and dangerous.

A foible of taste such as Peter III's for Vorontsova took on a more perilous aspect when gender roles began to wobble. Coup reports tended to empower and thereby masculinize Catherine and disempower and demasculinize Peter III. Russians, it was condescendingly suggested, liked "the regime of women."[41] After all, when Catherine seized control, women had ruled Russia for thirty-two of the thirty-seven years since Peter the Great's death. But Russia was not the only country with a woman ruler. In addition to Maria Theresa ruling the Habsburg territories, Portugal would have a queen regnant starting in 1777. A century earlier, Protestant Sweden had experienced a famous queen, Christina, though she had abdicated and then displayed her dangerously feminine capriciousness by moving to Rome and converting to Roman Catholicism. All of these women were understood to be exceptions, genealogically qualified stand-ins during dynastic interludes when no man was available, clear signs that "whatever else [a powerful woman] may represent, she always represents lack."[42] Yet because Catherine II had successfully pushed a man off the throne, the lack was reallocated at least in part to the man himself, producing the kind of self-fulfilling prophecy characteristic of how gender functions in society. The shifting gendering of the abdicating princeling and the robust usurper signals societies outside of Russia stabilizing their prevailing patriarchal ideologies by attributing conventionally feminine characteristics to the individual losing power and conventionally masculine ones, if only temporarily, to the individual gaining it.

A series of details in first-stage accounts of the coup signified Peter III's failed masculinity to a fascinated distant audience. His dawdling and vacillation when he learned that Catherine was leading a coup against him were labeled unmanly. His hasty retreat when he was challenged upon his arrival at the Cronstadt Fortress did not display masculine valor. During the whole coup, almost all accounts imply, too many women, including his mistress, and not enough men surrounded him. The one man identified as in his company, the aged Count von Münnich, was initially blamed for Peter's capitulation after Cronstadt, but that charge was soon reversed.[43] Instead, Münnich was credited with suggesting military options to the tsar, such as sailing into the Baltic, where he could perhaps have found asylum, or proceeding to northern Germany, where Frederick the Great's armies might have assisted him.[44] The unmanly tsar, however, according to one of his first biographers, probably Ange Goudar, made an "incomprehensible" choice not to resist but rather to "implore the clemency and pity" of his wife.[45] In another anonymous work, a pamphlet that took the antique form of a conversation among several dead rulers, Peter is asked why he got no aid from other supporters. His uncle Prince George of Holstein tried, the deceased tsar replies, but George's troops had turned against him and already sworn allegiance to Catherine.[46] Goudar, however, pointed out all the German men at court whom the tsar had generously rewarded but who failed to warn him of the menacing danger and neglected to assist him when the crisis occurred.[47] He concluded:

> If Peter had been a great man, he would have decided for the field [of battle], he would not have deluded himself, he would have seen the danger as it was and would have played a dignified part. But a mediocre man in the same circumstances remains uncertain, irresolute, indecisive, and of all the choices proposed to him, he ordinarily chooses the worst. This was what Peter did. He returned to Oranienbaum [after the Cronstadt debacle] and submitted to the discretion of those who would dethrone him.[48]

Representations of Peter III repeatedly and in various ways align him with lacks that are unsuitable for his masculinity: lack of decisiveness, lack of control over his own wife and other women, lack of bravery, lack of military skill, lack of political understanding, and, of great consequence, lack of virility. Sexuality again, that savory celebrity theme.

It was Peter's dynastic, masculine duty to ensure that heirs were born. But if Paul was a bastard, which the distant public could see that Peter as tsar at least implicitly alleged by not naming him successor, then Catherine's pregnancy nine years into their marriage was by another man.[49] Such an imputation raised questions about Peter's potency, about his ability to fulfill his procreative obligation. The assertion that Peter disclaimed Paul thus not only painted Catherine as adulterous but also inadvertently matched what the *London Chronicle* satire on his death had called "his ignorance, imbecillity, and impotence—to govern," with the dash neatly signaling that sexual impotence was meant as well as political. The *Gentleman's Magazine*, a monthly that functioned as "an indispensable source of news to its loyal readership scattered throughout the towns, villages, country houses, and parsonages of Britain,"[50] used italics to provide an ostentatious wink about Peter: "his private intrigues with one of the nieces of Chancellor *Woronzoff*, whom, it is said, he loved *as well as he could*, gave umbrage to the Empress whom he had never loved to much purpose."[51] The implications were enormous: gender did not automatically authorize a demasculinized Peter to be tsar. The delegitimating of Peter III as a man is thus part of the proof that he was incompetent to rule, and, for many readers and auditors, it must have been a thrillingly voyeuristic peek behind the imperial bed curtains.

Meanwhile, depictions of Catherine as powerful—in command, speaking and writing forcefully, wearing the insignia otherwise available only to men (and to ruling empresses)—masculinize her, as do references to cross-dressing and leading troops. If Catherine would be tsar, she had to be masculine. Yet, since Catherine was a woman she had to be feminine, so as soon as the overthrow succeeded, her dominant image reverted to femininity: a coup without bloodshed, a weeping and emotional empress mourning Peter's death, a protective male senate that endorsed her, statements in her second manifesto about "our maternal assistance" all contributed.[52] With celebrity frequently relying on actions that are accounted misbehavior according to dominant notions of what is acceptable and good, Catherine's breaches of norms for sexuality and her infringement of the conventional gendered distribution of power (which did not anticipate women becoming monarchs) was particularly potent material for conversation and critique, for engagement in front rooms and kitchens, in workshops and at the market.

The widely read English year-end review, the *Annual Register*, for the year 1762, solved the powerful woman conundrum by describing Catherine as "a woman with a masculine understanding,"[53] thus attributing to her the intelligence, good sense, and discernment that Peter was alleged most dismally to lack. Editor Gross used a different tactic in Erlangen. He slipped a short item into the August 28 issue of his paper, stating: "An epigram was sent to us with the last line, 'Now the woman locks up the Russian man.'" Gross commented: "The gentleman who composed it will not take it amiss that we for special reasons do not use it. The Russian is quite comfortable under the soft scepter of female rule and has been accustomed to it for some thirty years."[54] What the epigram's preceding lines were, one can only speculate, but the dephallicized "soft scepter" strongly hints that for Gross, as for others, Russia's eighteenth-century history of women rulers helped to legitimize Catherine. Reworking her gender to fit her position as tsar, she could be masculine and feminine at once. Such gender bending added to the elusive quality that is celebrity, what Joseph Roach calls "it," which he describes as "the power of embodying, apparently without effort, contradictory qualities simultaneously: strength and vulnerability, innocence and experience, and singularity and typicality among them."[55] In the first years of coup reporting, Catherine's textual persona could accomplish all this. If fans read more than one narrative of the coup, they almost certainly encountered inconsistencies in the characterizations, which could also serve as prods to further engagement with the tale. Thus, to a large segment of the empress's distant audience, its members mostly indifferent politically, the rousing story of a high-ranking couple locked in a marital battle in faraway Russia could provide entertainment, offer brief vicarious satisfaction of their own unfocused yearnings and vague hopes, and promote social solidarity from reading, listening, and talking among one another about the new empress.

In mid-September, amid many other references to Catherine's activities, a short passage in the *London Chronicle* mentioned that a postponement in the proposed coronation date for the empress had occasioned "much speculation," and for good reason, since all was in combustion at Petersburg; from whence they write, that the guards who partly contributed to place Catherine II. on the throne, are sorry that they were so precipitate in that affair; that the party which is formed for Prince John [Ivan VI] daily gathers strength; and that it hath already been insinuated to the Empress, and even spoke publicly in the streets, that she had no natural right to the crown.[56]

Based on these issues, "it is to be apprehended that this Princess's reign will not be long, notwithstanding the wise precautions she hath taken to establish her throne." Not much later, on October 4, 1762, another English paper asserted, "the Empress hath been put under Arrest, and that Search hath been made for Prince John, in order to his being placed on the Throne; but that he is no where to be found." The paper's Dutch source added that the Russian Minister to Holland had "dispatched an Express last Night to Paris; and as we cannot conceive on what Account, this too serves to make us not a little anxious to know what is transacting in Petersburgh."[57] The signs were being closely watched and the far-off rumbles treated as absorbing and exciting, full of possibilities to be pondered.

In mid-December, more mail from Holland announced that in Moscow, on November 8, members of a guards unit had confessed to "conspiring against the Empress's Life." The ringleaders "were sentenced by the Senate to be beheaded and the others as Accomplices to be sent to the Galleys"; the empress, however, had exercised clemency, demoting "the two principal Conspirators . . . from their Rank in the Army, and the Rank of Gentlemen" and banishing them for life to Siberia.[58] Such tales of Catherine's insecurity in power continued for years to come and kept the celebrity-fostering coup story buzzing. In 1764, Prince Ivan's status as a possible contender for the Romanov throne was brutally ended; in a complicated incident, he was killed by the guards assigned to prevent his liberation.

The conjugal squabbles of Peter and Catherine were savory celebrity fare because of what they seemed to reveal about the two participants. But it also mattered that the general public could fill in references to such problems with abundant familiar material requiring no expert political analysis, and, in the process, they might begin to identify with the new empress. Indeed, two years after the coup, the poet Anna Luisa Karsch's attitude toward Catherine had changed completely from political to personal. Karsch, probably the first person to get a divorce in Prussia after a law code change made such an action possible, wrote: "I am not so disinclined toward the Mistress of Russia as in the beginning. She seems to be not at all bloodthirsty and was perhaps forced to take that gruesome step just as I was forced to."[59] The poet drew forgiving parallels to her own life. Comparing Catherine's disposal of Peter III with Karsch's own deliberate arrangement of her husband's involuntary conscription, the poet accepted the proposition that the empress may have conducted her coup in self-defense. No more likening of Catherine to disreputable Livia or intemperate Mary Queen of Scots. Instead, again in an operation typical of celebrity, the empress had become a figure for moments of identification that overcame the huge social distance between her and her faraway audiences and that promised great, at least imagined, social mobility. The story of the coup that made Catherine II famous outside of Russia rendered her available for identification, glamourized her, and entered her into fascinating contests over gender norms, all of which furthered her international celebrity.

3

Media Workers and Their Commodities in Word and Image

Celebrities, like monarchs, are mediated creations. For eighteenth-century oglers who saw a king or queen in person, the presentation of the monarch's body had been carefully edited for public view by a swarm of attendants, from the marshals of the court to the hairdressers and dressmakers. For more distant observers, mediation by others, whether writers, portrait painters, or engravers, was even more inescapable. A famous person being mediated is, however, not sufficient for celebrity. Celebrities must also be commodified, "transformed ... into merchandise."[1]

The Venetian journalist Dominico Caminer wrote that Catherine II's seizure of power in Russia, which "created the most enormous uproar of our days," resulted in an inundation of "wicked and insolent books." Booksellers of all sorts, Caminer continued, sold their impudent products "for a high price";[2] he probably meant in comparison to their meretricious quality, their sometimes forbidden status, or their inexpensive production. An anonymous English scribbler was equally blunt when he explained that his retelling of the Russian coup in *The Beauties of all the Magazines Selected* was commissioned in the hope that "the writer would acquire an amazing reputation, and the publisher receive a much more substantial reward, *i.e.* he would get money by it."[3] Sometimes the rewards were indirect; Catherine's interactions with the French *philosophes*, for example, whom Cynthia Whittaker dubs the eighteenth century's "high priests of public opinion,"[4] were compensated with mixes of shared fame and her later pecuniary favors to them. Altogether, media workers—recycling and creating diverse materials about supposedly wonderful famous people for readers and auditors in cities, towns, villages, or farmsteads—along with all-important fans and a celebrated central figure giving some of her own input, were acting as crucial members of the troika that could and can create celebrity.

Representing the Empress

Over the course of Catherine II's reign, writers and publishers outside her realms produced roughly 600 books and pamphlets, costly and cheap, that purported to tell about her in a host of west European languages. In the first two years after her death, the foreign press was ablaze with accounts of her again; at least twenty-five new books, mostly biographies and some of them illustrated, appeared outside her country. The work of a prolific Spanish playwright, Luciano Francisco Comella, suggests how media workers sought to profit by writing about the Russian empress before and after her death. Many of his dramas were about dead rulers, including three plays about Frederick the Great and others about Peter the Great and Maria Theresa, but in 1795, while Catherine was still alive, he composed a three-act "heroic drama" entitled "Catalina Segunda, Emperatriz de Rusia." The result seems to have been especially successful, with multiple editions over the next years and indications of performances from Barcelona and Valencia to Madrid. Then, two years after Catherine's death, Comella wrote a second drama about her, "Catalina Segunda in Cronstadt," this one in two acts.[5] The plots of the two plays are different but equally fictional, serving mainly as devices to depict a grand and admirable Catherine engaging with her military staff, including in both cases Potemkin and a conveniently heroic Spaniard serving in her army. Comella was thus taking advantage of Catherine's fame, as were the theater companies that produced the plays and the booksellers that sold the scripts, complete in several cases with the names of performers of each role. Someone took this success even further afield because in 1805 the first of Comella's plays about the empress was also performed in Mexico.[6] To benefit from the widespread Catherine phenomenon, writers, actors, printers, and booksellers (these last two were often the same) all joined in commodifying representations of her.

Visual artists worked at this, too, hoping for gains by offering customers the chance to feel more knowledgeable about the appearance of the fascinating empress. The resulting prints and publications, along with the piles of articles in newspapers and magazines, addressed, reinforced, and, crucially for the cultural historian, recorded intense public curiosity about the empress during the decades of her reign and for years thereafter. With the proliferation of commodities, both the public's fascination with the empress and the eagerness of media workers to encourage and sustain it were manifest. When the heaps of inexpensive materials have characteristics that tend to promote identification with the empress, they signal her international celebrity; when other entrepreneurs invoke Catherine's name or title to advertise their various wares, that signals her celebrity too. Put differently, the makers, distributors, and sellers of these products were affected, even determined, by the possibility and gradually the reality of Catherine's celebrity status, which also, within the important limits of existing technologies, shaped what kinds of objects they made and how much such objects proliferated.

Making Visual Images

Depictions of a star can and could seize attention, offer pleasure or produce revulsion, raise questions, communicate values and beliefs, and yet leave enough openings for diverse beholders—literate and illiterate—to find points of connection to the depicted person or scene. The making and distribution of printed images intertwined artists' decisions, workshops' production choices, popular conventions, and sellers' undertakings. Catherine's coup against Peter III, for example, had immediately activated makers of printed portraits far from Russia. The young Pierre Adrien LeBeau in Paris

Figure 3.1 To take advantage promptly of public attention to the new Russian empress, Pierre Adrien LeBeau (1744/8–1817) revised an earlier image of Catherine as grand duchess and enriched the grandeur of the print with an elaborate frame. Source: Pierre Adrien LeBeau, *Catherine Alexiewna II*. Courtesy of the Bibliotheque Nationale de France.

produced a half-length frontal image of the new empress gesturing toward her heart and looking out past the beholder with a rather determined half-smile (Figure 3.1). To make the image commercially reproducible, with anonymous artisans employing a special press to "pull impressions," LeBeau used intaglio, one of the two available eighteenth-century technologies for printing pictures.[7] Relief, cutting away material from the flat surface of a plate and then inking the raised image, was the older technology; intaglio, incising grooves, scratches, and flecks from which ink transfers to paper, was the newer and, by Catherine's time, more common choice. Text on LeBeau's plate may have been produced by a different artisan within the atelier; to print correctly, it had to be crafted in mirror image.

The Genealogies of Types

LeBeau, never having seen the new empress, based his picture at least indirectly on a painting of her as grand duchess; it had been made in Russia by the famed Italian portraitist Pietro Rotari and then engraved there with a bilingual caption in Russian and German.[8] Once engravings such as these took the long journey west in mailbags and travelers' trunks, local painters may have been commissioned to devise portraits based on them, a possibility that could explain the range of coloring in the various painted revisions of the Rotari grand duchess that exist in small palace museums, in Germany for example, even today.[9] Most of all, once Catherine seized the throne, copies of Rotari's portrait spawned new versions on paper. In LeBeau's plate, the engraved empress still wears the source painting's sable stole over her shoulders, but her hand gesturing at her heart is an addition. An engraver in Berlin, on the other hand, Daniel Berger, using the same basic image, shows the empress with a sash of honor across her shoulder and a prominent badge of a chivalric order on her dress, signifying her new status as ruler, a status underscored by her conventional ermine-lined cloak and little crown (Figure 3.2). Berger's Catherine appears calm and confident and looks almost directly at the viewer.

Figure 3.2 Daniel Berger (1744–1824), in Berlin, relied on the same source image as LeBeau but depicted Catherine II wearing the insignia—sash, star, crown, and ermine cloak—that marked her new status as empress. Source: Daniel Berger, *Catharina die Zweite Käiserin und Selbstherscherin / aller Reussen*. Credit: bpk Bildagentur / Kupferstichkabinett, Staatliche Museen, Berlin, Germany / Jörg P. Anders / Art Resource, NY.

As befit celebrity commodities, which were aimed to reach a geographically and economically broad audience, prints of Catherine II varied in quality and price. That Berger's print was more skillful and thus probably more expensive than LeBeau's is suggested, for example, by the better modeling of Catherine's face, and by LeBeau's picture being a mirror-image copy of the original Russian-made engraving. The horizontally flipped orientation indicates a plate made by replicating a printed image directly, sometimes even by tracing it, rather than reversing it to recreate its original alignment. The abundance of printed images of Catherine II with various flaws and reversals shows that less skillfully made pictures were probably quite acceptable to eager buyers who were unfamiliar with the fine points of artistic portraiture.[10]

Both the Paris and the Berlin prints belong to the same "type." When multiple versions of a portrait derived ultimately from a single original, a "type" was born, a type of portrayal, a recognizable configuration of features, usually including basic pose, angle, face, and distribution of light and shadow. Recognizing types helps to show the flow of images over time and space in the eighteenth and nineteenth centuries. Portrait types depicting Catherine uniformly emphasized her well-tended appearance, rich clothing (unlike Frederick II, often in a dull uniform), elegant comportment, and breasts evident enough to signify her female body and its reproductive possibilities. Some types depicting Catherine II had mostly painted versions, some were mostly on paper, and a few, such as the Rotari, had numerous versions in each medium.

Figure 3.3 Georg Siegmund Facius rests his profile-in-braids image of Catherine II on palm leaves and a branch of laurel. Source: Georg Siegmund Facius, *Catherine II., Imperatrice et Autocratrice de tout les Russies*. Courtesy of Bereich Sondersammlungen, Universitätsbibliothek Leipzig, Germany.

Figure 3.4 An anonymous engraver in Paris provided an unusual printed cursive statement about his source being a print—he mangles the engraver's name, Radigues—of a painting by Erichsen. Source: *Catharina II. Gravé d'après le Tableau original de V. Eriksen Danois, Pientre du Cabinet de Sa Majeste l'Imperatrice de toutes les Russies.* Courtesy of the Bildarchiv und Grafiksammlung, Osterreichische Nationalbibliothek, PORT_00033945_01.

The first of the types to circulate extensively outside Russia was the Rotari grand duchess; it was copied, mostly after the coup, in a dozen print variations in cities from Paris to Prague to Berlin. About a decade into Catherine's reign, two new types were added that became especially widespread, a profile image in which her hair is in braids wrapped around her head, a style that was praised for its simplicity,[11] and a regal frontal image, based on a huge full-length painting by the Dane Vigilius Erichsen, in which she wears a small crown and looks directly at the viewer. The profile-in-braids type often showed the empress wearing fur trimming at her neckline and over her shoulders, a design that became a well-known visual mark of the empress.[12] Georg Siegmund Facius, in his etching of this type, offered two different captions, one in German and the other in French (Figure 3.3). Among the many prints based on Erichsen, one anonymous French engraver gave the empress a particularly open and approachable expression (Figure 3.4) and attempted to add credibility to his picture by including a few Russian words in Cyrillic lettering.

Eight months after Catherine seized power, the Treaty of Hubertusburg (signed on April 15, 1763) ended the Third Silesian War (a significant part of the Seven Years'

Figure 3.5 On this woven commemorative cloth celebrating the Peace of Hubertusburg Catherine is depicted second from right; how such textiles were used is unknown. Source: akg-images.

War) and precipitated new images of the empress, this time alongside other rulers. One instance was a material and visual object that had distinctive haptic qualities: a commemorative damask cloth in red and white, over a meter long and a little under a meter wide, displaying pictures of six key monarchs in the center, with winged fame hovering overhead (Figure 3.5).[13] Another instance was a broadside showing the Hubertusburg castle and a tree festooned with portraits of nine monarchs, with lines of poetry below.[14] For poorly printed and woven group images such as these, a close likeness was of little importance, and Catherine's face in particular was then, less than a year into her reign, still too little known for many to recognize.

Among both the six and the nine depicted in the groups with her were Frederick II and Maria Theresa. Artists in many locations, especially in Germany, had already created at least 200 printed pictures of Maria Theresa and probably somewhat fewer of Frederick II. Addressing regional demands that differed according to both political and religious disparities, pious Maria Theresa was venerated as the champion of Roman Catholicism[15] and as stalwart defender of her Habsburg dominions against the Prussian king's attacks, while Frederick was represented both as the champion of Protestantism, despite his personal disdain for religion, and also as a military celebrity, surprisingly admired even in his adversary's territories.[16] Catherine II's image, meanwhile, was still evolving.

Beyond Types: Inventions and Blends

In all the pictures of her, clothes mattered. Some, such as the middle-quality *Empress Catharine in the Habit in which she appeared at the Head of her own Regiment*, is, as its title indicates, fundamentally a fashion plate (Figure 3.6). Though the artist-engraver, Charles Mosley, represents the empress in regimental dress, or "habit," it is undated and depoliticized, showing her framed by a swirling drape, typical of eighteenth-century monarchical portraiture, with two tents and a few lances in the background, but no soldiers and no modern weapons. If it was meant to illustrate her participation in the coup, it modifies the story amusingly: as many newspapers reported and as the scene in Chodowiecki's picture sequence (Figure 0.1) would show in much later retrospect, Catherine appeared at the crucial event fully cross-dressed, in pants.

In this print, however, the tsarina wears a masculine military coat over her low-cut and frilly bodice and full skirt of expensively shiny fabric. Atop her wig or coiffed and powdered hair is a large three-corner hat decorated with a cluster of ostrich plumes, signs of luxury. Such supposedly were the garments in which, in contradiction to all prevailing notions

Figure 3.6 Charles Mosley, who worked mostly for booksellers in London, designed and engraved this postcard-sized print as a fashion picture of Catharine II wearing military "habit." Source: Charles Mosley, *The Empress Catharine in the Habit in which she appeared at the Head of her own Regiment*. Courtesy of the British Museum; Museum number 1871,1209.1308.

of femininity, Catherine headed "her own Regiment." The image offers a representation of this contradiction: a tightly corseted woman, located in a military camp, fingering a finely wrought sword with one hand and holding a commander's baton in the other. Despite these accoutrements and although she looks out over the heads of her viewers, as a commander should, she sits passively, not in a commanding, masculine stance. Yet such contradictions and inconsistencies are no problem in celebrity discourse.[17]

Mosley's print is an invented image of the empress. Other craftsmen mixed features of "real" pictures of the empress with imagined elements, yielding blends. An English printmaker, for example, simplified on an old-fashioned German picture, of Catherine as grand duchess by Johann Martin Bernigeroth, which was probably based in turn on a portrait of her at age sixteen by the Italian portraitist Louis Caravaque. The revised picture omits Bernigeroth's baroque framing, retains the basic shape of the empress's face but in reverse from the German print, repositions her hand, and, most of all, gives her a completely updated wardrobe (see frontispiece). The anonymous print of "the present Empress" thus blends elements of an older image with new taste. Blend images, like inventions, are indicators of celebrity discourse. They demonstrate printmakers striving to satisfy consumers' desire to savor gazing at the famed empress whom none of them in fact would ever behold.

Artists, Artisans, and the Impact of Celebrity

A whole array of artists worked to fulfill the craving for the visual that Catherine's popular fame induced during her long reign. At his workshop in France, for example, the Italian Giovanni Battista Nini made molds for elegant terracotta plaques with Catherine II's profile (Figure 3.7), while in England Josiah Wedgwood's catalogue of wares advertised bone china medallions depicting her,[18] and, late in her reign, in Germany Johann Friedrich Anting produced scenes showing the empress in the still new silhouette form. Not every kind of artist participated in celebrity production, however. Portrait painters, for example, who might be commissioned to copy an image of the empress for the palace of a ruler who was not on Catherine's gift list, did not significantly contribute to her popular celebrity, and, similarly, the most respected engravers, working to commissions like the painters, produced superior, often large-scale work that was mostly too exclusive and too expensive to add to her non-elite fame. Among more ordinary picture designers and engravers, however, some operated independently and at their own risk and others fulfilled orders for book or journal illustrations that might also be sold as separate sheets. At every step— from the size and shape of the artist's design, to the carver's, engraver's, or etcher's choice of technology, to the printer's selection of paper, to the distributor's decision on price, and more—the picture-making process had ramifications for the possibility of celebrity, and celebrity, in turn, had an impact on the pictures and their makers.

Competently made or not, and printed in towns and cities from Edinburgh to Venice and Madrid to Hamburg, most portraits of Catherine II fell into four subgenres: in profile, usually in head-and-shoulder format and alone, as in the picture by Facius; frontal portrait in head-and-shoulder to half-length, almost always alone, such as LeBeau and Berger produced; solitary central figure shown head-to-toe, such as in the Mosely print; a scene with other figures, such as on the damask or in Will's sequence about the coup (Figure 2.1). The promotion of Catherine II's celebrity lent itself well

Figure 3.7 The popular terracotta specialist Nini made plaques in several designs showing Catherine II in profile. Source: Giovan Battista Nini, Terracotta medallion. Courtesy of the Metropolitan Museum of Art, New York.

to all four formats, each of which had its own way of meeting celebrity discourse's promise of "spectatorial pleasure."[19] Profiles, reminiscent of coins, suggested an exalted leader looking intently into the future but resonated also with the familiar silhouette form that amateurs in the late eighteenth century could produce at home. Frontal head-and-shoulder pictures, on the other hand, relatively more intimate than the other three categories, gave at least a slight sense of a direct encounter between beholder and beheld and were not overwhelmingly grandiose;[20] the decreased sense of distance of many such portraits and corresponding increased access enabled viewers to gawk at the renowned figure's face, a pleasure that was enhanced by the eighteenth century's unprecedented interest in the individual. Full-length individual portraits accomplished something else, magnifying the success or failure of the depicted fashion, style, and regal comportment. Scenes in company with others added the attraction of narrative.

Starting in 1772, the scenes in which the tsarina appeared were often political prints, usually satires. Though celebrity discourse generally shuns overtly political issues, the sheer presence of the famed empress in these cartoons, many of them Dutch, could stimulate celebrity discourse too. By the 1780s, British visual satirists were developing a biting and vivid new style, using fewer words, reducing the number of figures in each picture, developing a system of identifying markers for key individuals,[21] and devising shocking new metaphors for their messages (Chapter 10).

Reaching an Inclusive Market: Captions, Frames, Backgrounds, Size, Paper, Color

To facilitate the conversion of pictures into celebrity commodities that attracted many buyers and fulfilled the hopes of a whole stream of profit-seeking craftsmen (and, sometimes, craftswomen), other factors mattered as well—caption language and contents, speed of production in some instances, framing and background, size, paper quality, and, occasionally, use of color.

Almost all printed pictures include words in languages that approximately signpost the intended audience. Since French was spoken among the privileged classes from Dublin to Warsaw, a fine print with a caption in that language might well reach audiences across much of Europe; a mediocre print with a caption in French would probably reach the middling classes in French-speaking regions but otherwise not travel far. Latin could address well-schooled viewers (which eliminated most women), or, because such captions were often rather short and full of cognates, could give less educated viewers and owners a sense of refinement. German was a familiar and usually not elite language from Northern Italy to St. Petersburg; even German royalty often did not and sometimes could not speak German. English, used in captions of the blended portrait, Mosley's "Habit" print, and many others, could reach a far-ranging population, both elite and non-elite, in several regions of the world. Captions in Dutch, Italian, and other choices usually indicated prints made for the home audience. A good version of the profile-in-braids type was made for customers in Spain (Figure 3.8), but its caption is so full of peculiarities that the person who devised it perhaps was not literate in Spanish (or possibly Catalan). Russian, little known west of the Oder and Neisse Rivers, was rare in Western prints aside from depictions of medals. The Parisian engraver who tried to use it as a guarantor of authenticity was an exception (Figure 3.4). In fact, although the Cyrillic inscription in the oval around Catherine's image reproduces her name correctly, it then veers into unreadable nonsense, wisely complemented by a label in Latin letters familiar to the printmaker's customers.

Images inevitably appear within frames, whether the Parisian's inscribed oval, LeBeau's elaborate garlands, the rim of a television screen, the sliced edges of a photographic print, or the white paper around a magazine picture. Frames matter, affecting the meaning and potential uses of the images. Some prints of Catherine II had, as Benjamin Schmidt calls them, "trompe l'oeil borders that mimicked the appearance of bona fide picture frames." Such frames "added depth and enhanced the visual impact" of the prints.[22] Backgrounds could be enhancing too and could influence meaning. The anonymous English blend of Bernigeroth and Caravaque omitted the earlier print's ostentatious palace setting and billowing baroque drape behind the figure, replacing it with a plain dark background and zooming in closer to the face and upper body of the empress. With that, the pearls around her neck and woven into her hair are more evident, while the bare oval frame, topped with a small bow, underscores the elegant simplicity of the image, reframed a last time by the blank margins of the rectangular paper. LeBeau's print showed no such restraint. He exhibited the empress's face in front of dramatic clouds, suggesting her elevated station both physically and metaphorically; he rested the oval frame, a common favorite for portraits, on a heraldic arrangement of bulbous Russian crown, crossed sword and scepter, and symbolic double-eagle shield, and reframed all of that with an outer, cross-hatched rectangle, setting his caption in a separate space below the picture.[23] Berger, in contrast, appealed to buyers with different tastes when he chose a classicizing frame, with a few small nicks on its edges, as though it and the empress it encircled already had the endorsement of time; her picture appears to rest on a slightly battered shelf, which is framed in turn by a plain, cross-hatched

Figure 3.8 A well-made version of the profile-in-braids type has a caption intended to reach an audience in Spain but anomalies in word choice and spelling suggest the caption writer was not fully literate in Spanish. Source: *Cathalina II, Czarina de Moscovia y Emperatríz de la Rusias nacio â 2 de Mayo de 1729*. Credit: Royal Collection Trust / © Her Majesty Queen Elizabeth II 2021.

rectangle. A crown tops the oval, its tip reaching just beyond the darkened rectangle, and at the base is a Russian double eagle with a coat of arms depicting a tiny equestrian St. George. A sense of depth is created by the frame's engraved shadow on the wall behind. Whether ornately grand or classically restrained, the frames within prints that occurred for virtually every close-up portrait of Catherine II from half-length to head and shoulders served to isolate the image and mark the transition from the featured face and richly dressed body of the empress to the mundane, plain outer edge of the paper and, with it, to the commonplace world of the viewer. The printed frame readied the picture for tacking to the wall, as records of middling-class homes show happened, or for inserting in an album of special treasures, all part of commodifying the empress.

Some publishers appealed to print collectors by tapping their impulse to acquire prints in a series.[24] Two early prints by Bause of Peter III and Catherine II (Figures 8.1 and 8.2), for example, are numbered 6 and 7 on the top edge of each image, signaling that they were part of a larger, evolving group that buyers might want to watch for. In another instance, a little over two decades into Catherine II's reign, a picture of her in an elaborate gown appeared in a set of French fashion pictures within a larger series of sets illustrating the dress styles of contemporary or historical roles and individuals. The savvy Paris publisher Duflos meant pictures of his figures, who ranged from Confucius to a

Figure 3.9 The publisher Duflos sold his fashion images in sets and offered them both plain and meticulously painted. Source: *Catherine II. d'Anhalt-Zerbst, Impératrice de Russie, d'Après un Medaille du temps*, in *Receuil d'estampes, représentant les Grades, les Rangs & les Dignités, suivant le costume de toutes les Nations existantes* (Paris: Duflos, 1784). Bridgeman Images. Image number: STC158928.

senator in Hamburg, to be collected and then bound together into a book. The group of six in which Catherine's picture appeared was the twenty-second installment, announced for sale in February 1784.[25] The empress wears an elaborate court costume, including wide panniers and an immense open skirt, with festoons of fur, familiar sign of the north (Figure 3.9). The colorist for at least one of the copies chose to make the outer skirt pink and the exposed petticoat pale green. The tip of one pink slipper peeks out from the middle of the hem. The caption of the fashion engraving claims that the image was based on a medal depicting the empress, but, in fact, it is another version of Erichsen's grand painting that had been circulating for more than two decades by then, complete with the cap-like crown. For well-informed fans, the golden hair of the colored image would have been a distraction: Catherine's hair was reported to be brown. Nonetheless, this glamorous, high-fashion concoction shows what a French print seller expected his prosperous, trend-conscious customers wanted the Russian empress to look like.

The generous size of the image and of the paper on which it was printed added to its cost, at a time when the best, most expensive pictures were always printed on large sheets of the highest quality of thick white paper. Familiar paper sizes in the eighteenth century ranged from the largest, royal, through the sequence folio, quarto, octavo, down to the very small duodecimo, and even smaller. Each one, after the first, represents another fold in the paper, and is thus half the size of the one before; specific measurements are hard to offer since sheet sizes were not standardized. Size then becomes one of several marks that can allow the inference of price and thus of intended market, with smaller pictures generally cheaper, though certain tiny novelty products were exceptions, such as an exquisite book about the size of a postage stamp containing portraits of nine rulers on heavy white paper edged in gold (Figure 3.10).[26] Some pictures—and some books—were printed on more than one quality of paper.

Identifying pictures of Catherine II that were available in a wide range of prices and that appealed to diverse audiences helps makes the case that she was an international celebrity. The cheapest prints, however, those designed to have the most popular appeal, were long of no interest to the connoisseurs whose collections became the basis of today's print rooms; such prints fell into the category of the (probably) most produced

Figure 3.10 An exquisite (now disassembled) miniature book depicted Catherine II among eight other, mostly German, rulers. Source: [Lambert], *Catarina R. I.*, in miniature book: *Bitte und Erhoerung* [Germany], 1779. Inv.-Nr. VI, 144,5a. Courtesy of the Kunstsammlungen der Veste Coburg/Germany.

but least preserved. One surviving example is a colorful little picture on brownish rough paper, approximately the size of a modern playing card. Varying the profile-in-braids type, it depicts Catherine wearing the fur-trimmed dress and looking purposefully straight ahead, but her hair, not in braids, is pulled back softly from her forehead and face and falls in a gentle curl over her near shoulder; to an audience of commoners, perhaps the replacement of braids with a looser coiffure suggested more expensive and thus celebrity-enhancing styling. Enlargement of her eyes and lips brings her closer to viewers, facilitating connection. But the most striking innovation of the print is that it ditches the subtlety of its uncolored cousins in favor of bright paints, probably stamped onto the image, rendering the empress's cheeks rosy, her lips ruby, the fur brown, her dress scarlet, and the neck ruff white. Undoubtedly the color raised the price, but with it the little print seized attention, especially for a clientele that seldom saw colored pictures on paper; those who could not afford the daubed versions could try for plain ones instead.

The print has more signs of this intended audience as well. One is the empress's diminutive, but obvious, crown. Engravers and painters making head-and-shoulders portraits for better educated, more experienced viewers could assume their audience would know that high rank was often signaled by a glimpse of ribbon or badge. In most images of Catherine, a ribbon crosses her chest, or an embroidered, jewel-encrusted, and star-shaped badge of an exclusive chivalric order decorates her dress. Even if, as in many prints of the braids type, one or both of these emblems were partly cut off by the edge of the picture or by a piece of drapery, for knowledgeable viewers the bit that remained was enough to signify her rank. Crowning the portrayed figure, on the other hand, made the visual code of the court easy for less experienced viewers and possible buyers to decipher.

The print's caption, furthermore, explains instead of assuming and places Catherine II firmly in a context that would have been meaningful to German audiences. In the band around the image the woman is identified as "Catherine II, Current Czarina," while two lines below the picture add: "Daughter of Prince Chris[tian] of Anhalt Zerbst, born May 2, 1729."[27] The brief text thus announces Catherine II's name and rank, allows a viewer to compute her age, locates her geographically by using the title tsarina, and notes the local genealogy that brings her close to the print's audience. Such explanatory information is redolent of the less sophisticated levels of non-elite buyers. The print's small size, cheap paper, bright color, redundant design elements (crown, star, and label too), relatively simplified engraving style, and explanatory caption all signify its intended audience as thrifty and not sophisticated, with basic levels of literacy, not familiar with the codes of court life, not attracted by the subtleties of skilled engraving, and yet fascinated by a German woman who had suddenly attained amazing power and status.

Picture Distributors, Sellers, and Price

The little colored print, LeBeau's somewhat bungled picture, Berger's better rendition, Mosley's invented "Habit" scene, and a varied assortment of anonymous prints—all of these joined a market for printed images that was flourishing spectacularly in the eighteenth century.[28] Art dealers helped their rich clients, including wealthy members of the non-elite ranks, to leaven their collections of old masters reproductions with more contemporary images, such as portraits and eventually political cartoons, with

Catherine II appearing in both genres. Booksellers, general shops, market stands, and local estate auctions sold prints to more middling-class purchasers. The colorful little print may have been in a peddler's pack. On some portraits of the empress were instructions explaining how to find the place where the pictures were sold; Berger, for example, specified that he could be found "in Spandauer Street near the Golden Anchor in Berlin," and the engraver who strove to use Cyrillic was on Gallande Street in Paris between a chandler and a crate maker. But buying was not the only option. At least a few shops posted notices in newspapers that they had pictures to rent, especially satires.

All commodification requires prices, and each price was the effect both of choices by the makers and distributors and of purchasers' anticipated preferences in particular categories. While celebrity discourse is always imbricated in the market economy, in most cases the prices of prints at the time of their initial distribution are missing now. Duflos's collectible French fashion print is an exception. The set to which Catherine's picture belonged cost nine livres if the six prints were colored and about half as much plain.[29] With tailors earning perhaps four livres per month,[30] such a purchase was impossible for most people, but to wealthy elite and non-elite segments of society the fashion prints might have been a charming and affordable acquisition.[31]

Overall, when both skilled and unskilled visual media makers produced pictures of Catherine II in large and small formats, on various qualities of paper, with and without color, they were enabling a range of prices great enough for celebrity discourse to function. Catherine II's potential distant audiences could acquire or at least encounter visual commodities that fit their economic diversity. Though amateurs may sometimes have used simple technology to craft representations of the empress that they then gave away—perhaps Goethe's plain plaster cast of a medal depicting Catherine II was of this type[32]—engravers and printmakers, but also professional editors, booksellers, writers, and pamphleteers who made representations of the Russian empress for general audiences far from her own territories were speculating on her marketability and thereby commodifying her. Most media workers in both words and images were unable to support themselves solely with commissions from elite clients and so intended to reach ordinary, less discerning, and more numerous customers. They tried to do so with products that met potential buyers' desire to believe themselves informed—correctly or not—about the empress, to have their imaginations roused, even to feel a personal connection to her.

Speed of production sometimes mattered. After Catherine's death, for example, Johann Erich Biester complained that his book entitled *Sketch of the Life and Reign of Empress Catherine II of Russia* had to be painfully truncated to meet his publisher's demand that it be ready for Germany's Easter book fair. Haste partially explains why in his and most of the other biographies that appeared soon after Catherine's death long passages were lifted nearly word for word from various previously published sources. Copying was the rushed writer's secret vice, as invention was that of the printmaker. But Biester recognized that his book was a "ware" that would be "worthless if it arrives at the market after the shops have closed"; all his efforts would be "completely in vain, if I with my industriousness arrive later than all my competitors."[33] Books, pamphlets, and periodicals purveying accounts of Catherine II were commodities. When such materials about Catherine II facilitated readers' engrossed attachments to her in a range of countries far from her dominions, they launched the empress into modern international celebrity.

Commodifying Further: Eighteenth-Century Celebrity Endorsements

Once Catherine II was famous across Europe, with her name and title conveying the enticing qualities of wealth, elegance, fashion, and social edginess on which celebrity thrives, she gained an additional commercial function, part of what Graeme Turner calls the "cultural pervasiveness" of a celebrity, "as the cultural meanings of and associations with the star leak into all kinds of locations in our daily lives."[34] Marketing could draw on the nimbus around her to sell almost anything. Advertisement writers in England might entice newspaper readers to buy "curious French pyes," supposedly from Catherine's British cheese merchants, to acquire the tooth powder sold by her dentist or the hairpieces with which she embellished her coiffure, or to attend an evening's entertainment watching "surprising and wonderful experiments" that she had (supposedly) enjoyed.[35]

In 1773, when Catherine II decided to acquire an English dinner and dessert set, the manufactory of Josiah Wedgwood also initiated a round of publicity that positioned royals as high-profile shoppers whose purchases might be of interest to a broader audience. The stipulation on Catherine's immense order that each of the 952 pieces should be decorated with a different English scene had swollen Wedgwood's need for designs and given opportunities to hosts of artists. When the work was finished, the canny entrepreneur, desiring to "complete our [the firm's] notoriety to the whole Island . . . & help us greatly . . . in the sale of our goods," placed an announcement in the newspapers that members of the high and low aristocracy were invited to an exhibition room of the company to see the service before it was sent to the empress.[36] The idea succeeded. Queen Charlotte was so curious that even she came to see the Green Frog Service, with its little amphibians alluding to the name of the palace for which it was destined. More than that, by seeing the announced display in the newspaper, members of the public further down the social scale could at least know about the display and might imagine what they could not see.

In 1780, one of Catherine's correspondents in Paris wrote about the many shop signs there for things Russian, including cafes and a hotel, and signs for places called "At the Russian Empress's."[37] A little undated piece of ephemera, an engraved slip of paper about four inches by seven, advertised such a shop in Vienna named "At the Russian Empress" (Figure 3.11). The text, first in German and then in French, announced that Ferdinand Leuthner, "Marchand bourgeois," middling-class merchant, at his shop on the centrally located Bauernmarkt, sold all types of silk wares, Batavia stockings and scarves, ready-made women's dresses, muslins, batistes, Dutch tulles, ribbons, gloves, "and every type of the newest fashionable wares."[38] The top half of the page displays a much modified image of Catherine II that gave her a distinct and friendly smile (not just the usual expression of gracious condescension or wise farsightedness) and updated her hairdo with increased volume and a curl over each shoulder. Though adorned with a crown and other imperial emblems, she appears as a happy and prosperous matron, gladly supporting Mr. Leuthner. It all belonged to mediating and commodifying the glorious empress and to constructing her as a celebrity for a large, sometimes surprisingly denationalized audience.[39]

Figure 3.11 A card for the shop "At the Russian Empress" in Vienna advertised in German and French the wonderful goods that could be purchased there. Source: Business leaf for Vienna shop: *Bey der Russischen Kaiserin. Ferdinand Leüthner Burgl. Handels Mann bey der Rusischen Kaiserin . . . verkauft alle Gattungen Glate, Fasionirte, und broschürte seiden Waren, Pattavia seidene Strimpffe und Tüchel, abgenähte Frauenkleider, Moussolines, Pattistes, Toule Niederländer und zwieren Spitzen Plondes Dünntücher Bänder, Handschuhe, und jede Art der neuesten Modewaren.* Courtesy of the Bildarchiv und Grafiksammlung, Osterreichische Nationalbibliothek PORT_00033949_01

In 1790, a London coach-maker followed Wedgwood with a printed invitation announcing that a carriage "Made For The EMPRESS of RUSSIA" was "now ready for inspection at Mess. Hatchett, Son, and Co's."[40] Since at least 1783 any passing literate gawker could see a storefront sign in Longacre Street announcing that Hatchett made coaches for the Russian empress as well as for the British king; the company's trade card announced the connection in English and French.[41] An article in the *European Magazine* for the same year described the carriage made for Catherine as a "magnificent" and "striking" example of "Mr. Hatchett's taste and genius," which had gained "universal applause" and yielded an immense reward for Mr. Hatchett, "if we recollect right," of 1,300 guineas.[42] When more about Catherine's coach appeared in the broadsides, any newspaper reader could have fantasies of the vehicle and its extravagant commissioner.[43]

Many eighteenth-century media workers, though not always the most skilled and most respected, participated in making the commodities that celebrity requires. That decision influenced their genre choices, affected the content they selected, flattened their levels of diction, and guided captions. In the case of Catherine II, over the three and a half decades of her reign and for almost fifteen more years after her death, the resulting items—books, pamphlets, pictures, puzzles, advertisements, poems and more—were crucial for stoking the interest and feelings of her fans and her anti-fans.

4

Fans and Anti-Fans for a Commodity Empress

Celebrity cannot exist without fans: an audience of people paying close attention to a famous contemporary who is usually of little or no practical consequence to them individually outside their captivation. Indeed, fans' knowledge of the figure is only or primarily commercially mediated, and yet many perceive themselves in an intense and personal though one-way relationship with the star. In 1762, when Catherine II seized the throne and—thanks to floods of newspapers that were produced by masses of media workers beyond her borders—interest in her burgeoned, exactly this attentive audience emerged. War and peace hung in the balance just long enough to make intelligence of the changed Russian leadership immensely important to ordinary people as well as those in power. With those issues soon settled, the suspenseful, unexpected, and conflicting accounts of the tsarina's personal story, the stuff of celebrity that had been present from almost the first days of reporting, could dominate for many readers and listeners. This chapter examines who the avid followers of the empress were, what forces drew them to her in a one-sided relationship, how the materiality of fandom registers the fans' existence, and how ambivalence and rejection could be incorporated into fandom.

Far looser than the bourgeois public sphere posited by Jürgen Habermas, audiences for celebrity discourse about the empress extended from the lower aristocracy and gentry to the untitled, but usually well-educated and sometimes very wealthy, upper layers of middling society, further to the traditional middle ranks in trade and guilds, on to lower-level urban workers, among whom most of Europe's thousands of free and enslaved Africans would be found, and, finally, to the urban poor, and, at least intermittently (on market days, for example), to the largest population segment, the peasantry. These diverse echelons from rich to poor were the intended customers of the media makers generating pamphlets, poems, and portraits of the empress throughout her reign. The stipulations that fans' knowledge of the central figure be indirect and commercial and that the figure have no or few practical implications for them as individuals explain why people of exalted rank are not significant as fans. For Catherine's world, this meant the exclusion of royals and aristocrats exalted enough in the social hierarchy to be informed at least partly through confidential (though leaky) diplomatic channels or to have ambitions vulnerable to actions of the empress; in a few corners of Europe these exclusions applied to hereditary patricians too.[1]

The conditions for fandom varied from country to country. England, with its early use of new sources of power, new materials, and new ways of organizing production, had rising numbers of people with cash, potential consumers of celebrity goods.[2]

The populace of the lower Rhine, though not especially engaged in early industrial development, was benefiting during this period both from their trade networks and from their roles as financial centers. Spain's economy, including its assortment of small businesses that sustained a traditional middle class, continued to profit, in varying degrees, from its involvement in the complex Atlantic trading system. France, amid its increasing economic problems in the second half of the eighteenth century, had at least some broad popular participation in consumer extravagance, as indicated by fashion purchases. But such a record can be misleading. In the German principalities, for example, periodicals that touted new products evidently gave readers more practice imagining luxury consumption than making acquisitions.[3] The same may have been true in fragmented Italy, with its highly uneven distribution of wealth and opportunity.

Direct documentation of Catherine II's fans is limited, but Gabriel Sénac de Meilhan addressed his letters about visiting the Russian tsarina (first published in 1792) to one of them. (Son of Louis XV's doctor, he had gone to St. Petersburg in hopes of an appointment at court but had rather quickly lost Catherine's confidence, a situation he never mentions in his glowing public account of her.)[4] Already his addressee's cryptic name, Madame de ***, stands in well for the anonymous mass of eighteenth-century fans. She had been, Sénac noted, an avid follower of another famous figure, Samuel Richardson, author of the hugely popular novels *Pamela* and *Clarissa*, and had acquired pens and a writing case that had belonged to him. These tokens of connection, Sénac wrote, she preserved like precious jewels. Knowing that Madame de *** would "treasure the least minutia" about Catherine II, the French traveler hoped with his book metaphorically to produce "Catherine's quills" and so to enhance her relationship with the empress, one-sided though it might be. The word "fan," from fanatic, had not yet entered the language,[5] so Sénac categorized his addressee's intense feelings as "curiosity" about someone "who has gained general attention and aroused admiration."

Among the components of this special curiosity was Madame de ***'s wish to receive from the author a portrait of the inspiring figure.[6] A much different fan of the empress, a poor, illiterate, working-class woman who appeared in a British magazine article about Catherine's overthrow of Peter III, also expressed interest in a picture of the empress. Goody Grogg, whose name invokes the vulgar, grog-drinking urban crowd and their supposedly low tastes, is described as the magazine scribbler's laundress. She may be an invention, but a plausible one. Goody, although already well informed about the basic outline of the momentous events that had just taken place in St. Petersburg, wanted to know more, telling the writer that "people love to hear . . . all about" the Russian story, and she urged him to include with his article a picture of Catherine II, or rather a picture for the imagination, because she added, "why you may get one easy enough," by buying "an old copper-plate" of another "outlandish" lady, then "rubbing out her name" and replacing it with the empress's.[7] One engraver, Johann Lorenz Rügendas, or perhaps his printer, indulged in exactly this fraud, re-labeling a picture of Maria Josepha of Bavaria; the nicely produced image does not actually resemble other portraits of either woman.[8] Such pictures provided an object to be looked at nonetheless, a person to encounter, and so offered a version of the "public intimacy" that celebrity promises.[9] So did entirely invented pictures labeled Catherine II—a particularly clumsy full-length image giving her a small head and overlong upper arms is a good example (Figure 4.1)—and they were

Figure 4.1 This clumsy invented image of Catherine II holding a huge scepter suggests an appeal to fans unfamiliar with state portraiture. Source: *Catharina II Jetzt Regierende Russische Kaÿserin geb. d.2 Maj 1729*. Print belonging to author, R. Dawson; photo by author.

likely to be cheaply made. Sénac de Meilhan's far more sophisticated fan, Madame de *** (if she was not also an invention), on the other hand, certainly knew authoritative prints of the tsarina from among the abundance available in France.

Fan Access to Celebrity Discourse

The mechanics of eighteenth-century fandom begin with access to celebrity discourse, primarily via printed representations. For Catherine II, the materials ranged from official documents reprinted in newspapers and magazines, to semi-official materials, to unofficial assortments, and, of course, a wide range of pictures. Official government materials, those that the empress or her agents commissioned or authorized in Russia and that made their way into general circulation outside the country, were unmistakably meant to minimize negative responses, gloss over problems, and, after the initial manifestos about the coup, exclude the personal details about Catherine that are crucial to celebrity. Semi-official representations that reached beyond Russian borders, those produced outside the government but presented either directly to the empress or indirectly at events sponsored by state organizations, were also excessively positive and sycophantic, as evident in orations that were given in Russia to honor the empress, then published, often in German, and sent abroad[10] or a tedious poem by Johann Gottfried Herder, an otherwise fiery young intellectual in the Baltic region who briefly envisioned himself becoming one of Catherine's reformist advisers.[11] Semi-official representations, deeply influenced by the great power of the empress, testified to her glory but lacked the edge and potential intimacy of the unofficial. Unofficial materials, those the empress and her agents could not control, at least not well, were the main stuff of fan discourse, whether in magazines, travel books, novels, letters, or biography, including memoirs and life histories of people close to the tsarina. Of all unofficial texts during the more than three decades of Catherine's reign, newspapers were the crucial medium in words for her celebrity and for eighteenth-century celebrity culture in general.[12] Newspapers were the first source of information about the empress after the coup, the one source that added frequently to her story through all the years, and the one most widely available to her distant fans.

An article under the heading "newspaper" in Johann Heinrich Zedler's highly regarded eighteenth-century encyclopedia of the time suggests how a large non-elite public of readers and listeners was drawn to Catherine II by newspaper stories. The original purpose of these weekly to daily publications a century earlier, Zedler correctly explained, had been to give merchants and traders the information they needed to conduct business, but to a broad audience now, he added ruefully, the gazettes were merely a source of entertainment. Of what value was it, the encyclopedia writer demanded, for an ordinary reader to know this: "In Petersburg a fireworks display is being prepared," or "Yesterday the king went hunting and then returned to Versailles in the evening." Useless information about the most privileged members of society and their doings, the very stuff of celebrity, was, the encyclopedist growled, of no benefit to ordinary people. Nor was this wastefulness confined to the literate, whose changing proportions of various regional populations scholars still debate.[13] Literate or not, a "common craftsman," the Zedler writer grumbled, or a laundress, the magazine writer might have added, could listen "the whole day to someone who wants to tell or read him" precisely such newspaper trivialities.[14] Though "excessive newspaper reading," the encyclopedist acknowledged, was creating profits for an extended range of media workers, from papermakers to printers, to postal services, and more, that did not justify the time-wasting frivolity the practice induced.[15]

By the middle of the eighteenth century, France had about twenty-nine papers, almost exclusively locally licensed versions of the *Gazette de France*;[16] they were augmented by independent French-language papers that were published in the Netherlands and Germany and then imported into France. In German-speaking areas, at least ninety-three gazettes were appearing regularly by 1750 in the local language. By 1785, with more papers appearing in both countries, the count was 151 in Germany and 44 in France.[17] Newspapers were expanding in the Low Countries and England too and in their far-flung colonies.[18] In Spain and Italy, the numbers were smaller, but newspapers emerged there as well. Adding to the coverage everywhere, individual issues of papers usually had multiple readers or listeners.[19] The result of all this newspaper enthusiasm was that there was "probably no permanent European settlement anywhere in the world where printed newssheets did not eventually make their way" in the eighteenth century. Furthermore, such gazettes were "printed in numerous European cities and towns that had no other major intellectual institutions: no universities, no academies, no book publishers."[20] Aside from particular central and southern regions of Europe with the smallest educated middling ranks of society, the newspapers at the heart of eighteenth-century celebrity were available.

Their late eighteenth-century readers, fans or not, were, of course, inevitably enmeshed in the broader political scene of their time, which, for much of Catherine's reign, included Britain's contest with France for power on the seas and over the seas, Spain's uncomfortable weakness, Italy's fragmentation, Germany's splintered form despite the nominally unifying leadership of the (usually Habsburg) Holy Roman Emperor, the awkwardly discontiguous and multilingual conglomerate of Habsburg hereditary lands that were scattered from the Southern Netherlands to Austria to Italy, and also, just east of the borders chosen for this study, both Poland's tempestuous internal instability and the Muslim Ottoman Empire's continuing domination over a large area of southeastern Europe (including all of Greece), as well as much of the Mediterranean rim. The gazettes were accordingly filled with political and military struggles. But readers could understand the same materials in different ways, some attuned to war news, political analysis, or economic content, and others finding material for celebrity discourse. Readers of no aristocratic or royal rank could engage in political debate in coffee houses and taverns, on street corners, or elsewhere, but, until almost the last decade of the century, they could only rarely convert debate into messages audible to the powerful.

Within that general political helplessness, celebrity culture could function as an alternative form of engagement, an apparently apolitical relation to, in Catherine II's case, a comfortably distant, but clearly formidable, ruler. Catherine's unfolding life as represented in the foreign press could induce quantities of gossip, and whenever people spoke of her, they helped concoct her celebrity. For ordinary non-elite women in particular, omitting political discussion from celebrity discourse was especially appropriate, given the eighteenth century's particular resistance to their political participation. Celebrity discourse—the whole range of ostensibly depoliticized talk, print, imagery and thought about a central figure—is exemplified by precisely the non-utilitarian quality that Zedler denounced when he noted that many newspaper readers and listeners "hardly . . . get or even seek any gain beyond being able to talk in society and passing the time." Yet, with representations of Catherine II reaching everyone, from working-class auditors such as Goody to highly privileged readers, an audience eager to talk together about the empress had immediately emerged.

Recounting what was happening at her house one morning in 1775, Fanny Burney had noted, "Charlotte was reading the newspaper."[21] Among the non-elite perusers of eighteenth-century newspapers were many women and girls, though scholars more often discuss men reading in coffee houses. Amalie Liemann, the eleven-year-old daughter of a wealthy German merchant-capitalist in Russia, was a newspaper reader and knew that her former governess, Helena Gatterer, having returned to Germany, had probably read in the gazettes of Prince Potemkin's visit to the Liemann family on June 16, 1791.[22] In a little collection of Liemann's letters that Gatterer published—it is the only book about the world of Catherine II's court that was written by a child—

Amalie's version of the Potemkin visit is exactly in the manner of an eighteenth-century newspaper report, composed in declarative sentences that cite a series of visible but impersonal signs. The Liemann house had been "illuminated" with lamps on all the window ledges and rooftops, the imperial names were fixed to the house and its gates in flowers, cannons were sounded as the prince arrived, bringing a large retinue with him, and the table was set for forty-five. Unfortunately, the letter omitted any note of the temper of the notoriously moody and imperious Potemkin or the topics of conversation at the grand dinner, or whether Amalia Liemann herself had sat among the privileged diners.

Changes in reading practices, especially for women and girls, also contributed to celebrity discourse. The old mode of intensive reading, concentrating on a small set of usually religious texts that were much reread, was being supplemented and eventually largely displaced by a new mode of extensive reading, reading widely, often

Figure 4.2 This crudely made woodcut, on a page labeled *Depiction of Russian Empress Catherine II*, appeared in a Swiss Limping Messenger almanac for 1773. Even pictures as simple as this one, disseminated especially to a rural populace, spread the empress's popular fame. Source: *Abschilderung der Russischen Kayserin Catharina II.* Courtesy of the Appenzell Ausserrhoden Kantonsbibliothek, Trogen, Switzerland.

for pleasure.²³ The memoirist Friederike Baldinger recalled reading the Bible daily with her mother but also constantly looking with her aunt for different, fresh texts to enjoy.²⁴ She was especially fascinated by the news of "kings and kaisers" that they found in both a scholarly newspaper from a nearby university town and a popular almanac, a so-called Limping Messenger (*hinkender Bote* or *messager boiteux*). This publication type, usually annual and produced in many different places in Europe, was intended to include the minimally schooled members of society (whose collections of printed material were so seldom preserved that copies of these "Messengers" are rare today).²⁵ Issues usually contained woodcuts; those depicting an important personage, even if crudely made, might promote celebrity (Figure 4.2).²⁶ For most fans, however, newspapers dominated, supplemented by pictures bought separately.

What Celebrity Offered Fans: From Entertainment and Identification to Fantasies of Social Mobility

In addition to requiring access to celebrity materials, the mechanics of eighteenth-century fandom needed to provide valued experiences, ranging from private entertainment to the sociable pastime of talking with others, the pleasures of identifying with a famous person, and on to visions of social mobility or of "intimacy at a distance."²⁷ Celebrity artifacts promoted these experiences. A distinctive visual genre of the time, for example, the engraved puzzle print, could contribute to both private and group celebrity entertainment with the invitation to seek and identify the profiles of prominent persons, mostly royals, concealed in an unrelated image, for example, of a vase or a garden. Catherine II's profile was a component of several of the surviving puzzles (Figure 4.3).²⁸ While solving them would seem to end the pleasure to the owners, it appears likely that these prints were brought out repeatedly as new visitors or friends could be invited to try the search together. Playing such games and gossiping about the hunts or fireworks displays in Petersburg or Versailles belonged to at least incipient celebrity discourse. But celebrity discourse goes far beyond this to what the scholar Graeme Turner calls "an important social process through which relationships, identity, and social and cultural norms are debated, evaluated, modified and shared."²⁹

Much of that process occurs through fantasy and identification and was promoted by texts and images inviting fans to relocate temporarily into different social worlds. Materials that incessantly represent the celebrity as having a special and noteworthy identity and yet also as having ordinary qualities entice fans into identifying with the spectacular subject. Sénac de Meilhan was attuned to this attraction and wrote astutely about how celebrity worked. Offering Madame de *** his portrait of Catherine II in words, he promised to "penetrate into her inner life and to know the details that give an accurate idea of her personally and of what motivates her." This did not include "the wars, conquests, and alliances that make Catherine's reign renowned"; those events were of no interest to him, to Madame de ***, or, implicitly, to the larger audience of fans who would buy Sénac's little pamphlet about the empress. His effort was to create an account of the tsarina not as the aloof, grand monarch but "débarrassée des

Figure 4.3 Puzzle prints such as this invited viewers to find silhouettes hidden in the scene and connect them with famous personalities, including the empress of Russia. Source: *Vier verborgene Silhouetten.* Getty Images. Landscape containing four silhouettes. Editorial Number: 1288013317. Credit: Sepia Times / Contributor.

habits impériaux" (freed of her imperial garments); such an account, Sénac crucially asserted, would promote identification with her. "Self-esteem tells us," he wrote, "that we, by thinking, feeling, and acting like them in ordinary things, would not be so very far from them in greater things either, if we played a role on the stage of the higher world."[30],[31]. Suddenly the text deploys inclusive first-person plural forms, suggesting that the writer was identifying with the empress too. This pathway of identification explained, he said, why the "smallest circumstances" and the "greatest trivialities" mattered so much. Especially for the relations of fans and incipient fans to the distant Russian empress, whom Sénac called "the star I came to see" (107), fans' condition of exclusion from her presence strengthened the importance of having a "mediated quasi-interaction"[32] with her and at least potentially with each other.

For fans, the culture of celebrity "forms a symbolic pathway, [giving] each aspiring individual [an] image of fulfillment: to be someone, when 'being no one' is the norm."[33] Thus, in addition to companionable discussion or argument, individual enjoyment, and identification, celebrity discourse proposes visions of upward mobility. This became part of the vocabulary of attributes that Catherine II's celebrity offered to the public. Her skill at conversation led the father of governess Helene Gatterer and her poet sister, Philippine Engelhard-Gatterer, to tell his witty and loquacious wife:

"Mama, . . . it's surprising that you didn't become a great princess; you could have turned into a Catherine!"[34]

An invented German print by the obscure J. P. Wolff tells her altered Cinderella story in its picture and caption, where Catherine's origin in a family that was indeed titled but otherwise insignificant underscored the chance to see her as almost "one of us." As a sixteen-year-old, she marries a prince, then actually becomes king, and now, as the image shows, stands there calmly and confidently in all the regalia of her high office. The explanatory text de-Russifies her, stressing her German connections through both her father and, in his role as a German duke, her husband. The caption alludes only circumspectly to Peter III's overthrow and omits his demise:

> Catharina. II. Empress and Autocrat of all the Russians; born May 2, 1729, a daughter of Prince Christian August of Anhalt-Zerbst, married to the Grand Duke of Russia and Duke of Holstein-Gottorp Carl Peter Ulrich on Sept. 1, 1745. Was declared empress of Russia in place of her husband on July 9 and was crowned at Moscow on September 22, 1762.

The picture that these words accompany deploys the accoutrements that could be expected of a state portrait, including a voluminous draped swag pulled theatrically to the side and a long, ermine-lined cloak swirling around the empress. The print's relatively large, quarto size, about the same as a modern business letter, probably indicates that it was meant for purchasers within the middling classes who could afford to spend money to acquire a rather splashy picture and who were perhaps drawn by its message of social mobility, always an important strand of celebrity discourse.

Complementing such visions, celebrity discourse promised fans a chance to move beyond the public construction of the star and to feel knowledgeable about the "real" person behind the glamour or grandeur, to mediate the unmediated. Charles Francois Philibert Masson, a writer in French who had spent years at Catherine's court near the end of her reign, published a much-translated account of her that confirmed how different she was publicly and privately. Masson emphasized her cheerfulness and friendliness in intimate settings, and the feeling of happiness and fun that surrounded her. He added, however, that anyone who was admitted to her private apartments could see that as soon as she put on her gloves to leave her rooms and appear in the public spaces of the palace, she changed. "She assumed a very different countenance and deportment. From an agreeable and facetious woman, she appeared all at once the reserved and majestic empress."[35] Catherine understood how to display gravitas and dignity, he asserts. But behind that impressive façade there was, as fans always hoped, a delightful, approachable person whom they could imagine knowing, whose gloves they could even imagine putting on.

An English traveler similarly presented a grand but friendly empress:

> In the morning, between prayers and dinner, she frequently takes an airing, according as the weather admits, in a coach or sledge. On these occasions she has sometimes no guards, and very few attendants; and does not chuse to be known or saluted as Empress. It is in this manner that she visits any great works that may be

going on in the city, or in the neighbourhood. She is fond of having small parties of eight or ten persons with her at dinner; and she frequently sups, goes to balls, or masquerades, in the houses of her nobility. When she retires to her palaces in the country, especially Zariskocelo, she lays aside all state, and lives with her ladies on a footing of as easy intimacy as possible. Any one of them who rises on her entering or going out of a room, is fined in a rouble: and all forfeits of this sort are given to the poor. You will easily perceive, that by her regular and judicious distribution of time, she is able to transact a great deal of business, and that the affability of her manners render her much beloved.[36]

Accounts of the private empress such as this "did not just follow the celebrity; they contributed to the production of celebrity,"[37] as Antoine Lilti suggests.

Since the non-elite public in the west of Europe had little or no unmediated access to the world of courts and, with limited exceptions, no access at all to the imperial court of the Russian tsarina, a dose of idealized unreality often clung to accounts of Catherine's world, as is common to celebrity discourse.[38] The representations by Sénac, Richardson, Masson, and others seemed at many points to display a near perfect empress. As one of her biographers wrote, she had won "the hearts of high and low, of the court and the people"—a routine topos in eighteenth-century descriptions of reigning princes—and "her mind, her cautious behavior, her pleasantness, her youth and grace, her effort to belong fully to the country to which she had been transplanted, the ease with which she learned the Russian language, her dignity when she attended church services, the beauty she brought to the national costume" supposedly made her into a model woman flawlessly adapted to her setting.[39] Such idealization, in texts claiming to offer details about Catherine II as a specific individual, crumbled her image into an ensemble of generic fantasies but was effective nonetheless. Invented portraits too, such as Mosley's "Habit" print (Figure 3.6), idealized the empress and worked to fulfill viewers' desire to identify with her. But celebrity discourse was also full of contradictions and inconsistencies, offering fans a figure who was often simultaneously idealized and transgressive.

Ambivalence and Rejection: Criticism, Anger, and Anti-Fans

As Rosemary Coombe contends, "The celebrity image is a cultural lode of multiple meanings, mined for its symbolic resonances, and, simultaneously, a floating signifier, invested with libidinal energies, [and] social longings."[40] There was never a fixed popular public notion of Catherine II, but rather an array of notions of her, positive and negative, that fans contested in various ways over time. Indeed, Chris Rojek argues that "celebrity is inherently bound up with transgression" and David Marshall, writing about movie stars, adds that certain kinds of transgression endow stars with the "autonomous subjectivity" that fans savor; when the best-known stars extend their impact through transgressive behavior, they appear to be subjects who make their own choices and exercise their own agency in contradiction to social norms.[41] Indeed, Catherine II's transgressions, beginning with the coup itself, offered fans endless opportunities for private identificatory dreams and for sociable interaction, including criticism. An Italian writer, commenting on distasteful accounts of the coup that had been "meticulously forbidden" and yet "reappeared over and over," added the obvious corollary: the prohibited materials "were greedily read."[42]

Catherine II's audiences of wealthy merchants, poor clergymen's widows, and industrious weavers, male or female, and many more were tugged differently according to their ranks and social identities, their wealth or poverty or stages in between, their gender and sexuality, their home countries' varied relations to Russia over the period from the end of the Seven Years' War to the rise of Napoleon, and their changing attitudes toward court society, especially after 1789, when the French Revolution ripped apart many conventional pieties. After all, popular culture, to which the materials of celebrity discourse overwhelmingly belong, is and was always unstable. Indeed, popular culture is, in the words of contemporary scholars, "a site of struggle, a place where conflicts between dominant and subordinate groups are played out, and distinctions between the cultures of these groups are continually constructed and reconstructed."[43] For women celebrities, the norms being challenged are typically construed as breaches of gender or sexuality or both. The sexual behavior ascribed to the empress both in distant media and in the public's collective mind, seeded, as it was, by long-established myths about powerful women, became a common point of attack on her; poet Anna Luisa Karsch's first reaction to the coup news had been to associate Catherine with Livia and Mary Stuart, two women emblematic of power hunger and sexual voracity.[44]

Much though viewers and readers might often happily imagine being in the slippers of the minor German princess who had become rich and famous, they could be critical of her and angry too. Fans were and are often ambivalent about celebrities, swinging with gusto from adoring to despising, glad to shed the envy that lurks around their affection but still fascinated by the attention-grabbing figure. Some could be emotionally engaged but hostile enough to be called anti-fans. Catherine's repelled and engrossed anti-fans, living far beyond her jurisdiction, resisted accepting her transgressions; they could justify their feverish and furious rejection of her emotional tug on them by condemning her political, military, and economic failures if they did not want to address her supposedly personal ones. Yet even when a critique of the empress was mainly political, it could add to celebrity discourse by being "productively consumed by audiences and fans."[45] Conversation-inspiring images were exactly the specialty of the golden age of caricature in Britain, which often deployed metaphors of sexuality to make adversarial appraisals and so gave Catherine's anti-fans a chance to immerse themselves in voyeuristic indignation at her (reported) deeds (Chapter 11).

Popular representations could assume distinctive meanings when the "floating signifier, invested with libidinal energies [and] social longings" is or was a woman. For adventurous distant women and girls who read about the empress from the time of the coup onward, identification with her could offer both a tempting chance at social mobility and imagined transgressive sexual experiences. When Sénac de Meilhan promised to "penetrate" Catherine's private life and "disrobe" her, he seemed to recognize that fans particularly sought not just private but intimate information, hoping to savor the closest possible, though one-way, relation with her, imagining having her most personal feelings, or those of someone near her, such as a lover (even if the particulars about such men were long only suspected); their desire to pry out intricacies of the featured person's temperament, inner life, and private world served to find contact points for aligning the fan's self with the other. Sénac, in his fundamentally unremarkable account of the empress, did not deliver on the promise of revelations, although access to rumors and claims was probably not difficult. During her whole reign, sexual gossip about Catherine II was stuffed into diplomatic pouches for high-ranking readers outside Russia, and other visitors to St. Petersburg asserted that people there spoke openly about the empress's paramours.[46] Details appeared in private writing inside Russia too, as seen in the lively personal letters of Elisabeth von Sievers. Writing to her husband, a Baltic German who held a high post in the Russian government outside the capital, she told about Grigory Orlov's fall from Catherine's favor as it was happening[47] and, a little over a year later, recorded signs of Potemkin's rise. Among the chatty details, she mentioned that the new man had received 3,000 serfs in Poland, "which is not very much," 50,000 rubles in cash, a table service for twenty-four, and a house near the palace, to be furnished at the cost of the court."[48] Later she noted more elements of the lover-favorite sign system—Potemkin's coach drawn by six horses, the sashes of various orders he received, and his seat in the theatre.[49] Frank letters such as hers quite possibly reached addressees outside the country, not through the post, which was monitored, but carried out by travelers. Such accounts, if they did arrive in Western countries, would have been widely read, but they were unlikely to be preserved and published unless they had a famous author or a well-recognized addressee; the only letters of Elisabeth von Sievers known still to exist are those excerpted in a biography of her husband.[50]

The distinguished Horace Walpole in Britain immediately sensed the libidinal possibilities Catherine's alleged behavior offered within his aristocratic set, writing jokingly of a woman friend who imagined herself as Catherine with the same extensive choice of lovers.[51] For men readers and writers, fantasies of being her lover intertwined sexuality with an upward leap in status and wealth. Nor did the decades in which details about the imperial lovers were kept out of print smother such conjurings. In 1775, Goethe, toying with the idea of writing a second novel about the earlier life of his tumultuous character Werther, composed a scene in which the young man and his friends play a game involving imagined marriages; Werther is assigned the role of Catherine's "life companion."[52] Stories or even hunches about the amazing social mobility of the men who became imperial lovers could make them alluring figures for identification. As Elisabeth von Sievers's letters suggested, gaining wealth was intrinsic to the men's sexual stories.

For women within the asymmetrical structuring of middle-class gender in early modern Europe, sexual norms forbade acting on their own sexual desires outside of marriage and muffled their responses to institutionally powerful women whose sexuality was less constrained. Middle-class men's overt and sometimes overwrought reactions to Catherine's insinuated sexual transgressiveness registered both their desire for her and their repulsion. "There is no sight more infuriating," a pamphleteer mentioning the empress declared, "than a woman who has left her destined path, has desecrated the beautiful duty of gladdening and blessing others, due to unbridled passions, a wild desire to dominate, unnatural attitudes and temperamental instability, and who repulses our hearts, which she should be attracting."[53] Though the writer claims to wish merely that his heart be attracted to the empress, the references to unbridled passions, wild desires, and unnatural attitudes adds a sexual dimension that suggests he did protest too much in his search for a relationship with Catherine II. He exemplifies one of the strands of anti-fan feeling directed at her that was closely tied to her gender. Yet for some in the middling classes, the incompatibility of Catherine II's gender and her situation as autonomous individual par excellence was at least partially remedied by celebrity itself when the seemingly personal and especially the sexual elements of celebrity discourse displace the political and institutional from attention. Catherine II's power as a celebrity, being unofficial, was more socially acceptable than her formal power. It was also correspondingly more acceptable for women to be fans of such a figure.

"Europe's Tsarina"

Throughout Catherine II's reign, news items offered accounts of her that readers and listeners of every ilk might enjoy, admire, dislike, or revile, and their responses were varied. The search for the personal in an abundance of purportedly intimate and/or transgressive stories, lack of interest in the (overtly) political, fascination with trivia, the proliferation of visual images, a lively narrative that was intelligible even to illiterate members of her audience, apparent opportunities for a parasocial (one-way) relation of fans to the "star," often to the point of identification—all these belonged to fandom, to Sénac's notion of "curiosity," which was fueled by passionate feelings and the "sentiment de vénération"[54] and entails audiences emotionally engaging with commodified representations of a famous person.

Shelf-loads of visual and textual images of the empress produced in non-Russian languages, mostly outside of Russia's borders, confirm the public demand and thus the existence of Catherine II's large audience of anonymous fans, part of the eighteenth century's new "culture-consuming public," which was suddenly growing, though in socially and geographically uneven ways.[55] The sheer profusion of commodified representations of the tsarina, especially those designed to appeal to less-privileged groups of consumers, indicates a fan audience that could make no practical political or economic use of what they saw and read about her and who evidently responded to her with minimal political interest—to them she was a celebrity. Having achieved a "form of status that serves the interests of capitalism,"[56] she became a collection point of purchasable representations in picture, text, or both.

The discourse of "news," as it seeped into popular culture, invited vicarious pleasures of excitement as readers, hearers, and beholders took advantage of their ability to refocus texts and images away from their official or political or military purposes and onto the personal, private, and intimate instead. The very improbability of a girl's Cinderella ascent from an obscure little European principality to the fabulous and exotic world of the Russian imperial court, to her attainment of power as well as wealth by shockingly dumping the prince, could invite distant audiences to imagine being lifted out of their ordinary circumstance into almost inconceivable opportunities. Celebrity discourse emphasizes the imagination of fans, stimulated by themes such as vast personal wealth and luxury, freedom from convention, and opportunities for transgressiveness. For some, Catherine II was an appealing and inspiring invitation to identification, but for others, an affront to common sense and a case of unacceptable and dangerous patriarchal incoherence—simultaneously masculine and feminine. Indeed, since the beginning of Catherine's reign, writers and artists had struggled to represent the dilemma the empress posed to social expectations: powerful and yet female. Precisely Catherine's gender and her sexual behavior were often the levers, during her life and posthumously as well, for criticism of the all too autonomous empress.

In one of the first biographies of Catherine II published after her death, a writer emphatically amended his phrase "Russian tsarina" to "Europe's Tsarina."[57] Just as international fans two centuries later treated thoroughly commodified Princess Diana as their "queen of hearts," Europeans in the last third of the eighteenth century and for a few years into the nineteenth were also coaxed to consider the scrutinized, scandalous, criticized, and glamorous distant princess in Russia as their flawed but fabulous celebrity tsarina. "Craven and inspiring, obsessive and mercurial, transcendent and debased: celebrity is a tangle of contradictions."[58] When people followed the lure of celebrity discourse about Catherine II to gain individual entertainment, to enjoy group sociability, to savor imagined possibilities that she inspired, or to relish the pleasure of detesting her, readers and listeners far from the empress both in status and in geography became her fans and anti-fans, some ardent, others desultory, some admiring, others abhorring, many ambivalent, and most of them changeable over time. They flocked around the person whom Sénac de Meilhan called a star.

5

The Star as Contributing Subject and Living Object

The third indispensable member in celebrity discourse's troika of participants, along with media workers and fans, is the "star," the central elevated figure. The star must at least minimally engage in behavior that makes her or him visible, directly or indirectly, to the scrutiny of outsiders to the star's circle. Thus, a celebrity must have a flesh and blood body, available to the gaze of contemporaries. This in turn means that—although celebrity status can continue for a limited time after death—the celebrity's life must significantly overlap with the lives of fans, no matter how great or small the geographical or social distance that separates them. Accordingly, fans usually want to believe that they can recognize the star, can discern the individual body, face, or at least the style coded as hers or his. With the material body as a necessary component of celebrity discourse, the star functions both as agent of publicity and object of the gaze, and so becomes a bundle of signs, many elements of which are produced by media workers and fans.

In the eighteenth-century context, a star's willingness to be publicized did not have to indicate a deliberate engagement in emerging celebrity discourse. Catherine II's keenness was part of her desire for *Ruhm*, or *gloire*—as it was called in German and French—for monarchical glory. This was a system in which individuals of the highest ranks competed for status with their superiors and their peers through the grandeur of their persons, the splendor of their surroundings, and the magnificence of their deeds. For rulers' displays of *gloire*, the sociologist-historian Norbert Elias argues, the immediate intended audience was often the nobility. Court festivities, for example, were held to exhibit the uniqueness of the monarch's office, "to set the King apart from his people," and to subordinate "the nobility—and, by extension, the state—to more effective royal control."[1] But it was meant as well to impress and, in some cases, intimidate other rulers. Moments of great *gloire*, another scholar argues, provided "a paradigm of absolute royal authority in action."[2]

In this context, Catherine II's typical monarchical prestige fetish, palpable from the moment she seized power until stroke felled her, was not only inescapable but also well founded, given her many vulnerabilities. It offered a symbolic demonstration of her power, wealth, and fortitude to any possibly recalcitrant members of the highest Russian aristocracy, to other rulers, and to her own and other populaces. This was especially urgent because she was both a foreigner and a woman and thus not conventionally qualified to rule the Russian Empire, also because, having seized power through a coup, she lacked traditional legitimacy, and, finally, because, as the empress of Russia, she belonged to a dynasty that did not always get full recognition in its dealings with the rest of Europe. She was interested in everything that increased the reputation of Russia and its rulers and thus enhanced her political standing. To Catherine II, the value of pursuing *gloire* was unmistakable.[3]

Yet during the three and a half decades of Catherine II's reign (1762–96), long-standing feudalistic regimes were already in decline, and power was slipping in some regions from the *gloire*-seeking highest ranks of eighteenth-century society to less exalted, but more productive, categories. The meanings of "representation" and of "public" were changing too, as Habermas argues, sliding from realms of aristocratic discourse to new communicative and structural forms being developed by the middling levels of society.[4] In 1780, for example, the obscure J. G. Mayer lightly satirized the glorious and glamorous activities of Catherine II meeting with the Austrian emperor Joseph II in the White Russian city of Mogilev. In a dialog between an observing and a questioning voice, neither with access to the inner world of the court, Mayer first describes the scene of *gloire* and then cautiously speculates about the Russian monarch's political agenda of gaining Austria's acquiescence in her planned attack on the Ottomans:[5]

> At the high table for luncheon both high persons ate on golden tableware, the other high guests being served on silver.—On the fourth of June, in the evening, at 6 o'clock, both high rulers with the whole court attended an Italian opera, which was performed in a theater hastily built at the Empress's command. The encounter at Mohilow went well?? It is already over? Yes!! It is over.—What was decided? I don't know.—I see, I see!! Hm, Hm!—That is all that we other people know for sure. One can guess this or that.—That the good Musselmen aren't in a very fine mood one knows for certain.[6]

While politically informed readers, those aware of anxious Muslims, must have dismissed the myriad accounts of inexpressibly magnificent court events as boringly familiar, for others the brilliant superficialities of gold and silver dishes, temporary theaters, and special opera performances were evidently engrossing and inspiring. Most important for Catherine II's status as star, when she merely pursued her own dedication to *gloire*, she colluded in the continuation of her celebrity, because grandeur required spectators, even spectators with little or no social standing. Publicity provided spectators, real and virtual.

Celebrity did not arise out of nothing in the eighteenth century. The attention-grabbing story that thrust Catherine II onto the eighteenth-century world stage, together with the inevitable publicity about her participation in the royal rivalry for fame, inadvertently turned into modern international celebrity when distant media workers far from her imperial territories commodified (purported) accounts of her activities and (purported) images of her face and body for large general audiences in distant punch houses and market stalls, in dining rooms and back kitchens. Her sudden popular fame outside Russia, a by-product of many forces—rising capitalism, increasing literacy, the burgeoning of newspapers, and a growing though still small middling class—occurred in confrontation and collaboration with the old courtly system of aristocratic and monarchical fame.

Where Regal *Gloire* Meets Popular Celebrity

Grand state portraiture was one of the traditional tools of *gloire*. Especially in large format, showing a full-length figure, and filled with allusions to mighty Rome, with that ancient empire's connotations of order, power, and great respect, portraits were a particularly prestigious genre, nectar to elite fame. Early in her reign, Catherine commissioned the admired painters, Stefano Torelli and Vigilius Erichsen, each to depict her at her awe-inspiring coronation. In both, she stands alone in a majestic setting, wearing a dress with wide panniers. She holds a scepter and an orb, is bedecked with an immense bulbous, jeweled crown, and, gazes at or beyond her viewers. To impress her monarchical rivals, such as Frederick II of Prussia,[7] she sent them copies. Frederick decided this glorious gift deserved glorious reciprocation and, as one of Europe's first monarch-capitalists, he selected a response that was particularly shrewd, ordering his newly acquired royal porcelain works, for which he wanted to rally business, to translate the coronation painting into a one-of-a-kind porcelain centerpiece for Catherine's dinner table. It was a gift that would signify his wealth, power, and modernity and also acknowledge hers. It was also a gift that eventually turned the grand empress, agent of her actions, into an object for non-elite others to behold.

While porcelain, like painting, was an elite medium, the shift from one to the other was accompanied by a shift in style, one that matched the improbable taste of the virulently misogynist king, who remained dedicated to playful, airy, unmasculine rococo long after taste for it was receding elsewhere. The design choice and the (relatively) diminutive size of the porcelain table decoration lessen the grandeur of the empress and feminize her; she gestures delicately and leans slightly forward and to the side, with downcast eyes, not looking directly into the eyes of her beholders. Additional figurines compensate for the diminishing effect and justify the pose: she is responding to both a crowd of adoring porcelain subjects representing the diverse tribes and peoples of her empire and a cluster of picturesquely defeated Ottoman Turks.[8] All are positioned in attitudes of submission, overwhelmed or perhaps enchanted by her glory.

To accomplish his capitalist goal, Frederick II took an additional step, one in which he helped link the glorious porcelain representation of Catherine, which was indirectly also a glorious representation of himself, to inglorious celebrity. Before shipping the pieces to St. Petersburg, he put them on display in Berlin so that potential buyers would see the high quality of the workmanship. Little though the king otherwise cared about the opinions of such people, he nonetheless wanted the elites high and low and the middling classes to become purchasers of his porcelain and so exhibited Catherine's image to them. By thus mixing his *gloire* as a splendid gift giver with early capitalism, he both objectified the empress and compounded the audience that a splendid image of her could reach. When Frederick II publicly associated his porcelain product, furthermore, with the famous woman, he staged an eighteenth-century celebrity endorsement of his manufactory.

Nor was that all. Yet another layer of effects occurred, distributing the buzz beyond Berlin. The poet (and letter writer—Chapter 2) Anna Luisa Karsch, seeking, as she often did, to inveigle compensation from potential noble benefactors, wrote and published a poem that digressed into a description of the "precious table set":

Eternally great will Catherine remain
In the hero-worshipping world
Eternally beautiful, and eternally preserved
The gift of Frederick of Berlin.
Pale trembling figures,
Conquered Ottomans kneel

Figure 5.1 Charles Turner Warren projected the braids print to full length to invent a luxurious and exotically Russian fashion—and a stiff pose—for the empress in 1789. Source: Charles Turner Warren, *Catherine II. Empress of Russia*. Getty Images. Catherine II. Editorial Number: 50698202. Credit: Time Life Pictures.

> Before the porcelain throne
> White, like a snowfall,
> And in earnest grace
> From beneath the laurel wreath
> The empress watches.[9]

Casting Catherine II as the object of hero worship and as a victor in battles with the Ottomans, the lines erase some of the disempowerment suggested by the fragile porcelain. Most of all, through the poem's description, readers of German poetry far outside of Berlin or St. Petersburg could envision this elegant picture of the empress at least in words.

The porcelain empress is exquisitely dressed. Because she was a rich woman, but also because she had worn an officer's uniform as she rode to arrest her husband, fashion was a frequent part of discourse about Catherine II and well suited to building her celebrity. Johann Bernoulli III (1744–1807), a Swiss mathematician from Frederick the Great's Prussian academy, reported seeing Catherine in a violet and silver version of her Russian dress in the morning and in celadon green in the evening.[10] A print of the empress that projects her familiar fur-trimmed bodice or vest into full-length image awkwardly combines the much-copied profile-in-braids type (Figures 3.3, 3.8) with a rigidly frontal body dressed in a complete fur-trimmed ensemble (Figure 5.1). But one unimpressed writer declared Catherine out of fashion when she chose designs with hints of indigenous features, though he conceded that her well-chosen colors meant "the unpleasant cut is not so noticeable."[11] Another writer noted that non-Russian designs and fabrics on the body of the foreign-born tsarina were a potential political problem to her.[12] Gender, power, and national identity were the constant subtexts of Catherine II's clothes.

Court Rituals of Seeing and Being Seen

"I have seen her today, stood close to her, clearly heard her speak—the first and most prominent person of the whole contemporary world," the German traveler Johann Jacob Bellermann (1754–1842) proclaimed in his anonymously published book about Russia.[13] A small number of travelers, diplomats, and others came from the west of Europe to see Catherine II in person, and she regularly made herself available to scrutiny. The Englishman Nathaniel William Wraxall (1751–1831), in his much cited and often reprinted account, wrote dramatically: "I felt a pleasure corrected with awe as I gazed on this extraordinary woman, whose vigor and policy, without any right of blood, has seated and maintains her in the throne of the Czars."[14] Some observers failed in their effort to comply with correct behavior at the moment of seeing. The young Frenchman Charles François Philibert Masson (1762–1807), one of her posthumous biographers, wrote, "My eagerness to examine her person caused me successively to neglect prostrating myself before her with the crowd." Yet, he argued, "the homage I paid by gazing at her, was surely more flattering."[15] Given that the body, and particularly the female body, is a common object for taboos, it is not surprising that opportunities to gaze at the powerful woman "in the flesh" were highly regulated and ritualized encounters

Writers frequently described their accomplishment of access to Catherine II as almost heroic acts of exposure. In September 1781, Bellermann considered the effort required for proximity as an important part of the seeing: "In order to make the feelings at least somewhat comprehensible that her power, greatness, and extensive authority produced and that still agitate my soul, I need to tell you how I got there."[16] Like most would-be spectators, Bellermann's entry into the palace required assistance: an acquaintance who knew the ways of the court had offered to help him come close to the powerful woman. His text works to produce Wraxall's "pleasure corrected by awe" in the reader by recounting that procedure. As the narrator waited for his friend, he looked at the maps on his wall and realized how much larger the Russian Empire was than the other countries. He pondered the greatest empires in history, those of Cyrus, Alexander, Caesar Augustus, Constantine, Genghis Khan, Timur, and more; he declared them small in comparison to this one that stretched from Riga to Alaska and yet was ruled by a single person. Impressed by this awareness, Bellermann went to see Catherine as she returned to her apartments from a Sunday church service. Innumerable grand coaches already stood in rows before the palace as he arrived. When one of the guards asked Bellermann in Russian who he was, his friend replied (untruthfully) that the traveler was "a German cavalier," a status that made him eligible for prompt admission (311–12). They stepped into "a jumble of ribbons, stars, uniforms of every kind" and the clamor of representatives from "all the European nations and the different peoples of Asia, from Cossacks and Kalmucks to Crimeans and Persians" as well as handsome Russian men (313). When the door opened for Catherine's entry, the foreign ministers and other most distinguished persons formed into two rows on either side of her way (313–14) and a "sacred silence" fell, as though no one dared draw breath aloud.

Sénac de Meilhan, the writer who had so well identified important elements of what fans seek from a celebrity, noted the complex relation between beholding and being beheld. Writing of the empress, he noted, "One sees that she feels that all eyes are on her" and that her distinguished audience did not come to see "a private person lost in her own thoughts but a Princess on whom their fates depend." Unlike many princely persons who walked through their palace reception rooms without a glance at the hordes of courtiers, he asserted, Catherine looked around carefully, "distinguishing some people with an affirmative glance or some kindly words."[17] Catherine II was the aware object of the gaze and equipped with a powerful gaze of her own.

Distant readers realized that public settings were staged events that did not "free" her from her "imperial garments," as Sénac had wished. The German-Czech aristocrat Joachim von Sternberg (1755–1808) asserted that she possessed "the art of rearranging her facial expression into a friendly form and of affecting cheerfulness of spirit."[18] Masson vividly confirmed that Catherine II left behind her private persona when she put on her gloves before entering the public spaces of the palace: "She assumed a very different countenance and deportment. From an agreeable and facetious woman, she appeared all at once the reserved and majestic empress. Whoever had seen her then for the first time would have found her not below the idea he had previously formed, and would have said, 'This is indeed the Semiramis of the north!'"[19] As Patricia Spacks observes, "Good manners constitute a tax paid by individuals to society, a widely condoned form of hypocrisy."[20] Some observers claimed to detect moments when the empress found the etiquette tax wearisome. Bernoulli, as part of the audience watching her eat at a state dinner, noted that she "drank some red wine with water and ate very little." (A truculent account of Catherine from 1800, in contrast, maligned her for being as dedicated to drink as to sex.[21]) Bernoulli continued that he could detect from a few of her glances toward one of her court officials "that she was very tired and that her uniform was too tight and too warm." He added hastily that her face nonetheless revealed no annoyance.[22]

Everyone in Catherine's presence watched for moments when emotion—especially sorrow or anger—might intervene in her well-regulated exterior. Bernoulli told his readers that the empress, having made it a principal not to display anger but always to project a friendly appearance, withdrew into her private chamber if she felt angry until she could return with a calm countenance (89). Weeping was a different matter and had been since the beginning of her reign, when she reportedly announced Peter's death with tears streaming down her face. But that performance, the French observer Rulhière declared, occurred the day after she had learned of the murder; on the night when she first received the information, she had left the dinner table to be given the news and then returned to her party in all gaiety.[23] Tears, cynical Rulhière implied, signified nothing, though the anonymous composer of an eighty-eight-page-long heroic poem about Catherine wrote of the "most precious, noblest tears" that she wept and advised: "Heroine, do not press them damagingly back into the most sensitive/ Heart of the tenderest mother from whom they run!"[24] Indeed, Catherine's tears are a common topos in the various narratives of her behavior in crisis and are an example of a bodily event that is frequent in texts but absent in images. Tears showed emotional involvement but did not seem to disqualify her from ruling, especially because men rulers too were described as weeping. Either way, tears were yet another opportunity for distant readers and listeners to try to peel back surface appearances for hidden meanings about the celebrity woman.

Impolitic but Indispensable Body and Mostly Male Watchers

The envisioned empress was, of course, a gendered and sexed being. Overtly or covertly, celebrity is always sexed and gendered, with multiple effects. Women celebrities are discursively inspected, weighed, measured, re-weighed, and re-measured, dressed and undressed, and always judged. On one level, fans want and wanted famed women to be beautiful and sexually attractive; on another, they often disparage and deride women for exactly those qualities. Celebrity discourse, so often ambivalent, plays avidly to both impulses and constantly encourages the urge to see. In a period, furthermore, when producing a visual portrait required skill and effort with paint or ink, the very act of picturing a woman such as Catherine II, and not someone else, hinted at a disruption in gender relations; it marked the power her body possessed over media workers and ultimately over the beholders of such images too.[25]

In 1787, Philippine Engelhard-Gatterer wrote in a poem for children:

One more princess I would like to see
Going there by foot would be fine with me
    To Russia's great tsarina!

With no opportunity to make the trip, however, Engelhard-Gatterer left the description of Catherine II to the almost exclusively male band of writers and printmakers. The writers, evidently feeling it was less acceptable for men openly to scrutinize women's physical appearance than for women to scrutinize each other, often prefaced their descriptions of Catherine with a rather guilty and thoroughly gendered explanation, such as declaring they were acting at the request of a woman acquaintance. Sénac de Meilhan, for example, explained that, after going to Rome explicitly to view St. Peter's cathedral, he had proceeded to "the North" to behold one of the world's other most interesting sights, Catherine II,[26] and he presented his account of her as answering the request of Madame de ***.

Shape, Appearance, and Decorum of the Visible Body and Face

The empress, according to a book that appeared in 1766, was "of ordinary height and fairly stout. It is not a mistake to call her beautiful. She is brunette and very well built. . . . Her glance and appearance are majestic and her mien is full of marvellous courtesy and cheerful friendliness. Whoever has the good fortune to look at her is immediately stirred to respect and love."[27] Like this one, most descriptions of the empress's body addressed an inventory of height, weight, and breasts, or, less blatantly, body shape, often adding hair and eye color, and always also extrapolating her personality, conduct, and demeanor from her features. Some writers acknowledged their sexualizing male gaze. Bellermann, for example, identified three aspects of the imperial body that he could not omit mentioning and acknowledged that these were the aspects which "men are accused of usually noticing first about the other sex—I know not whether with justice." He then specifies that Catherine's large breasts are hard to see well because of the high necklines of Russian dresses, that her waist is thick but shown advantageously by her choice of clothes, and that he was not able to glimpse her feet.[28] Breasts, waist, feet—Bellermann is striving to look beyond the garments to the naked body.

But, of course, except in the satirical images late in her reign, the fabled empress was always represented as literally and figuratively dressed up and made up. Makeup itself is a standard means of concealing unwanted bodily signs and producing other more culturally desirable or more fashionable ones, all the while also impeding close observation. Bellermann asserted that Catherine II's cheeks were rouged a bright red (315), while her hairstyle he described as "low," of three fingers height at the forehead, with "some braids hanging down in back" and topped with the small diamond encrusted crown, as shown on the coins" (316). The rather simple coiffure—omitting the entwined pearls—in images such as a small one by Cornelis van Noorde (Figure 5.2), might enable viewers in diverse cultural and geographical locations,

Figure 5.2 Unlike the anonymous French head-and-shoulders excerpt of Eriksen's grand portrait of Catherine II standing before a mirror (Figure 3.4), Cornelis van Noorde added a sumptuous backdrop to his Dutch-captioned image. His empress has an expression that is sober and astute, yet also pleasant. Source: Cornelis van Noorde, *Catharina II. Keizerin van geheel Rusland.* 1773. Public Domain. Courtesy of Rijksmuseum, Amsterdam.

from Italian cities, French towns, and the servants' rooms of English estates, to feel connected to the grand lady despite the lavishness of her dress.

The Rude Body Visualized

While the focus on beauty, groomed good looks, and elegant, sexuality-erasing comportment was enough to induce fantasies in some members of the distant public and at least to ignite conversations among others, it is evident that several aspects of the female body were taboo. Menstruation and menopause, for example, were proscribed topics, about which none of the foreign visitors to Catherine's court published any words. Yet, since she belonged to a religious tradition that required women to modify their ritual behavior based on their periods, it was not impossible for various people at court to be informed. The number who could both know and write about it, however, was distinctly limited.[29] In the absence of clear references circulating outside Russia during her lifetime and in the first years thereafter, menstruation and menopause played no traceable role in her celebrity (and remain mostly taboo in such discourse today as well).

But a closely related topic, Catherine's reproductive body, was of critical public interest, despite also being silently implicated in exactly the taboo matters. The two (purportedly) legitimate pregnancies before the coup and the resulting births of a son and a daughter had invited widespread rejoicing and perhaps encouraged some pre-coup moments of celebrity identification. Paul and short-lived Anna were routinely mentioned in biographical material about Catherine as soon as she came to power.[30] But beyond that—historians variously assert that Catherine had an additional one or two children more—her pregnancies were carried out in secrecy, though Bernoulli's identification in 1780 of Count Bobrinski as a "natural" son of Orlov may have made some readers suspicious, if they knew or guessed Gregory Orlov's past status as Catherine's lover.[31] Such speculation, however, was probably too oblique and limited to have reached most of Catherine's distant audience. Late in her reign and after her death would be a different matter.

In the 1780s, as various local political tensions rose in Europe, jeering visual inventions of her sexual behavior and misbehavior began to appear in satirical images that energetically reversed the decorum usually haloing the empress. Here was the opportunity to laugh or scoff at images contradicting the reverent cant about the mighty woman's beautiful looks and fine manners. In the satires, Catherine II's disruptive female body resisted the reassurances pressed by official portraits that smoothly integrated femininity with imperial rule. To eighteenth-century shop girls and delivery boys, artisans and farmers, housewives and husbands, caricatures of the empress in words or images were enjoyably impolitic—breaking her body and her status as empress apart and showing them as incompatible. Satirical prints, for example, sometimes made coarse jokes. In one, the British prime minister Pitt sings three lines:

I made war with Kate,
a buxom Northern Lass:
But such my cruel fate—

Another figure nearby completes the rhyme:

"She bid you kiss her A------!"[32]

Maria Theresa had already led the way as a female target of political cartoonists, especially in Britain. The attacks began in 1741 under the impetus of the War of the Austrian Succession, when Frederick II of Prussia and others, rejecting Maria Theresa's claim to rule the Habsburg territories, invaded and occupied her territories. Between 1741 and 1763, at least forty-two visual satires depicted Maria Theresa, mostly made in Britain.[33] Several of the early ones are distinctly bawdy, including a design showing her, posed like a Venus statue, being stripped naked by the Prussian king and his allies. Another design portrayed her, under the supervision of quack doctors who represent the rival monarchs, as she sits on a portable toilet and vomits. Yet another pictured her urinating onto a knife sharpener's whetstone.[34] The situations and confrontations in the pictures were drastic, but the representation of the queen herself was always generic, with no markers specific to Maria Theresa. After 1762, as her wars with Prussia drew to an end, the wave of satires about the empress-queen ceased. British cartoon makers lost interest in both Central and Northern Europe at precisely the moment when Catherine II came to the throne. For the first ten years of her reign, she was spared satirical attention, and for the next fifteen years, starting with her participation in a huge land grab partitioning Poland in 1772, the depictions—French, British, Dutch, and German—were relatively decorous. Then, in the 1780s, starting with her entanglements in both Holland and the Austrian Netherlands during the Fourth Anglo-Dutch War (1780–4)[35] and soon continuing with another Turkish war, the situation changed. Vulgarity had become the order of the day, much exacerbated within a few years as the French Revolution got underway (Chapter 11).

The caricatures gleefully disrupted descriptions of Catherine II as a paragon of courtly comportment. The German traveler Bellermann had reported: "She carries her body with much decorum, very straight, without appearing forced,"[36] and Sénac de Meilhan too mentioned her "serious and unforced pace," affirming that "her gestures, her walk, her conduct, and the tone of her voice are all in perfect harmony with each other."[37] Satirical images depicting the empress, however, attacked all three of the key interrelated body themes that mattered most to eighteenth-century audiences: the shape and appearance of her female face and body; her presentation of self using cosmetics, jewelry, hairdo, and fashion; and her success or failure at demonstrating desexualizing restraint and feminine demeanor.

Aging

When the French Revolution began, forcing a great caesura in the history of many European monarchies, Catherine was sixty; being of flesh and blood, her body had aged, a reality that media workers and fans often ignored. One of the less remarked requirements of celebrity discourse, that fans and star overlap in time, inevitably entails aging, much though both parties may seek to fend off that fact, especially in the case of a female celebrity; for an eighteenth-century figure such as Frederick II, depictions of a wrinkled face and stooped posture added authority and admiration. Not so with eighteenth-century women of popular note, whose mortal bodies were expected to decline in attractiveness. Eventually too, death would obtrude and, swiftly or slowly, change the discourse. When Catherine II was about fifty-three, Bellermann wrote condescendingly that, given her age, "one could not expect youthful beauty. She is however far from ugly; one can see in her face many marks of her former beauty and visible indications on the whole of corporeal charms."[38] He was in his twenties; the writers who described the aging Catherine for publications in the middle and west of Europe were all significantly younger than she was. Ten years later, Sternberg, thirty-seven when he was in St. Petersburg, suggested that the empress, then sixty-three, must have been very attractive when she was younger and noted her eyes as blue, the contours of her face as "somewhat long," the chin as prominent, the lips as "promising friendliness," the nose as well built and somewhat rounded, "giving the face an air of seriousness." He added that her age was largely concealed by artful decoration, splendor, and plenty of rouge.[39]

Stoutness was a feature of Catherine's described body. Wraxall noted in 1775: "Though she is now become rather corpulent, there is a dignity tempered with graciousness in her deportment and manner, which strikingly impresses."[40] Bellermann later cautiously stated that she was "somewhat robust in chest and body."[41] Sternberg, in 1791 and 1792, mentioned that the empress had become "fleshy" enough to be bothered walking.[42] Masson at about the same time wrote: "few women . . . with her corpulence, would have attained the graceful and dignified carriage for which she was conspicuous."[43] While fat was not desirable, it was not, except in political cartoons, made shameful (Chapter 11).

Engravers and designers sometimes sought to keep up with the changes they knew must be affecting Catherine's appearance, but, lacking authoritative sources from Russia itself, they simply attempted to age the images they already had. In the 1780s, for example, the Parisian Augustin de Saint-Aubin (1736–1807) designed, engraved, and then added his name to a medium-sized print (13.1 × 8.7 cm) of Catherine that seems meant to show her in updated detail (Figure 5.3). Saint-Aubin, who had never beheld

Figure 5.3 Augustin de Saint-Aubin's print, made in Paris between 1784 and 1790, classicizes Catherine II and faintly suggests her aging. Source: Augustin de Saint-Aubin, *Catherine II*. Getty Images. Augustin de Saint-Aubin, Catherine II. Editorial #: 1162532806. Credit: Sepia Times.

her in person, slightly modified existing pictures in his treatment of Catherine's eyes and throat to hint at the passage of time. The portrait shows a richly dressed woman in profile against a very dark, almost black background, her eyes looking forward, her hair styled in loose curls embellished with both laurel wreath and crown.

While deferential graphic images addressed the topic of changes in Catherine's appearance gently, satiric representations were not so restrained, as a French example shows. In *Jeu de quilles républicain* (Republican bowling), the bowler is a healthy young man under the protection of both a woman representing the revolution and an angel of fame, and the pins he hopes to topple with his bowling ball are European monarchs, all of them disfigured and debilitated by age. Catherine appears as a hideous witch-like figure wearing an extravagant and out-of-date gown, her ankles showing, her legs wide apart, and her mask-like face bearing a long, unmistakable, downturned handlebar mustache (Figures 5.4 and 5.5). This was a distorting caricature indeed.

One of the last descriptions of Catherine II's appearance, when she was well into her sixties, exemplifies both the close attention observers paid to the mighty empress

Figure 5.4 Neatly capturing the anti-monarchical spirit of the French Revolution, *Jeu de quilles républicain* uses a bowling game to satirize Catherine II as an ugly hag in an old-fashioned court dress and standing in the absurd and offensive colossus pose from an earlier satire, *An Imperial Stride!* (Figure 10.1). Source: [Jean-Pierre Berthault?], *Jeu de quilles républicain: encore un moment ils seront abbatus*. Public Domain. Courtesy of Musée Carnavalet, Histoire de Paris /Les Musées de la ville de Paris.

and the anxiety they felt about being deceived by her. Charles François Masson, writing after her death, radiates ambivalence. He detested her successor, Paul, who had evicted him from the country, and wanted to detest Catherine as well, but kept coming back to the attractions of the cheerful, kind, and witty woman whom he had admired on a daily basis: "never did a crown sit better on any head than hers. . . . In her private life, the good-humour and confidence with which she inspired all about her, seemed to keep her in perpetual youth, playfulness, and gaiety. Her engaging conversation and familiar manners placed all those who had constant access to her, or assisted at her toilette, perfectly at their ease."[44] This is the empress on whom he so much liked to gaze that he forgot the requisite deep bow. He notes with admiration that "when she let a foreigner kiss her hand, she did so with much politeness and usually said a few words to him about his arrival in Petersburg and his journey." Yet exactly at that point, his description turns to gall because suddenly, when she began to speak,

> all the harmony of her countenance was instantly discomposed, and for a moment the great Catharine was forgotten in the sight of the old woman; as, on opening her mouth, it was apparent that she had lost her teeth, and her voice was broken, and her articulation bad. The lower part of her face was rather rude and coarse; her grey eyes, though clear and penetrating, evinced something of hypocrisy, and a certain wrinkle at the base of the nose gave her somewhat of a sneering look.[45]

The allure of the celebrity empress's body had vanished.

Among the ingredients that celebrity requires is a star who is willing to contribute to her or his own fame. For Catherine II, the competition against rival rulers for great

Figure 5.5 The details in *Jeu de quills républicain* invite the viewer to look closely and see Catherine II depicted as a hideous and aged empress with a mask-like face and clawed hands. Source: [Berthault?], *Jeu de Quilles républicain* excerpt. Public Domain. Courtesy of Gallica/Bibliothèque nationale de France.

gloire induced her to engage in the kinds of self-display a star must offer; some, such as the commissioning of painted portraits, were intended for distant elite audiences, and others, such as the routine processions through her own palace, were intended for both Russian and foreign viewers in person. Amplified far outside her empire by media workers struggling to earn a living and reinterpreted by potential fans seeking entertainment and imagining alternate lives, Catherine's popular fame could build on the dramatic launch into her distant audience's awareness that the extraordinary coup story had provided. Her actual female body, its valence changing over time and in different observers' eyes, was always part of the discourse about her.

II

Engaging Themes, Sustaining Celebrity

The dramatic overthrow of Tsar Peter III prepared the celebrity of Catherine II, but a ragout of other events and themes enlarged and nurtured her popular fame over the next more than three decades of her reign. Several of the stew's components the empress provided with her well-chosen and well-publicized decisions involving the two dissimilar ingredients of Enlightenment and extravagance; she had reasons of self and of state to engage with French *philosophes*, for example, and to make profligate purchases. Two other key ingredients, gender and geography, unavoidable products trussed with particular eighteenth-century social meanings, she attempted to season carefully. Most of all, the success of the recipe, or "the secret of the nature of celebrity," as Robert van Krieken writes in his study of this kind of prominence, "is primarily a matter of the accumulation and distribution of attention."[1] Catherine received plenty of that, both good and bad. Media spread the tidings of how she engaged in the Enlightenment movement, how she used her vast new wealth, how she positioned herself as a woman ruler, and how she attempted to steer the meaning of the Russian Empire to audiences far to the west; they also disseminated the news of how these efforts sometimes scorched or soured. But even amid details of blunders and streaks of aversion, media attention to these themes sustained and enlarged the distant public over the years from the coup until almost the last decade of her life and thus were essential to her celebrity.

6

Woman Philosopher on the Throne

For some non-elite readers and listeners in distant parts of Europe, the coup had been enough to catapult Catherine first into fame and then into celebrity; for others, the connection of the new empress with the Enlightenment precipitated the shift into this modern form of popular reception. The most optimistic among her audience hoped the new empress would be willing not only to pursue Enlightenment schemes and goals that they valued but might even abandon monarchical practices incongruent with Enlightenment ideals. As one encomiast recklessly declared, when Jove asked Catherine what gifts he should give her, she answered first with what she did not want: Not magnificence scratched from the marrow of the country, not laurels dripping with blood, the kind that crowned the enemies of humanity and that tyrants lusted after, not wealth that gleamed with the sweat of the poor and made only flatterers laugh. "Do not give me these!" she said. Instead, the idealized tsarina asserted the new values, coding them as a desire for "the wisdom of Solomon" so that she would be a blessing to her country, thanks implicitly to an activist Enlightenment agenda. Because she was a woman she also wanted and received a mother's heart.[1]

For ordinary readers and listeners from Aberdeen to Madrid or Berlin, representing Catherine II as enlightened provided a theme that could assist importantly in the construction of her celebrity. Enlightenment ideas that appeared, for example, to make social boundaries porous might inspire feelings of affiliation with the empress on the part of potential fans, both readers and listeners. Exchanges of letters in which the august empress on the Russian throne communicated more or less politely with a person of no aristocratic rank could validate a feeling of connection to her even among members of the public who knew nothing about the Enlightenment and were perhaps illiterate as well. They could be drawn too when Enlightenment projects occasionally seemed to reveal Catherine's private world, or when some of her Enlightenment values or projects appeared to have ordinary motivations, such as maternal feelings. In addition, for the better educated fans or potential fans of the middling social levels and gentry, Enlightenment representations of the empress could offset some of the transgressiveness of the coup and of Peter III's suspicious death, especially if they felt that their Enlightenment tastes and preferences were gratifyingly endorsed by similarity to hers, confirming their self-images and agendas and so providing another of the satisfactions of celebrity discourse. Thus, to a whole range of observers outside Russia, the Enlightenment projects and commitments of Catherine II could offer the validation and dream-inducing parasocial (one-way) relationship that celebrity discourse promises. Soon after the coup, a pamphlet gushed to readers: "If you would only come here, you would see a true philosopher on the throne."[2] By 1764, her Enlightenment activities sometimes overwrote the coup, as in the *Journal des Dames*, which emphasized her generosity to a project of the French *philosophes*.[3]

European newspaper readers and listeners had learned of her generosity to learnedness when, within a few months of the coup, the Russian empress invited Jean Baptiste le Rond d'Alembert, the French co-founder of the great encyclopedia project in France, to be the tutor to the next tsar of Russia, her young son. After D'Alembert rejected three offers from her officials, Catherine herself wrote to the scholar on November 13, 1762. Her letter, full of peculiar and imperious twists, made its way quickly into the European press in multiple languages, including the French original.[4] She began by attributing to the philosopher a dismissive attitude toward mere "grandeur and honour" and by claiming to agree with him, and then she asserted presumptuously that his talents and his philosophy imposed obligations on him and "that to refuse to serve mankind, whilst it is in your power, is to miss your aim."[5] She surmised none too flatteringly that he was motivated to decline her proposal by his "love of ease, and leisure to cultivate letters and the friendship of those you esteem." To this she offered a generous solution that also addressed the trouble he was having with the censor in France. "Come, with all your friends," she wrote, promising them "every conveniency," and adding, "perhaps you will find more liberty and ease here, than in your native country." She concluded in a courteous and respectful tone, claiming: "I have the education of my son so much at heart, and I think you so necessary to it, that perhaps I press you with too much earnestness. Excuse my indiscretion for the sake of the occasion of it; and be assured that it is my esteem for you that makes me so urgent. Moscow, Nov. 13, 1762. CATHERINE." But a postscript returned to the omniscient and self-assured judge: "In this whole letter I have argued only from what I have found in your writings; You would not contradict yourself."

Crucially for the emerging celebrity of the new empress, the letter could promote identification, admiration, and fantasies about Catherine II, as well as suggesting a possible need for caution. It showed her in the commonplace eighteenth-century role of a concerned parent organizing her child's education. At the same time, it demonstrated a monarch of the highest rank corresponding with a commoner; and, to adherents of the Enlightenment movement, it showed a wealthy and generous ruler offering an impressive opportunity to one of their own, igniting dreams that they too, or their countrymen, might also become her beneficiaries. The letter thus reintroduced the upstart empress in new and enticing terms that continued to earn esteem and even veneration for years, moving beyond the official manifestos that had announced and rationalized events around the coup. Written, furthermore, in Catherine's own hand, a token of her personal interest, the invitation to educate the next absolute ruler of Russia was an unmistakable mark of distinction for the *philosophe* and produced an abundance of commentary, public and private.[6] In Russia, she was already having herself depicted as Minerva—"embodiment of enlightenment," in Richard S. Wortman's analysis—on a medal cast to celebrate her accession to the throne, although this representation would not seep into prints (and eventually caricatures) outside her country for several more years (Figure 6.1).[7] Although Catherine, in a probably disingenuous display of modesty, complained to one of her influential French correspondents, Madame Geoffrin, that

Figure 6.1 A Russian medal that signaled Catherine's dedication to both learning and war by depicting her as Minerva was copied on a complex plate, engraved by Pauquet, along with the slogan: "It is the joining of authority and Enlightenment that must bring prosperity to the people." Source: Jean Louis Charles Pauquet, *Catherine II. / C'est de la réunion de l'Autorité et / des lumières que les Peuples doivent / attendre le bonheur.* https://commons.wikimedia.org/wiki/File:Profile_engraving_of_Catherine_II_of_Russia_04.jpg.

her communication had been published without her permission, writers across Europe could expect their readers to know of the empress's message.[8] It was included in a letter-writing manual published in London the next year.[9]

Boundary Breaking Relationships

In the early years of Catherine's reign, public discourse about her included a long menu of Enlightenment projects, large and small, and an array of relationships, some brief and some extended, between the empress and Enlightenment figures. They ranged from the famed Madame Geoffrin and even more famed Denis Diderot to the utterly obscure Madame Büsching. This German woman, living in Catherine's capital city, experienced the kind of social rather than parasocial relationship of which fans dreamed. Polyxene Christiane Auguste Büsching née Dilthey (1728–77) was in St. Petersburg with her husband, a Lutheran pastor and schoolmaster who later became a famous geographer, well known for his expertise on Russia. When Catherine II learned that in 1751 Madame Büsching had been named a poet laureate by a university in Germany, where there was a short-lived practice of honoring women writers, the empress three times sought the commoner's advice about her literary efforts. Madame Büsching wrote about these remarkable encounters in letters to a friend in Germany, Johanna Charlotte Unzer (1725–82), depicting Catherine as by turns pushy, friendly, brusque, sympathetic, peeved, generous, and encouraging. The letters offered precisely the kind of apparent truth about the presumed "real Catherine" that celebrity fans yearn to achieve, but because the discreet Madame Büsching was not inclined to trumpet her experience to a broad public, the dissemination was only local, in the circles around herself and Johanna Charlotte Unzer.[10]

Publicity about Catherine's connections with figures in the French Enlightenment was quite different. With the empress's assiduous coaxing and flattery, oiled with her money and often with an invitation to become a member of the Academy of Sciences in St. Petersburg, these relationships granted Catherine II widespread admiration and glory abroad.[11] In 1765, for example, when she purchased Denis Diderot's library, he became linked in the public mind to Catherine, as D'Alembert had been before. The *Gentleman's Magazine* explained to its broad readership that "Monsieur Diderot, so well known for his share in the *Encyclopedie*," had needed to raise money by selling his books, and a "friend" wrote of the sale "to a correspondent in Russia." The correspondent notified the empress, who "become the purchaser, offering a thousand livres more than the sum at which the collection was rated, and insisting on M. Diderot's further acceptance of an annual salary as her Librarian, in which character she directed that he should still retain the books in his custody."[12] The magnanimous gesture was promptly reiterated in every form of news periodical—the most respected international newspapers, local sheets in the provinces, monthly magazines, and annual summaries of the year's events; it was retold in biographies after her death as well.[13] It was a story of generosity and kindness to a scholar and thus at least nominally signified the empress's great respect for learning and for the Enlightenment. A snag followed the library purchase, however, as subsequent reports revealed, when months passed without payment of the pension and Diderot thought he had been forgotten. Finally, a letter from the empress arrived and all was well again; she apologized for the delay and prepaid the pension for the next fifty years, so that such a problem would not recur.[14] Catherine's letter to D'Alembert had shown a huge public the social bridging possibilities of the Enlightenment, and her bounteousness to Diderot underscored its monetary value.

A different early relationship must have especially interested distant women. From 1763 to 1768 Catherine corresponded with middling-class Marie Thérèse Rodet Geoffrin (1699–1777), who had gained fame in Paris by fulfilling the main function allowed women within the Enlightenment movement: using her salon to promote sociability among educated men. Charming passages from Catherine's letters circulated in Paris in the early years of the acquaintance[15] before Geoffrin made the decisive mistake of inviting Claude-Carloman de Rulhière to read his harshly critical account of Peter III's overthrow at her salon (Chapter 12).[16] She tried to rectify matters by offering Rulhière a bribe to suppress his scandalous manuscript, but when the effort failed, the *salonnière*'s correspondence with Catherine was effectively over. Memories of the empress's fabulous gifts to Geoffrin lived on—the caustic English aristocrat Horace Walpole described them as "three sumptuous robes of ermine, martens, and astrachan lambs, the last of which the Czarina had, I suppose, the pleasure of flaying alive herself"—and were repeated, for example, in a German book about distinguished women.[17] Such ongoing dissemination of the image of Catherine engaging with writers and intellectuals of no exalted social rank, people somewhat like the readers (though famous for their accomplishments), confirms that cultural producers expected popular fascination with these moments.

Redemptive Early Projects

Stories of the empress's letters and generous deeds to the compatriots of distant readers and listeners could easily become celebrity discourse, keeping her name in the news, seeming to say something about the kind of person she was, and hinting at the possibility of a relationship with her. Furthermore, once Catherine could be seen as pleasingly enlightened, then it could be argued that by having the intellectual capacity and judgment necessary to rule an enormous country she deserved the throne. This innovative justification of the coup by intellectual qualification could have made little headway before Enlightenment arguments succeeded in posing the desirability of a monarch being enlightened and in placing a premium on a ruler's reason and intelligence, as opposed to genealogy or even the predecessor's blessing (which was how an earlier foreign woman, Catherine I, had been able to succeed her husband, Peter I, to the Russian throne). Now the Enlightenment provided an alternative and one congenial to a woman ruler, especially a woman ruler struggling to legitimize her power: The very notion that having a philosopher on the throne might be advantageous not only diminished the conventional qualifications of dynastic genealogy but also reduced the usual concomitant insistence on a male monarch. Ambitious projects—a home for abandoned children, legal reform, population growth, smallpox inoculation—all added to the alluring aura gathering around Catherine II.

1763 Foundling Hospital

News of her new institution for the care of abandoned, often illegitimate, children began reaching the Western areas of Europe late in 1763. As the French-language newspaper in Vienna explained, she was building a foundling "hospital" (or hostel) at Moscow where "mothers or other persons" who brought children there, day or night, would be subjected to no incriminating questioning, asked only whether the infant had been baptized or not and whether they wanted any record made of their connection to the child.[18] Seen through Enlightenment lenses, foundling hospitals, which the French had reintroduced in the seventeenth century and the English in the middle of the eighteenth, were expected to increase the population of a state by preventing infanticide (since many of the mothers were single) and so preserve the lives of vulnerable infants. For Catherine's empire in particular, it was argued, such institutions could be the "kind of school where the Russians gradually become accustomed to the concepts of freedom, property, and trade," middling-class values central to the Enlightenment.[19] Seen through the lens of celebrity, the foundling hospital and the lying-in facility connected with it could suggest to distant reading and listening cobblers and cooks, bureaucrats and housewives, that the new empress had attractive and familiar maternal qualities that might invite identification.

Catherine's own publicity efforts helped make the new institution famous outside of Russia; she sent, for example, a second letter to D'Alembert reassuring him of her continuing goodwill and, in tribute to his educational interests, enclosed a gold medal commemorating the new "hospital." Parisian newsmongers were soon gossiping and singing about the deed, and coffee houses and drawing rooms were presumably sharing the buzz.[20] By 1772, wealthy book buyers could enjoy engraved prints of a whole series of such medals commemorating key moments in Catherine's reign collected, along with other Russian medal prints, into an expensive volume.[21]

More broadly accessible were accounts of the Moscow foundling home that appeared in words. The Englishman William Coxe, who visited four times, extolled it first in a pamphlet and then again in his much-translated and often republished book about Russia and neighboring countries. He exulted that "each foundling has a separate bed; the bed-steads are of iron; the sheets are changed every week, and their linen three times a week," and, most of all, he claimed the children seemed convincingly happy, contented, and healthy.[22] Struggling to find something to criticize, Coxe decided that it was a mistake for the young charges to perform plays and operas, activities that distracted from their work and training, but he acknowledged that the empress considered "that species of entertainment . . . a means of civilization."[23] Another often well-informed writer, August Ludwig von Schlözer (1735–1809), who became Catherine's persistent critic once he returned to Germany after years working in Russia, alleged that because the children were excessively exposed to cold and the infants were fed on cow milk, mortality rates were high.[24] But most commentary, such as that in Florence's respected *Gazzetta Universale*, which named the foundling home in Moscow as among Catherine II's most notable accomplishments[25] supported the image of an apparently maternal and caring empress worthy of her fans' fervent esteem.

Codifying Russian Law

The law code reform project that Catherine started in 1768 was a more cerebral matter, but the guidelines she wrote for this favorite goal of Enlightenment statecraft, the *Grand Instruction*, were published in a range of editions at different price ranges and in all the major European languages and sent a giddy celebrity buzz through newspapers and magazines across Europe. Distant readers, talkers, writers, and cultural moneymakers extolled the feat. One German scribbler, writing for women readers, proclaimed

Catherine's scheme for legal reform "the bravest plan that had ever entered the soul of a monarch,"[26] and the often belligerent author of the twice weekly *Deutsche Chronik*, Christian Friedrich Daniel Schubart, named the empress one of the "great benefactors of the human race" and claimed she demonstrated "the greatest respect for life, property and freedom of all her subjects" and would ban slavery (as Russian serfdom was often labeled).[27]

A French novelist took up the new code plan as well. According to the analysis of Robert Darnton, Louis-Sébastien Mercier's futuristic, utopian *The Year Two Thousand Four Hundred and Forty*, was the supreme best seller among France's forbidden books at the time.[28] Mercier's discussion of the legal system begins with his time-traveling eighteenth-century narrator's praise for the twenty-fifth century's "amazing alterations in our laws." The response from his twenty-fifth-century interlocutor is immediate: "Your laws! Stop there. How could you give that title to an undigested mass of contradictory customs, to those old shattered papers that contained nothing but ideas without connection and grotesque precedencies?" When the speaker in the future continues that Catherine II had played a key role centuries earlier with her groundbreaking legal reforms, his eighteenth-century visitor reports the bad reception of the empress's work in some quarters, writing that an entire print-run was "privately burned at Paris . . . except a single copy, that I by chance, saved from the flames."[29] (In one of her letters to Voltaire, Catherine herself had proudly announced the banning of the *Instructions* in both Paris and Constantinople, a claim he confirmed to her later.[30]) The law project gained its own celebrity-enhancing whiff of the forbidden.

Most of all, Catherine II's fame always derived in part from the incongruence of her gender with her actions. Men of the Enlightenment, who in an early, more inclusive phase, had championed women as scholars and writers, had by Catherine's reign generally decided that women's ability to reason was inferior to their own and so chose to treat her as an exception whose skills and accomplishments signified nothing larger, but whose wealth and political power implicitly corrected the deformity of sex. Frederick II, for example, in magazine versions of his supposedly leaked assessment, designated Catherine's *Instruction* as "worthy of a great man" and unique among women rulers,[31] a much-repeated judgment. The protofeminist Theodor Gottlieb von Hippel, on the other hand, belonging to a less misogynist strand of the movement, praised her "nobly independent soul," and argued that, unfettered by limiting prejudices, "she shows what a woman can become."[32] Though celebrity talk, pressing at least occasionally against convention, can sometimes help a society shift its dominant discourse, Hippel's version of such a shift did not prevail. Overwhelmingly in Enlightenment texts, Catherine was treated as an exception who reinforced rather than questioned society's underlying low esteem for women. Pieter van Woensel, for example, wrote, "She has a solid judgment, penetration, strength of mind free from prejudices in general, and particularly those of her sex."[33] Catherine could be described as outstanding to the extent that she differed from other women. Sweeping praise for her was wrapped in condescending generosity, and dominant gender schema were salvaged by packaging Catherine as exceptional. In her Enlightenment image, the gender unruliness that was a significant part of Catherine II's celebrity elsewhere was not prominent. As for legal reform, after the lawgivers whom she impressively summoned to write the new code met for a time in Moscow, their assembly unobtrusively disbanded, but travel writers continued to mention seeing the original copy of the *Instructions*, written in Catherine's own hand and carefully preserved.[34]

More Well-Publicized Early Projects and the Visit of Diderot

In 1765 the *Annual Register* emphasized Catherine's Enlightenment credentials and called her court "the asylum of the sciences, to which she invites learned men from every part of Europe."[35] Ideas poured in, and publicity gushed out, keeping talk of the empress humming. One of her correspondents proposed tobacco companies and cheese making,[36] another suggested the empress purchase a "universal calculating machine" that had been devised by a village pastor in Germany,[37] and Voltaire offered the design for a new machine for transporting artillery.[38] As one contemporary observer of Catherine's court put it, "Foreigners who felt themselves qualified to be the reformers of Russia and so of maybe half a world" streamed to St. Petersburg.[39] Projects that for years generated almost continuous clamor about Catherine outside her territories addressed the themes of implementing medical discoveries, exploring the empire, encouraging population, improving transportation, and, in many forms, educating her citizens. Several had elements that lent themselves to the seemingly personal components of celebrity.

In 1768, for example, readers from Ghent to Madrid and beyond encountered surprising news that, on October 13, the empress of Russia had submitted to inoculation against small pox. It was a disease feared by eighteenth-century readers and listeners. As one writer, feminizing the contagion, asked:

> Who does not tremble, when this inexorable enemy of the human body spreads her contagious breath everywhere and slinks invisibly on from house to house? . . . Who does not tremble, when she brands even those who believed they were safe from her gruesome ravages with her hideous marks . . . sowing the surface of the smooth skin with her boils, swelling the body, deforming its regular shape; making the face, the noblest features, the place of beauty, unrecognizable, enveloped in confluent pustules.[40]

The deaths from smallpox of Tsar Peter II in 1730, Queen Ulrika of Sweden in 1741, and Louis XV of France in 1774 showed that exalted rank provided no protection. Yet a ruler's choice of whether to risk the new inoculation, deliberately infecting the skin with pus from someone whose smallpox case was mild, was still difficult. (Vaccination, a safer approach using cowpox, was developed only at the end of the eighteenth century, in the year of Catherine's death.)

As a host of newspapers reported once success was certain, Catherine II was treated by an English doctor, Thomas Dimsdale.[41] The procedure took place on October 13, 1768, but "had no visible effect till the 19th, when, the weather being fine, and the ground covered with snow, her majesty took a walk in the morning for the air." Soon she had "symptoms of a fever, which continued till the 31st towards six in the evening, when the eruption first began to appear." She recovered and promptly ordered Paul to be inoculated along with a dozen gentlemen and ladies of the court.[42] Once additional groups had also received the treatment, she crowed to Voltaire that "more people have been inoculated here in one month than in eight at Vienna."[43]

To the distant crowd, most of whom were not wealthy enough to afford the expensive procedure, the celebrity potential of the story focused on what it seemed to reveal about the empress herself as a brave, determined, and generous person. According to "Curious Anecdotes" in *Town and Country Magazine*, Doctor Dimsdale had inoculated the tsarina, "when the symptoms were as favourable as possible," though her "corpulency" worried him. Knowing that doctors were always suspected if anything went wrong with an important patient and fearing "banishment for life in Siberia," Dimsdale was terrified when she abruptly summoned him ten days later, but when he arrived at the palace, "the empress came running to him in an Amazonian dress, in full health." She invited him to go hunting, "as he had been lavish in his praises of the excellence of his countrymen in that diversion" and "rallied him smartly upon his groundless terrors and apprehensions." To distant readers the newspaper item may have been another reminder of the capriciousness of autocrats, the frightening image of Siberia, but also the generosity and spirit of the powerful monarch, as well as her unusual status, a ruler in "Amazonian dress." The anecdote concludes: "It were needless to add how magnificently, nobly, and generously, the czarina has rewarded the doctor, as his honours, titles, and presents, have been repeatedly published."[44]

Acclaim for Catherine II's inoculation appeared in literary forms that might extend the audience for her as a celebrity, both because such texts were often reviewed[45] and because they might appeal to the matrons and governesses, for example, who did not care for the travel books or biographies that contained other extensive accounts of the event.[46] As Jean-Joseph-Thérèse Roman (1726–87) wrote, mothers were the key people to persuade if inoculation were to be widely accepted, and a pleasing poetic form, he thought, was most likely to reach them.[47] The dedicatory stanzas to his poetic "L'Inoculation" in four cantos are addressed to Catherine, who was, he asserted, "much more courageous" than other leading royals: "You had it done on yourself, and you repeated it/ On your son, your only hope for your vast state."[48] This and other texts bade readers to admire the supposedly caring empress and identify with her maternal feelings.[49]

Improving and spreading education was another of Catherine's Enlightenment projects. One writer was so impressed with her schools that in the midst of his description, he switched suddenly to poetry:

—Did she, did Catherine this?
   For this one act be all her sins forgiven,
   And bless her, bless her heaven where'er she goes.[50]

Improving education was yet another topos likely to please distant audiences who thought of themselves as ever more enlightened.

Mid-Reign Cracks in Catherine's Enlightened Image, 1773–89

The euphoric first phase of Catherine's popular image as an enlightened monarch, the initial decade of her reign, included her Enlightenment-inspired project of luring new settlers to her huge territories, thereby increasing the wealth, status, and power of her empire.[51] Already in 1763, the year after the coup, European newspapers reprinted two manifestos of invitation that mapped out the "very advantageous conditions" for settling "in any section of the country." One magazine used fanciful imagery, on which celebrity discourse thrived, to describe the empress's determination to make her "empire blossom as much as her court gleamed." Meanwhile, worried German princes attacked "the ambrosia of beautiful promises" made by Catherine's recruiters and said that new arrivals were "hated by the natives," a statement that at least acknowledged the existence of unspecified "natives" on the supposedly empty land.[52] Gradually, it became widely known that people from many parts of Europe, especially Germany, were moving to Russia.

Then a more mixed, cautiously critical second phase of Catherine's Enlightenment fame began, extending from 1773 to roughly 1788. Nonetheless, throughout Catherine's reign, fantasy-inducing stories appeared about the gracious enlightened ruler. In one, according to a newspaper item, Abbé Raynal, a well-known *philosophe* at the time, asked a Russian general to beg the empress to send him some of her tea. When she heard the request, the "crowned Philosopher" promptly sent him, the newspaper asserted, "an ample provision" and "a letter, expressive of her high opinion of his merit and talents."[53] In another instance, a woman in Frankfurt am Main sold the empress manuscripts of the great seventeenth-century astronomer, mathematician, and astrologer Johannes Kepler, which Catherine then donated to her Petersburg Academy.[54] Likewise, a German educator, J. B. Basedow, working on a four-volume encyclopedic work for schoolchildren, with a costly fifth volume of illustrations, gladly accepted a subvention from the empress and included a version of Russian history that glowed with enthusiasm for her and her patronage of artists and writers "without regard to nationality or creed."[55] Catherine's Jewish subjects wrote flattering poems to her in an effort to gain attention for their issues. Isachar Falkensohn Behr, for example, proclaimed Catherine II "the wisest of all the crowned wise" in his long German birthday poem for her and avowed: "And if the great princess most graciously grants/ a listening ear to the singer of Israel, / and appoints the stranger to be a subject / lifting him most considerably out of the dust!!—/ . . . should such a blessing ever delight me/ then grant me just this day of happiness." If he had the joy of being a fully recognized imperial subject, he would die happy.[56] The poems, tales, and dreams of imperial generosity and good nature, even mixed with rejection and criticism, were all nectar for celebrity discourse. Diderot's visit to St. Petersburg seemed at first to provide more.

In 1773, the already much-repeated story of Catherine II purchasing Diderot's library reappeared in the news along with the announcement that "Monsieur Diderot is now gone to Petersburgh" to thank his benefactress. The "genuine Anecdote of the Empress of Russia" reiterated "Monsieur Diderot's distressful situation" before Catherine made her dramatic intervention in the role of munificent fairy godmother, stimulating exactly the kind of fantasy that wealth can suggest within the unrealistic discourse of celebrity.[57] Yet the Frenchman's Russian trip represented a quiet tipping point in Catherine's public relations. After the crescendo of Enlightenment praise in 1768 came a decrescendo five years later at a moment that should have been a triumph: Diderot's visit.[58]

Relations between a judgmental empress and even the most distinguished scholar were almost inevitably delicate. When Melchior Adam Weikard, as a doctor newly arrived from Germany, had his first conversation with her, she asked him which scholars were currently most significant in Germany. He praised his then friend Johann Georg Zimmermann, of whom Catherine had already heard something, and mentioned a recent work on the philosophy of history by Johann Gottfried Herder.

> Who is this Herder, she asked hastily. He is a clergyman, said I, in Weimar. A clergyman, she said, then this cannot be a philosophical work. If the man is a philosopher, she said, then he cannot be a clergyman, and if he is a clergyman, then he cannot qualify as a philosopher. Of course, the supernatural nonsense that passes for philosophy in some quarters today does fit better with clergymen, Jews, and heathens; only it does not tally with common sense.[59]

The "philosopher on the throne" was confidently dismissive of the man whose ideas still influence philosophy, history, and anthropology.

Whether Diderot had the same experience of a disparaging but genial empress, the general public did not find out. Competing with several more urgent events, including turmoil in her central Asian provinces and her participation in an act of territorial aggression in which Prussia, Austria, and Russia took convenient slices out of their mutual neighbor Poland (Chapter 9), reports of Diderot disappeared from the papers. After his departure again from St. Petersburg, newspapers printed hints that the *philosophe*'s relationship with the empress was not a success. On May 9, 1774, a Frankfurt gazette announced: "Diderot, whose speedy departure surprised everyone, is thought to have done some thoughtless things which led to the order that he clear out within a few hours."[60] Though the *General Evening Post* also suspected that, like other "modish philosophers," Diderot might have unwisely tried to "fathom and discuss religious points," it more firmly proclaimed: "That such a favourite of the Empress of Russia should experience so singular a disgrace, is a fresh instance of the fickleness of Court favour."[61] Whatever the cause of "this wonderful alteration," Diderot himself published virtually nothing to clarify the matter,[62] and the encounter of the two celebrities sank into obscurity.

In 1786, readers of French were told that Catherine had sent another famous visitor packing, the eighteenth century's most notorious practitioner of esotericism, self-declared "Count" Cagliostro. That year, just as the pre-revolutionary diamond necklace affair at the court of Louis XVI was making Cagliostro infamous, a salacious "genuine report," supposedly by his runaway servant, described the effort of the purported mystic and his wife to draw Catherine into their scheme. She, however, allegedly declared that "miracles do not comport well with the philosophy that I am trying to introduce into my states" and directed the couple to leave.[63] She had in fact already had the debunking

News of the Notorious Cagliostro's Stay in Mitau, in the Year 1779, and of His Magic Operations There[64] by Elise von der Recke published in Russian[65] and had written a play of her own lampooning Cagliostro. Though the printed record of Catherine II's literary reception is mixed,[66] later editors of a collection of her plays wrote that her writings were interesting precisely because of what they show about her, not about their ostensible topics. The editors added that "we," as the distant public, "love to see [the famous] in their private lives, so to speak, not dressed up."[67] The empress's literary texts, they were arguing, could facilitate the parasocial relationship, the intimacy at a distance, to Catherine II that celebrity promised.

Further Intellectual Engagements

For many distant adherents of the Enlightenment, Catherine II's most dramatic action in the middle of her reign was the appointment in 1783 of Princess Yekaterina Romanovna Vorontsova-Dashkova to head the Russian Academy of Sciences. Western gazettes were agog over the amazing position for a woman, who many readers could remember from her role in the coup in 1762. It was further stuff of celebrity, exploring the boundaries of the acceptable. In Britain the *Monthly Review* purred: "It is not uncommon to see the fair-sex cultivating the flowery shrubs of Parnassus, nay sometimes peeping into the temple of science; but it is a rare phenomenon to find a lady at the head of a learned academy, whose labours turn, for the most part, on the most difficult and severe parts of natural philosophy." Yet such "is exhibited to us by the appointment of the Princess Daschow to the place of directress shall we call her, or director of the academy of Petersburg." The appointment was firmly marked as an exception, but, the *Review* reported, "the labours of the academicians are now resumed, and will be hereafter carried on with new vigour."[68] Though other writers too, such as Madame Büsching's husband, expected that "the scholarly men will feel comfortable under female direction,"[69] Germany's best-known woman novelist of the period, Sophie von La Roche, writing years later, recalled "derision and complaints raised on all sides" against the choice. One of Catherine's almost apoplectic critics, Caspar van Saldern, for example, declared that Dashkova was "childishly vain" when she accepted the position "and imagined herself a scholar"; he argued that "having fallen into hands that should be running a spinning wheel," the academy became "insignificant."[70] La Roche, however, contended that if the empress "can select generals and ministers and give orders, why shouldn't another woman have gathered enough knowledge to listen to, judge, and fund the ideas of fifty academists. . .?"[71] With such stuff for sociable discussion, even an academy directorship could join celebrity discourse.

It was happening at a time, distant gazettes showed, when the empress's relationships abroad with the *philosophes* had ebbed and she had become more accessible to German intellectuals,[72] such as Johann Georg Zimmermann (1725–95), George III's official physician in the English king's German territory of Hanover (which he never visited). In a personal crisis, Catherine had found comfort in Zimmermann's book about loneliness and had sent him a splendid reward. Trumpeted in German newspapers, this became a fabulous celebrity endorsement for the doctor.[73] Over time, he and the empress also developed a regular correspondence, as he proclaimed in 1788 in *Doctor Zimmermann's Conversations with the Late King of Prussia: When He Attended Him in His Last Illness a Little before His Death*.[74] To some readers far from the territories of the rich and powerful tsarina, the book exposed Zimmermann's compulsive fawning over rulers and his excessive pride about his correspondence with Catherine.[75] Many noticed the contradiction between the Enlightenment movement's egalitarian implications and its members' frequent search for royal sponsors. Critics guffawed over the amusingly titled satire *Zimmermann I and Friedrich II*, which sarcastically praised both the doctor's assiduous stress on his correspondence with the empress and the didactic tone he adopted toward the brilliant king.[76] Another writer suggested the doctor's volume should have been called "About me on the occasion of my conversations with Frederick the Great,"[77] though one of his defenders retorted that the relationship of the doctor with the empress "was costing all of us a droplet of envy."[78] Zimmermann, undeterred by the ridicule, soon copied the Catherine passages into a second book about Frederick, added a longer comparison of the king with the empress,[79] and thus did his part in stimulating her fame among the educated reading public.

Celebrities often both gain and maintain their status by performing notorious misdeeds, but among women stars prolonged transgressiveness is uncommon. For Catherine II, famous first for shockingly dethroning her husband, engagement with the Enlightenment provided early chances of public redemption. Representations of her as an Enlightenment figure long helped to sell books, opening doors in the imagination, suggesting shared interests and hopes based on learning and reason, seeming to show a maternal and usually affable woman in private, hinting at passageways that could overcome the status gulf separating readers from her, arousing awe as well as envy of the valuable tokens of imperial esteem that she sent out, but also causing disappointment when projects were dropped and when tales of an entirely different sort—uprisings and wars—shadowed the empress's image. Over the same years, media workers and their audiences were pursuing yet another celebrity-inducing theme, Catherine II's immense wealth and how she used it.

7

Consuming Catherine II

Gender and Wealth

"Posterity will be at a loss which to admire most, the great power of Russia, or the magnificence of its empress," the widely distributed and highly respected *Annual Register* proclaimed in 1773 to readers in Britain, emphasizing that despite the long and expensive war she was conducting with the Ottomans, "her expences, whether in rewards to her generals and officers, in presents to learned men, in the encouragement of arts, or in the purchase of libraries, statues, pictures, antiques, and jewels, infinitely exceed those of any late or present European prince, except Lewis the Fourteenth."[1] Since Catherine was a parvenu ruler who claimed to be empress over a parvenu empire that claimed to be European, the extreme deployment of magnificence and opulence to signal the grandeur and hence supposed legitimacy of her court was another politically logical enhancement of her *gloire*—her imperial fame, glory, and grandiosity. If her spending was publicly compared with that of a renowned and notoriously spendthrift French king, a key purpose of the purchases was accomplished.

Because courtly display, *gloire*, had to be flaunted, remote observers from many different social classes and with no line to the court could read or hear much about Catherine II's extravagant choices too. To the matrons and nursemaids, grandfathers and man-servants, far from her capitol, the costly splendor that marked the world of any distant royal or imperial court could—especially before the French Revolution erupted near century's end—arouse a range of reactions, extending from boredom to disgust to pleasure at being lifted out of their own narrow sphere, even to identifying with one of the successful players, imagining what it would be like to be Catherine or to be close to her. In the discourse around Catherine II, the theme of wealth, in stories of her extravagant display, purchases, presents, and patronage, reverberated widely to the benefit of her celebrity, her engrossing fame among ordinary people.

Celebrities are always entangled with money not only because they are themselves invariably commodified but also because—with rare exceptions—they are almost equally invariably posed as consumers, particularly of costly luxury goods and services. Much as fans seek commonalities with a celebrity that enable identification, they also treasure certain differences that make identification alluring, often differences in wealth. Catherine II's attainment of prodigious affluence despite the obscurity of her family made it easier for a non-elite audience to imagine that something at least a little like that might also befall them, especially since a woman's access to great wealth was almost always improbable and contingent. When Catherine's grandiose and imposing self-representations to other rulers and to her own nobility spilled over to a wider, non-elite audience, she became a fantasy consumer, one seemingly without monetary or geographical limits, evoking the dreams and creating the vicarious pleasures that an audience derives from the celebrities it accepts and creates. Even distant folk with mere pennies for a broadsheet or minutes for listening could learn of Catherine II's extravagances in acquiring precious adornments for herself, making luxury purchases, becoming glamorous, building an especially audacious monument, and granting generous patronage, including to the distant audience's countrymen.

As its prime example of Catherine's lavish consumption, the *Annual Register* cited "a diamond of an enormous size which she purchased this year."[2] The rumors were sketchy, but the magnitude of the diamond was amazing and its price stunning—some said 450,000 rubles and others as much as 700,000. Catherine appeared willing and able to transfer a treasure house of silver for a stone she could hold in the palm of her hand. This was exactly the stuff of price tag glamour, which connects publicly announced, or presumed, exorbitant prices with particular individuals, usually already famous celebrities. Disproportion maximized the gem's imaginative potential for readers and auditors with little, less, or no disposable income. A fanciful poem, "Story of the Great Diamond in Petersburg," by a German poet with a popular rococo flair, Johann Wilhelm Ludwig Gleim, told of Jupiter noticing a fleck of dust and turning the fleck into a diamond that fell into Catherine's lap and became the topmost ornament in her imperial crown.[3]

Newspapers, of course, quickly published more realistic accounts. "About six years ago," according to the *Notizie del Mondo* in Florence, "a Greek gentleman named Georgio Souffras, came from Isphahan [to Amsterdam] and brought with him a diamond of extraordinary size and immense value."[4] Mr. Souffras deposited the gem in the bank, *The Annual Register* stated in its breathless account of Catherine's magnificence, "till he could meet with a purchaser; the greatness of the price would have made this difficult, if the Empress of Russia had not existed. She has paid upwards of 100,000 £. Sterling for it, besides settling a pension for life, of 4000 rubles, upon the gentleman, which amounts to little less, than a thousand pounds sterling a year."[5] Over the following years, the diamond acquired its own exotic itinerary and its own detailed and adventurous, but inconsistent, narratives, all of which signaled the continued interest—and probably the sociable conversations—of distant audiences.

Louis Dutens, a French expert on precious stones, for example, vaguely acknowledged that the stone's story was, as scholars today note of many luxury acquisitions, "intrinsically ... part of a colonialist discourse."[6] Dutens claimed Catherine's immense gem, which was incorporated into the imperial scepter (where it remains today), had formed one eye of a famous statue in a Brahman temple in India until a cunning French grenadier pried it out and sold it to a sea captain for 50,000 livres.[7] Peter Simon Pallas, an explorer and ethnographer, on the other hand, wrote of a cruel Persian emperor, Shah Nadir, whose throne was adorned with two Indian diamonds that, after Nadir was assassinated, were "secretly disposed of by the soldiers who shared the plunder." The sale to Catherine offered a further saga, with the seller variously identified as Greek, Persian, or Armenian and then generally given a name—Souffras, Shafrass, Suffras, Saffras, or Safras. Or he is identified as a Jew, in which case, he remains nameless (and Jewish readers and listeners would have been aware that gem dealing, since it was not controlled by a guild, was one of the few trades open to them in eighteenth-century Europe). Some accounts of the diamond added a dollop of seemingly romantic intimacy by asserting that Prince Orlov, whose status as Catherine's former lover was probably known in scattered parts of her foreign audience, purchased the precious jewel and gave it to the empress as a birthday present,[8] a claim of generosity that simultaneously signaled the enormous value of intimacy with the empress and showed Catherine's court as an astonishing place where "such presents can be made by subjects to their sovereigns."[9]

The Complex Mix of Wealth and Gender

Interpreting huge expenditures as signs of affection and benevolence obscured the role of such gestures in draining the nobility's potentially dangerous energies and resources into symbolic activities, such as "gift"-giving and bargaining for jewels, and ignored the exploitation of serfs and wars as the sources of money to pay for such costly trinkets, also glossing over the expectations of courtiers that outlandish extravagance would be rewarded in time,[10] part of what Marcia Pointon calls "the slippery relationship between gift and commercial transaction."[11] The larger political function of gifts in demanding deference is obfuscated too. Maria Theresa of Austria's supposed rage "at seeing her own reputation eclipsed by the superior splendor of Catherine" lost its potential political bite by being personalized as a conventional case of "female jealousy" that allegedly "heightened the aversion between the two empresses."[12] Orlov as giver yields a conventional narrative that inscribes onto Catherine's acquisition of the diamond an orthodox eighteenth-century gender relationship between a man, who is a capable agent bringing gifts, and a woman, who is a presumably passive object of attention. To fans of the empress who sought confirmation of familiar gender pieties, Catherine could be the feminized recipient in the gift story and Orlov the masculinized, gallant, and immeasurably rich donor, commemorated even now in the name of the diamond, the Orlov.

Similarly, decades later, Sénac de Meilhan, with women readers especially in mind, wrote in detail about a lavish party given for Catherine by another lover. The writer marveled at "the illuminations, the most fabulous clothing, diamonds, dances, music." Prince Potemkin, "the first among the greats of the empire, richer than all the others, and famous for his victories, wearing his field marshal's uniform glittering with jewels," threw himself at her feet when she arrived at his palace (see also Figure 0.6). This sight, Sénac claimed, showed "the power of beauty" and of the "kindness that appears to be characteristic of the female sex"; modeling a fan's worshipful admiration, he too wanted to adore the empress "like a benevolent goddess."[13] Though Catherine's extravagant world was far from the mundane situations of distant readers, they could recognize the relationship's purportedly conventional gender outlines.

More than that, parading the disbursal of great sums was and is a form of power that women of great privilege could exercise somewhat less objectionably than other forms (perhaps because most such rich women came to their money only through a rich father or husband). Thus Catherine II's demonstrations of a consumer's fondness for luxury or a patron's fondness for munificence were not as great a deviation from familiar eighteenth-century gender expectations as were her actions employing military might or displaying immense political authority. Particular demonstrations of wealth, furthermore, could have their own gendered qualities, sometimes enabling members of the middling sort to imagine connections that class and rank differences otherwise negated. Buying pictures, dishes, dresses, or diamonds enabled at least some women readers to assimilate their wishes, if not the size of their expenditures, with the empress's. Catherine II as consumer blended with Catherine II as celebrity in a pattern that has become characteristic of celebrity discourse.

Glamour

To many fans, prodigal princely behavior must have seemed glamorous. As John Berger explains in *Ways of Seeing,* glamour is "the happiness of being envied" for a look or style that seems both distinctive and effortless.[14] Distant writers and artists concocted and publicized representations of Catherine to dazzle her non-elite audiences and capture their imaginations, associating her with theatricality, beauty, and wealth, not to mention the themes of sexuality and notoriety that also clung to her name. All of these were and are qualities that combine to produce glamour in the eyes of less-privileged observers.[15] Women celebrities in particular are almost always glamorous, but in the eighteenth-century context, when glamour in its modern form lacked a name and celebrity was still in an early stage, the concept sometimes peeked through terms such as "taste" and "magnificence." One admirer, for example, described Catherine's "personal taste" as revealed in "her clear fondness for everything that is noble, great, and beautiful" and asserted that it "shows itself in the projects she has ordered, in the public buildings in her gardens and palaces, in the decoration of her rooms and chambers, yes even in her choices that are fanciful and capricious."[16]

Reports of the costliness of her dress and accoutrements could provide readers and listeners the fantasized momentary lift out of their everyday world that celebrity discourse augured. In 1780, when she journeyed to meet another ruler, Emperor Joseph II, she presented herself in "the most charming Amazon outfit, decorated with all her orders and the whole dress spangled with diamonds."[17] Earlier, one visitor claimed, "She does not like excessive grandeur at all," but added, "Her clothing is splendid and superior."[18] Another described her as bedecked with "Diamonds, rubies, emeralds, and so forth, of unusual size,"[19] and another wrote that the gold and diamond chains around her shoulders made her into a fortress of precious stones and metals.[20] A portrait that Catherine commissioned from Alexander Roslin late in 1776 or early the next year depicted her indeed as laden with precious metals and stones and dressed in a style denoted as "Slavic."[21] The picture gained her approval enough to begin the process of having copies painted and sending some of them abroad, where engravers far from St. Petersburg reproduced them on paper. Their prints, mostly excerpts of the tsarina's face and upper body, yielded a new picture type showing a middle-aged or older, richly dressed and bejeweled Catherine, a figure confident enough as monarch to smile slightly and look kindly at the beholder (Figure 7.1).

One such exorbitantly costly choice with the distinctive aura of glamour was the enormous dinner service that Catherine II commissioned from Sevres entailing 797 pieces ornamented with handcrafted cameos.[22] For faraway customers in ordinary shops and marketplaces to find pleasure in such lavish consumption, a major cultural change was necessary in the eighteenth century. The indulgence in luxury or thoughts of luxury by anyone outside the aristocracy had for centuries been vilified as a plague that produced "indecent softness, indifference to great deeds, little feeling of sympathy and humanity, [and] a destructive tendency to go from one lust to the next"; according to such complaints and the classical sources on which they drew, luxury in the wrong places caused poverty and led to depopulation.[23] But exactly around the time of Catherine's reign a new strand of argument was gaining attention with the claim that when ordinary folk bought or built things richer than the standards traditionally conceded to them, they stimulated commerce and helped the general

Figure 7.1 Catherine's costly chains of office and other jewels are shown in a print made by Caroline Watson in 1787. One of the few women fine print makers in the eighteenth century, she based her elegant picture on a variation of Roslin's decade-old portrait, the same portrait type that Ferdinant Leüthner had used—but made more fashionable—for his business card (Figure 3.12). Source: Caroline Watson, *Catherine II. Empress of Russia*. Portrait of Catherine II. Image ID:2B0C10N. Credit: Artocoloro/ Alamy Stock Photo.

public welfare.[24] With this newfound economic function of spending, readers and listeners in the middling and even lower classes could acceptably enjoy vicarious pleasure in the empress's profligacy and opulence. In London, they might even pay to see a supposedly lifelike representation of it in the form of a traveling waxworks, "just arrived from Paris." A paid newspaper announcement for the show stresses the chance to see Catherine II, and other rulers, doing something very familiar to viewers, sitting at dinner with her family, but here "in a most august and splendid manner."[25]

More than making the sight of Catherine's riches attractive, the ebbing of moralizing about spending meant glamour could offer viewers a proposal of self-transformation by, as Berger bluntly states, "buying something."[26] Part of the less-privileged public contemplating accounts of Catherine's ostentatious purchases could envision luxury not as a self-indulgent pleasure forbidden to their class but as a transformative way of cultivating their own taste and enhancing their freedom, autonomy, and agency.[27] To laud Catherine II's discrimination in buying was to laud her and to assign attributes to her that lowly viewers, readers, and auditors could acquire in their imaginations or, miniaturized, by making purchases of their own.[28] In short, attention to Catherine II as a super-consumer could promote early capitalism and thus contribute to the production of capitalist subjectivity. Thus, to the middling classes of the eighteenth century, the real or imagined acquisition of material goods was taking on new meaning for the self, and when they bought certain kinds of things, they could see objects such as plates and teacups, at least occasionally, as resembling Catherine's not in cost but in kind. Purchasers could begin to imagine a continuum in which the notion of good taste joined their frugal choices, whether waxwork and lecture tickets or patent medicines and false teeth,[29] to Catherine's expensive and glamorous ones.

Extravagant Display

Glamour usually happens in settings of luxury that involve expenditures with a price disproportionate to what is being bought. In one form, a colossal price is unbalanced by the ephemerality and transience of what is purchased. In another, the price of the exclusive item vastly exceeds the price of something similar that is equally functional. In yet another form, a high cost combines with lack of ordinary utility, as in the instance of the diamond and, as will be seen, of art purchases too.

The squandering of riches on short-lived pleasures occurred conspicuously in lavish court rituals, theatrical events, parties, and fireworks. At a dynastic festivity for the birth of Catherine's grandson, for example, the highest-ranking members of court were "invited by the favorite Moor of the empress" to play "a game of dice in which each player who threw a nine received a diamond of a particular size."[30] Performances of music, theater, opera, and dance accompanied festivities, as at all but the most threadbare princely settings further west. Periodicals noted Catherine's recruitment away from rival courts of great stars from France and Italy,[31] such as the celebrated Neapolitan Giovanni Paesiello. After his debut, readers of the *Courier de l'Europe* could learn, at a "magnificent dinner and ball" magnificent presents of "diamond necklaces, snuff boxes, etc." were given to "the virtuosos of both sexes." The detailed account ended with a slightly apologetic postscript: "In the absence of political news, we thought we might please you by passing on this type of notice." On the next line is the editor's reply to his correspondent, projecting the imagined voice of readers savoring such tales of luxury: "Oh! Yes, in truth, the greatest pleasure."[32]

The compensation for artists coming to St. Petersburg was a moment for price tag glamour that illuminated both the artist and the empress. The acclaimed singer Caterina Gabrielli, herself a celebrity,[33] turned her negotiations with the empress's Milan agent into a much-repeated quip. When she demanded "7000 rubles (or about 1500£. Sterling) a year, besides a house and carriage" and would not "relax the least article of this sum," the negotiators "remonstrated with her at the unreasonableness of so enormous a salary, and to induce her to diminish it, informed her that a field marshal had no more. 'If that be the case,' said she, 'I would advise her majesty to make one of her marshals sing.'"[34] Wit, like details and differing opinions, could make accounts of events and their participants more vivid to distant readers and auditors and provide material for their entertainment or indignation.

Catherine II clearly accepted and sometimes solicited publicity for her court festivities, which, one writer asserted, she considered to be "the tribute that monarchs owe the public."[35] When she went to meet Joseph II, the king of Austria and emperor of the Holy Roman Empire, at Mogilev (now in Belarus), she arrived in her fabulous state coach and was preceded by twelve postilions. Readers of a pamphlet entitled *The Exalted Eagle in the Mask of a Falcon, or Journey of Emperor Joseph II to Russia under the Name Count von Falkenstein* by J. G. Mayer were told that she had an "almost divine appearance, fluttered about by a thousand graces."[36] Not for her the budget touring that Joseph practiced on this and other occasions by traveling "incognito," using one of his lesser titles, so that both he and theoretically his hosts could circumvent much of the protocol and costs of a formal state visit. In a telling instance of inventive artists fulfilling audience wishes, however, a print in the pamphlet shows Joseph, despite his incognito, in an elegantly bordered coat, not the determinedly plain garments he preferred, as he meets a slim, regally berobed and gracefully dressed, glamorous version of Catherine II.[37] Buyers almost certainly preferred glamour to factuality.

Catherine's role as a model consumer applied especially when she selected functional products in versions far more costly than what gentry wives or shopkeeper families far from the empress's court bought for their homes and their tables. Middlemen, merchants, dealers, collectors, craftsmen, artists, and writers scrambled to stimulate imperial acquisitions and to use the endorsements that such purchases implied to their advantage. Josiah Wedgwood's publicity about her huge table service (Chapter 3) meant that middling-class consumers, buying in a Wedgwood shop, could feel a connection to the celebrity empress's luxuries.[38]

Art, Literature, Learning, and Patronage

The English-language *Italian Mercury* called Catherine II "the Elizabeth of our day, . . . collecting whatever is curious in every part of polished Europe, nay, in the whole universe."[39] Durable objects that had no utility beyond display could function as "positional goods." Valued for their symbolic utility, they confer status on the possessor because they are rare, highly desirable, and, of course, expensive,[40] and, for full effect, their ownership must also be known to a public. In *The Wealth of Nations* (1776), Adam Smith noted that for the owners of vast wealth "the chief enjoyment of riches consists in the parade of riches, which in their eye is never so complete as when they appear to possess those decisive marks of opulence which nobody can possess but themselves."[41] Among quintessential positional goods are original art works by a desired artist or in a preferred genre. Intriguing to Catherine II's distant non-elite audience were the prices of such goods and the possibility that they might offer hints about one of celebrity discourse's quintessential topics, the wealthy buyer's private personality. The empress made many widely touted purchases that conferred prestige on herself and her country and added to the new appraisal of Russia as becoming enlightened.[42]

Art collecting was an especially well-publicized aspect of the luxury discourse that enhanced Catherine II's celebrity. Word soon spread of her participation in this "process of actively, selectively, and passionately acquiring and possessing things removed from ordinary use and perceived as part of a set of non-identical objects or experiences,"[43] as Russell W. Belk calls it. The *Annual Register* for 1771 noted that she had purchased paintings in Amsterdam collected by "that celebrated connoisseur Mr. Bramcamp" and had paid "upwards of 100,000 guilders" for them, a sum that belonged unmistakably in a realm of fabulous wealth.[44] For the distant reading public in tea rooms and coffee houses, Catherine's acts of "competitive connoisseurship,"[45] buying up collections of deceased owners in Germany (Count Heinrich Bruel), France (Louis Antoine Crozat, baron de Thiers), and Britain (Sir Robert Walpole), offered enticing material for both praise and disgust.[46] Soon, whenever expensive art came up for sale, predictions were made, not always correctly, that Catherine would make the purchase.

Despite problems with payments and safe transport,[47] publicity about Catherine II's patronage inspired numerous artists, craftsmen, and dealers, and presumably the watching general public as well. The empress, receptive to new art as well as old, bought paintings by Angelika Kaufmann, gave a commission, as *The World and Fashionable Advertiser* noted, to Sir Joshua Reynolds,[48] became an early continental patron of Joseph Wright of Derby, acquired 500 drawings of Sicily by the French painter Jean Houel (1735–1813),[49] and purchased "lots and lots" of the miniatures of Theresia Concordia Maron, a German painter in Rome.[50] On September 3, 1774, a newspaper mentioned orders from the Russian empress for eight portraits by Anna Dorothea Therbusch (or Therbouche) nee Liszewska (or Liscewska or Liszewski) (1721–82), one of the rare women members of the French Academy of the Arts.[51] But Therbusch's contact with the empress also could notify the public of its pitfalls. On her own speculation, the artist produced an ambitious painting depicting Catherine's son, Grand Duke Paul, meeting the king of Prussia and surrounded by both real and allegorical figures. The picture was expedited to St. Petersburg and presented, as usual through an intermediary, to the empress. But then it fell into limbo. The artist perhaps did not realize that, while Catherine II needed the heir for the security of her own reign, she also feared he might launch an initiative against her. Four years later the painting had not been returned, a promised medallion had not reached Berlin, and the impoverished Therbusch was dead—some said of starvation.[52]

Occasionally, chambermaids, cordwainers, and cooks far away from St. Petersburg might glimpse price increases that Catherine's purchases induced for other art buyers and how the new prices magnified attention to the artists, provided them with funding for other projects, and awakening hopes or disappointments in their competitors.[53] Johann Heinrich Wilhelm Tischbein, working in Italy, wrote excitedly to a correspondent in Germany, about the picture he was painting for the empress—he planned to include the famous countenance of Emma Hamilton in it several times.[54] He emphasized the generosity of Catherine's agent, who "was ordered to buy up everything that I had available; for a head, just a sketch of a portrait of Paris, she paid 1000 rubles."[55] Through such accounts, Catherine kept the dreams of contemporary artists alive.

Her most famous commission, however, was the production of a large public sculpture, not of herself but of Peter the Great, the much earlier predecessor of her husband. The monument boosted celebrity discourse around her with comments on its design, its allegorical meaning, the technology of its casting, its sculptor, Étienne Maurice Falconet (1716–91), and the woman, Marie-Anne Collot, who was his unexpected assistant. Even the statue's extraordinary stone base received extensive comment. The huge rock, found in a swampy area many miles from St. Petersburg, was conveyed at enormous cost—one writer called it "a great deal of squandered money"[56]—to the Neva, then shifted onto a barge and "towed by boats to the city," a process that the brilliant engineer, Marin Carburi, recorded in an expensively illustrated book, including a tiny image of Catherine amid an assortment of other tiny figures watching the rock underway.[57] The huge glacial erratic itself became part of her celebrity. Travelers went to observe masons shaping it as it was moving, while creative entrepreneurs swept up the chips to make jewelry. Bernoulli, the mathematician visiting from Berlin, picnicked in a village on the road to a workshop that produced rings, necklaces, earrings, and buttons from the fragments. Another traveler promised to bring fragments home, providing a new way for distant admiring observers to link their social identities with the ruler of Russia,[58] and soon a medal depicting the sculpture on its base was available in cheap and conveniently portable casts in wax, plaster, or papier-mâché, all signaling the celebrity-infused desire of buyers to link themselves to Catherine's bold project.[59]

Media workers far from St. Petersburg also saw the profitability of words and pictures of the ostentatious, hypermasculine statue that connected Catherine with her awe-inspiring predecessor, whose grandson she had married and then deposed.[60] While Russian engravers showed the monument's bilingual inscription in Cyrillic letters, print makers elsewhere showed the Latin letters used on the stone's other side, its savvy means of addressing audiences in both east and west: "Peter I [from] Catherine II." The two names, displayed in exactly equal size and style, seemed to erase all the rulers between them, establishing a simple sequence of first and self-legitimating second, dramatically publicizing Catherine II's claim to be Peter's successor, completing what he had started (Figures 0.3 and 7.2). Only in these words does the audacious commissioner of the statue, the powerful but out-of-place woman, the shocking usurper of masculine prerogatives, become visible. Art thus became another way of dealing with gender. One writer took the lesson: "I consider Russia as an immense landscape, in the fore-ground of which appear the statue of Peter the Great, and the living figure of Catherine II."[61]

That living figure also dazzled her distant audience with her displays of patronage to writers, poets, and other (ostensibly) deserving individuals who were their countrymen.

Figure 7.2 Catherine II used commemorative medals as a form of publicity within and beyond her domains, in this case, celebrating her famous statue of Peter I. Copied abroad as engravings, the medals became believable and relatively inexpensive depictions of her and thus sources of new picture types as well. Source: F.C. Krüger, [Catharina II medal.] Berlin. Public Domain. https://picryl.com/media/katharina-ii-kaiserin-von-russland-df99f4?zoom=true

Discussing her courtly *bienfaisance*, a commentator asserted, "it is not enough to give and to give much; the art consists in choosing when, whom, and how one gives," and by such measures, he continued, Catherine "will probably never be topped!"[62] The Swiss bookseller, idyll writer, and painter Solomon Gessner was a typical case; a package unexpectedly arrived for him containing a gold medal and a letter from the empress.[63]

Of course, like much of celebrity discourse, the glitter screened out a different reality. Hidden behind newspaper reports of Catherine II's "liberality and respect for men of talents" was the reality that in many cases valuable gifts constituted remuneration for services rendered or compensation for costs that hopeful individuals had incurred. When she "settled a handsome pension" upon the impoverished widow of a historian who had spent his life working for Russia, for example, it was not the "striking proof" of her generosity that the *Public Advertiser* claimed[64] but rather a form of posthumous salary rectification.

The notion of generosity, however, nourished the dreams of fans, who might not recognize that such "liberality" was a way of keeping payment arbitrary and encouraging flattering attention to the powerful people who gave the supposed presents. When aristocrats and royals interacted with artists and writers, it was a vertical patron-client relationship that depended on a poorly defined exchange with no clear obligation for remuneration, as the painter Therbusch's experience showed. From the point of view of a patron, the conferring of favors has the greatest effect on the recipient when the largesse is unpredictable. A scattering of unexpected gifts, made public, could and, in Catherine II's case, did have widespread influence.[65] Her conduct of artistic and literary patronage fit exactly this pattern, eliciting many hopes, much submissive and fawning behavior, and often ending in disappointment, usually swallowed in silence.

Canny contemporaries plotted ways to become recipients. Friedrich Benda, a musician at the Prussian court, induced the gift of another large gold medal by sending his compositions to Catherine.[66] Just enough artists and scholars benefited from these gifts to give many others hope. For women writers and artists in particular, dreams of gaining Catherine's attention probably helped induce their efforts at gender solidarity with her. A Dutch poet and playwright, Juliana Cornelia de Lannoy sent a cloying epistolary ode and received an imperial acknowledgment in return. (She then used that as an excuse to publish the poem for all to read.)[67] The best-known German woman writer of the time, the successful novelist Sophie von La Roche, seeking a bigger prize, approached the empress indirectly, through another woman, the German aristocrat Juliane Franziska von Buchwald.[68] With her help, Catherine was persuaded to subscribe for 500 copies of her new monthly for girls and then included in one issue an uncharacteristically brief and reticent reference to Catherine II, commending her for making German women proud of themselves, knowing that "the great, wise monarch of Russia is a German princess."[69] Two years later, having terminated *Pomona*'s publication because of both financial difficulties and the workload all the writing imposed, La Roche hoped to pay the journal's debts by dedicating to Catherine a republication of the didactic, advice-filled letters to a fictionalized girl, Lina, that had been a regular feature. Such a dedication, as a public demonstration of respect, was yet another means by which authors attempted to impose an obligation for compensation on the renowned empress. But so many German writers had tried to reverse the patron-client relationship by making unwanted dedications that in the summer of 1785 a Russian Ukase appeared in the newspapers forbidding all further dedications to Catherine from Germany. Eventually, after activating intermediaries once more, La Roche dedicated the first and second editions of the Lina letters to the empress and was presumably rewarded, though not in public.[70]

Celebrity discourse usually covered only the winners in this game, but there were losers too. One was the obscure Karl Ernst Christian Müller, who made a prodigious effort to fill more than 200 printed pages with ornate inanities such as: "Catherine's scepter is soft and mild; it is nourishing, fruitful, heavenly dew that causes the flowers and fruits of human industry and human happiness to sprout forth"; the imperial recipient (privately and correctly) pronounced it boring and left it unrecompensed.[71] A British cartoon of 1783 entitled "The Italian Poet" showed a downcast, stooped man apparently struggling to survive; he has a paper or letter in his pocket inscribed "Empress of Russia." Evidently, no help had arrived for him.[72]

The most famous and most remunerated writer-recipient of Catherine's imperial largesse and the biggest flatterer was Voltaire (1694–1778). In the pointed words of the *London Chronicle*, the once renowned and incisive satirist now, in his old age, celebrated princes who "pay him for his adulation."[73] For the first months of Catherine's reign, he had waited to see if she would survive longer than Peter III, but soon they began fishing for connections to each other, and their correspondence began.[74] In 1765 when he dedicated his *Philosophy of History* to the "Empress of all the Russias and protectress of the arts and sciences," he implicitly wanted something in return, starting with a relationship with the richest woman in the world. He got it.

In two phases, readers outside Russia learned about the epistolary bond of the empress and the wit, first, when letter extracts found their way into print, and, second, in 1784, six years after Voltaire's death, when the whole exchange was published, revealing the symbiotic and carefully gendered relationship between a major ruler and a famed intellectual. In a performance of masculinity modulated by age, Voltaire presented himself as an articulate, old, and physically impotent man, platonically seduced by a desirable great empress. As part of his performance, he engaged in ceaseless flattery with frequent profit-seeking digressions. Catherine presented herself as lighthearted, in control, successful, and confidently at ease ruling a huge, multicultural empire. But the reading public could easily discern that the clever French Enlightenment writer had become the Russian tsarina's informal publicist,[75] and that she compensated him generously.

By buying his library after his death, she also made famously generous arrangements for his niece and heir, Madame Marie Louise Mignot Denis. The *Journal historique et politique*, for example, reprinted Catherine's letter to Madame Denis about the sale and itemized the "feeble testimonies" to her good intentions, as the empress called them, including "a golden box, decorated with a portrait of her imperial majesty, some very expensive furs, and fifteen thousand *ecus*."[76] But Catherine's gifts to writers sometimes produced bad publicity too, as when a French recipient, Constantin François de Volney, returning his gold medal to the empress in 1791, asserted her "pecuniary assistance" to the monarchist opponents of France's radical new government meant her present to him no longer seemed "a noble instance of what power ought to be."[77]

The vision of Catherine II's wealth and glamour, mediated through pictures and text to onlookers far from St. Petersburg, brightened and dimmed along with the changing reception of royal *gloire* that it signified, and debates about her extravagance could fulfill one of the functions of celebrity, enriching discussion among ordinary readers and auditors about a social issue. Yet while luxury and profligacy, central to dominant notions of courtliness, became increasingly irreconcilable with the growing force of bourgeois notions of thrift and economic prudence, it is unclear that the critique ever dimmed the glamour of the celebrity tsarina.

8

Disconcerting Mother of Her Country

Gender and Power Again

Despite Maria Theresa's decades reigning in the Habsburg territories before Catherine II came to the Russian throne, the notion of a woman ruling over a vast empire was still gender-jarring and outrageous. Before the coup, Catherine had seemed in representations published abroad to be an ordinary, and thus successfully unremarkable, crown prince's wife. When she overthrew her husband, however, the ordinariness abruptly and shockingly ended. When Peter III died, no representations—aside from a few lines in the newspapers about her supposedly excessive grief—showed her in the role of widow; no images depicted her in mourning for him.[1] The jolting clash between prevailing gender expectations for women and Catherine's immense power and authority as the Russian monarch became a key theme of her celebrity, as writers and artists struggled to locate the empress on the map of gender, with its many variations based on culture and class. One author, striving to fit Catherine II into expected models, advised readers to imagine her in gendered terms as a "mother of the family" but with greater responsibilities,[2] and another proposed she could be considered a model *Hausfrau* for women of every rank.[3] But many reports of Catherine as empress seemed to show her both avoiding women's traditional roles and doing what men, and specifically men rulers, were expected to do, such as making war.

Because two key gendered expectations, motherhood and remarriage, could jeopardize her power, they were problematic to Catherine II. On the other hand, conventional language of men rulers as paternal was readily adapted for women rulers as metaphorically maternal; readers in distant countries could see Catherine herself using this language in one manifesto after another. Yet being an actual mother—and unlike being a father—especially of a male heir, was supposed to relegate a woman to the diminished status of regent, a temporary placeholder from which her son would dislodge her as soon as he came of age. In a world in which men had automatic legitimacy as rulers, Catherine II's status as mother, specifically as foreign-born mother of a son, entailed special hazards to her power. For her Habsburg contemporary, the risks and rewards were quite different. Maria Theresa, repeatedly portrayed surrounded by her children or accompanied by her eldest son, emphasized her role as mother and thus reassuringly confirmed her status as transitional between her father and her son; this bridging operation, after all, matched her goal of preserving the multiple elements of her dynasty's power.⁴ Catherine II had no such stake in a transitional status and would have been weakened by it; none of the many portraits that she sent abroad to foreign courts showed her with Paul.⁵ Soon, the notion that Catherine II would be a mere regent disappeared. Decades later, writing and publishing little books for her first two grandsons—though nothing for her granddaughters—Catherine became a public grandmother.⁶ Yet to the end of her reign and afterward, perceptive distant fans could see that actual, rather than metaphorical, motherhood remained problematic for her legitimacy on the throne.

Official accounts always claimed Catherine's love for Paul, but speculation in parlors and coffee houses about their relationship must have been varied. A particularly negative construction that appeared in 1802 in a *roman à clef* may have been long in circulation. The novel *Staub der Erste*, "Dust the First," by Johann Friedrich Ernst Albrecht, attributed a completely instrumental view of motherhood to Catherine, called Miranda in this and Albrecht's several other novels about her and her court.⁷ In her years as grand duchess, the novelist asserts, Miranda secured her status as wife of the crown prince by nefariously passing off "the very ordinary product of a different marriage" as her son, Staub/Paul.⁸ Once she seized the throne, she deliberately neglected the child and allowed others to spoil him badly so that potential opposition leaders would not be tempted to replace her with the willful young man.⁹ Albrecht's representation showed motherhood as having no allure to Catherine and her heir's very existence as a threat to her power.

Elsewhere, remarriage was also portrayed as unappealing to her and for the same reason of disempowerment.¹⁰ For a male monarch, remarriage after the death of a spouse would have been a routine step, but the "rumour of a marriage being intended between Major Orlov, of the life-guards, and a person of the highest rank in the empire" had occasioned "several tumults and commotions" in St. Petersburg in 1764, according to the *London Magazine*. The magazine added that the gossip "was grounded upon some odd appearances," but provided no details, merely adding that this rumor had now been replaced by—unspecified—others.¹¹ Much later, a junior French official in St. Petersburg, Marie Daniel Bourrée de Corberon, wrote home to his brother in France about the story. To consolidate her rule after the coup, Corberon explained, her advisers allegedly argued she needed a husband, implicitly a Russian husband, and when Orlov received the title of prince, he thought himself about to wed her. With that status, the Frenchman burbled, Orlov would "rule the Empire, and though the first subject, he would have had the power." Marriage, after all, is one of society's chief mechanisms for gendering the distribution of authority. Small wonder that on the day intended for the marriage, "the Empress withdrew her hand," an act of self-interest that the young French observer could fathom only as womanly weakness: "She waivers, she hesitates, in a word: she is a woman."¹² Corberon missed the point of his own observation about Orlov's expectations: marriage would have sucked power and authority from the wife. The witty Lord Chesterfield in England had mentioned this problem in a comment about the other obvious candidate for Catherine's hand, the long-imprisoned, twenty-one-year-old Ivan VI, the Romanov great-nephew of Peter I who, as an infant, had briefly been tsar before another Romanov, his aunt Elizabeth, deposed him. Chesterfield quipped of Catherine and Ivan that she "would murder or marry him, or probably both,"[13] and indeed, in 1764, two years into Catherine's reign, Ivan was slain during a plot allegedly to liberate him.

With public remarriage problematic for the retention of her command, as distant observers could see, Catherine's marital options were either, like Elizabeth I of England, not to marry at all, or, like Elizabeth of Russia, to risk marrying secretly (thus reducing the sharing of power that a public husband could have demanded); a biography of Potemkin soon after his death and during her life mentioned rumors of just such a secret marriage to him[14] (as many scholars now also suspect).[15] To the distant public, mighty Catherine's apparently complicated, gender-bending choices could add intriguing twists to familiar matters of childbirth, marriage, and remarriage, topics that still today, as any supermarket checkout rack confirms, invite rumors and conjectures and fuel the fires of celebrity discourse.

Little of the controversies about gender and rule are evident in the portrait prints that Catherine II's distant fans might acquire over the course of her reign, although exactly this clash would become a vivid motif in the caricatures of her in her last decade and would be hinted at in broadsheets earlier. Portraitists, however, minimized the complexities of Catherine II's gender status, mainly by using the same visual vocabulary of state authority for her as for male rulers, casting her as admirable and worthy of fan enthrallment. Two prints by Johann Friedrich Bause (1738–1814) make the point, one of Peter III when he ascended the throne and the other, made a few months later, of Catherine II (Figures 8.1 and 8.2). Both appear in the same simple oval frames within darker rectangles and resting on plinths that seem to give the pictures the air of timeless, three-dimensional solidity. Both figures are angled a quarter away from the plane of the picture but with their pleasant faces turned toward the viewer. Illuminated against unadorned backgrounds, both are expensively dressed and wear ermine-lined cloaks and shoulder sashes signifying their high rank. Gender is indicated by the rest of their garb, their hairstyles, and, more subtly, by their gaze. Peter, looking beyond the viewer, is made flatteringly masculine-aloof, while Catherine's gaze toward the beholder, as in many positive full-face images of her, appears feminine-accessible. Peter is also closer to the plane of the picture, making his face larger in the frame; Catherine is further away, a bit lost. Subtler still is a slight difference in pose between the two. Bause, like a number of print makers far from Russia, drew on a much earlier portrait, by Pietro Rotari, of Catherine as grand duchess. The other print makers, however, also revising Rotari to show Catherine as empress, straightened her posture (Figures 3.1 and 3.2), while Bause retained the flirtatious tilt of her head that weakened her authority yet strengthened the message of femininity. Within the clear conventions of the state portrait genre, even in two such apparently parallel images as Bause's of Peter and Catherine, gender could matter in multiple, often understated, ways that might appeal to fans and potential fans.

Russia's "Petticoat Government"

When Catherine's incongruous status as a powerful woman was addressed in words, it was sometimes contextualized as part of Russia's curious acceptance of "petticoat

Figure 8.1 and 8.2 Printmakers such as Johann Friedrich Bause used standard monarchical portraiture to depict both Peter III and Catherine II, but with subtle gendered differences beyond dress and hairstyle. Source: Johann Friedrich Bause, *Petrus III. Russorum Imperator*. AKG images. Identifier: AKG89263. Berlin Sammlung Archiv für Kunst und Geschichte.

government."¹⁶ Baffled distant observers, noting that four women had already occupied the throne there during the eighteenth century, regretfully concluded women were apparently the right rulers for this peculiar empire, though the inexplicable practice, they hastened to add, had no validity elsewhere.¹⁷ A Swiss writer, for example, with years of experience in Russia, Charles François Philibert Masson (1761–1807), charged that the tsarinas' reigns were "prolific in wars, revolutions, crimes, disorders, and calamities of every kind." In a footnote, he fumed further: "An army of five hundred thousand men was at the disposal of Catharine, yet she would not entrust another woman with a single company! She directed the politics of Europe, and gave it peace or war though a woman could not enjoy the most trifling office in it! Is there not great inconsistency in this conduct?"¹⁸

Of course, it was precisely a ruler's ability to make war that collided most completely with expectations of femininity. For Catherine's partisans, when the goals or outcomes of her military interventions met their approval, that was justification enough for the mighty empress. Applauding her steps to "liberate" Greece from Ottoman rule, one magazine published a heroic poem in which Greeks were aided by a light-bringing figure who blended Catherine II with Athena.¹⁹ The poem provided a fantasy, well removed from political realities, of an all-gracious, emancipatory empress. Equally fanciful was the dedication of *Lasting Peace to Europe. The Dream of an Cosmopolite* that used the trope of women as bringers of peace. Motivated by the tsarina's role in bringing an end to the Bavarian War of Succession in 1779, the writer averred, "You, Madam, who, while all Europe seem to combine together to shed human blood, you are the only one who has courage and magnanimity enough to stretch out the healing hand of Humanity, and offer the mediation of Peace." The text also claimed, with equally unfounded certainty, that Catherine "would be the first to abdicate, in favour of the people," if she thought other princes would follow.²⁰ At the very start of Catherine's reign, she had indeed seemed peaceable, winning esteem for her decision not to reenter the Seven Years' War.

Not peace-making, however, but war-making underwrote the widespread assumption that the position of monarch was quintessentially masculine; either a woman ruler, who had the authority and capacity to make war, was merely a front, or the woman ruler was not, or not completely, a woman. Louise de Kéralio, writing early in the French Revolution, stated this starkly. Denouncing French queens in a book entitled *Les Crimes des Reines de France* (The Crimes of the Queens of France) (1791), Kéralio wrote: "A woman for whom all is possible is capable of anything; when a woman becomes queen, she changes her sex."²¹ Read pragmatically, a woman ruler needed an abundance of masculine qualities, and one eighteenth-century way to endow women with such qualities drew on physiognomy, the notion that a person's traits and abilities were discernible in the face and head (Figure 8.3). Johann Kaspar Lavater, the foremost advocate of this aspiring science, confidently muddled through the exact elements of Catherine's face that were manly: "Except the smallness of the nostril, and the distance of the eyebrow from the outline of the forehead, no one can mistake the princely, the superior, the masculine firmness of this, nevertheless feminine, but fortunate and kind countenance."²² The logic was circular: if Catherine II was successful in the male role of tsar, she must have visible manly qualities, and if she had visible manly qualities, she

Figure 8.3 Lavater, in his *Physiognomy*, illustrated his claims about Catherine II's "manly spirit" with a profile portrait that gave her a close physical resemblance to both Frederick II of Prussia and, below him, Voltaire. Source: *Empss of Russia*, in English translation and abridgement of Lavater's *Essays on Physiognomy* (1806). Public Domain. Courtesy of Hamilton Library, University of Hawai'i, photo by author.

would be successful as tsar; yet her femininity could be conveniently asserted too. All of this could readily stir celebrity discourse.

Debut in Satires, Both Textual and Visual: Poland 1772–3

The makers of visual satires in the European countries west of Russia found more vivid ways than portraitists to depict the powerful empress, and yet the contribution of political cartoons, as they are often called now, to Catherine's celebrity is complex. The artists' motivation was almost always to censure, not approve or defend. Institutional power and authority and especially war were topics not inherently conducive to celebrity, and, when the aggression or conflict being satirized harmed or threatened to harm the countries where her audience lived, a severance from celebrity seemed even more likely. Yet that was not exactly what happened. The satires often reduced the conflict to something amusing rather than threatening; the representations of Catherine were often both energetic and clever and thus appealing; and she was almost never the sole rogue in the picture, but just one of a cluster of figures being lampooned.

Her debut in pictorial lampoons happened tentatively in 1772 and then unmistakably in 1773. The launch occurred in two large prints that were included, in folded form, in a French satirical pamphlet, *Congres Politique*, in which European monarchs discuss giving balls, by which they mean wars. The first print shows the assembled potentates sitting against three walls of a large, elegant room facing the improbable conveners of the group, the Ottoman sultan and the pope; across the room sit Catherine and Maria Theresa, furthest away, quite small, and lacking any satirical distortion. The second print, ridiculing the hypocrisy of church and state, depicted no identifiable specific culprits. The pamphlet and its prints seem to have appeared and disappeared almost without a ripple.[23]

The next year a political cartoon appeared in response to Russia joining Austria and Prussia in the land grab that became known as the first Partition of Poland. In one of her vividly written formal manifestos, widely distributed abroad, Catherine loftily asserted that she was seizing a slice of her neighbor's land in order to protect Polish non-Catholics, "dissidents," who had been increasingly deprived of their rights until the only liberty they still shared with the Catholic majority, she claimed, was the freedom to breathe the same air. Many observers in continental Europe, including leading members of the Enlightenment, approved the partition,[24] but to others the pious cant about religious tolerance masked blatant aggression. Soon media workers in France, England, Holland, and Germany were converting Poland's disaster into the diverting words and images that would provide a new element in the growth and maintenance of Catherine's celebrity among distant merchants, journeymen, market women, kitchen maids, and more.[25]

The best-known result, a mildly critical bilingual political cartoon, entitled "Le Gateau des Rois" in French, and "The Troelfth Cake," in garbled English, showed a seemingly sociable gathering at which the chief participants met around not a cake, as the title said, but a large map of their intended domains (Figure 8.4). In the picture, Frederick II of Prussia and Joseph II of Austria confront each other a little too closely and not entirely peaceably, with the Prussian king pointing aggressively at the map with his drawn sword and aiming at his most contentious claim, Danzig. Catherine faces her old lover Stanislaw August Poniatowski, the Polish king, who clings awkwardly to the slipping crown that he owed to one of her earliest blatant shows of force. Perhaps because Jean-Michel Moreau, the Paris artist on whose drawing the engraving was based, was in the employ of the French government, he apparently knew of Catherine's old love affair with Poniatowski; the drawing as engraved by Nicolas Noël Lemire shows the Polish king's undone hair flowing loosely down his back, thus transferring a conventional sign for the sexually undone woman to the sexually and politically undone man.[26]

Just as portraits of the empress were refashioned and tweaked to fit changing purposes, visual satires of her showed their popular appeal by being repeatedly copied and modified for new audiences and different settings. A prolific German printmaker, Johannes Esaias Nilson reused Moreau's image but bowed to Prussia's involvement in the partition and omitted the visual critique, showing a properly bewigged Stanislaw August posing proudly and pointing heavenward, as though the excision of large segments of his

Figure 8.4 "Le Gateau des Rois/The Troelfth Cake," in its several versions, showed a mocking representation of Catherine II and the kings of Austria and Prussia planning to seize territory from Poland, to the shock of the Polish king, who grabs for his slipping crown as Catherine looks on. Source: Lemire, Noël. *The troelfth cake. Le Gâteau des Rois*. London: Printed for Rob. Sayer, 1773 Public Domain. Wikimedia Commons: https://upload.wikimedia.org/wikipedia/commons/f/f0/Allegory_of_the_1st_partition_of_Poland.jpg

territory were the will of God rather than an assault on his country and throne; Joseph and Frederick look at each other calmly. By revising the Polish king's figure and sheathing Frederick the Great's sword, Johannes Nilson transformed Lemire's satire of the Polish Partition into a celebration, avoiding a critique of the three partitioning powers.

While serious, reasoned analysis of statecraft and of state relations lacks the individual and intimate components necessary for celebrity discourse, satire in the form of a print or a private conversation among insatiable monarchs could completely change the equation, adding the personalizing components that graft celebrity discourse onto power politics. The mocking pamphlet *The Polish Partition, Illustrated in Seven Dramatic Dialogues*, published in multiple editions between 1773 and 1775, excerpted in newspapers,[27] and translated into at least six other European languages, became probably the most widely read political satirical text in all of eighteenth-century Europe. Given that the pamphlet's denunciation of the partition was not the dominant response at the time, one of the reasons for its popularity was surely that it depicted three of the eighteenth century's monarchical celebrities in unrestrained confrontation with each other: Frederick the Great, Maria Theresa of Austria (not her rather colorless son and co-regent, Joseph II, shown in most visual representations of the event), and Catherine II, the most attention-grabbing of the trio.

Supposedly by Gotlieb Pansmouzer, a mocking pseudonym redolent of a stereotypical German pedant,[28] the dialogues argue that the high values invoked by the partitioning powers were a cynical screen for the rapacious desires of the "Empress of R-ss-a," the Prussian king, and Maria Theresa. The three struggle to compose a manifesto that, in Frederick II's words, will perform "that political chemistry that can melt down contradictions" and provide "that optical magic, that can make illusion pass for reality and put upon truth a garment of many changing colours" (2). The text avoids shrillness by placing its condemnation of the attack on Poland in the mouths of the perpetrators and by using both irony and ridiculously elaborate language to demonstrate the cupidity of the partition and the fraudulence of the rulers' justifications. Although the Russian empress briefly makes the feminized accusation that Frederick had misled her into the deed and taken advantage of her, she nonetheless feels "something between . . . repentant vexation and the agitation of ambition, that has just conquered remorse, but has been ruffled in the combat" (17). Hoping to avoid a reputation as one of "the plagues and scourges of mankind," Catherine worries that she and Maria Theresa both "look like fools in the eyes of Europe,—as dupes led by the nose," and she continues: "we can scarcely get rid of the imputation of imbecility without incurring one of a heavier kind: we cannot, in a word, cease to be *ridiculous* without becoming *odious*. Fy—fy" (18—italics in the original). When the other woman notes that Catherine is blushing over this thought, the Russian empress explains, "I blush but at few things. I have got far enough in philosophy to have triumphed over *remorse*—but I have a passion for *glory*—and glory is not attainable without some *appearance of virtue*" (18–19).[29] Pansmouzer's Catherine II is a model of hypocrisy, displaying qualities that distant readers and listeners could relish denouncing or defending around the workbench or over sewing baskets.

Touches of sexual innuendo add to the satire. The dialogues include, for example, a glancing reference to Frederick's lack of desire for women, whereupon the two women rulers "look at each other with much expression, and take out their snuff-boxes to conceal their embarrassment" (49–50). They also react uselessly to the news of widespread rape in Frederick's new territories, supposedly to increase the population: "the two Empresses squinted at each other, and called up a frown, for which the muscles of the two countenances were so little prepared that it might have almost passed for a smile" (56). But the pamphlet's most damning claims were not about such abuse but about the three monarchs as duplicitous, manipulative, dishonest, and greedy.

Catherine is depicted as mindful of the contradiction between her public appearance and her action: "From a declared protectress of the Republick of Poland," as she puts it, to "one of the avowed vultures, that are preying upon its vitals." The situation "looks ill," but the supposedly enlightened ruler counts on philosophy to help her overcome her qualms, and she is eager for Diderot to arrive and teach her "more of this elegant subject." Her recurring instants of doubt in the *Dialogues*—such as her claim that "at certain times, my heart rises against our proceedings and there are moments in which I am tempted to fall back into the belief of such a thing as conscience" (57–8)—helped readers see how repugnant the thoughts and deeds of the monarchs were, even as the emphasis on Catherine's attention to her public image could alert distant observers to the many ways their view of the empress might be influenced.

The desire to please that is attributed to Catherine II here (and by other writers elsewhere) feminized her and possibly enabled her audience to better rhyme her power with her gender. She wants, she says, "to be loved by the publick, to be *esteemed* and respected as well as dreaded" and so is anxious about the partition's impact on her reputation: "I had made some progress in fame—I was looked upon as a declared patroness of the arts and sciences—I had acquired by my plan of legislation, a reputation of equity and wisdom, that effaced many little transgressions and covered *some great ones*—I set out, even in these affairs of Poland, upon honest principles" (66). Frederick, in contrast, is willing to be hated, provided he is also feared (61). When Frederick belittles her hesitations, her incensed retort, reinforced by the included stage directions, begins as an echo: "*Female inconstancy and weakness* forsooth—[*She bites her lips*] these terms are insolent and your conduct begins to be overbearing." After a moment of considering herself as Frederick's victim, she fights back: "the more I yield the more you grow overbearing—But I would have you to know, that the tone of authority and contempt you assume at present is not made for my spirit—I will not bear it" (69). In a harsh aside about his manipulation of the two empresses, the king of Pr—ss-a hisses: "The poor woman! How little does she perceive, that she and her sister of Hungary are, at this very moment, the laughter of Europe." Catherine meanwhile plunges ahead with her tantrum by invoking the theme of forcing people to be happy: "Besides my design is to render the Lithuanians happy and free, for I will,—yes I will,—I will—I will have the reputation of clemency" (71).

The great success of the cleverly written dialogues certainly derived at least in part from its effectiveness in delivering an imagined behind-the-scenes account of the famous monarchs and in giving readers and auditors the feeling of personal insight that celebrity discourse claimed to provide. It probably also helped that, by not rendering the two women rulers as totally vicious, the pamphlet allowed admiring readers to retain some of their esteem for them. Clever as the pamphlet was, public response in the West to the Polish Partition remained mixed, more a product of the larger political system than a reaction to the misfortune of the Poles.

"Astonisher of All Regions," from Constantinople to Amsterdam and Antwerp

Whenever displays of power and acts of war were discussed and illustrated in terms that seemed to offer celebrity's magic of glimpsing the "real" character of a famous person, responses could range from abhorrence to identification. Early in her reign, Catherine's power plays could become part of the transgressiveness that is inherent in celebrity, endowing stars with the "autonomous subjectivity" that fans relish, or loading them with the guilt that anti-fans may insist they have amassed.[30] Since the transgressions of women celebrities are often construed as breaches of gender, Catherine's activities could be construed to enthrall audiences with the promise of scandal.

Catherine's war against the Ottoman Empire from 1768 until 1774 generally aroused the enthusiastic approval of faraway intellectuals. Voltaire expressed astonishing blood thirst toward the Turks, enthusiastically envisioning Catherine's Christian Russia ridding Europe of these barbaric, oriental, Muslim invaders.[31] A German poet in 1773 addressed Catherine as "Empress! Astonisher of all regions! / You, for whom Mars & Minerva are / preparing immortality."[32] She was long construed as a Turk-fighting heroine immune from moral considerations about killing. Recalling a Russian naval victory that produced "joy in the whole educated world," Goethe noted that people reacted "as though no human beings were being sacrificed when non-Christians fell

Figure 8.5 *Vorstellung und Abbildung* (Presentation and Illustration) is a woodcut broadsheet printed in Copenhagen by Johan Rudolph Thiele and partly painted. Its German text—it was published again years later with a Danish text—questions the value of war but nonetheless admires Catherine's fight against the sultan, "enemy of Christians." Source: *Vorstellung und Abbildung von Catharina Alexiewna, Keiserin von Rusland, und Achmet der Vierte, türkische Keiser oder Großsultan, als vorhin in viele Jahren krigführende Potentaten* (Copenhagen: Thiele). Public Domain. Shelf mark Billedsamlingen. Kistebilleder. Cl. 208. Box. Courtesy of the Danish Royal Library.

by the thousands."[33] The single satirical image that addressed this point was "Merlin: or, A Picture of Europe for 1773," published in the *Westminster Magazine* in December 1773.[34] On the right edge of the picture stands Catherine, wearing her fur-trimmed gown, waiting in a long line of other rulers to consult the wizard, and blandly holding the severed head of a Turk in one hand. Of all the figures standing with her, only the Ottoman sultan reacts.

A different print, a colored broadsheet published in Copenhagen with a German-language text, showed Catherine, crowned, holding her scepter upright, and the turbaned sultan holding a flag in one hand and stabbing a small crucifix with the other (Figure 8.5).[35] The nine stanzas beneath the picture suggest Catherine's defense of Poland's religious dissidents had been a pretext meant to induce the sultan's declaration of war. It worked, but none of the conflict was depicted in the woodcut image, an omission that made the print match easily with the discourse of celebrity.

Meanwhile other wars and disputes were erupting. From 1780 to 1789, the Low Countries, made up of a republic in the north and a group of provinces still under Habsburg rule in the south, engaged in a variety of disputes, for which they sought Russian aide. In at least ten of the cartoons about their struggles, written in Dutch and Flemish (though at least once also with a French version), Catherine appeared in the form of a slender and well-dressed, crowned figure.[36] But the lack of the "iconoclastic bravura and anti-authoritarian energies" of caricature[37] meant that most such broadsheets—depicting card games, cheese cutting, and the like—invited at most a smile, not laughter, and would have contributed to Catherine II's celebrity only locally.

Outbreak of the Second Russo-Turkish War: More Political Cartoons

In 1787, Catherine II went to war once again with the Sublime Porte. By then, her armies having repeatedly proved themselves, many outside observers believed the infidel Turks were a useful check on the aggressive Russians, and more makers of political images showed her with her Muslim adversary. A Danish printer, who had acquired the carved woodblock showing side-by-side images of Catherine and the sultan, put it in his press again, this time with verses in Danish (Figure 8.5).[38] At about the same time, German printmakers cautiously experimented with satire, a skill they seemed to drop after the early years of Maria Theresa's reign. In one picture that added Joseph II to the other two rulers, the empress's scepter aims at the sultan's sword, specifically its phallic knobbed handle (Figure 8.6).[39] The three rulers, posed as in many eighteenth-century paintings of individual monarchs, stand upright, one hand tucked into the waist or holding the hilt of a sword (or in Joseph's case, touching a map), the elbow jutting obtrusively, in fact often aimed at the viewer, to demonstrate bold and masculine impunity. Women rulers did not swagger across the canvases of their official portraits sticking an elbow out, but in this unofficial portrait, with German and French captions in verse below the three figures, Catherine II signals her power by cocking her arm like the others. A different printmaker devised a fully satirical image by adding action to a scene about Catherine II compelling Joseph II's assistance. The tsarina, recognizable in her fur-trimmed dress, manfully pushes the emperor in a wheelbarrow. As the sultan and the king of Prussia (by then it was Frederick William II) ask where she is taking her passenger, she replies, "Into the mud."[40] Femininity transgressed is a routine trope for satirizing an empress.

Cross-dressing particularly signaled such transgression, which made it a valuable motif for satire. In yet another German print, an elegant woman, identified as Catherine by the sash of office across her chest, sits before a desk (Figure 8.7).[41] On the walls around her are four paintings. She ignores the framed canvas labeled Bannat (Banat) that shows no fighting and perhaps refers to the Turkish re-occupation of that region belonging to her Habsburg ally in 1789. She also disregards portraits of two apparently murdered men, their heads drooping to the side and their eyes closed, probably Peter III and Ivan VI; their mustaches meant they were not from the west of Europe. Since hard-to-trace rumors of Catherine as murderous had continued to circulate—a usually well-informed, middle-class German woman, companion to a countess, wrote, for example, in 1785 that "the rumor she killed her lover, a general, ... with her own hand using a dagger in her room has been confirmed"[42]—it is possible

Figure 8.6 In belligerent German verses below their images, Catherine II and Joseph II speak with each other about their eagerness to attack the sultan, who stands apart, proclaiming his own military might and asserting in his verses that Mohamed is on his side. The untitled print is another product of Johann Martin Will's prolific workshop in Augsburg. Source: Will, Johann Martin, *Wenn Achmet noch so stolz auch wäre* (Augsburg: Nürnberg). Public Domain. Inventar-Nr. HB 8178, Kapsel-Nr. 1314a. Courtesy of Graphische Sammlung, Germanisches Nationalmuseum, Nürnberg.

Figure 8.7 In *Kriegs Theater*, the possible meanings of "theater of war" suggest more than merely an elegantly dressed woman in a fine private room. Two paintings on the wall depict the current theater of war in 1789, and elements in the room that represent fighting may be props that the woman used for her (inappropriate) role in the theater of pretense that is the court or the media. Source: Boluzion, *Kriegs Theater*. Public Domain. Courtesy of Biblioteca Panizzi in Reggio Emilia (Italy), "A. Davoli" Collection.

that one of the portraits refers to this piece of horrific gossip, itself a strong signal of the incompatibility of women and power. What the woman in *Kriegs Theater* (Theater of war) points at is a painting of the massive, blood-soaked battle at Ochakov, a key event in Russia's ongoing war.

On the sofa where the woman sits is a surprising, discarded pair of men's knee britches. The combination of pants and paintings seems to propose that Catherine is a recently un-cross-dressed Amazon involved in the notorious Ochakov victory. The glaringly un-Germanic names on the print, designer Nic. Menses and engraver Boluzion, taken together, add to the suggestion that the seemingly sedate picture draws on the ancient tradition of the bloody devouring female. Viewers needed little erudition to know that the word Menses could (and did) refer to menstruation or to suspect that Boluzion was a twist on *pollutio* (Latin), pollution (German and English), a persistent take on menstruation.[43] The Catherine of this print is thus suggested to be simultaneously a ladylike figure, a martial cross-dresser, and a source of enigmatic and dangerous bleeding pollution. Yet the broken sword (signifying peace), amid other military paraphernalia, and the location, at her feet, of her plumed hat hint that the bloodshed is over. Strange names, a Russian victory and an Austrian defeat (although this is ambiguous because the Habsburgs retook Banat later); a scene in which a woman appears to have just changed out of the clothes of a man; reminders of two murders—what does all this mean? The political messages of continental prints, produced in areas where artists, printers, and printsellers could be jailed for incautious publications, were sometimes almost indecipherable. Perhaps *Kriegs Theater* was intended to express an uncomfortable, almost unwilling, admiration for the tough and dangerous Russian empress at the expense of the Habsburg Empire's seemingly ineffectual leaders. Catherine, the print suggests, is a bleeding-polluting (thus female) ferocious and murderous creature masquerading as a high-ranking and seemingly proper, elegant woman, who, having abandoned her ruined weapons and reclaimed a long skirt, is possibly even a peacemaker.

Over time, ever more skillful cartoonists, using a newer, brasher style, paid attention to the mighty woman, whose transgressions by 1787 against gender and against the European balance of power were fast accumulating. Soon, German visual satires of Catherine II stopped appearing, overtaken by brilliant English cartoons of the mighty woman. One potent choice for representing the disconcerting anomaly of a woman exercising state violence was to show her as a virago, defined in Samuel

Figure 8.8 The anonymous *Christian Amazon* of 1787 shows the threesome of Joseph, Catherine, and the Ottoman sultan again. Catherine seems here to be a man masquerading as a woman, though the men (except Joseph) and the monkey react to her as a woman. Source: *Christian Amazon*. Public Domain. Courtesy of https://lccn.loc.gov/99404748. Courtesy of the Library of Congress.

Johnson's eighteenth-century *Dictionary of the English Language* as "A female warrior; a woman with the qualities of a man . . . commonly used in detestation for an impudent turbulent woman."[44] Whether the emphasis was on her imputed male qualities or on her female verve and turbulence, the gender of the virago empress was strangely and always captivatingly unsettled, as in the arresting and irreverent "Christian Amazon" (Figure 8.8). Using the well-known classical precedent of a woman warrior, the unknown artist showed Catherine II and the Turkish sultan battling hand-to-hand, while Emperor Joseph II (Maria Theresa had died in 1780) hides behind his wild-haired female ally. Catherine has the strong arm of a man, her chest is ambiguously flat, and her dress is tucked at the waist to reveal the stance and especially the knee pants of a man beneath her skirts. As Marjorie Garber argues, cross-dressing is not a matter of either/or, either masculine or feminine, but rather both at once, in an unstable and unpredictable combination.[45] Here, despite the sword-fighting empress's seeming masculinity, three of the other figures react to her as the female object of their sexual attention. Thus, the sultan's phallic bayonet, complete with balls, aims directly at Catherine's suggestively depicted crotch, the monkey's punning tail points similarly, and an unidentified third figure behind them, a generalized European man, leers at Catherine's exposure through his lorgnette.[46] Looked at in isolation, the portrayal of "Catherine" seems to show a man cross-dressed as a woman, but the reactions of the figure's audience suggest a woman behaving as a man dressed as a woman, the two simultaneous possibilities making her gender undecidable.

The notion of a woman exercising ultimate authority over huge armies, making decisions about war and peace, confronting bellicose neighbors, and doing all of this without a husband was a challenge to eighteenth-century expectations about gender, a challenge that could spark exactly the kind of lively discourse that promotes and maintains celebrity. In the case of Catherine II, that discourse was further enhanced by the distinctive setting of her reign, in an empire that mixed the exotic with the barbaric.

9

Empress of the Other

An elegant, but rather silly, Parisian engraving that paid tribute to Voltaire after his death depicted the Russian empress at full length almost in the center of the picture; she is pushed slightly to the side by D'Alembert representing Europe and yet is more fully shown than he is. Catherine, though she is dressed like an eighteenth-century version of a Greek goddess, represents Asia in the image (Figure 9.1). Her gown is wafted open to the hip on one side, showing a nude leg, matched by both the knee-panted leg of D'Alembert, representing Europe, and the naked leg of Benjamin Franklin, representing America in a bearskin tunic and his signature coonskin hat; meanwhile Afra Behn's fictional Oroonoko, signifying Africa, remains in the back of the group, turbaned, vaguely cloaked, and overall a discreetly secondary figure. Unlike the other three, Catherine is "Asia" only because the caption designates her so and because Russia was automatically the Eastern other to the wealthy (but not necessarily aristocratic) viewers of carefully engraved and etched prints that might circulate in France or Austria, in Italy or Ireland.

Russia, of course, included a great tract of Asia, and to many Western observers Asia infiltrated all of Russia, despite the well-known efforts of Peter the Great to produce a capital city that looked otherwise. The signifiers Asia, Asian, Asiatic, and Oriental conjured up a cabinet of curiosities and a whirlwind of dangerous forces, but also the original source of precious porcelain and fabled silks and furs. When a traveler wrote, "The richness and splendour of the Russian court surpasses description," it was not surprising that he continued, "It retains many traces of its ancient Asiatic pomp, blended with European refinement."[1] Altogether, as a place supposedly profoundly alien to more westerly, less "Northern" and less Asian sensibilities, Catherine's empire oscillated between the delightfully exotic and the atrociously barbaric.[2] Once she added Polish territories to her domains, another people seen as representing stigmatized otherness, Jews, played a more prominent role in the exoticizing stories of Catherine II's territories that reached faraway readers and listeners, some of them of course themselves Jews. The empress's relations with diverse groups often (though not always) gave an additional intriguing tint of the Other to the empress.

Russia—Exotic or Barbaric?

To her distant audiences, Catherine II was not just the ruler of a foreign country, but of a deeply alien empire. The French were foreigners in England, the English were

Empress of the Other 133

Figure 9.1 An allegorical print about Voltaire's death used Catherine II to represent Asia, although her clinging gown was more reminiscent of classical Greece. Source: C. M., *Le tombeau de Voltaire / Dedie a Madame la Marquise de Villette, Dame de Verney* (Paris: Alibert, 1779). Digital Id cph 3a45632 //hdl.loc.gov/loc.pnp/cph.3a45632. Courtesy of the Library of Congress.

foreigners in Germany, but the Russians were foreigners of an entirely different order. Their literature was unknown, their artistic and architectural styles were in most cases deplored, and their church rituals censured. Even the beards of Russian men were disturbing visual markers of Russian otherness. Words from their language had no place in the vocabularies of the cultures further west than Russia's Polish neighbor, their history was less tied to that of readers and observers from Berlin to Aberdeen or Madrid, and Russia's ethnic diversity was inscrutable.[3] The Frenchman Sénac de Meilhan wrote about awaiting his introduction to the empress in

> a great and magnificent room ... in the midst of a jumble of courtiers ... most of them in uniform, as is customary at all the northern courts. But what was striking and what one only finds in Russia was the multiplicity of costumes. Among the generals there are Cossacks, Turks, Georgians, Tartars, Circassians, in long robes, with and without beards, and from this difference of clothing emerges a feeling of amazement produced by the thought of a monarchy ruling over so many different peoples.[4]

Friedrich II too, when he decided to make the ostentatiously costly porcelain table decoration for Catherine, included figurines representing both conquered Turks and indigenous ethnic groups making satisfyingly submissive gestures (Chapter 4). But distant observers were ambivalent whether the Russian Other over whom Catherine II presided was a neutral or even positive force, as in exoticism, or a frightening and perilous one, as in barbarism. Uncertainty as to which Russian otherness prevailed added to its interest and helped propel the decades of celebrity discourse that swirled around Russia's ruler.

When the other is understood as exotic, a realm of unaccustomed social and aesthetic norms is invoked, and, with its unleashing of imagination, an exciting though at least potentially unsettling interchange between "us" and "them" is suggested too. For readers and listeners in Europe's bustling big cities, steady provincial towns, and conservative villages, Russian exoticism could offer a particular visual pleasure, deriving both from images of unfamiliar people—their faces, gestures, hair styles, and fashions—and strange objects—with unusual colors, shapes, and design—all of them savoring of fantastical distant places. Also, as Benjamin Schmidt, writing about the sixteenth and seventeenth centuries, notes, "Exotic geography . . . reflected a basic commercial imperative: it appealed broadly, and it sold widely. It was an attractive product. And it was a salable product."[5] The commercialized exotic could also alluringly evade taboos, especially those connected with sexuality or privilege; its peculiarities could be rendered less dangerous or offensive by distance and aesthetic qualities.

The discourse of barbarism, on the other hand, is about blatant abuse and brutality, untempered by pleasantness. In barbarism the Other is perceived as profoundly dangerous, with alien individuals or groups indigestibly disrupting the highly regulated standards of civilization, standards in which newspaper readers were generally immersed. Barbarism implies a threat, a shift toward coarseness; it positions the readers or their like as potentially vulnerable to harm. In narrative, when effects of antipathy and revulsion are not mitigated by an appealing aspect, when the strange and alien is only revolting or frightening, when it is acted out on sympathetic figures who resemble the readers, the barbaric slips toward horror. Evoking and then purging the feelings of fear and loathing, horror narratives have an entertainment value that diverse eighteenth-century publications showed themselves capable of exploiting. Depending on external and internal circumstances that affected reader perceptions, the distinction between exoticism and horror could shift, with some readers consuming texts as exotic that other readers perceived as inspiring horror. This variable swirl of otherness around Catherine II added to the celebrity discourse about her.

Already in the 1760s, soon after Catherine II seized the Russian throne, when notions of Russia wavered between optimism about the country's acceptance of "European" civilization and pessimism about its "Asiatic" barbarism, a litany of alleged defects in the empire was well established. It included harsh social practices, startling gender relations, misguided sexual customs, and the brutishness of the populace—standard elements of any barbarian discourse. Late in her reign, a radical German periodical, *Das neueste graue Ungeheuer*, proposed designating the Russian "mix of animosity, barbarism, and contradiction with the word Catherinism."[6]

Throughout Catherine's years on the throne, travelers scrawled their versions of familiar primitivist and barbaric topoi. The abbé Jean Chappe d'Auteroche (1728–69), for example, forcefully recirculated the Barbaric Russia notion in his vividly written, well-illustrated, and splendidly produced *Journey into Siberia*; it appeared in 1768 in

French, in 1770 in English, in two translations, and in Dutch in 1771–2. The colorful, but harshly critical, picture of social and cultural conditions in Russia was written with the authority of an eyewitness who was a member of the French Academy of Sciences; he was soon echoed by an Englishman, John Williams. Chappe wrote, for example, that the peasants lead a "languid and inactive life" and are "artful, cunning, and greater rogues than any other nation."[7] Williams opined that "The common people . . . are naturally lazy, dishonest, and fond of drinking strong liquors to excess" and that "the severity of the climate" inured ordinary Russians to adversity and made them "strong and robust."[8] Another traveler, Joseph Marshall, stressed that "they make nothing of hardships, and will bear in continuance what would destroy in a short time other people of less robust constitutions."[9] To emphasize the raw loutishness of the people, Chappe cited Montesquieu's brutal phrase that you must flay a Russian before you can bring him to feeling.[10]

Two Russian social practices that Western discourse found particularly barbaric were serfdom and punishment with the knout. Chappe's book described the brutal lashing of a gentlewoman with the knout for a seemingly minor crime, and some editions included an illustration of the event. To Western observers, to readers leaning over the picture or simply imagining what was graphically described in journals such as the *Monthly Review*,[11] the incident exemplifies barbarian harshness but also exoticizes the woman's sado-masochistic exposure (and her heavenward gaze in the print). This, the travelers in their books and articles seemed to say, was the world of Catherine II about which celebrity discourse was curious.

Descriptions of other unfamiliar practices, especially those that did not inflict bodily pain, could often be read either way, as repulsively (but also fascinatingly) barbarian or appealingly exotic. Russian saunas and baths with their seemingly wanton mixing of naked men and women are represented in one early book as both attractively suggestive of a state of innocence (as though one were "in America among the savages") and appallingly conducive to animal behavior (which "hinders reproduction").[12] Marriage customs, including a process for confirming that the bride is a virgin, also drew salaciously ambivalent attention. The *Monthly Review*'s thorough summary of Chappe's book, which circulated much of the shocking material further in England, must have stimulated many readers' fantasies by enticingly proclaiming the Frenchman's account of Russian marriage customs "too gross and indecent" for its pages. Travelers, newspaper correspondents, and politicians writing about Russia echoed and re-echoed the preexisting catalog of exotic and barbaric tropes and topics, always with the general tendency to reconfirm the superiority of the rest of Europe, either by deploring Russia's distance from European standards or, as in Voltaire's view, which was nudged toward optimism by rich Russian subsidies, by admiring the country's movement toward a European vision of civilization.[13]

Accounts of Catherine II occasionally included exotic details alongside the message of a westernizing, progressive Russia. In 1767, at one of the stops on her inspection tour along the Volga River,[14] according to the *Berlinische Nachrichten*, 600 people came to kiss her hand, and some of the women, the jewels in their headdresses glittering, were also allowed to kiss her cheek. A few issues later the paper announced her arrival in the city of Kazan, where Catherine gave a diamond-encrusted watch to the Kyrgyz prince whom her government held as pampered hostage and met a select group of Tatar men "and their wives and daughters." At the archbishop's palace, she was greeted by delegations of Volga-region children from ethnic groups with names that must have seemed remarkable to distant readers: Tatar, Chuvash, Votyak, and Cheremiss.

The next year, a speaker at the German Society in Göttingen declaimed enthusiastically:

> What a picture, gentlemen, of royal Kazan, to see this astonishing confluence of people from more than twenty different nations, all recognizing the great empress as sovereign, and yet so different in language and customs and partly also in religion. At the sight of the daughter of heaven, the heart of the barbarian beats for the first time with noble feelings, becomes self-aware and senses the happiness of more cultured peoples, and brings the descriptions of his ruler from horde to horde.[15]

Exoticism of this kind could thrill the hearts of the empress's distant fans. Yet based on the infrequent later references to the voyage, it made no lasting impact outside Russia, and seven years afterward, when Kazan was burned to the ground in the course of the Pugachev rebellion, Catherine's earlier visit was not mentioned.

The year after the Volga journey, Chappe's book appeared, powerfully reinscribing barbaric images of Russia. It was probably Catherine II herself, perhaps with other contributors, who produced a long refutation of the French astronomer. Her uninterestingly titled *Antidote* (French original in 1770; English in 1772) was written in a harshly acerbic style and obsessively, tediously enumerated every individual fault of its target.[16] Published anonymously, furthermore, and so lacking the credibility that a well-informed author could provide, the treatise had the unintended effect of eliciting reviews that repeated Chappe's main charges, and it was these that were then cited for decades.

Along the Rhine, the Seine, the Thames, and other cords of communication, contesting notions of Russia as profoundly non-European and barbaric or as becoming Europeanized, though with exotic touches, persisted through Catherine's whole reign and tinged her popular fame. The salience of one or the other varied according to additional factors that were considered newsworthy. Among these, the great rebellion that the newspapers began reporting in the last weeks of 1773, eleven years after she seized the throne, strongly impacted representations of Catherine II and her reign by recirculating images of barbarism and horror and piling them onto an exciting new serialized story about the celebrity empress's survival on the throne.

Pugachev Rebellion, 1773–5

A report from Hamburg dated December 13, 1773, of an insurrection in the center of the empire and of the dispatch of a Russian general to quell the trouble was republished on January 3, 1774, in the *Gazette de France*.[17] Attention to the most alien aspects of Catherine II's territories quickly rekindled and soon concentrated on the rebel leader, on the distinctive ethnic groups who followed him, and on the remote locations where the upheaval was occurring. By January 22 cautious Vienna papers were referring to the rumors. Though the Russian minister in The Hague at first refuted "false and scandalous reports which have been propagated by the News Writers in this country, and from thence have spread all over Europe,"[18] a few days later, the scandalous reports were officially confirmed.

By mid-February newspapers were printing competing supposedly official reports based on a manifesto signed by the empress proclaiming that "a certain Cossack by the name of Jemeljan Pugachev" and a band of pillagers had been conducting "the most horrible robberies" and murders; they had disturbed public order by promising simple folk that they would be liberated from subordination to authority. After the upstart, who claimed to be Peter III come out of hiding, and his followers committed vicious crimes, such as killing captured garrison officers in what Catherine called "a barbaric manner," she issued a manifesto pledging to exterminate the whole gang.[19] By the end of the year, the *Gazzetta Universale* was comparing Pugachev to Attila the Hun.[20] Within the accounts of dangerous events in Russia's "Asiatic" provinces, the papers emphasized the roles of a whole range of steppe peoples, depicting them as fearsome others, not the adoring exotics of the Volga trip or of Friedrich II's elegant porcelain gift. The story of their uprising would accompany Catherine for the rest of her reign, becoming the lingering byword for the barbarian aspect of Russia until, thirteen years later, Catherine's Crimean trip would become the publicity counterpoise to the upheaval. In 1773 and 1774, however, the political stakes within Russia and in Russia's relations to other governments were enormous at a moment when the first partition of Poland was recently concluded and peace with Turkey was being negotiated once again. To readers who cared nothing for politics, however, the story could simply provide an exciting narrative about the parvenu yet enlightened empress embroiled with a marauding band that was both exotic and barbaric.

Class and geography were further salient elements of the events. The middling classes and the lower nobility of eighteenth-century European society were full of anxieties about seditious behavior among the social groups below them. Vienna's main newspaper posed the rebellion in central Russia as the actions of "mutinous peasants from the lowest level of humanity."[21] Any questioning of possible Russian abuses that might have induced fury among the subject ethnic groups of central Asia was strikingly missing from the newspaper accounts, with the Western press skipping opportunities to criticize either Catherine or her policies. Western dislike of Russian serfdom almost vanished, even though Catherine herself had noted in her *Instructions*, that if "slaves" are "used with too much Severity," they may "rebel in their own Defence."[22] Journalists failed to mention the drastic action taken a short time earlier by 150,000 Kalmyk nomads, disgusted by the Russian court's persistent unwillingness to act on their needs. Warned of their possible departure by her officials and then inadvertently displaying how poorly she understood her nomadic subjects, Catherine II made no adjustments either to her massive demands on the Kalmyks for military service or to the colonization policies that were squeezing them out of their migration pastures along the Volga. The main force of the Kalmyk responded by packing their tents, gathering their herds, and setting out on the long and deadly trek from Russia back to a region of western China that they had left over a century before.²³ In fact, although this immense and terrible exodus had occurred in 1771, it was not widely reported in the West until 1773, just months before the larger rebellion erupted.²⁴ But no lines were drawn to the discontent of the Cossacks or other herder groups, much less to the assorted serfs.

Furthermore, although Catherine's first public announcement about the rebellion acknowledged that Pugachev had promised his followers liberation from subordination, newspaper writers and editors gave the rebels' political agenda almost no attention in the many articles that followed over the next months, though a few papers correctly, but incompletely, specified the rebels' motivations as opposition to "the new and insupportable taxes" and forced military recruitment.²⁵ Newspapers sometimes briefly mentioned that the nobility were especially targeted and that the atmosphere in Moscow was alarming, since the "blind mob" there might support the rebellion,²⁶ but the ignorance of internal policy botches and the othering of Pugachev and his band apparently produced a sense of collective identity among distant observers in at least provisional solidarity with Catherine as the representative of order, reason, and the Western way of life, opposing the disorderly peasants and nomads. With such mechanisms in place, the rebellion became exciting material, an "adventure" as one paper put it, for distant readers.²⁷

Exotic geography spiced the story too, with the rebellion occurring on "the lawless plain / Where Tartar clans and grizly Cossacks reign," as a British poet had long before described central Russia.²⁸ News accounts described the regular Russian army, sent out to suppress the uprising, encountering huge distances, woefully inadequate roads, towns with strange new place names, such as Kongour, Kransnoiar, and Kouvatskoi and few cities.²⁹ By retreating in many directions into the vast territory around them,³⁰ the rebels—described in one source as 50,000 fighters and in another as 100,000 "Seditious"³¹—stretched the army's skimpy supply lines and inadvertently stretched the patience of curious Western readers as well. A German account with the dateline "Kaminieck, 28 February" explained that it was difficult for news reports "to pierce through such an immense space as the deserts of Asiatic Russia are, without having the descriptions either gain or lose something."³²

Not that everyone was sympathetic to the difficulties. An Englishman traveling during this period, Nathanial Wraxall (1751-1831), scoffed at the imported English newspapers he read in Russia as "the avowed vehicles of falsehood over all Europe."³³ Yet the confusion of information as it trickled out of Russia created its own form of unsettling narrative excitement, with publications repeatedly thematizing the contradictory nature of the rumors.³⁴ The July issue of the Spanish *Mercurio historico*, for example, published official triumphalist news of the rebellion on one page and a far grimmer story in "letters that escaped the vigilance of the Russian Government" on another.³⁵ For newspaper printer-editors, the chance to speculate was rich, with a weekly paper in Belgium, for example, mentioning and then dismissing a shocking rumor that the general sent to suppress the insurgents had been forced by his troops to join the rebellion instead.³⁶ In March, the *General Evening Post* reprinted a report not only that "the rebels have taken Casan" but also that they "are arrived at Moscow."³⁷ Some papers reported that talking freely about the rebellion was not permitted in

Russia,[38] and soon a news item claimed that Catherine had promulgated an ukase forbidding discussion of public events on pain of death.

The plot of the Pugachev story was driven forward by the notion of his capture, his rebellion brought to an end, order thus satisfyingly restored, and tragedy turned to comedy. But this narrative was repeatedly foiled. In early March 1774 came a report in the Frankfurt newspaper that the rebel leader, in this instance called Monsieur Purgar, had been captured,[39] and on March 14, a report asserted that Pugachev's wife and children had been caught.[40] But then on March 22, an item appeared stating that a reward in the amount of 100,000 rubles was being offered for Pugachev's capture, dead or alive.[41] In May, newspapers reported that Russian forces had scored a major victory (in April), though Pugachev himself had escaped with either four comrades, as reported on one page, or four horses as reported on the next.[42] At the same time came the disturbing news that the much admired General Bibikow had died of a fever.[43] In June papers were still struggling to sort out conflicting reports. They began suggesting that Pugachev's influence, having reached Moscow, would now spread further. In fact, the same French report asserted, Pugachev was now having ruble coins struck bearing his image and labeled "Peter III, Emperor of all the Russias, 1774," with a Latin slogan on the reverse.[44] In mid-September "Letters of good authority" reported "that the famous rebel Pugatschew is fallen into the hands of the Russians."[45] Finally, in early November, they got it right, based on a Petersburg report dated October 7.[46] The Frankfurt paper rejoiced that the "monster" had been turned over to the commander of the city of Yaik and would soon be sent to Moscow, "to end his life in a tragic scene."[47]

Many comments about the struggle between Catherine II and the Cossack rebel gave the story extra punch by structuring it in gendered terms. At one point a London paper printed a rumor that, compelled by the rebellion, Catherine had conceded the throne to Paul, but added that "it is hard to believe that a woman of her fortitude would resign her Crown but with her life."[48] A report forwarded from Warsaw claimed that the purpose of Pugachev's "insane daring," as Catherine's widely cited manifesto called his pretense to be the deceased Emperor Peter III, was to wrest power from Catherine and return it to the male line, in the form of her son.[49] Another paper satirized the rebels' biblical imagery to align Pugachev as the resurrected Peter III with Jesus, claiming he "arose from the dead, and was sent from Heaven, in order to procure his son, the present Grand Duke, the Russian diadem, who is kept from it by the craft and violence of his mother."[50] Posing Catherine II as a crafty and violent mother reconfirmed the illegitimacy of institutionally powerful women.

When the media represented Pugachev as attempting to push Catherine II from the throne as she had pushed Peter III, they made him her dark double. He even gained elite status in some reports. Dubbed "Prince P--------w," he was described as supported by "several great men of the empire."[51] Soon "the Chief of the Insurgents" was such a danger that "the Empress hath promised a considerable sum and the ensigns of the order of St. Andrew to any person who shall arrest him."[52] A Frankfurt newspaper reported that reliable sources indicated Pugachev was only the figurehead leader for a group of foreigners who were actually running the rebellion. A page later the story about "Monsieur or Marquis Purgar" gives him a whiff of Frenchness, adding that he is "supported by 500 notorious louts."[53] Western papers, baffled by the rebel's success, sometimes attributed the movement's leadership to members of the Russian aristocracy. One paper insisted that the rebellion would be nothing more than a straw fire if some of the elite were not participating and indeed that one such person had just been beheaded by the Petersburg court.[54] Another rumor asserted wildly that Catherine's old friend from the coup, Countess Dashkova, was leading the revolt.[55] Some involved Paul, claiming, "The grand of the empire actually murmurs to find the lawful successor deprived from his right and to prevent any further dissatisfactions of the kind, the Empress has politically resolved to share her authority with the Grandduke."[56] Opportunities to speculate were numerous. Even if Pugachev were not the instrument of Russian conspirators, for example, Russian aristocrats might take advantage of his movement: "It is suspected that many of the principal men in the empire will lay hold of this opportunity, and that a total revolution will be the consequence of it."[57] Soon the speculation had almost become fact: "Private letters from the Hague by the last post advise, that a strong report prevailed there of a great revolution in Russia, where the Empress was said to be dethroned, and the Grand Duke her son raised to the Imperial Crown."[58] The crisis for Catherine appeared dramatic.

Claims of foreign involvement contributed yet another stirring narrative element. A London paper asserted: "We are well informed that the disturbance in the government of Orenbourg hath been raised by the secret enemies of Russia, and that Pugatschew, the chief of the mutineers, is assured of a retreat in case he fails in his attempt."[59] The London *Gazetteer and New Daily Advertiser* for April 5, 1774, stated bluntly, "several French officers are with Pugaschew, and command the chief band."[60] One paper published a report that Pugachev himself was from a "far more civilized nation" than the Cossacks, but had just modified the ending of his name to give it a Cossack sound.[61] It seemed that European observers struggled to imagine a major insurrection in Russia unless it derived power from aristocrats or the West.

The last incident in the captive rebel's story, his trial and execution in Moscow, was as contradictorily reported as the previous events. According to Vienna's main paper, after "the scum, Pugachev himself," was excommunicated (a step that made it possible to kill him), he became rueful and begged forgiveness.[62] Other papers labeled him aloof and indifferent,[63] or, in the version composed far from the scene by the energetic German poet and journalist Christian Friedrich Daniel Schubart, the rebel died with "the defiance of a barbarian" and the stoicism characteristic of either "animal stupidity or angelic wisdom."[64] Many papers asserted that the executioner, instead of starting by hacking off the Cossack's hands and feet, decapitated him first, an act variously presented as merciful, accidental, or the result of a supporter's bribe.[65] A later version recounted not Russian barbarity but Enlightened notions of punishment, with the empress countermanding the plan of the investigators to torture Pugachev into a confession and ordering his beheading before quartering because she wanted to avoid letting her reign "be stained by any atrocity."[66]

With his death, Catherine's supremacy was supposedly fully restored, but the revolt as a massive demonstration of discontent showed that Catherine II was not as admired by the Russian populace as distant readers may have thought. It positioned Pugachev not only as an alternative to Catherine but also as her dark shadow, different from her in his open violence, but like her in his grasp for ultimate power. His pretenses, recirculating the story of Peter III, reminded readers of the shaky legitimacy of Catherine II's rule and corroborated the Otherness theme in her celebrity.

Others Who Spoke for Themselves: Catherine and Her Jewish Subjects

Few, if any, members of Catherine II's distant audience belonged to the ethnic groups who clustered around Pugachev. Quite different was the situation of another group, the Jews in and out of Russia, who were also marginalized as Other, though stigmatized rather than marked as exotic or barbarian. Given the inclination of fans to identify, positively or negatively, with the celebrities available to them, reports about the empress's relationship with the Jews in her domains must have especially intrigued faraway Jews reading and listening in households and workshops further west. The responses of this group of potential fans, however, were probably mixed and mobile.

Stigmatized status, evident, for example, when a group's very name is execrated, was signaled in the publicity about an ukase that Catherine issued forbidding the use of the word "Jew" as an expletive.[67] Stigma, its circumstances, and ramifications were topics in eighteenth-century analysis, though without the term. William Richardson paused in his book about Russia to discuss peoples, such as Finns and Jews, who differed from the rest of the nation "in language, customs and religion." He stated bluntly: "Such differences will expose them to contempt; the contempt they meet with will in time make them deserve it: treated with no respect by others who have power over them, they will lose all sense of character, and have no respect for themselves." This deplorable situation, Richardson added, feminized such unfortunates, who did not dare "to express their resentment in a resolute and manly manner." The consequences, he believed, were devastating, because people in this predicament "will harbour sentiments of latent malice; they will indulge ignominious vices; become mean, insidious, and deceitful."

Having sketched a social-psychology of exclusion that blamed the circumstances of stigmatization for eliciting negative characteristics among the victimized and insufficiently manly people, Richardson, writing from the perspective of the dominant group (not Jews, not women, Jewish or otherwise), emphasized that historically the situation of the Jews in Europe was dire and their choices few: "Contemned and detested for their origin, their religion, their hatred of Christianity, and their persecution of its holy Author, they felt that they had no character to lose, and betook themselves for subsistence to such employments as the Europeans despised." Richardson then described the wealth of the Jews and their business successes as "advantages, which compensated for the contempt they suffered, and reconciled them to their condition."[68]

Though Catherine II's impact on the "advantages" of her Jewish subjects received only intermittent and inconsistent notice in Western publications, it may have been of special interest to Jewish readers and listeners outside her domains. Papers announced that she permitted Jews to practice their religion; they reported an ukase in 1764 allowing Jews to participate in trade. A German who wrote about these developments noted that since Catherine II usually tried to follow the policies of Peter the Great, who had been quite harsh on Jews, she must have had very good reasons to deviate from his approach.[69] The first partition of Poland added, various writers quickly noted, several regions with large Jewish populations to Catherine's territories. Soon after the partition was implemented, in November 1774, newspapers were reporting that "that almost all the trading Jews of any consequence have left the Polish dominions, and gone to settle in Russia, where they have great encouragement given them by the Empress."[70] Using language typical of stigma, William Coxe, journeying through the newly acquired Polish areas, noted "being struck with the swarms of Jews." What especially shocked him, and must have interested his Jewish readers, was the diversity of occupations they were allowed to practice:

> If you ask for an interpreter, they bring you a Jew; if you come to an inn, the landlord is a Jew; if you want post-horses, a Jew procures them, and a Jew drives them; if you wish to purchase, a Jew is your agent: and this perhaps is the only country in Europe where Jews cultivate the ground; in passing through Lithuania, we frequently saw them engaged in sowing, reaping, mowing, and other works of husbandry.[71]

But the limitations imposed on them were also recorded. In 1780, for example, when Catherine visited her new lands, the obscure J. G. Mayer recorded that she was met outside the gates of various towns by delegations of Jews, the area inside the gates being reserved for citizens.[72] When the evening's entertainment included a display of public buildings illuminated with candles, most of the lights were on churches—Jesuit, Dominican, Franciscan, and Basilian in the case of Polatsk. Amid all the dazzlement there, Mayer observed that the Jews managed to organize a boat displaying the image of an eagle accompanied by the words Hope and Loyalty and the phrase "under the shadow of your wings" in Hebrew and Latin.[73]

Indeed, printed words, often in languages familiar to readers well beyond her borders, were an important element of the Jewish interaction with the empress and so became available to readers much further away. Texts such as a song of joy of the Jews of Sklov describe Catherine II from a stigmatized position, yet as a people who exuberantly, though abstractly, praises the "Crown of Heroines," the one who radiates inextinguishable light, who, they significantly assert, brings justice and prosperity to all. The twelfth stanza is slightly more explicit both in its depiction of the group's desired image of Catherine, calling her "the one who binds up broken spirits" and begging her not to distain a humble people but to have mercy on them, like a mother to her child. The final, fourteenth stanza asserts that this humble people, like her other subjects, cherishes her greatness, is filled, like the others, with her immortal fame, and is glad, like the others, to be her subjects.[74] Published in German, the poem makes an argument for better, more equitable treatment based on similarity with the dominant and thus non-stigmatized group and on a flattering depiction of the powerful woman treating all with equal justice.

The "Song of Praise and Thanksgiving of the Jewish community of Mohilow at the Entrance of her Imperial Majesty Catherine II, Autocrat of all the Russias," appeared in two languages, first Hebrew and then German, and is likewise laden with sublime images of Catherine.[75] Echoing the Psalms, it begins: "Praise the Lord this day! Sing to him a new song" and quickly shifts to Catherine: "She arrives, the earth's delight, the joy of all eyes / Catherine! the magnificent crown of the daughters!" This poem too undertakes a wishful description of Catherine from the perspective of the community, praising her for the attributes they hope she will demonstrate to them: "Comfort to the wise and to the dominated," and "Comfort also to us, the witnesses to your great good will." The agenda is clear: "She is mercifully maternal to Jacob's weak remnants, / placing princes over us who are full of goodness and honesty. / Her scepter protects justice, frightens evildoers. / She dissolves the bindings of injustice, relieves whomever is oppressed by profanity." The poem concludes with hope for Catherine's life to be long, for Paul to remain safe and for his wife to have many children. To what extent distant eighteenth-century readers and listeners, Jews and non-Jews, encountered these words or responded to them is unclear in retrospect, but corresponding reports about Catherine's encounters with Jews on her travels were available in newspapers everywhere.

1787: Crimea Trip and the Staged Exotic

In 1787, as all followers of newspapers and journals in the west of Europe learned, the empress planned a great junket through her empire, where she would meet many of her most exotic subjects. This much publicized journey to her newly acquired territory, the fabled Crimea, activated notions of Catherine again coddled in exotic "Asiatic" luxury and invited fans and potential fans to indulge fabulous dreams about a trip that covered 6,000 kilometers and lasted six months. Altogether, the imperial progress to the Black Sea and home again was a vast and enthralling, spectacularizing encounter between a glittering Westernized monarch and a large clutch of diverse, well-packaged, and thus aestheticized ethnic groups in a mysterious distant landscape. This was an event that could provide celebrity's boost to fans, lifting them out of their everyday worlds and into an imagined realm of wealth and luxury.

For years, rumors circulated of an expedition being planned to the recently founded city of Kherson on the Black Sea and on to the nearby Crimea.[76] Catherine had been on the throne almost a quarter century when she finally set out. One purpose of the trip, editors (correctly) speculated, was for the empress to meet for a second time with Emperor Joseph II of the Holy Roman Empire.[77] Papers such as the carefully monitored Spanish monthly *Mercurio histórico y político* conjectured that the two rulers were hoping to carry out a partition of southeastern Europe, as they had done in Poland.[78] The *English Review* mused about "that enterprizing and magnificent princess" attracting "the attention of Europe" when she becomes "the foundress of a new Greek empire."[79] Other writers guessed that Catherine wished to irritate the weakening Ottomans into hostilities, or that her most famous courtier, Potemkin, wanted to show her that Russia's new southwestern territories, over which he ruled as governor-general, were not just costly and worthless projects, as his enemies in St. Petersburg said.

To many readers, however, the reason for the trip probably mattered little; it was the trip as a months-long performance of exotic grandeur that counted, with extensive publicity that was easily readable as celebrity discourse about great extravagance, alien places, exotic transportation, and extraordinary participants, including two kings, Joseph II and King Stanislaw August Poniatowski of Poland. When contemporary reports mentioned crowds of other highly privileged foreign watchers joining the trip, it appeared that even the elites of society far to the west were acting as Catherine's fans. In Kiev, the prolonged first stop on the journey, according to trip accounts, foreign visitors from as far away as Spain joined the local crowds to gawk at the celebrity ruler.[80] Various rich aristocrats from the French court were reportedly so thrilled by the prospect of the empress's extravagant outing to the Crimea that they sought their king's permission to attend it. An unnamed Paris correspondent commented: "It is hard to believe: our French gentlemen do not like traveling for pleasure," but the desire to experience the celebrity-enhancing, glamorizing presence of Catherine II in the exotic Black Sea setting supposedly offset the strenuousness and discomfort of the long journey.[81] However many foreigners actually came, these Western would-be spectators, along with numerous less-privileged local watchers, could stimulate the imaginations of vicarious travelers at home.

Another participant was important as well. Years after Catherine's death, when discussion of her sexual life was rampant, one member of the expedition, Melchior Adam Weikard, emphasized the presence on the trip of her new young lover, Alexander Mamonov. To the choleric Weikard, the immense expedition was a pleasant pastime for the spoiled empress and a sweet classroom in which she could be schoolmistress to her ignorant young pupil and paramour.[82] For distant readers at the time of the journey, however, only hints about previously obscure Mamonov appeared in print. It was noted, for example, that he conferred the diamond-encrusted St. Andreas order on Poniatowski;[83] and when the king then bestowed the White Eagle on him in return, the paper called him the "very wealthy, young Mr. Momonov," thus giving the unfamiliar gentleman attributes that would have alerted at least some readers to his status as Catherine's privileged and well rewarded lover.[84]

Many other people came to see the events too. In an imperial progress, spectators "enhanced the authority of the performers" and so were an important element of the occasion both in words and in images.[85] On one evening, for example, when Catherine planned to have her dinner with Potemkin, "visitors great and small were allowed into the dining room to see the imperial magnificence that the prince had prepared for the empress. Silver dinner ware with the crowns and representations of the empress's magnificent deeds filled the hall."[86] The visit even by such unnamed spectators made the whole scene more significant for readers, for whom almost no visual accounts of the trip were available. One exception shows a flat landscape that is represented as the place where Catherine and Joseph met on the trip (Figure 9.2); it is a shockingly barren site, abated by a few tufts of grass but unlikely to inspire any sense of exotic aesthetics. The print was the work of a popular Viennese engraver,

Empress of the Other 145

Figure 9.2 One of the few attempts to depict the Crimea trip, a hand-colored print by Johann Hieronymus Löschenkohl, shows Joseph II and Catherine II meeting together, with members of their entourage, in an empty landscape. Source: Johann Hieronymus Löschenkohl (publishing house), *Zusammenkunft Joseph II. mit Katharina II. am 18. Mai 1787*, 1787. Courtesy of the Sammlung Wien Museum, CC0 (https://sammlung.wienmuseum.at/en/object/319504/).

Johann Hieronymus Löschenkohl, who probably displayed it in his much visited showroom in the center of the city.[87] Using his preferred format of full-length figures with faces in profile, the engraver depicted the emperor in the upper middle on the left, hat in hand, reaching toward Catherine in the middle on the right. Wearing a wide skirt and a big hat, she gestures slightly toward him. Four witnesses direct their attention—and the viewers'—toward the rulers. On the right edge of the print, the tall man standing behind the empress is Potemkin, grand master of the entire journey,[88] and the other three are additional members of the rulers' entourages. Their place toward the front plane of the print draws in the viewer to complete the circle and be a witness too.[89]

The trip they were observing gained part of its fascination from its immense cost, which clearly riveted media workers, who perhaps suspected the topic would also attract readers in the drawing rooms and alehouses of their countries. With Joseph's participation, delicious bits about the lavish preparations came from the Habsburg lands as well as from Russia.⁹⁰ Even for the comparatively impoverished King of Poland the journey meant huge costs. When Catherine sent a lieutenant general to welcome Poniatowski, the king rewarded him with a portrait set with diamonds and valued, the newspapers assiduously reported, at 8,000 rubles,⁹¹ though perhaps the costs were not as great to Poniatowski as it appeared: British papers reported "his expences are defrayed by the Empress, who has made him a present of a considerable sum, said to amount to two millions of rubles."⁹² Triumphal arches were built, bells rung, cannon fired, palaces speedily constructed and furnished, gardens equipped with peacocks, swans, and nightingales. Fireworks were set off in an almost literal display of having money to burn.⁹³ Potemkin's accomplishment in organizing these events was rewarded with both a special title, Tauritscheskoi or Potemkin-Taurian, and a purse of 100,000 rubles in cash.⁹⁴

The reward was also for Potemkin's arrangement of transportation on the challenging journey. For observers outside Russia, the movement in comfort of a large party in a

Figure 9.3 A few years before the empress set out for Kiev on the way to the Crimea, a print dated 1784 depicted her comfortable means of riding along bonfire-lit tracks in winter. The engraver, who signed the print only Walker, was probably James Walker, who was recruited to St. Petersburg that year to serve as "engraver to her imperial Majesty." Source: Walker, *The Empress of Russia's Travelling Equipage*. London: Harrison, 1784. Getty Images. The Empress of Russia Travelling. Editorial Number: 464425971. Credit: Heritage Images.

region where such travel was rare added significantly to the amazing character of the event (Figures 0.5 and 9.3). By proceeding as far as Kiev in winter, the empress and her party could travel in carriages fixed onto sleighs, "the motion of which over the beaten snow was perfectly smooth and even."[95] Catherine's, drawn by twenty-four horses, was reported to have two or three heated rooms.[96] With the strange notion of comfortable travel over great snowy distances, an air of enchantment shimmered over the story.[97] Beyond Kiev, newspapers told of Catherine traveling hundreds of kilometers by water on "fairy-like" galleys that floated down previously unnavigable cliff-lined stretches of the Dnieper.[98] Catherine's ship, named for the river, shone with gold and included a bedroom, living room, boudoir, dining room for forty guests, and two reception rooms, all of them done up with silk and mirrors.[99] Potemkin likewise had a ship of his own, as did the foreign ministers; the ladies in waiting had one "fitted up like a Cloyster," with cells lining both sides of an oval vestibule.[100] Two ships accommodated the imperial kitchen, two more were for horses, and many others were for the rest of the entourage.

Correspondents frequently noted the unfamiliar, but supposedly gracious, peoples whose well-choreographed rejoicing at Catherine's visit must have fascinated many faraway readers and auditors: "The Tartars, and even the Mahometans . . . were eager to shew every civility to the illustrious travelers. They frequently furnished horses, and even lent their own carriages. The Popes [i.e. priests], the Cossacks, and the Greeks, where they lodged, vied with each other in the splendor of their entertainments."[101] These were scenes to erase memories of Pugachev's bloody rebellion thirteen years earlier. "A deputation of ten Kyrgyz Tatars . . . with a sultan at their head" were given "new red caftans with silver borders and white damask vests" and "were admitted to an audience, where they sat in a circle awaiting the arrival of the empress."[102] A much-reprinted letter from Sebastopol mentioned the troops of Cossacks and "a thousand regularly trained Tartars, armed with lances, and otherwise completely mounted, [who] came to meet her and escorted her as far as Batchiasary, where her Imperial Majesty lodged in the palace of the Chans."[103]

This thoroughly exotic scene placed Catherine II in proximity with the traditional quintessential group of Others to the Europeans, the Ottoman Turks, with their flamboyant costumes, sensationalized sexual customs, infidel religion, alleged cruelty, strange architecture, and more. A handsome print, by the obscure F. M. Will, shows Joseph II and Catherine confronting the massively beturbaned and bearded sultan, all their swords drawn (Figure 9.4). In the matching French and German text below the picture the three exchange taunts. Many observers read in bewilderment about the provocation to the Ottomans that the meeting of the emperor and empress represented; she was visiting exactly the lands on the Black Sea she had recently appropriated, and the Porte had notified her that she could be crowned queen of "Tauris" in Petersburg, or Moscow, or any of her other northern provinces, but they would consider it a specific public insult if she persisted in Cherson in the rumored coronation plan.[104] Published references in the west to a coronation plan silently disappeared. Even so, Catherine's trip entailed provocation enough and afforded her the chance to secure Joseph's support against the empire to her south. The second Russo-Turkish War broke out soon after she was back in St. Petersburg. Outside Russia, Catherine II appeared to be

Figure 9.4 An undated allegorical print of Joseph II, the sultan, and Catherine II depicts the three rulers together, each under a symbol that seems to promise European victory in their coming war: the benevolent eye of Providence for Joseph; a sickle moon, associated with the Ottomans, ominously partly obscured over the sultan; and the sun dispersing small clouds over Catherine, who rides demurely sidesaddle. Source: F. M. Will, *L'Empereur Joseph II: Ennemi de Chretiens! qui tu es fiers de tes Troupes*. Courtesy Early and Rare Printed Books Department, Research and Special Collections Division, National Széchényi Library, Budapest, Hungary.

both an exotic celebrity and a worrisomely "Asiatic" despot, sometimes still shadowed in the imagination by her terrible double, the marauding, murderous, and charismatic Cossack who claimed to be Peter III. Even though various pro-Russian factions among her distant observers saw her as a champion bringing Enlightenment to her population and combating the conventional Asiatic threat to Europe, a more apprehensive camp helped to launch the often-derisive last phase of the living Catherine's distant popular reception.

III

Transgressions Accruing and Secrets Revealed

The attention of a distant public to Catherine II's reign continued in the late 1780s and beyond, but awareness of her threats and transgressions was accruing. Her earlier projects were subjected to disillusioned reassessments, as faraway media workers outdid themselves with savage and clever satires on each jolting new misdeed by the mighty woman. Refurbished stories of her marriage with Peter III and her seizure of his throne appeared anew in the bookshops and on the margins of political cartoons. Titillating, but long suppressed, versions of her sexual behavior were offered up for readers, listeners, and viewers to discuss, disparage, and envision. The French Revolution, which was recalibrating attitudes and expectations across Europe during the final eight years of the tsarina's life, 1789–96, deepened the stains on her foreign reception and tarnished her image for years after her death, until a new tsar and new conditions in Europe made room again for directing both admiration and ambivalence at "Europe's empress."

10

Final Eight Years

Reassessment and Satirical Critique

By the last decade of Catherine's reign, disappointments and failures in areas such as ending serfdom, nurturing colonies, and improving education seemed to be increasing. Back at the beginning of her reign, even a contemptuous French writer had hoped "the empress of Anhalt-Zerbst" would extend "the privilege of freedom . . . to all her subjects."[1] Another writer had added, "No country yet has regretted abolishing serfdom and Russia would certainly also not be sorry. Of course, such a step is laden with difficulty, but to Catherine II nothing is too challenging."[2] Mid-reign, in 1777, an anonymous analyst was still confident that she would free the serfs because she recognized the importance of liberty and inalienable human rights.[3] Ten years after that, however, the lack of progress was unmistakable.[4] Serfdom continued in Russia until 1861.

As pronounced in the periodical press, Catherine's colonies, under the management of Prince Orlov, also lost Enlightenment luster. A biography of Orlov in 1791 described the fiasco of colonists being provided with flour full of worms and maggots, horses that were wild ponies not broken to the plow, housing promised but not built, harsh winters spent in "miserable tents," the colonists' petitions for help only serving to heat the ovens in Orlov's cozy Petersburg office. Many of the settlers, allegedly, even chose suicide over the desolation of their lives.[5] A Lutheran pastor corroborated this grim account, describing the dilapidated condition of his church and house, the wild attitudes of the German "trash" who were supposed to be his congregation, and the lack of protection he experienced both from them and from marauding Kyrgyz bands.[6]

Some new smudges on the lore about Catherine II circulated privately. The rumor that she was vindictive, for example, spread when one of her correspondents in Hannover, Dr. Zimmermann, passed the word to a Göttingen university official that the empress was extremely distressed about an item in an obscure newspaper published in their town. The journalist should be ordered to retract the piece and apologize immediately as Catherine was "known to be very vengeful," and, if she did not get "complete satisfaction," she might forbid her subjects from studying there. Public retraction and apology followed promptly.[7] Such incidents did not match the image of the gracious, tolerant, and enlightened empress of the early years.

Metaphors of Gender and Sexuality and the Dominance of *An Imperial Stride!*

The most important political elements in the late-reign reassessments of Catherine II were the troubling impact on the power relations among European states of her wars, her land annexations, and her threats against revolutionary France. When her second war with the Ottomans erupted, both Britain and France, anxious about Russia's further aggrandizement, backed the Sublime Porte. Then, in 1793 and 1795, along with Prussia and Austria, she partitioned the final chunks of Poland, crushing Polish resistance and imprisoning its famous leader, Tadeuz Kosciuszko. Criticism of these exploits provided journalists, artists, and printsellers with abundant material. Also conspicuous in the news were Catherine's professions of support for royals and royalists in the unfolding French Revolution, though in fact she sent no troops for the campaigns that a coalition of European powers conducted against the French army.

Amid all of this, media workers in Britain, where freedom of the press was generally better protected than on the continent, engaged in raucous commodification of such politics, producing England's "golden age" of caricature in the 1780s, 1790s, and later, and using Catherine II as part of it. Once their guffaw-inducing political satires mostly replaced the mildly amusing (and sometimes flagrantly pornographic) prints produced for the Dutch, Belgian, and German-speaking worlds of the 1780s (see Chapter 9),[8] the British craftsmen were joined from 1791 to about 1794 by French cartoonists, French pamphleteers, and soon French playwrights as well. The resulting new satires—"liberated, farcical, transgressive, carnivalesque,"[9] and sometimes again pornographic—belong to what has been called "the most influential art of the 1790s and early 1800s."[10] Their exposés of the powerful Russian ruler with a female body could entertain well-off folk standing in printshops, impoverished passersby gazing at outdoor displays, and a core of wealthier viewers enjoying at home the often expensive prints they had rented or purchased.

Indeed, though the varied military-economic issues and shifting political positions of the contending governments were fundamental to the existence of each print, pamphlet, or play, that was now, as earlier, only part of what interested the audiences, who often ignored international politics, over which they generally had no iota of control. Each of the texts and pictures had a political message, sometimes one the makers were specifically commissioned to communicate, and most of the works reacted to a specific event. But well-drawn, obstreperous political cartoons in particular had an impact that far exceeded their political content. Because of this excess, because of the pictures' crucial "ability to subvert and transcend their perceived ideological affiliations," such visual satires could join celebrity discourse almost shorn of their topical political references. Gabriel Sénac de Meilhan had noted in his prescient account of celebrity that reports of "wars, conquests, and alliances" were not what his correspondent, Madame **, expected from him.[11] Of concern in this chapter are the elements of celebrity discourse evident in the growing pile of satirical prints of the empress, and many satirical words as well; the details of their political and military contexts are largely omitted.

One print in particular fed into celebrity discourse about Catherine II and became famous across Europe. *An Imperial Stride* was cited in the House of Commons on the day it was published, April 12, 1791,[12] which was about the time when Sénac's letter was being written. With English political satires usually more obviously transgressive than recent continental ones and their jokes easier to decipher, they could be attractive to be copied in other countries. Of roughly twenty-five political cartoons depicting Catherine II that were produced that year mostly in Britain, some in France, the *Stride* image, or *L'Enjambée Imperiale*, is one that was apparently published in nearly simultaneous English and French editions (Figures 10.1 and 10.2).[13] Although its creator is uncertain, many scholars today think it was probably Thomas Rowlandson;[14] it was prominently displayed in William Holland's printshop, as seen in a watercolor painted by another maker of visual satires, Richard Newton.[15]

The *Stride* image has a distinctive triangular composition, with Catherine's crown forming the apex, her dramatic skirts giving the triangle volume, and a miniaturized pack of "European Powers" along the bottom of the print establishing the base. The posture of the enormous, central figure, the lone woman, is memorably incommensurate with proper eighteenth-century femininity: she lunges forward, with one foot just reaching the tip of a minaret in Constantinople and the other atop a rock resembling the pedestal of the famous Peter the Great statue in St. Petersburg. Though the print does not name her, this depiction of the empress as a gigantic female version

Figure 10.1 *An Imperial Stride* satirizes Catherine II's aggression against the Ottomans as a giant step she is taking over the heads of amazed monarchs from St. Petersburg to Constantinople. Source: *An Imperial Stride!* Courtesy of the British Museum; Museum number 1868,0808.6035.

Figure 10.2 *L'Enjambee Imperiale* is the French version of *An Imperial Stride*, but whether it came first is unclear. Both satires, but especially this bare-breasted French one, became immensely well known and were repeatedly cited by French and English visual caricaturists. Source: *L'Enjambee Imperiale*. Digital Id cph 3b51421 //hdl.loc.gov/loc.pnp/cph.3b51421. Courtesy of the Library of Congress.

of the Colossus of Rhodes is easily identifiable via the emblematic royal crown and the Russia-coded, fur-trimmed overdress that engravings of Catherine II had used for decades. As political commentary, the print warns of Russia's aggression against the Ottoman Empire and elsewhere. Reread as celebrity discourse, it is an invitation to shock, fantasy, and contempt for Catherine II.

Adding significantly to the cartoon's bite is its deployment of gender and sexuality, emphasized by the row of small head-and-shoulder portraits of a series of men potentates gazing up the empress's skirts and making bawdy remarks. Their venomous double entendres, in phallic-like speech balloons aimed at her crotch, label her as sexually aggressive and insatiable, thereby reinforcing the unacceptability of her power. Britain's iconically stuttering George III, for example, makes both the physical-sexual and geopolitical comment, "What! what! what! what a prodigious expansion!" The doge of Venice, the pope, the king of Spain, and Leopold II of Austria all similarly exclaim, while the sultan remarks viciously: "The whole Turkish Army wouldn't satisfy her." The unmistakably dominant female figure above them, in contrast, says nothing and seems unaware of these diminutive, leering, sexual connoisseurs. The viewer, drawn close to the image by the miniscule texts, peers from intimate proximity at the controversial celebrity empress's sexualized body and so partially joins the male rulers' intrusive gaze. At that moment, the social distance between her and her non-elite audiences is symbolically erased, and their norm-reinforcing condemnation of her scandalous transgressions, both political and personal, is encouraged.

Similar though the French and English versions of the print are, they also differ in several ways, large and small. The empress in the better known of the two French versions faces right and in the English one left; both French prints show eight rulers and the English only seven; the French versions age her face by squashing it and adding a suggestion of toothlessness; her hair flies loosely in the French images but is better groomed in the English ones. But the most glaring and most significant difference is the empress's breasts. The English print masculinizes the empress, flattening and covering her breasts, while the French editions, in dramatic contrast, underscores Catherine II as a dissolute woman by offering the spectacle of her bright, plump, bare breasts, emphatically framed by thick, dark bands of fur and positioned just above the midpoint in the image. Most scandalous, however, in all the versions are her disgracefully splayed legs, an unmistakable and vulgar signifier of sexual impropriety in a woman and one that was repeated several more times in satires of the empress.[16]

Created far from Russia by culture producers aiming to make saleable goods, the *Stride* cartoons exemplify the anxieties about sexuality and gender that Catherine II's great power induced. This image became the most famous and most often appropriated satirical representation of her, reappearing in numerous memes, not only in other attacks on Catherine II but also on Marie Antoinette and later Napoleon too, and in France it gave Catherine the name Madame Enjambée, a title applied to her in two plays from 1793 that imagined the confinement of all remaining European monarchs to a remote island where they are then devoured by a volcano; stage instructions in one of these scripts—and both plays were in fact performed—specifically mention the empress taking long strides as she comes on the stage.[17]

Force Unsettling Gender: The Indeterminate-Androgynous Woman Ruler

Caricaturists sought to devise representations of Catherine II that offered their beholders and especially their purchasers not just critique but also amusing individual entertainment, conversational matter for sociable interaction, and stimulus for their intimate sexual fantasies, all the stuff of celebrity. Any widely seen version of the tsarina drew attention to her and fostered her fame, but caricatures that satirized her allegorically as sow, hen, or bear, for example,[18] were less likely to fit with celebrity discourse than those showing her in human form. As the French Revolution challenged the norms of public discourse and skewered deference toward powerful rulers, inspirations for depicting the norm-violating empress abounded, evidently to the relish of viewers across Europe and Britain. Because hers is usually the only female figure in a satirical scene, gender was always part of the effect, drawn from a whole cupboard of readily combinable misogynous tropes, old and new, from androgynous freak to ridiculous heroine, from scatological warrior to lascivious woman, and, ultimately, to the monstrous-feminine fiend.[19]

The theme of her gender—and sex too—as unsettled appeared frequently. Already the German *Kriegs Theater* had hinted at this in 1788, showing the empress as a cross-dresser, disturbing her socially construed and constructed gender. New images seemed to revise her biological body, a notion in alignment with Louise de Kéralio's claim that being a ruler changed a queen's sex[20] or made the status of her sex and gender an undecidable mix.

The Prussian Prizefighter is one instance of such undecidability. This print, produced like the *Stride* image, early in 1791, exposes Catherine's entire upper body and shows her participating in an activity reserved for men, a boxing match (Figure 10.3). But despite the flat chest, pronounced biceps, and heavy face of a man, her gender remains ambiguous in the picture. She wears the shoes and skirt of a woman and is accosted, as with the monkey's tail in the *Christian Amazon* (Figure 8.8), by a serpent-like, phallic braid, this time belonging to the Prussian king, who is "attempting to tame Imperial Kate," as the print's caption puts it. (Many of the English satires allude to lines from Shakespeare.) The print shows her as a man, but, importantly, the figures looking at her in the picture respond to her as a woman.

The image was successful enough to be replicated in a smaller format too, made by a less skilled engraver who merely copied the original picture as he saw it and so produced it in print as a mirror image, though the text engraver produced the legible reverse.[21] Evidently, using muddled sex and gender to represent Catherine's gender-bending power had sufficient frisson to be worth crafting the cheaper reproduction so that more viewers could be enthralled by the flagrant unsuitability of the powerful woman. Masculinized versions of Catherine concentrated on her face, giving her the heavy jaw, jutting nose, and prominent eyebrows, also seen and interpreted in an illustration from Lavater's books of physiognomy (Figure 8.3). The unruly ruling virago beckoned eyes and imaginations.

Figure 10.3 In *The Prussian Prizefighter*, though the half-naked Russian empress looks powerful, her sex is indeterminate. Source: *The Prussian Prize fighter and his Allies attempting to tame Imperial Kate | or the State of European Bruisers*. Digital Id cph 3g06765 //hdl.loc.gov/loc.pnp/cph.3g06765 Courtesy of the Library of Congress.

Final Eight Years 157

Ridiculous Heroine

The incongruity of eighteenth-century aristocratic femininity with fighting provided many of the gags that media workers used late in Catherine's reign, as earlier in both *Kriegs Theater* "Theater of War" (Figure 8.7) and *The Christian Amazon*. In *La Mascarade*, an anonymous French print maker satirized the very title "heroine of the north" that Voltaire had given Catherine II long before (Figure 10.4). The preening empress, one of the least distorted figures in the ensemble, greets caricatured figures of émigré supporters of the ancien régime who are fleeing for their lives. Portrayed with diminutive bodies and oversized heads, in the manner of Jacques Callot's dwarves, they wear masks with fixed grins and grimaces as they trundle toward Catherine, who looks up to the top of the approaching cart, where a huge rat labeled Louis XVI sits. At her feet kneels one of the highest-ranking members of the French royal family outside of France, the notorious womanizer Count of Artois, a brother of Louis XVI and a leader of the émigrés, and she fondles the masked count's large nose, an allusion both to his sexual reputation and to hers, an insinuation again of her alleged all-devouring sexual insatiability. Made diminutive in this picture, the empress could arouse more scorn and less fear. It was evidently a successful technique; a

Figure 10.4 In the anonymous *La Mascarade* (1791), Catherine II, receives dwarfish émigrés from revolutionary France; their identities are specified in a key below. Source: *La Mascarade* (1791). Public Domain. RESERVE QB-370 (26)-FT 4 [De Vinck, 4360] Identifier: ark:/12148/btv1b6948184g. Courtesy of the Bibliothèque nationale de France, Département estampes et photographie.

pirated copy of *La Mascarade* was also produced, hastily and crudely in reverse, and she appeared in a different later French print in similar style too.[22]

Lascivious Libertine

For a long time, allusions in print to Catherine's actual sexual behavior after the coup had been suppressed, though at least one oblique satirical reference to Catherine as a lascivious woman had been made in Britain as early as 1783. *The Ladies Church Yard* is based on the supposedly common use of graveyards as trysting spots for prostitutes with their customers. Among many tombs with epithets mocking the sexual behavior of famous British women is one in the background topped with a miniaturized portrait of the empress wearing her signature fur-trimmed dress. Her presence in the scene is a suggestion of libertinage, even though the words on her stone carefully refer only to her extravagance with money.[23] By 1787, such constraints on prurient depictions of the empress were ebbing, as indicated by the sexual allusions in *The Christian Amazon* and in James Gillray's *Amsterdam in a Dam'd Predicament*, in which she proposes a licentious reversal of the Ottoman Sultan's sexual economy, saying to him, "Blast you, you old Goat! to keep so many women shut up in your Seraglio. I'll turn over a new Leaf and allow every Woman 2000 Men."[24] Scurrilous sexuality, whether openly depicted or disguised, was an inherent element of celebrity discourse, and illicit sexual behavior was a favorite weapon of attack among caricaturists depicting the Russian empress.

It was the theme as well of a clumsily drawn print from 1789 or 1790 supporting the Brabant Revolution, an area of present-day Belgium that was part of the Habsburg Empire (Figure 10.5). In the image, an unimpressive Joseph II approaches Catherine, who, lounging under an outdoor canopy, her knees wide apart, lifts her skirt and casually invites the sexual attention of the distraught emperor. He shields his eyes from the sight of her genitals and complains in rhymed lines about the embarrassing loss of the Habsburg Empire's "beautiful low countries":[25]

> The Sultan laughs at me; the French King, Prussia,
> The English, the Dutch, You Madam in Russia,
> You all sold me for gold
> Yes, all, I see that I am fooled?

Catherine dismisses his accusation but demands,

> Look under my skirt. You will find them there,
> Else do not seek low countries anywhere.

The joke is not just that he will find only a map of the Austrian Low Countries rolled up near her feet, but more blatantly that beneath her skirt he will encounter her own lower regions between lasciviously spread legs. Her bland gaze directed at Joseph II and her allusive language indicate that the nonchalant sexual encounter would be nothing new to her.

Figure 10.5 *Tous mes beaux Pays-bas* (All my beautiful Low Countries) uses a pornographic image of Catherine II to depict the Austrian emperor's helpless inability to counter Belgian independence. Source: *Tous mes beaux Pays-bas*. Public Domain. http://hdl.handle.net/10934/RM0001.COLLECT.506443 Courtesy of the Rijksmuseum, Amsterdam.

Catherine's posture in the image resembles that of the urinating Maria Theresa in The *Queen of Hungary's Whetstone*; since none of the four male figures in that picture look toward the queen, however, the effect there is scatological rather than salacious.[26] By 1789 to 1790, however, with the publication in France of pornography that diminished the authority of the social elites, the obscene image of Catherine lifting her skirts both belittles the whining Austrian emperor and demeans and de-sanctifies the whore-like Russian empress.

Depictions of the tsarina as a lascivious libertine announced power between men and women as both exercised and represented in the form of sexuality, and thus readily available for celebrity discourse. The numerous prints that cited the *Stride* image, which was made a year or two after the Low Countries picture, implied this message and gave viewers the pleasure of knowledgeable recognition. In *An Amusing State of Uncertainty*, for example, Catherine is drawn as a composite from the prototype's two forms, her head taken from the English version and her bare breasts from the French (Figure 10.6). In the print, she is ready for bed and must choose between two suitors,

Figure 10.6 *An Amusing State of Uncertainty*, citing the head and bare breasts of *L'Enjambee Imperiale*, shows Catherine with two competing illicit suitors, the British politicians William Pitt "the Younger" and Charles James Fox. Source: *An Amusing State of Uncertainty*. Public Domain. Courtesy of The Lewis Walpole Library, Yale University.

two British politicians; foppish Prime Minister Pitt stands barefoot, bewigged, and half-dressed before her, while his hirsute archrival, Charles Fox, tries comically to hide under her chair, or, in another version, under her bed.[27] Strikingly, she is never the victim in these images. Often, she is physically large and in *An Amusing State* she is armed with a dagger as well.

Fox, famed womanizer whose politics the empress briefly admired, appeared in many satires with her. His name occurred also in the satirical sayings and verses about Catherine II that newspapers, lacking political cartoons, occasionally offered. In London, for example, *The World* satirized Catherine's imagined physical attraction to Fox by announcing the motto she had supposedly affixed to a bust of him that she had commissioned at a moment when the British politician appeared to be supporting her: "This Man, whom dearer than my Life I prize; / Charms by black Hair, black Eye-brows, and black Eyes."[28] Another issue of the paper sexualized Catherine's reception of the bust both in commentary and in rhymes, including one by "Countess of Friskiwowsky" that uses italics both for emphasis and to signal double entendres as it concludes:

> In *eloquence* he might prevail,
> But what's a *head* without a *tail*?[29]

Figure 10.7 Politics is represented as sexual activity in an anonymous British satirical print, *Saint Catharine and St. George*, with a whorish Catherine in charge. Source: *Saint Catharine and St. George*. Public Domain. Digital Id cph 3g06754 //hdl.loc.gov/loc.pnp/cph.3g06754, Courtesy of the Library of Congress.

Of course, such visual and textual metaphors of imagined amatory relations were different from the stories and gossip about actual love affairs that were gradually appearing in print, especially on the continent.

On April 15, 1791, three days after the *Stride* cartoon appeared, another anonymous print translated the maritime political struggle for control of the Black Sea into a carnal assault by Catherine II on the supine British king (Figure 10.7). To viewers who were already appalled by the empress, especially this late in her controversial reign, the image of the full-bodied and unsaintly empress astride George III, his phallic lance flat on the ground beside him, was legible to any slightly informed audience, literate or not. The offensive scene, degrading to her and to the king, could offer a satisfyingly severe and multilevel condemnation of Catherine. The accompanying words add entertaining puns, asserting she will "ride Saint George till he has fairly entered the Black C," a play with her name and her often dark reputation as well as with the military venture to the body of water shown in the background as a lake. The representation of Sweden has a similar salacious edge with the Swedish king, standing second from left, punning that the empress "shall have my Stock home"; it is, as Vincent Carretta remarks, "a promise his sword seems visually to reiterate."[30] Despite these clear allusions, however, the print offers no hint that the unctuous figure in the left foreground, Catherine's controversial and powerful minister, Prince Potemkin, had been or might still be her lover. There were lines yet to be crossed—mostly after Catherine's death.

Such pictures invoked men's anxieties about a woman in power and the power of women. They communicated a desire to punish the empress and, more broadly in many cases, to undermine the ruling class. As part of celebrity discourse, however, such pictures could carry the parasocial relation between empress and distant audience further into the realm of voyeurism, offering sexual stimulation or gratification by visual means, as Lou Charnon-Deutsch suggests.[31] The numerous fictional depictions of Catherine's sexual behavior, sometimes in veiled terms, enabled eighteenth-century audiences to enjoy what Cashmore calls the "collective voyeurism" typical of modern celebrity.[32]

Indecorous and Abject Being

Eighteenth-century political prints were, in Albert Boim's words, "a social weapon unmasking and ridiculing the pretensions of the powerful."[33] Grasping "at the gross material conditions of ordinary life" could be another way for caricatures to debunk the embodied empress. Her status as a paragon of courtly comportment could be jubilantly disrupted. In *Imperial Salute, or invitation to Peace Rejected*, for example, another anonymous print in near simultaneous French and English renditions, the imperious empress stomps indecorously toward a scabrous scene of Louis XVI kissing the large bare buttocks of a female figure personifying the French Revolution.[34]

Even more vividly, a rude and undignified Catherine, furious at the unexpected failure of the Prussians to defeat the army of the French Revolution, appears in Isaac Cruikshank's *Bobadil Disgraced or Kate in a Rage* (1792); the title refers to the cowardly braggart Captain Bobadil from a much-performed English play by Ben Jonson (Figure 10.8).[35] Here again, the tsarina is a fierce termagant, violently breaking all decorum by kicking at one man and forcefully toppling another; the kick, yet another *Stride* allusion, reveals not only an ankle but also one leg up to the garter above the empress's knee and a shocking tiny fraction of flesh beyond as well. While her clothing—especially a distinctive Russian head-dress, copied from a serious Catherine portrait,[36] and a white scarf modestly covering her décolletage—suggest proper femininity, her words indicate something quite different. She castigates a cringing general by saying, "I suppose you was frightened at their Naked A------sses," a reference to the popular name, sansculottes, of the male supporters of the revolution, wearers of working men's pantaloons rather than elite knee britches. She concludes, "Get out of my sight, or I'll send you and your Army------after my Husband," a reminder to viewers of Peter III's unforgotten sudden death. Nor is the unfortunate duke of Brunswick, whose phallic sword is given the usual thrust toward Catherine's crotch, the only target of the imperial ire. The other officer, whom she grasps by his pigtail, is, in the English print, the hapless king of Poland, who had just been intimidated into backing out of his country's most recent effort to resist Russian aggression. A French version was also made but retitled and with the pigtail figure labeled Francis II, the young new Habsburg emperor, whose aunt, Marie Antoinette, the French had guillotined just a few months earlier.[37]

Other differences between Cruikshank's original and the French copy in mirror image underscore that the scandalous depiction of the livid empress was the main interest in both. The impudent words of the English print are gone in the French one,

Figure 10.8 Cruikshank's *Bobadil Disgraced or Kate in a Rage* depicts a fierce and determined Catherine mistreating two military officers and transgressing the strictures on upper-class feminine decorum. The image turns the indecorous action of the *Stride* into an even more norm-flouting high kick. Source: Isaac Cruikshank, *Bobadill Disgraced or Kate in a rage—For Brunswick's Duke with Ninety Thousand men March'd into France and then!!—then March'd out again*. Courtesy of the British Museum; Museum number 1868,0808.6231

unnecessary because the image itself is so strong. The map in the background has lost its meaning, partly because it is confusingly shown in reverse, but mostly because the imperialist label "my share" above the line through France is missing. Most of all, in both images, the whole inventory of signs—Catherine's high kick, her fierce face and brawny outstretched arms, her attack on two men at once, and her harsh words—made her into a brazen and ill-mannered woman who must have evoked caustic laughter from many in her multinational audiences.

Both French and British visual satirists gloried in depicting not just misbehaving but abject royal bodies, excreting, farting, and vomiting. Farting, often represented as a blowing feather, and defecation became common motifs. Two French prints, one a reversed version of the other, with different figures under assault, depict rows of bare bottoms squirting excrement toward a crowd of rulers that includes Catherine II (Figure 10.9). In the version with the longer caption, three ranks of deputies to the French National Assembly aim their buttocks at the assembly's opponents; the representation of Catherine is again copied from the *Stride* print. Naked from the midriff up, she is prominent above the other targets of the spray, reaching forward as in the *Stride*, but this time with both hands. Opposite her the French king, sitting in the mouth of a canon, vomits downward toward his peers.

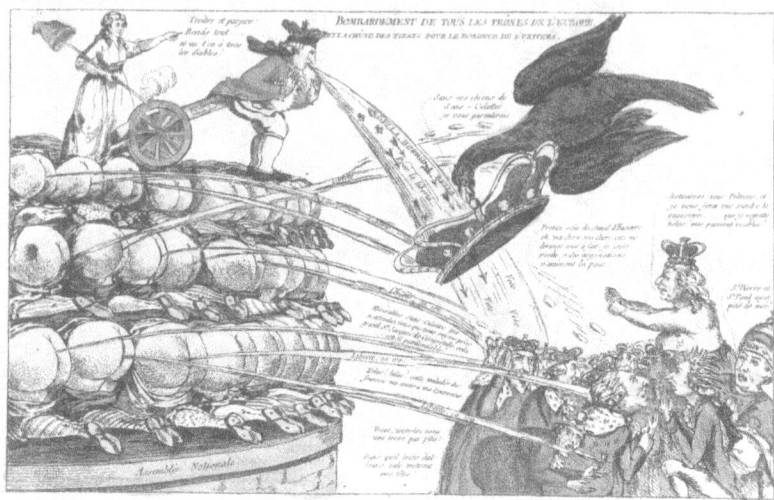

Figure 10.9 Catherine II, her upper body again echoing *L'Enjambee Imperiale*, is inserted here into a whole scene of abject revolutionary bodies raining excrement down on the rulers and leaders of Europe, who are only partially protected by a black imperial eagle and crown. Source: *Bombardement de tous les trônes de l'Europe et la chûte des tyrans pour le bonheur de l'univers*. Public Domain. Courtesy of The Elisha Whittelsey Collection, The Elisha Whittelsey Fund, 1962, Metropolitan Museum of Art, New York.

Monstrous-Feminine Body

There were other punitive satirical versions of the empress too, all keeping her vividly before the eyes of the public. From early in her reign, Catherine II had sometimes been understood as a horrific example of the monstrous-feminine. Her insipid readiness to hold a severed head in *Merlin: A Picture of Europe 1773* had been depicted roughly two decades before the often-savage satires connected with the French Revolution (Chapter 8). In *Jeu de Quilles*, for example, she is not just a representative of the old-fashioned ancien régime, as her dress signals; she is a hideous crone, her legs wide apart in tribute to the *Stride*, hairless except for her masculinizing mustache, but still threateningly wielding her scepter (Figure 5.5). She is an object of horror.

Another representation of Catherine II as horror is *The Northen Bugga Bo* (1791), again criticizing Russia's second war against the Turks (Figure 10.10). The colloquial word "bugaboo" in the anonymous print's triply misspelled title meant "a fancied object of terror."[38] Why the tsarina was terrifying is partly explained by her war aims, which seem modest at first but quickly become, like her figure dominating the page, vast and formidable: "The Empress only wants to secure her Back frontiers, and then she will Stretch over the Black Sea, Embrace with her Arms the Baltic, and deluge the Ottoman Empire."[39] Her disturbing immensity is then increased by the print's bold offenses against her gender and her sex. As viewers could notice at first glance,

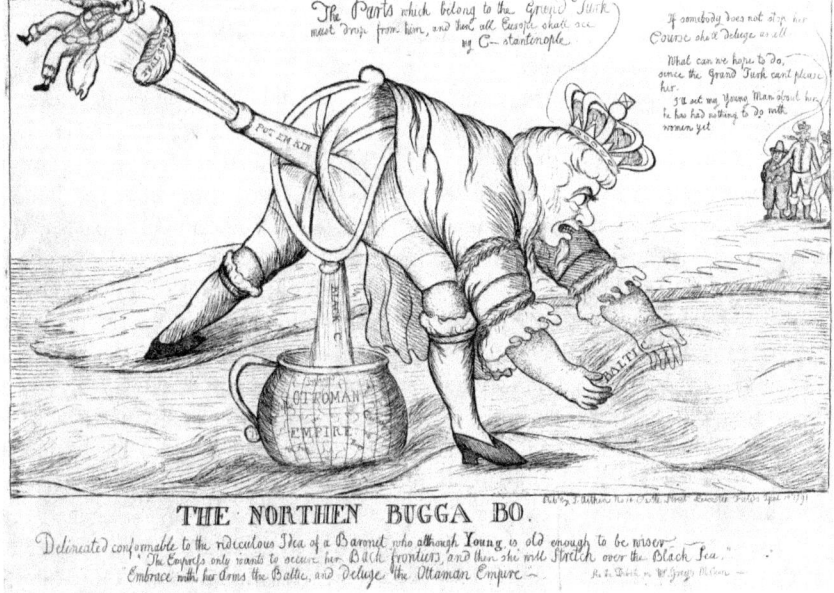

Figure 10.10 *The Northen Bugga Bo*, addressing Catherine's second war with the Ottomans, depicts her as a penis-equipped, gigantic, crowned figure wearing the empress's iconic dress and a peculiar, canon-like undergarment (the reverse of the canon in Figure 10.9). Since many elements in the print point clearly at the identity of the central figure, it is unlikely that the misspelling of "northern" was meant to reduce the danger of libel. Source: *The Northen Bugga Bo*, Courtesy of the British Museum; Museum number 1990,0623.19

though she wears the iconic fur-trimmed dress with frill-edged sleeves and feminine slippers, the etching allots masculinity to the empress by giving her a coarse face, hairy forearms, and a madly unfeminine posture: legs splayed again and bending over, her buttocks in the air. A second glance shows that she is pissing the punning "Black C" into a map-decorated pot labeled Ottoman Empire and that the piss gushes from the tip of her penis. Here is a bugaboo indeed.

And there is more. Although her dress is hitched up to the waist, her bottom is not bare; instead, she wears a bizarre undergarment of wrappings from which a canon-like protrusion emerges labeled Pot En Kin, a slight coding of Potemkin. A fiery fart explodes from this misplaced phallic contraption, blasting a small figure part way out of the frame of the print; it is the sultan, his turban decorated with an oversized feather labeled "Grand Turk." Adding to this, the varying sizes of the words, the capitalizations, and the abbreviations all seem to make Catherine's speech, as she reaches into the Baltic, sexually suggestive: "The Parts which belong to the Grand Turk must drop from him, and then all Europe shall see my C—nstantinople." Two other figures make clear that this masculinized bugaboo is still simultaneously a sexually insatiable, devouring female. A tiny figure on the right edge of the image asks, "What can we hope to do, since the Grand Turk can't please her," and another answers: "I'll set my Young Man about her. He has had nothing to do with Women yet." In this extremely hostile, sexualized discourse, the powerful empress had become a man and yet again also an insatiable all-devouring monstrous woman.

The monstrous, all-devouring female could appear hiding behind proprieties too, as in Isaac Cruikshank's sardonically titled *Royal Recreation*, inspired by an event that occurred on November 4, 1794 (Figure 10.11). On the outskirts of Warsaw, in the town of Praga, the Russian army carried out a notorious massacre of some 20,000 civilians.[40] Europe answered with revulsion, much of it directed at Catherine. In Cruikshank's merciless cartoon, a muscular and demented-looking general is reporting to her about the Polish town, his still bloody sword tucked under his arm. In his hands he holds by the hair two clusters of severed heads of women and children; three assistants follow bringing more loads of heads. Catherine, nicely dressed, with a modest covering over her hair and a frock that is not low-cut, sleeves to the elbow trimmed in a frilly ruffle, sits demurely on a throne. Scepter, ermine mantle (although in one rendering it is colored to look more like leopard), and a bear, squatting tamely beside her to signify Russia, must have made her identity unmistakable at a glance. Opposite the bear, observing gloomily, is the unfortunate sculpted bust of Charles Fox.

Yet even the attack on Praga's civilian population, which concentrated viciousness into a single repellant episode, could contribute to Catherine's always ambiguous celebrity

Figure 10.11 Late in Catherine II's reign, Isaac Cruikshank's *Royal Recreation* satirized her repulsively celebrating the slaughter of Polish women and children. Source: Isaac Cruikshank, *Royal Recreation*. Public Domain. Courtesy of The Lewis Walpole Library, Yale University.

among fans and anti-fans; to both groups, the formidable empress in *Royal Recreation* may have exhibited the elusive "it," the combination of seemingly incompatible qualities that, as Joseph Roach claims, a celebrity brings together.[41] Cruikshank's image of the empress entwines maternity and cruelty, dominance and submission, potency and vulnerability, and matches fastidious femininity with the ancient notion of a monster female's pleasure in ghastly devourings. The image of the improperly striding colossus empress made in 1791 had been shocking, but it was less repulsive and frightening than the decorous empress presiding over the grisly scene that Cruikshank devised.

This Catherine II does not look ugly or depraved and has no grotesque bodily characteristics, not even a vile face like her general. Yet she is depicted as utterly cruel and vicious. She accepts her general's tribute with evident enjoyment, and, savoring her power, reaches out to finger one of the bodiless heads on the chin. The gesture and her visible pleasure can only be read as monstrous, revolting, and despicable. Cruikshank's caricature effectively represents gender issues that long swirled around many constructions of the mighty empress, that added shocked buzz to the celebrity discourse she evoked, and that late in her reign often provoked horror as well.[42]

In 1795, some months after the Praga massacre, George Galloway's angry poem "Tears of Poland" furiously criticized the empress, deploying familiar tropes of sexual enthrallment to warn of her aggressiveness:

This Cleopatra holds you as her own;
And courts no more now deem their State secure,
From this arch Amazonian, Babylonian whore.[43]

Galloway was referring to Rev. 17.1-2, which states, "the kings of the earth have committed fornication" with this "great whore," and "the inhabitants of the earth have been made drunk with the wine of her fornication." Little wonder that the Scottish poet continued irately in the next line by admonishing his readers to "mark her monstrous strides." With these words, he was reminding them again of the political cartoon that long fueled attention to Catherine's sexuality.

A particularly obscene Polish cartoon, entitled *Catherine's Mealtime*, apparently survives only in a written description, vivid in its extreme savagery:

The empress sits alone at the table. From one side some Cossacks offer her the still bloody limbs of Swedes, Poles und Turks, whom they have just murdered. On the other side lies a row of young, naked men side by side, like barrels in a wine cellar, and by means of a specific manual operation an old woman draws from these living kegs a juice which she catches in a goblet and hands to the empress for her to drink. Below this despicable caricature are some verses worthy of it. One can with a little decency translate them thus: Since you love men so much, eat their flesh and drink their purest blood![44]

This is a visual satire of utmost debauchery and depravity, depicting Catherine as practicing cannibalism and drinking semen, as made clear in the verse the narrator paraphrases. It is a ferocious representation of men's fears of being devoured by the insatiable libertine empress, fears that can only be contained by being rendered visible and shown as horrible. Lynn Hunt, in her studies of eighteenth-century pornography, stresses the philosophical and political elements of such images and texts during the ancien régime, arguing that they make vivid "the irrationalities of the ancien régime moral system" and suggest "the feminization of both the aristocracy and monarchy."[45] A print such as this Polish one may have had very limited circulation, but if it did reach celebrity's non-elite public further west, it gave its viewers an extraordinarily potent opportunity to revile the powerful woman and her alleged voracity.

Some accounts of the Russian empress's willingness to use blood-spattered force probably elicited a level of revulsion that celebrity discourse could barely absorb. Yet Galloway's "Tears of Poland," though it aims to excoriate the empress, used such rich language and energetic metaphors, that it perhaps roused imaginations as well as ratified indictments at least among well-educated readers. His label of Catherine as "Hercalian Jezebel" alludes both to the dangerous feminine sensuality of the Biblical woman and to the Byzantine emperor Hercalius, who, like Catherine, fought against Islam; the warrior empress, however, flame-breathing, also wages war on men:

Far to the North, . . . Where pining frost grasps an eternal hold, . . .
'Tis here resides the 'Hercalian Jezebel,
Who's mouth breathes war, hot as th' flames of hell:
For since she slew her husband,—the just Czar,
'Gainst Adam's Race she's wag'd eternal war.

In addition to calling Catherine's murdered husband "the just Czar," the verses vividly describe the fearsomeness of her military engagements with border areas.

See! bounding Baltic pours a crimson flood,
From coasts where human carcases are strew'd.
See! Poland's streams, their fertile banks run o'er
Luxuriant field! now dy'd with human gore.

To Galloway, Catherine II is a grotesquely over-powerful and oversized female ruler, whose "awful feet" tread on "Europe's isles," whose fist squeezes Sweden and Denmark, and who makes "Whole Empires tremble, Kingdoms, Kings, and States." With the assertion that Catherine "wallows in blood, fair Poland to deflow'r," her cruelty is tied to her loathsome appropriation of masculine aggression in the form of rape, classic indicators of the monstrous-feminine.[46] The poem is an elaboration in words of such visual satires as the "Royal Recreation" and "Catherine's Meal." Grabbing one item after another from history's well-stocked misogynist supply of depraved female examples and images, the poet proclaims Catherine II the almost unnamable "vile infernal she." Even though the varied satirical representations of the empress—as androgynous, ridiculous, lascivious, abject or monstrous—could not offer the usual "spectatorial pleasure and identification" that celebrity discourse promises,[47] it could claim to unveil her secret motives or make plain her horridness, and this could be the compelling stuff of celebrity too.

11

Still Relishing the Failed Marriage, the Coup, and Its Deadly Aftermath

Far from Russia, in the early years of the French Revolution, the Austrian police confiscated a poem containing a brief and slangy reference to the "the Russian Kathy / who is so precious to ye," but who deposed and murdered her husband.[1] The verses assumed that the general populous of listeners in Vienna would know enough to understand the poem's condensed reference to Catherine the Great's long-past history. A book for a more privileged French audience a few years later, in the last months of Catherine's reign, likewise asserted "tout le monde" still knew about the overthrow that the dysfunctional marriage had helped precipitate thirty-four years earlier.[2] From 1762 until 1765, a scandalized first round of coup narratives and accounts of the imperial marriage had reached a large European audience in ephemera such as newspapers, magazines, and pamphlets, most of which disappeared as scrap once they lost currency.

For almost the next two decades little new was added to the story in print. When it began to reappear, it was embedded in larger narrative forms: autobiographies, travel books, current events accounts, schoolbooks, engraved political satires, novels, newspaper items, political tracts, and more. After the death of Catherine II in 1796, and until 1810, a cascade of piquant new versions of the marriage and coup was published as additional biographers, playwrights, and novelists—often taking a severe tone—joined in the posthumous commodification of the empress. Most of all, after the initial reporting about Catherine's marriage and the ousting of her husband, succeeding narratives offered her distant public the potentially enthralling intimate disclosures, fictive or factual, that are characteristic of celebrity discourse.

When fantasies about the renowned tsarina wafted toward the private and intimate, three pleasures in particular were offered to readers, listeners, and beholders. First was the voyeuristic frisson of prying (even just imaginatively) into an area that people ordinarily kept out of public view. Precisely because celebrity is "mediated," not conducted face-to-face, it could (and can) enable fans to attain a feeling of intrusively private, secret knowledge of a famed person, indeed more intimate than occurred among real-life acquaintances in ordinary interpersonal circumstances. In celebrity discourse, this prying includes savoring stories of innermost relationships, both thriving and crumbling, whether depicted in words or images, whether invented or factual. For Catherine II's fans and anti-fans, the story of her marriage provided that indulgence. Second was the pleasure of penalty-free identification with characters in the stories—in Catherine's case, with her, with her husband, or with her paramours. Third was the often self-righteous happiness, and sometimes the challenge, of being the judge but from a safe distance. Media workers produced representations of the empress that beguiled audiences with exactly these three pleasures, and the sheer numbers of accounts in different languages and genres, their staggered publication over time, their skillful use of narrative, and their diverse and often scandalous content meant that Catherine II's distant audience remained familiar with her long-ago marital strife and its drastic consequences.

The Dribble and Then Flood of Curiosity-Stoking Texts

Among the new versions of Catherine II's marriage story, the one that was probably most read was first published in 1784. Its author, a Cambridge-educated Englishman, William Coxe, visited Russia in 1778 and snooped eagerly for fresh details about the relationship between the tsar and his wife and about Catherine's takeover of power.[3] Coxe's much-reprinted version of events, tucked into his *Travels into Poland, Russia, Sweden and Denmark*, fit celebrity discourse's notion of stars who were simultaneously fabulous and ordinary. After its publication in London and after it was promptly pirated in Dublin, Coxe's book appeared in a second edition in 1785, a third in 1787, a fourth beginning in 1790, a fifth in 1802, a sixth in 1803, and yet another in 1808, with the number of volumes per edition ranging from two to five.[4] Meanwhile translations were also popping up, again in multiple editions, and extracted versions as well.[5] Coxe claimed that his book contained "the first circumstantial account ever published of this extraordinary revolution."[6] Because many of his sources were still living in Catherine II's Russia, where the writer's brother and part of his wife's family also resided, Coxe delayed publishing part of the information until after Catherine's death.[7]

In 1788 and 1789, two other reports of the marriage and the coup appeared, also in multiple editions and translations. One was the autobiography of Johann Ludwig Hordt (1719–98), a Swedish count who wrote favorably about both the tsar and the tsarina. Taken captive by the Russians during the Seven Years' War while he was serving as a Prussian military officer, he had been freed by Peter III and was invited often to his dinner table, an opportunity for detailed observations.[8] The other account was in a book of caustic political analysis, *Du péril de la balance politique de l'Europe*, published in English translations as *The Danger of the Political Balance of Europe*. The identity of the understandably anonymous author provoked immediate speculation.[9] A German reviewer of the French original had heard that the author was a Geneva political pamphleteer, a description that could fit Jacques Mallet du Pan, to whom the book is now often attributed.[10] But an English reviewer accepted the proposal that *Danger* might be the work of the king of Sweden, Gustav III, "or, at least, that it contains his sentiments, and that it is, therefore, in some degree, if not wholly, to be considered as his majesty's performance."[11] Royal author, or not, the little book shows that details of the imperial coup d'état still grabbed attention almost three decades after it happened. The very proliferation of inconsistent, but delectable, stories added abundantly to the celebrity buffet of transgressive treats that seemed to grant readers and listeners the intimate information and connection they sought.

With Catherine II's death in 1797, an additional crop of coup narratives appeared, some containing calumnies that her agents previously had blocked from publication. When her son and successor Tsar Paul attempted to restore the reputation of his putative father, he signaled the end of enforced respect for his mother and allowed old slanders to reappear. Publications ranging from the untidy *Fragmens historiques sur Pierre III et Catherine II* (Historical Fragments about Peter III and Catherine II) to a basket of biographies of both Peter III and Catherine II could sustain the ongoing commodity value of the two contending monarchs, but especially of the empress. Some of the concoctions were bland, such as two by the Germans Seume and Andrä, who lifted long passages from the same sources so that at many spots their books were almost word for word alike. Some reinforced representations of Peter III's bizarre personality, adding claims about his sexual failure and reporting an operation intended to address it, and some provided new grounds to harbor dark suspicions of Catherine II.

One of the most popular later narratives, often reprinted and retranslated, was the long awaited little *Histoire, ou Anecdotes sur la révolution de Russie en 1762*, by Claude-Carloman de Rulhière. It had been written with blithe coquettish verve in 1768. Anecdotes, as a form of brief story about specific individuals in real places, were popular in the eighteenth century and, then, as now, could be conducive to celebrity, especially when picking up the themes of troubled relationships, fabulous wealth, exoticism, transgressive gender, and even transgressive sexuality and crime. Catherine's deputies had wrested an agreement from Rulhière that his account would not be published during her life, but Rulhière, reading his manuscript aloud in the salons of Paris and beyond, had publicized it in the space between public and private where current events could be discussed and where eye witnesses could be raconteurs. "I was upon the spot," Rulhière proclaimed in the opening sentence of his text, "and an eye-witness of the Revolution, which hurled the grandson of Peter the Great from the throne of all the Russias, and placed a female stranger upon it."[12] After Catherine's death, the book immediately appeared in print, and, though some readers supposedly met it with "scorn and contempt" because of its "shallowness, insipidity and addiction to slander,"[13] the volume gave audiences in countries across Europe chances to snicker and talk. Newspaper advertisements for the book, as well as the editor's preface, cannily stressed its previously forbidden status, a claim that was repeated in the French, German, and Dutch editions in 1797 and the English one in 1798,[14] and it soon served as an unacknowledged treasure trove that others plagiarized, summarized, and excerpted.[15] (Its details about Catherine's love affairs as grand duchess are treated in Chapter 13.)

Meanwhile, Jean-Henri Castéra, an agent in the French diplomatic service who had worked in Poland and visited Russia during Catherine's lifetime, rushed a biography of the tsarina into print in France, and his well-informed English translator, William Tooke, made additions to the text that were then included in all future editions, in multiple languages. Their account, written with lubricious flair and using motifs similar to those in lascivious novels such as *Les Liaisons Dangereuses*, became the definitive biography of Catherine for the end of the eighteenth and the first half of the

Figure 11.1 The stipled illustration in one of the numerous biographies of the empress brings Peter and Catherine together again and notes that, while he was emperor for six months, she reigned for thirty-five years. Her head is an iteration of a much used type on one of her medals (Figure 7.2), but here she is clothed in the fur-trimmed dress and given an older appearance. Source: John Chapman, *Peter III. Feodorovitch, Emperor of Russia, reigned VI Months. Catherine II. Alexievna, Empress of Russia. Reigned xxxv Years*, frontispiece in [Castéra and Tooke], *Life of Catharine II*. 3rd ed. (London: Longman, 1799). Public Domain. Volume belonging to author, R. Dawson; photo by author.

nineteenth centuries. Most editions were enriched with portraits of the key participants in Catherine's life. Peter III's image had long been suppressed in most publications, but now he reappeared (Figure 11.1).

Another of the posthumous narratives that readers might consume about the marriage of Peter and Catherine was a book published in both German and French and allegedly composed by a German former employee of the Russian court, Caspar von Saldern (1711–86). As one of the few Germans of his time who rose from the lower classes into the honorary aristocracy, Saldern had smuggled himself into Russia late in Elizabeth's reign, quickly insinuated his way into Grand Duke Peter's circle, and become Russia's representative at a peace conference in Berlin in 1762, an appointment that kept him away from St. Petersburg as the overthrow occurred; Catherine sent him packing in about 1774.[16] According to the preface, Saldern, having supposedly written the manuscript for Paul's later enlightenment about his much maligned father, dispatched it to an unnamed friend, who then gave it to an editor after Saldern's death, though with the suspicious stipulation that it not be published until after Catherine had died too.

Obviously dubious are the references that "Saldern" makes to situations occurring long after his demise.[17] As in the complex authorial and editorial truth claims of many eighteenth-century epistolary novels, the book evidently had either a ghostwriter or an amplifying editor. In its effort to disparage Catherine—"victorious iniquity hoisted itself triumphantly onto the throne"—it decried all the texts that criticized Peter III after the coup as the "despicable work of paid traitors," whose pens were "dipped in the poison of calumny, in order to write a defamation of the victim and give themselves the appearance of justice before the amazed eyes of Europe."[18] The former tsar's adherents could only sigh, "good, noble man, you deserved a better fate and a better wife." This book, despite its title as "biography of Peter the Third . . . for the unbiased scrutiny of the effect of the . . . revolution and for correcting the judgment of Catherine II's character," contains mostly censure of Catherine.

Further important additions to the growing library of volumes that could promote Catherine II's posthumous fame were by another anonymous defender of Peter III, Gustav Adolf Wilhelm Helbig. A lesser diplomat from Saxony about whom remarkably little is known, he reached Russia only about 1787 but nonetheless eagerly sniffed out new details about Peter and Catherine and included them in two books, one a series of biographical sketches of the many women and men who had been favorites of the tsars over the whole eighteenth century and the other a digression-filled, scandalous, and sometimes brutally critical biography of Potemkin,[19] that was first published in serial form beginning in 1797.[20] Re-shaped into a book, it was translated, still without attribution, into French, Dutch, and, much-revised, into English.[21] Jean Charles Thieboult de Laveaux, the French consul in charge of commercial relations with Russia from 1761 to 1773,[22] quarried both Helbig and Rulhière to write his "secret history" of Catherine II's lovers.[23]

Both Rulhière and Laveaux announced that their books belonged to this popular genre, which emphasized the revelation of things previously concealed. Indebtedness to sixth-century prototype, Procopius's *Anekdota*, was acknowledged whenever titles contained either "secret history," as in Laveaux's *Histoire secrete des amours et des principaux amans de Catherine II*, or "anecdotes," as in Rulhière's *Histoire, ou Anecdotes sur la révolution de Russie en 1762*. Readers' enjoyment of such books, and passages in books, required no foreknowledge of Russian history, no interest in European political issues, and no sober analysis of ethical dilemmas. Composed in a tone of light conversation, secret histories, a superb vehicle for celebrity discourse, claimed to tell truthful though scurrilous stories of real contemporaries in positions of power, typically positing powerful men as vicious and powerful women as sexually promiscuous.[24] As scandal memoirs that either openly named the individuals allegedly depicted or disguised them in ways easily recognizable to the public, secret histories were designed for the pleasure—not the intellectual or moral edification—of the reader, who was often privileged and female.[25] Still, the claim that hidden, private forces had powerful political effects provided a sheen of legitimacy to the sexual material that the new accounts included. The tomes by Coxe, Hordt, and the *Danger* author before Catherine's demise, and Rulhière, "Saldern," Helbig, Laveaux, and others after it, all revel at least partly in secret history.

Skillful Narratives

Beginning a few years after the coup, texts about Catherine II's marriage and seizure of power faced the difficulty of effectively retelling a story that much of the public already knew, at least in outline. To increase the salability of their texts to broad audiences, the writers of such accounts resorted to a wider range of narrative techniques than the initial reports had used. To their two intriguing primary characters, Peter and Catherine, they added a platter of better developed secondary ones, including some who had become well known in the meantime; they used well-chosen narrators, noted unresolved questions, and offered multiple plots, all well spiced with scenes, digressions, and retarding moments that make narratives interesting. They also tended to note transgressive behavior in the compelling realms of gender and sexuality. Tumultuous relationships, often in the form of tensions between norms for (gendered) individuals and those for (also gendered) pairs, are common themes in celebrity materials, enthralling areas of negotiation between hyperindividualized figures. The feelings and behavior toward each other of the central agents in the coup narratives were a rich opportunity to depict an unhappy marriage and to add titillating sexual stories that earlier hints of son Paul as a bastard had only implied. The new accounts added further salacious material: medical detail that undercut Peter's masculinity and peculiar conspiracy theories about Peter's death.

Choice of narrator mattered. Many of the texts that appeared after the first few years of Catherine's reign use an external narrator, one who is not a character, and who can thus jump between events happening simultaneously in different locations. Rulhière's use of such a narrator enabled him to obscure the question of exactly which coup events, if any, he had actually witnessed; his external narrator maintains the same authoritative, though mildly japing, tone throughout.

Other texts deploy a personal narrator, a character internal to the story. Such a narrator is almost obligatory in an autobiography, and Anton Friedrich Büsching's example, probably written with the aide of diaries, shows the effectiveness of a personal narrator in writing about Catherine. Büsching's long passage about the coup begins as the narrator, pastor of one of the Lutheran churches in St. Petersburg (meanwhile he had become a school director and geographer in Berlin), was returning in his coach from making calls on the sick. Hearing a distant rumble that sounded disturbingly like a noisy crowd, he ordered the coachman to take him home. Once there, he and his wife Polyxene Christiana (who would soon be writing to her friend in Germany about discussing literature with Catherine II—Chapter 6) hurried to the corner room of their apartment:

> We opened the windows toward the Kazan Cathedral across the way where we saw an immense crowd, with uniformed and half-uniformed members of the guard regiments on foot and on horseback mixed together with the crowd of common people. In their midst was a simple coach drawn by only two horses. After a few minutes a lady dressed in black and wearing the order of St. Catherine came out of the church and seated herself in the coach, at the same moment that the bells of the cathedral began to ring and the priests and their attendants emerged from the church, holding their crosses, and surrounded the coach. Now we recognized the empress, who greeted the people on both sides.[26]

This is a recognition scene with a good choice of detail.

Coxe had sought to validate including "little circumstances" of a kind that might be thought "unworthy of the historian's notice" by arguing that "great events frequently turn upon [such details]; and they often discover the true character of the principal personages concerned in the scene."[27] This notion justified the composition of accounts that meshed with celebrity discourse, narratives full of personal and supposedly telling details that give the reader a sense of familiarity even with someone at great geographical and social remove. Büsching, from his exactly described viewpoint, provides the precise information and trivial details that could enable fans to fantasize themselves as present long ago in Saint Petersburg too. Within the flow of Büsching's narrative, the combination of setting and event and even sound at the cathedral make a textual "scene," a passage that "clearly attempts to imitate the space and time inhabited by events and characters"[28] and implicitly invites readers to join in the experience in their imaginations. Both external narrators, who figuratively stand outside the events, and internal narrators, who are simultaneously characters in the narrative, appear frequently in celebrity materials, then and now.

The internal narrator's specific angle of view can add to the credibility and visual effectiveness of a scene, as when Büsching reports: "The procession passed in front of our house, past the new stone winter palace and then the old wooden one, and common Russians called scornfully to us: Your god (they meant the tsar) is dead! Others said: he is gone, we don't want to have him any longer."[29] The derisive words of the passersby retard the narrative's advance in the Büsching text and increase the scene's memorability for readers while also providing them exactly the sense of inside knowledge that nurtures celebrity. The best coup narratives are full of such scenes. Büsching's internal narrator provides the corresponding anxious point of view of a foreigner in a city undergoing a dangerous transition.

Coxe, on the other hand, used an external narrator, one who does not question Catherine's methods or motives at the coup and thus subtly signals his sympathy with her, probably bending the perception of readers toward that point of view as well. The narrator in the text by Helbig, reporting the same events, is slightly cynical, suggesting Catherine's behavior before the soldiers was a deliberately manipulative performance in which "she employed all the feminine arts for arousing sympathy and gaining followers. It was successful. The crowd enlarged around her like a snowball."[30] Narrators who, like Helbig, suspect the truthfulness or sincerity of a star are not rare in celebrity discourse and appear most often when there are transgressions to report.

Büsching's inclusion of the distinctive implications of the coup for himself could further draw readers into his experience, especially with brief instances of dialogue, which, according to narrative theory, produce small "detours" that generate suspense.[31] On the second day of the coup, for example, just before he was to step into the chancel to preach, an official arrived with the command that people in the church were immediately to begin swearing fidelity to Catherine as tsar. Büsching knew that Catherine was claiming the crown, but he argued the coup might even then be collapsing, to which the official retorted: "'Herr Doctor, you are too anxious.' 'What,' said I, 'can one be too anxious in such circumstances? Who had freed us from the oath that we swore to the Emperor, to risk and sacrifice even the last drop of our blood for him?'" The official however was undeterred. "'Oh,' he said, 'don't you know the emperor? Do you think that he will resist? For certain, everything at Peterhof and Oranienbaum has been worked out already and he is no longer our emperor.' And that in fact seemed probable to me (and was confirmed by that evening)."[32]

Büsching's narrator's understated agreement that Peter would offer no effective resistance and the parenthetical confirmation of that assessment are powerful messages about the low esteem of both speakers for Peter's competence within dominant eighteenth-century expectations of political figures and gender schemas. A tsar should defend his status and a man should resist submitting to a woman's authority, especially his wife's. The two speakers' verified expectation of Peter's spinelessness was simultaneously a confirmation of Catherine's tsar-like, but unfeminine, fortitude and another moment in the celebrity-sustaining gender shock that had marked coup reports from the beginning and that still could be effective with readers decades later. It was a moment especially suited to an "I-witness" narrator.

The manageably short list of other characters served as contrasts to the two vivid protagonists and performed useful functions in the plot, and their roles in several cases were reevaluated in the later accounts. Princess Ekaterina Dashkova, for example, whose performance during the coup was mostly admired in first-stage reports, found her participation disparaged later as a romantic exaggeration. Her sister, Elizaveta Vorontsova, Peter's mistress, continued to be vilified, especially by Peter's supporters, who blamed her for the tsar's panic at Cronstadt.[33] In many accounts, the old warrior, Burkhard Christoph von Münnich,[34] whom Peter had only recently recalled from exile in Siberia, became a hero, seeking to encourage the disheartened tsar: "'Go forth,' said he, 'put yourself at the head of the troops you have with you, or go forth alone; address the two regiments that are marching against you: Tell them you are their sovereign, the grandson of Peter the Great; ask them if they have been aggrieved, and assure them of full redress.'"[35] But Peter was shown as incapable of such audacity. At a key point, according to Coxe's version, Catherine may have vacillated too, though it was never held against her. When wakened with the news that one of the conspirators had been arrested, she "shuddered at the advice to precipitate the hour of action: her resolution at this awful crisis, when immediate decision was necessary, seemed for a moment to fail, and she hesitated to assent." Having neatly evoked the common narrative motif of time running out, the account continues that Catherine "traversed the garden to the place where the carriage was waiting for her [and] was conveyed with all speed to Petersburgh."[36]

Unhappiness, Weakness, and Discord

For readers interested in celebrity discourse, the multiple late accounts of the coup and the posthumous accounts as well continued the previous depiction of the relation of Peter III and Catherine II as an unhappy marriage, a theme that has become standard fare in celebrity discourse. Peter III, Catherine's main narrative foil, provided a contrast to her words, personality, emotions, desires, and relationships; material about him was a late-arriving bonanza for fans, anti-fans, and potential fans, anyone wanting to ascertain more about the empress. Now they could ponder again the conduct and emotions of each spouse. Count Hordt stated bluntly: "Nothing can better exhibit the character of Peter III. than his foolish behaviour to Catharine."[37] Peter forced her, for instance, to invest his mistress with a chivalric order reserved for women; the result, Hordt speculated, may have been that Catherine, "much indisposed," began planning the overthrow.[38] Some writers tried to offer the couple belated advice. Basedow's schoolbook asserted Catherine could have been "a leader" to Peter, though under the more gender-appropriate "appearance of a companion," adding enticingly but vaguely that Peter "had the particular weaknesses that are not compatible with absolute power (if the empire is not to decline)."[39] Coxe, emphasizing the contrast between clownish emperor and decorous empress, noted that Peter's insults, no less than his deference, equally attracted opprobrium to himself, and popularity to Catherine. Because Peter was indiscrete and his mistress imprudent, Catherine, having quickly learned of his dangerous intentions, could "seize the decisive moment of enterprize, and secure her safety by preventing the designs of her husband."[40]

Overconfidence, *Danger* argued, led Peter to overlook "the first clouds" of the tempest that ruined him, including rumors deliberately circulated by Catherine's side that "poisoned the public discourse, and prepared the way for a revolution."[41] But *Danger* also defended the tsar by blaming his military obsession on his unsatisfactory relation with Catherine and arguing that the lack of understanding between Peter and his wife left the prince without domestic solace; in this setting, compulsively exercising his German troops was his only recourse.[42] Coxe contrasted Peter's military fetish with Catherine's simultaneous effort at self-education, when she "employed her hours of leisure in a course of assiduous study, and particularly applied herself to those authors who were most eminent for political knowledge."[43] The English writer ascribed qualities to her that were likely to fit the preferences of distant middle-class readers, mentioning her "mild and insinuating manners, her engaging address, the graces of her person, her unwearied assiduities, and a perpetual fund of interesting conversation."[44]

The coup further garishly illuminated the differences between husband and wife: "The vigor and celerity with which the empress acted in effecting the revolution, could only be exceeded by the pusillanimity and meanness with which Peter resigned the crown."[45] One narrator scolded that instead of facing his renegade wife, Peter "fell to the feet of the empress in the garden at Oranienbaum, covered his face with his hands and begged with a stream of tears for his life and the retention of his Holstein domains."[46] As it had been in the very earliest accounts, Peter's ineffective performance of eighteenth-century royal masculinity remained a theme.

His passionate admiration for the king of Prussia, for example, could be read as confirming his masculinity and dominance—until carried to excess, suddenly producing the effect of submission and effeminacy. When Peter III as tsar spoke publicly of Frederick II "in a tone of exultation, under the appellation of 'the King, my master,'" he bizarrely undercut the expectation of strength that prevailing gender schemas would have granted him.[47] Peter so idolized the Prussian king—even while Frederick II was Russia's key enemy in the Seven Years' War—that he sometimes wore a Prussian military uniform the king had sent him and typically wore an at least Prussian-inspired one. According to Rulhière, the effect of this highly political version of men's clothing, still innovative in the mid-eighteenth century, was ridiculous: "His spatterdashes, which he wore continually, were so tight that they cramped the motion of his knees, and obliged him to sit and to walk all in a piece. A hat, of prodigious size, fantastically cocked, covered a small, ugly, and crabbed countenance."[48] After watching Peter III riding with a contingent of soldiers, sitting straight and "stiff as a wooden image" with his face turned rigidly to the right, Büsching commented: "At that time and when I saw him in a Prussian regimental uniform, he seemed so dim-witted (*kleingeistisch*) that I would have been depressed if I had not already known from history that regents more often have small minds rather than great ones."[49] Such published characterizations of Peter III's appearance told against him as ruler and man.

Worse yet, during the coup itself, Peter's pretensions to military greatness vanished pathetically. New details about the distraught tsar's hours of useless dithering include Coxe's claim that when he eventually sailed to Cronstadt Fortress seeking assistance, he was wearing his Prussian regimentals, but for his humiliating return, "too late," he put on Russian military garb.[50] Meanwhile, as was well known, Catherine from the start of her march against her husband "dressed herself in the ancient uniform of the [Russian] guards"[51] and thus communicated her dedication to Russian values. Indeed, Peter's most energetic defender during Catherine's lifetime, the author of *Danger*, simply omitted the Cronstadt calamity from his account of the coup.

Catherine's cross-dressing, unlike Peter's Prussian masquerade, signaled her ability to assume a masculine role. As usual, given the higher status of masculine qualities in patriarchal societies, it was (and is) not rare for a woman of influence, such as cross-dressed eighteenth-century Catherine, to gain by appearing to have such abilities. Peter, in contrast, when he seemed in any way feminine, demonstrated qualities generally less admired, especially in a man whose masculinity was dented and damaged. Cross-dressing thus strengthened Catherine (given her status as a woman), whereas notes of femininity seriously weakened Peter (given his status as a man).

Portraits of the husband and wife, various writers suggested, reinforced the issue. Coxe described a painting he was told bore "a striking resemblance" of Peter. It depicted the tsar "in his Holstein uniform; the complexion is fair, and the hair light; there is no expression in the features, and the countenance is effeminate."[52] In contrast, another writer, Nathaniel William Wraxall in his travel book, described the huge painting that Catherine commissioned of herself after the coup:

> She is habited in the Russian uniform, booted, and sits astride on a white horse. In her hat is the oaken bough, which she wore at the memorable revolution which placed her on the throne, and which was likewise taken by all her adherents. Her long hair floats in disorder down her back; and the flushing in her face, the natural effect of the heat and fatigue she had undergone, is finely designed.[53]

Still Relishing the Failed Marriage 179

Figure 11.2 The volume of Voltaire's correspondence with Catherine II included the first print, by Jean Baptiste Fosseyeux, that showed a small excerpt of Erichsen's great equestrian painting of the empress conducting her coup against Peter III. Source: Jean Baptiste Fosseyeux, *Catherine II. Imperatrice de toutes les Russies*. Courtesy of the British Museum; Museum number 1891,0511.284.

The traveler Bellermann wrote in 1788 of having seen versions of the picture several times in different places and asserted, "it made such an impression, that I am not surprised that this illustrious person's real appearance, along with the most advantageously chosen accompaniment, inspired as much trust as fear in the confused public at the time."[54] Starting in 1784, when the first of many editions of Voltaire's correspondence with the empress was published, a head-and-shoulders excerpt of the painting was provided as the frontispiece (Figure 11.2); it showed her military hat but omits the pants and the sight of her riding astride.[55]

Sexual Difficulties

Mixed in with the marital crisis and allegedly contrasting personalities, the late accounts of the coup addressed specifically sexual issues. The birth of Paul had settled the unpublished question of whether Catherine was fertile, but not necessarily the companion question about Peter. Rulhière, describing the start of the imperial couple's married life in his usual suggestive language, wrote: "The nights, which they always passed in each other's company, did not appear sufficient to exhaust the vivacity of mutual endearment; and many hours were daily stolen from the formalities of a court, and devoted to an intercourse of a different nature." Playing with his audience's expectations, Rulhière continues: "The whole Russian Empire was eagerly looking forward to the birth of a second heir, not imagining it possible that a youthful couple should be all the while employed only in practicing the Prussian [military] exercise, and doing the duty of a common sentinel under a shouldered musket." Catherine, in this telling, "by observing a profound silence respecting her husband's whimsical delights, ... got the complete government of him."[56] A few pages (and years) later, according to Rulhière, Peter successfully fought back: "Utterly contemptible as the grand Duke was, he did not degrade himself so far as to submit longer to the government of his wife."[57] But that breach of gender norms was succeeded by another, the possibility that Peter was the cause of Catherine's failure to get pregnant.

Since, as Nancy K. Miller notes, "Publicly known failures of masculine sexual performance demolish (manly) reputations in literature and society,"[58] this topic was discussed cautiously in print. Rulhière stated emphatically that, "although nature had not totally denied sensibility to the grand Duke, the intelligent were able to demonstrate, by infallible tokens, that the line of succession was 'not to be expected from this quarter.'"[59] In 1797, Castéra provided details, asserting that, although Peter "gave reason to think that he had various adventures of gallantry, he was not perhaps therefore the fitter for obtaining an heir." To eighteenth- and early nineteenth-century readers this might seem to hint at syphilis or another venereal disease, but Castéra suggests a problem in anatomical development: "By an operation . . . which he had undergone in the first years of his marriage, he was freed from an obstacle without procuring greater means."[60] The later English translation and augmentation of Castéra clarified that the operation was "in a small degree similar to that of the judaical rite."[61] One of Peter's defenders described the problem somewhat differently and disagreed about the effectiveness of the cure. Helbig, as Peter's best early biographer, stated vaguely that the "bodily constitution of the Prince was very weak and so wrongly organized that it was thought he would only get the necessary strength through an operation." Yet after the unspecified procedure, he was "strong."[62] For non-elite eighteenth-century readers, this must have been a fascinating debunking of dynastic bloodlines.

Another of Peter's biographers, writing after Catherine's death, enmeshes the grand duke's surgery with Catherine's infidelity. In this tangled plotline, the grand duchess's secret lover, Sergei Saltykov, needed to enact a bit of clever stagecraft to explain Catherine's sudden and unexpected pregnancy. According to Laveaux, Saltykov told a surprised Empress Elizabeth that Peter had an "obstacle that prevented him from fully enjoying his spousal rights";[63] he suggested an operation might make a difference and she urged him to persuade Peter to proceed, which he did. Following the surgery, the biographer asserted, Catherine could more plausibly announce her pregnancy, though still not without raising suspicion and gossip. When Paul was born, both official and unofficial comments in print and available to distant audiences made no references to any doubts, but by the time of the coup, they were part of the overthrow's transgressive thrill, and after Catherine's death, alleged details could become yet another riveting scandal.

Peter III's Mysterious Demise

Another compelling and shocking rumor was that the Russian empress was responsible for the murder of her husband. This obloquy too was perfect celebrity fare, and the possibilities offered in print were numerous, each a potential stimulus to more scandalized celebrity talk. The variably named Mr. de Beauclair, a French professor of pedagogy at the German university in Marburg, stated a dozen years after the coup that the memory of Peter III would have been "a matter of indifference to posterity" and "his gentle shade would have descended tranquilly to the abode of the dead . . . if the moment that ended his dismal career had not thrown the world into wonder and compassion." Peter's sudden descent from holding "one of the most brilliant scepters of the universe" to being "instantly stripped of everything, thrown into a dark prison, and reduced to perish a tragic death"[64] provided a shocking and riveting conclusion to most coup narratives. Peter's abdication, the *Danger* account argued, imposed obligations for his safety on Catherine, "who, during fourteen years, had the honour to be the partner of his bed."[65] The honor was dubious and the protection failed, but conjectures about Catherine's role in the failure escalated.

Already in 1769, a German pamphlet of "friendly letters" had warned against "the tale of poisoning told in seaports by [Peter III's] escaped valet" and claimed that when this allegation was not sensational enough the valet offered "the story of strangling from behind on a chair."[66] Caminer in Venice, in 1771, claimed that the dismayed and disheartened Peter died a natural death, but he added a footnote naming two German books that called the matter murder.[67] In 1774, Beauclair called the death "still today a mystery to the public" and added blandly that the announced cause met with incredulity among many people.[68] Some commentators offered excessive drinking as an alternative cause that removed all guilt from Catherine.[69] Richard Turner's 1787 schoolbook assertion that Peter "expired [. . .] of what was called an haemorrhodial colic" was undercut by his further assertion that the death was "universally expected" since "princes dethroned by their subjects, are seldom allowed to languish long in the gloom of a dungeon."[70]

In 1792, James Gilray's humorous visual reference in a political cartoon had linked the official claim that Peter died of hemorrhoidal colic with the rumor that he was murdered. It presents a satirical version of Catherine's art collection, including sculpted portraits and fictitious paintings on the wall. The central piece shows a noose displayed in a circular frame on which two sardonic phrases are inscribed: "Conjugal Love" and "A Cure for Haemerrhoidal Cholic."[71]

The conflicting accounts and many reminders gave the distant public plenty of material for discussion and speculation, including about the various actors "in this horrid tragedy."[72] Both John Sinclair, writing in 1787, and Coxe named Aleksey Orlov and one of the Bariatinsky brothers.[73] Peter's biographer Laveaux, who alleged that Peter was first poisoned and then strangled, added to these participants Potemkin, who thus makes an early malevolent appearance.[74] Casanova, in his manuscript account—which remained unpublished, but not necessarily undiscussed, until the middle of the nineteenth century—claims to have met one of the killers, "Teploff, whose vice was that he loved boys, and his virtue that he had strangled Peter III."[75] The additional characters added more color and possibilities for speculation.

Some writers stirred attention by explicitly blaming Catherine. Voltaire's English translator composed a lurid footnote about Peter's demise as resulting from "the resentment of a slighted woman, whose affection (if ever she had any for her husband) was changed to extreme hatred," adding that she and "the priests . . . glutted their fury, by making him expire under the most horrid tortures."[76] The *Danger* volume was equally certain of her guilt: "Europe, and posterity, will never forget the cruel fate of this monarch, in the flower of his age—dragged into captivity, and expiring in the ferocious hands of his wife, and his own confidents."[77] The ever-contentious "Saldern," disputing the widespread claim that Catherine was reluctant to approve of Peter's killing, demanded, "who can believe that?" He asserted that all three Orlov brothers plus five more members of the murder conspiracy went to the house where Peter was imprisoned and, after a boisterous sequence of failures involving both poison and gunshots (with one bullet hole "still visible today over the door"), strangled the tsar with a handkerchief.[78] "The thin veil" that the supporters of the empress tried to hang over the deed, the text claimed, using a metaphor well suited to celebrity discourse's fondness for revelations, was not enough to "whiten the black of her character." [79]

Among the angry condemnations of Peter's assassination that appeared after Catherine's death was a vivid one in an Italian pamphlet containing Catherine's "last confession," in which she tells her confessor of her sleeplessness, haunted by the shade of her "betrayed consort," his face livid, his lips "still soaked and gross with his blood," and threatening her with "his most dreadful revenge."[80] Remarkably, however, one of Catherine's bitter posthumous critics, Gustav Adolf Wilhelm Helbig, nonetheless insisted that accusing the empress of ordering the murder was an insolent slur: "Catherine could not fall so deep." He argued that, despite her confident face, she had been deeply fearful during and after the coup, sleeping every night in a different secret place, but "definitely" not ordering her husband's death. Yet even without the murder charge, he contended, there was "material enough to un-deify Catherine," including her failure to use all possible resources to protect her vulnerable husband's life. He blamed the Orlovs for the murder, done, Helbig conjectured, to make it possible for Catharine to marry the eldest of the brothers.[81] Coxe, who in a late edition of his book had "no doubt" that "this unfortunate monarch was put to death," also firmly stated "that the death of the emperor was not perpetrated by the command, nor even with the knowledge of the empress."[82]

A murder scenario much like the one historians today accept[83] is presented in a travel book by a French duke, Alphonse-Toussaint-Joseph-André-Marie-Marseil le Fortia-de-Piles. He visited Russia three decades after the coup and published his account in 1795, the year before Catherine's death. Acknowledging the uncertainty of his story, which turned the killing into an impulsive deed by Aleksey Orlov, the French writer depicted the depressed ex-tsar and the bored nobleman who was guarding him becoming inebriated, arguing, and starting a fight that gave Orlov the sudden idea of putting an end to Catherine's anxieties and bringing immense benefits to himself and his brothers. He tried to strangle Peter, but the victim put up so much resistance that Orlov had to call for assistance from two other nobles nearby, the Bariatinsky brothers.

Peter finally succumbed under a pile of pillows. Fortia-de-Piles noted that the three assassins he identified were still alive three decades later, yet he too concluded, in the conventional language of mystery: "The death of the prince is one of those events over which the veil will probably remain forever impenetrable."[84]

A postscript to the various death accounts comes from sturdy Pastor Büsching's 1789 autobiography. After Peter III's corpse was brought to the Alexander Nevski monastery, he and his wife followed a seemingly deferential order from Catherine's government to show the tsar their last respect by going to witness the body, thereby, of course, confirming his demise. They went through the room twice, he wrote, in order to have a good look at the controversial corpse, but he did not record their conclusions, only adding that on the next day, supposedly due to the increasing decomposition of the body, Peter was buried.[85]

Murder stories lingered on, some in works of fiction. The most unusual of these was the weird and chaotic *Fragmens historiques sur Pierre III et Catherine II* (Historical Fragments about Peter III and Catherine II). As the book opens, the first-person narrator declares his wish to speak with the shade of the deceased emperor:

> At these words, a shiver ran through me, the sweet sound of the treetops seemed to announce his presence, an indefinable feeling in my inmost being was struck by the sounds of a plaintive voice speaking: "It is I who—since my death under those known but secret circumstances and whom your heart still mourns—hang over these regions as the guardian angel of a dear son and an innocent wife."[86]

That the death of Peter III occurred "under known but secret circumstances" was, of course, part of the event's fascination, but that the Peter character in this narrative might call Catherine his "innocent wife" was an unexpected twist. *Fragmens*, however, perhaps written by the obscure Jean Goebel and published anonymously in Paris the year after Catherine's death, claimed a vicious murder had been unfairly pinned on the deceased empress. This book announced that the new tsar, Paul I, would now put it right. The ghost declared: "During moments of solitude the heart of my dear Paul is already meditating a plan for calming the ghost of his father and reclaiming his memory." The moment has come, the ghost adds, to tear off "the veil that covers the tableau of my death" (25). The narrator immediately sees what his role should be, performing "the sacred task of writing the history of the life and death of unhappy Peter III," revealing a truth that "will astonish the universe" (26). Never mind that what he actually produces is one of the strangest and most ridiculous books related to the coup, a hodgepodge of inconsistent arguments tied together by a conspiracy theory laden with contradictions. It tries to avow the fundamental innocence of both Catherine and Peter since they were unknowing pawns (4) in the hands of murkily identified villains who seem to be Grigory Orlov and the court of Versailles (22, 115).

Two dramatists added their own quirky notions to the hum of argument about Peter's end. The Dutch playwright Andries Kraft's *Czaar Peter de Derde* (1801) recounted the overthrow and its culmination in five acts. His selection of scenes, use of complex motivations, and unexpected reinterpretations of who played what role possibly offset the play's undramatic reliance on long expository speeches. In this version of events, Peter's mistress Vorontsova warns the emperor repeatedly about popular discontent and argues that Catherine is stirring it up, but overconfident Peter naively refuses to listen.[87] Almost as soon as Peter learns of the coup in progress, a messenger from Catherine brings him the chance to leave immediately for Holstein if he signs the abdication document, which he promptly does. But in the next act, when Catherine learns that a mob outside the palace wants to see the deposed tsar, the possibility that she will allow him to depart disappears. Consulting with the Orlovs about how to treat their unwanted potential prisoner, Catherine worries aloud that killing him would have a bad effect on her reputation; then Gregory offers the cover story of illness (88).

While Catherine never explicitly approves the murder, the play depicts her foreknowledge of the plan. It is then carried out on stage in a remarkable last act. The curtain opens with Peter establishing an admirable relationship with his servant, fittingly named Constant, and ruminating on the visit he paid in act II to his imprisoned predecessor Ivan ("Why did I not foresee what has now turned out to be true?" 98). Orlov arrives, jovial, friendly, and reassuring, claiming that the populace was demanding Peter and Catherine should share the throne, a demand to which Catherine, he says, already consented. Despite some initial suspicion, Peter agrees to the division of power and Orlov prepares a quick supper on stage. Assuming a hospitable tone, he offers Peter a glass of poisoned wine. "Moved by your spirit," Peter responds, with unwitting irony, "this drink is dedicated to you." He continues philosophizing until he realizes what has happened. The faithful servant tries to intervene and is stabbed to death. "Monsters!" Peter exclaims dramatically, "You pushed me from the throne, ruined my honor (this hurts me worst), betrayed me, end my life. And cut me off from my last friend, innocent Constant. But . . . (raising his voice) I forgive you. O God, receive my spirit" (111). Orlov and his assistant hear the guards coming and depart. Kraft's play ends as the bodies are discovered. Of particular interest in the drama is the abrupt ending, leaving much for the audience to evaluate.

Six years later, in 1807, an obscure French dramatist named Godineau, who specialized in plays about recent historical figures, concocted a "tragedy" in verse about the coup that vindicated Catherine but gave Peter a completely new end: he engages in courageous military combat against the conspirators. Severely wounded in battle, he is brought before his wife on a stretcher. Although he alludes to Catherine's ambition and her desire for power (while she insists her motivation is protection of herself and her son), he forgives her, as Kraft's Peter had forgiven Orlov. Before dying on stage (and thus foreclosing any hint of murder), the tsar in Godineau's play willingly passes the rule to his wife, and not to his aggressive mistress with whom he had previously been plotting. Whether this muddled concoction of motives and relationships was ever performed is unclear, but copies seem to have been widespread.[88]

With typographical shrieks indicated in eighteenth-century German texts by widely spaced letters, Caspar von Saldern had sputtered: "*Catherine the woman* places herself at the head of an army; *Catherine the wife* marches against her husband!"[89] Assorted narratives and dramatizations of the coup had enthroned the empress from the start in celebrity discourse and maintained her there even after her death. Not only did the basic story include a murder mystery with multiple solutions, but it was laden with gender shocks and sexual peccadillos that offered the pleasures of savoring salacious sexual material. Every coup narrative provided a vehicle to tackle the issue of Catherine II's gender transgressiveness, the question of how it was that a woman again ruled Russia. Every effort at an answer kept Catherine's celebrity-making story in circulation.

12

The Lovers

Dabs of Fiction, Grains of Truth, Gobs of Scandal

During her lifetime, after her death, and until today, erotic fantasies and suspicions, with or without evidence, have ignited the public's fascination with Catherine II. They were prominent in the satirical pictures that skewered her in the last decade of her life; they were conspicuous in the retellings of her original coup against Peter III that appeared after her demise. They became especially important as biographers and novelists, poets and historians began composing reams of material about her lovers, often using sexuality as a weapon to sully her reputation, but also including it because, in the eighteenth century, such material had "acquired market value,"[1] as E. D. Jones has pointed out. Already in 1787, in an expanded edition of the fictional Baron Munchausen's popular tall tales, the title character recounts Catherine II thanking him for his gift of bearskins by "inviting me to share the honours of her bed and crown." There it is, a storyteller's imagined opportunity for sex with the powerful empress, expressed in the first person and soon reprinted in numerous further editions and an array of translations. Although Munchausen "declined her majesty's favour in the politest terms," the text left ample room for the reader's fantasy to proceed where he retreated.[2]

Tales of erotic possibilities added to Catherine the Great's celebrity, giving her audiences chances to ogle, condone, or condemn the allegedly misbehaving empress from imagined proximity. They provided yet another rich lode of storytelling that nurtured her celebrity. The famously insubordinate and destabilizing woman was and is imbued with the power to generate fantasy, especially sexual fantasy, and so to provide audiences with the accompanying pleasures of mediated voyeurism, identification, and appraisal. These pleasures, already examined as stimulated by sexualized visual satires, are read in this chapter as they appeared in words—tales and novels, biographies, travel books, and epic poems—but not plays, not on the stage for decades to come.

Phases of Lover Publicity

The stories of imperial sexuality appeared in several phases. During Catherine's life as grand duchess, political considerations had legitimized the monitoring of her sexuality.

When bearing a son was an urgent demand made on the grand duchess, decorous public discussion of her sexuality had been acceptable, as it was for the consorts of all kings and crown princes; without their heterosexual activity, dynasties changed branches or died off. As part of the wish for Catherine's reproductive success, a German wedding poem could attribute sexual desire (*Brunst*) to her, though regulated (for her as a woman) by chastity (*keusche Brunst* "chaste sexual desire").[3] After she ruptured gender rules by overthrowing her husband and becoming famous across Europe, many in her distant audiences promptly assumed she had also breached the limits of propriety imposed on female sexuality, especially its allocation to patriarchal marriage. Yet, during the mid-reign decades from 1766 to 1786, such material about Catherine II mostly disappeared from the distant press, though in Russia itself, she reportedly did not conduct her amorous affairs surreptitiously.[4]

She followed the "strange singularity of living without any affectation of mystery with her lovers," Rulhière asserted, as Empress Elizabeth had done before her, he added. Diplomatic correspondence, as always, and private letters by foreign residents of the Russian capital passed sexual gossip about the powerful woman on to selected readers far to the west,[5] and sometimes recipients with privileged connections shared the chatter with others. Louis XV's diplomat Count de Broglie, for example, wrote to a well-connected *saloniste* about Catherine's arranging for Stanislaw August Poniatowski to become the king of Poland: "If she means to be equally generous towards all his successors, there will not be crowns enough, in Europe, to decorate the brows of her lovers."[6] Beyond such private remarks, there were few mid-reign hints in print to the general public. One exception was a 1780 French book of satirical political analysis in the form of a trial of monarchs, in which Catherine obscenely declares, "je puis bellement être enculée" (I can be well fucked). Her diction contrasts radically with that of the other queen in the lampoon, Maria Theresa.[7] Still, pressured by censorship on the continent, libel laws in Britain, and the demands of Catherine's diplomats, most mid-reign books and gazettes contained little of this kind and nothing about paramours. Then, within a few years, satirical images became bolder, and more scandalous words appeared as well.

To Catherine II's faraway non-elite audiences, women monarchs had two main sexual options: either the choice made two centuries earlier by Elizabeth I of England to stave off her sexuality with her public performance as virgin queen or the recent decisions by Maria Theresa of Austria to display herself first as fertile wife, then as widow queen in mourning garb. Many observers, however, imagined or knew or half-knew exotic Catherine as a kingly queen, a ruler with multiple lovers.[8] In the mid-reign hiatus of sexual reporting, some well-practiced distant readers and some with special knowledge might have deciphered the sexual implications when newspapers reported that a man in the empress's circle was receiving flurries of gifts and large promotions in rank. Then in the summer of 1784 a young courtier, who incongruously held the rank of general, Alexander Lanskoy, suddenly died. Subsequent newspaper items hinted, sometimes strongly, at his status as lover and recipient of unearned privilege.[9] Yet a rhetorical question that was asked almost immediately after Catherine's death twelve years later suggests that secrecy about the imperial lovers had been far from complete: "Who knows them not, the changing unconstrained masters of Catherine's heart,

Orlov, Potemkin, Lanskoy, Zubov?"[10] Apparently, scattered published intimations had been enough—amplified no doubt through discussions in informal social settings far from Catherine's domains—to create a general sense of the empress's relationships with men whose names appeared in print in assorted different roles.

In 1787, the packed crowd in a London courtroom heard Lord George Gordon, on trial for libeling Marie Antoinette, assert that the accusation was impossible because the Queen of France "is as great a whore as the Empress of Russia."[11] Newspaper readers merely learned of his assertion that the two women were equally notorious.[12] There was a whole literature in English of whore biographies, and eight years later Galloway would publish lines calling Catherine "this arch Amazonian, Babylonian whore." But that was not the trope that became dominant in biographical texts about the empress. Whore was a step too far; it could not accommodate the great institutional power, high social status, and enormous wealth that were essential to Catherine II's particular aura as a celebrity. For long stretches, sexuality was a minor, almost absent, theme in representations of the faraway empress.

Lovers Slipping into Print in Catherine's Last Decade

From the late 1780s to the early 1790s, in addition to the fanciful sexualized caricatures that beguiled audiences remote from Catherine II's realms, only a few plausible erotic hints appeared in print, all of them for regional audiences, mostly in German-speaking areas. There, Catherine's most powerful lovers—Grigory Orlov, who had died in 1781, and Grigory Potemkin, who died a decade later—were the subjects of three minor biographies. Two of the three books cautiously sprinkled the intoxicating perfume of the still living empress's illicit sexual history onto the pages of their accounts. Although *Anecdoten zur Lebensgeschichte des Ritters und Reichs-Fürsten Potemkin* (Anecdotes about the Life of the Knight and Imperial Prince Potemkin), for example, linked Catherine II to unspecified libidinous and bloodthirsty male monarchs "who bathe themselves in lust with mistresses on their sofas at the moment when thousands of their subjects swim in blood, lying on the battlefield with lacerated limbs,"[13] the book offered no application of this repulsive image to any particular scene in the tsarina's life.

Once Catherine's demise removed her from the world stage, political cartoonists, with one exception, stopped drawing her. But, at a time when Europe's newspapers otherwise were filled with military news of the young General Napoleon Bonaparte's Europe-altering exploits, writers turned out plentiful sensational textual accounts about the tsarina addressing her sexual life, real or imagined. Castéra with Tooke, Helbig, Laveaux, Saldern (with his editor), and Albrecht, as inveterate composer of biographical *romans-à-clef*, studded their volumes, most of them supposedly serious, with vivid and extensive narrations of Catherine II's allegedly libertine ways. Charles François Philibert Masson, whose 1802 memoir was much read, concentrated on close-up observations of Catherine's last years on the throne. The Marquis de Sade, the greatest pornographer of the eighteenth century, invented gruesome-libidinous episodes involving Catherine the Great for his new novel, *L'Histoire de Juliette* (1797), and other novelists joined the fray as well. Of course, some writers resisted sensationalizing the private life of the deceased empress. Johann Gottfried Seume, for example, wrote blandly (and yet anonymously) that it was no secret the empress was "somewhat passionate in the physics of love," but he added: "All who have been much in the company of the empress insist that they have never seen a woman more modest in her conversation and conduct." He added that Catherine's lovers may have been expensive (due to her generous gifts to them) but were not a harmful weakness. Since Catherine had practiced leniency, Seume argued, her critics should as well.[14]

Celebrity Appeal of Sexuality Reports

All the attention to lovers before and after Catherine's death occurred during a time when non-elite notions of libertinism, women's sexuality, and marriage were evolving, under pressure both from the French upheavals and from other slower discursive and societal changes. Secularization was weakening the force of earlier religious constraints in some parts of European society; urbanization in several regions was bringing unaccustomed mixes of people closer together and providing them a degree of freedom from surveillance, and the growth of print culture was spurring previously taboo discussions.[15]

A transformed discourse of passion and intimacy had been emerging in Europe over the seventeenth and eighteenth centuries too. As the middle class, in the analysis of Niklas Luhmann, gradually gained cultural strength and reacted against their ostensible betters, they swerved toward a new ideological grounding for both sexual passion and marriage. They rejected the libertinism associated with royals and aristocrats, which notably avoided any promise of marriage, and they were not satisfied by the privileging of economic and status considerations in their own marriage traditions. For a time, new notions vacillated between seeking a foundation for marriage either in friendship or in passionate love, until the non-elite middle ranks chose, Luhmann argues, passionate love, transformed, however, from a libertine sensation that was fleeting, extramarital, and aristocratic, to a romantic emotion that was eternal, marital, and bourgeois.[16] This drastically reversed the valence of passionate love from an option of the aristocracy that the middle class expected but did not approve to the principled foundation of middle-class marriage. Introducing new notions of marital fidelity, family intimacy, and tender, faithful womanhood, they sharpened their sententious attacks on libertinism. This new discourse could readily mesh with the French Revolution's denunciation of privilege in inducing changes to social norms for marriage and sexuality. Many media workers' accounts of Catherine II's lovers shifted accordingly, from the quietly tolerant images in the first decades of her reign to vilifications later. This shift fit too with the structure of celebrity, in which, as Heather McPherson notes, "calumny and vituperation were the flip side" of the obvious admiration.[17]

The offensiveness of libertinism to the middling levels of society meant that tales of Catherine's sexual behavior could function to condemn the empress and her reign but could also signal her personal agency and thus emphasize the quality of individual autonomy that fans tend to admire in their stars. Indeed, the increasing rejection of monarchical libertinism by much of Catherine's distant non-elite audience produced exactly the transgressiveness that could heighten her celebrity as fans shifted back and forth between finding her alluring and appalling. Thus, accusatory or not, late-reign and posthumous reports in narrative forms ranging from newspaper accounts to travel books, novels, and biography about Catherine's lovers added to the celebrity discourse about her, inviting sociable interactions among the heterogeneous readers and listeners in coffeehouses, at tea tables, and around market stands, providing them entertainment, helping to examine social boundaries, offering them a chance to identify with a special figure, occasionally proposing a vision of something better (perhaps in reaction against her), and selling publications. The French writer Fortia-de-Piles noted of the tsarina's sexual behavior: "Sovereigns are human beings, and thus subject to the same caprices, slaves of the same weaknesses" as the empress's distant publics.[18] With such seeming similarity between ordinary readers and a great empress, bolstered by the sheer excitement that the lovers elicited and by the alluring visions of social and economic advancement that they seemed to propose, fans could deploy even the scantest information to imagine entry into Catherine's world.

Love Affair Trajectories

When overt published reporting on Catherine II's sexual life was scarce, rumor could thrive. In 1785, for example, middle-class Luise Mejer, after reading newspaper items about the death of Alexander Lanskoy (although she named him incorrectly), heard not only that the young man was an imperial lover but also that Catherine had killed him "in her room with a dagger." She considered reports of the empress's conspicuous generosity to the man's relatives as corroborating the murder rumor, compensating them for his wrongful killing.[19] Such speculations eventually disappeared, but awareness, informed or not, of Catherine's lovers persisted.

Celebrity-fueling glimpses in print of her private world told how the trajectories of her favorites were configured and what they stood to gain—and lose—from intimacy with her.[20] Probably the earliest published account of a lover's displacement appeared in the first biography of Orlov. Written in German in 1791, at a time when British and French attention was directed more at bloody events in Paris, the book looked back at Orlov's role in the coup, at the long continuation of his affair with Catherine for over a decade, and at his abrupt and unexpected replacement: "All Petersburg was amazed at the sudden change and at the advancement of a man who was previously unknown and lowly."[21] As readers and listeners would soon learn, this account of a new lover's arrival and a predecessor's eviction provided an approximate template of lover narratives yet to appear and made alluringly scandalous material for celebrity discourse.

"When the renowned Prince Orlov lost the special favor of the empress in 1772 and the gentleman of the chamber Alexander Vasilchikov took his place and his apartment at court, Potemkin readily saw that this was not the man to keep the empress's favor for long."[22] So stated *Anecdotes for the Life History of the Knight and Imperial Prince Potemkin* (1792), one of the pair of German biographies of Potemkin that appeared within two years of his death. The anonymously published *Anecdotes*, with its narrative perspective from within the culture of the Russian court, offers a blunt, practical explanation for Catherine's reliance on favorites: "At a court such as Petersburg's, it is not easy for a woman to sit on the throne unless she has a man at her side whom she can trust and who, through his talents and knowledge, would support the intentions of the regent to carry out . . . her plans" (4–5).

Seemingly unmarked by lust or seduction, such a man has an administrative function within a patriarchal system, and the obligations of trustworthiness and responsibility that his role implies provide the *Anecdotes*' standards for repeatedly censuring Potemkin's overweening grasp for power and influence and for Catherine's failures to curb him. Although the book vaguely acknowledges that Potemkin was Catherine's lover, the insignificance of their sexual relationship in this accounting is illustrated by the consignment to a footnote of a previously unpublished and explosive rumor that the empress and her courtier may have secretly married (231). That possibility must have created much talk among contemporary readers; the evidence and probabilities are still discussed by historians today.[23] Mostly, the two earliest Potemkin biographies—despite the first words in its title, *Private Life*,[24] the other one omits Catherine almost completely—offered abundant details about Potemkin's personal foibles and public successes and failures but lacked the favored ingredient of celebrity discourse, attention to his intimate relationship with the powerful empress.

That relationship was precisely the focus of the far better-selling *Pansalvin, Prince of Darkness*, a German *roman á clef* about Potemkin. In this, the first of the prolific Albrecht's set of five novels about Catherine and her circle, sexuality loomed large. Published anonymously, and clearly intended to titillate non-elite readers, *Pansalvin* contains a basically accurate account of Catherine II's most ambitious courtier and includes extensive material about their complex love affair.[25] In 1795, the book was reportedly outlawed in all the Prussian states at the request of the Russian court,[26] although Potemkin's later biographer, the well-informed Helbig, claimed Catherine herself read *Pansalvin* and found it sufficiently flattering that she made no endeavor to have it confiscated or to identify the author for recrimination.[27] Banned or approved, a second edition with an amplified title was published that year,[28] and Albrecht often used "author of *Pansalvin*" as his substitute for a pseudonym.

The book, a reviewer in an influential German literary magazine declared, should be considered a "history half-novel," because "even its hypothetical fictions have . . . such a high degree of probability that one is tempted to believe the author was an eyewitness to scenes that surely only came from his fantasy."[29] Scandal-packed, *Pansalvin* was an excellent vehicle for celebrity discourse, construing Catherine's presumed intimate feelings toward Potemkin in detail and unabashedly suggesting erotically charged events happening behind closed doors, though in terms respectable enough not to offend possibly prudish readers. *Pansalvin* provided abundant gossip with just the thin tether to facts that could enable celebrity to prosper.[30] More than any of the other accounts published during Catherine's lifetime, and more than most published afterward too, Albrecht's *Pansalvin* and later his *Miranda* celebrated sex, as Faramerz Dabhoiwala puts it,[31] and offered his celebration to middle-class readers.

Eighteenth-century literature offered an abundance of tales of aristocratic predators beguiling unwitting victims. Gender was one factor that ensured the early accounts of Catherine's love affairs resembled none of them. The closely watched empress was not portrayed as a highborn seducer, nor were her male lovers ruined prey. Instead, the functional account of their relationship that the *Anecdotes* about Potemkin articulated seemed to provide an acceptable framework for understanding favorites and their rivalries; moral commentary about them could focus on the abuses of privilege that they practiced, not on the nature of their intimate connection to the empress. This was a phase of discourse about Catherine's lovers that could offer celebrity-stoking eroticism, as Albrecht showed, and entailed almost no censure of the sexual morals of the ruling woman or her lovers; the men were criticized more for qualities such as greed, vengefulness toward others, arrogance, and incompetence. The travel writer Bellermann, for example, belittled Alexander Lanskoy, claiming that his ability to remain Catherine's lover for over three years meant that "either he was extremely sly and good at pretense or other powerful people must have decided that he would never get in their way." Meeting him in St. Petersburg in 1781 or 1782, Bellermann called Landskoy "the handsomest man I have seen in my life, tall, marvelously well built" and with something "very promising" in his eyes. A footnote in the account (published in 1788) records the lover's death three years later but with no details about how it happened (and certainly no reference to the murder that Luise Mejer had alleged).[32]

In 1796, a few months before Catherine died, Fortia-de-Piles's travel book was published identifying several lovers (but cautiously spelling out only the first three to five letters of their names). He added a new procedural element to the story of a woman with a sequence of lovers, describing the bureaucratic screening mechanism for the "fortunate mortals": "The empress goes to dine with a woman from her intimate circle where the man is invited whom she is considering to fill the vacant place. H.M. [Her Majesty] talks with him, examines him, tries to ascertain his temperament and the turn of his spirit." If the empress likes the man, the confidante "prescribes when he is to arrive, at a particular time, in one of the apartments of H.M., who intimates to him her wishes." At that point, Fortia-de-Piles encouraged reader fantasy and identification by teasing coyly, "we will not say what happens; these memoirs do not extend that far."[33] He also estimated the lavish sums that Catherine expended on her lovers and the fortunes they amassed,[34] another topic a general public could easily understand and find thrilling or repulsive. For the buzz of celebrity discourse, great expenses for intimate purposes amplified the allure of details about Catherine's paramours.

The Gush of "Revelations" Posthumously

Once Paul was on the throne, caution about describing or ascribing his mother's lovers mostly vanished. New accounts, especially those in the genre of secret history, treated illicit sexual affairs as the hidden explanations for the central figure's public behavior. Amatory episodes packed with concealment, discovery, reversal, ambition, miscalculation, dismay, and success are characteristic of the genre and make up its appeal to the middling levels of society and the unranked masses below them. The whiff of intimate disclosures, the shocking breaches of social norms for both gender and sexuality, the titillation for a society that was supposedly pursuing other norms—all turned the far from exalted secret histories about Catherine II's favorites into excellent material for celebrity discourse, and the profusion of such publications signals that media producers expected readers, listeners, and, with the occasional inclusion of

CATHARINA II GAAT POTEMKIN, IN ZIJN EENZAAM
VERBLIJF BEZOEKEN.

Figure 12.1 Catherine's pursuit of Potemkin in his monastic cell is depicted in Laveaux's *Histoire secrète* and in its translations, such as here in the Dutch version. Source: Lambert Antoine Claessens, *Catherine II gaat Potemkin, in zign eenzaam verblijf Bezoeken* in Laveaux (in Dutch), *Minnarijen van Catharina II. Keizerin van Rusland; en geschiedenis van haare voornaamste minnaars* (Amsterdam, 1780). Public Domain: http://hdl.handle.net/10934/RM0001.COLLECT.95823 Courtesy of the Rijksmuseum, Amsterdam.

images, viewers to be interested in how she chose her favorites, what happened when each was selected, how she rewarded them, and how and why a lover lost her favor. The texts and pictures—Laveaux's volume, for example, reinforced its allure with a frontispiece picture of the empress visiting the supposedly reluctant Potemkin in his monastery cell (Figure 12.1)[35]—offered erotic adventures that could nurture any audience's desire to identify with the lovers, the powerful tsarina, or her angry critics.

Completing the Record of Catherine's Intimate Life

Scandal mongering thrives on and revels in suspenseful discrepancies as much as in consistency. Immediately after the coup, readers from Aberdeen to Naples had learned that Peter III accused his wife of adultery, but the identity of the offending lover was nowhere to be found until Rulhière's publication gave the affair exactly the stereotypical arc that celebrity discourse favors: from illicit love's bliss to its disintegration. According to this account, the empress Elizabeth, worried about establishing a succession of crown princes and tired of waiting for Catherine and Peter to produce a baby, decided to assign the grand duchess a secret lover, Sergei Saltykov, and then sent him abroad as soon as Catherine's pregnancy was certain.[36] The variant provided by Castéra and Tooke identified the same first lover but assigned the initiative for the affair to the rake, who detected the vulnerability of the grand duchess to a sexual adventure and set about seducing her; they claimed Empress Elizabeth was horrified when she learned of it.[37] It was a story that provided Catherine II's fans and anti-fans copious material for sociable chat about marital fidelity, family intimacy, and tender, faithful womanhood.

Slow trickles can be part of the pleasure that fans appreciate in sharing their lifespans with the lives of the star, and sometimes with the star's afterlife as well, and the grand duchess's second pre-coup lover, the handsome Pole Stanislaw Poniatowski, was the subject of just such intermittently dribbled disclosures. In 1772, for example, a shilling pamphlet announced that Poniatowski, for whom Catherine had recently arranged the kingship of Poland, had years earlier "attached himself to the great Duchess, and insinuated himself into her favour."[38] The accounts that appeared after Catherine's death but during his life narrated embarrassing and ridiculous situations involving him. In one instance, according to the version attributed to Saldern, for example, Poniatowski disguised himself as a tailor for a nocturnal visit to his beloved at the Oranienbaum palace. He was intercepted and dragged before the supposedly amused grand duke— "Saldern" always strove to put Peter III in a favorable light—who pretended at first not to recognize the worried would-be tailor. Rulhière in his version claimed that when Poniatowski "fell into the hands of the injured husband," Catherine went to Peter, "boldly acknowledged the whole truth," and then succeeded in quieting him by promising not only to treat her husband's mistress "with all possible respect" but also to pay the woman "an annual pension from her own pocket."[39] In a much different version, that of Helbig, Poniatowski was disguised as a hairdresser, and Empress Elizabeth, enraged by news of the shenanigans, considered putting the grand duchess in a convent. According to Helbig, after Peter's mistress urged him to intercede on his wife's behalf with the empress, Elizabeth warned that Peter and his mistress would "regret this—I know Catherine!"[40] A neat bit of prophesy, of course, in a retrospective text that narrates the affair as an infuriating moral affront to good society; yet the comedy of a grand duchess's suitor masquerading, whether as tailor or hairdresser, remained.

The raft of new publications treating Poniatowski's successor, Grigory Orlov, gave readers across Europe ample material to savor after Catherine's death. Rulhière described the scandalous affair of "the handsomest man of the north" with the disguised grand duchess, whose true identity Orlov purportedly only learned when he saw "the beauty he adored" at a palace ceremony.[41] After Peter's overthrow, Orlov surprised the court by sitting down in Catherine's presence and thus revealing their secret affair. To Helbig, Orlov's move "into a number of rooms in the imperial winter palace, very close to the new monarch" meant he was "ceremonially represented to the whole court as openly declared lover."[42] To the distant public at the time, such gestures were left unreported, and even after Catherine's death, a few patches of anxiety remained about the dangerous fruit of sexual revelations concerning Orlov. *Fragmens historiques*, apparently seeking to protect Catherine's reputation, did not say he had been her lover,[43] and the *Monthly Review*'s long analysis of Rulhière likewise referred to the long-dead courtier only as O****.[44]

Most writers and publishers by then displayed no such qualms however. Indeed, belated gossip circulated of Catherine's illegitimate secret pregnancies by Orlov during Peter III's reign and later and invited logistical speculation.[45] Helbig enlivened his version with the claim that, to conceal her labor from Peter as the "crisis of the condition" approached (in April 1762), one of Catherine's courtiers deliberately set something ablaze in a remote part of the city to draw Peter, fascinated by fire, away from the palace to watch. Adding to the naïve goodness of the cuckolded emperor, Helbig added that before heading to the scene Peter came to Catherine's room and called to her not to worry about danger because the blaze was so far away.[46] "Saldern," in his vicious attack on Catherine, dated the birth after the coup: "Everyone in Petersburg knows that she wore the uniform of Field Marshall Butterlin, a man of unusual corpulence. This uniform could hardly fit the shapely Catherine well. But her advanced pregnancy made this uniform necessary."[47] Sordid though Saldern meant such an accusation to be, in celebrity discourse, disgust with arrogant libertine behavior could blend with relishing a famous person's transgressive promiscuity.

One repeated theme in the accounts is the lovers' opinions and treatment of the empress. Laveaux energetically derided her for being "reduced to the contemptible toy of her lovers, . . . submitting to the most degrading insults and the most humiliating debaucheries."[48] His book reinforced that disempowering account by concentrating for almost two thirds of its pages on arrogant and ambitious Potemkin. Masson, trying as he usually did to balance the attraction and repulsion he felt toward Catherine, called the later lovers "rapacious as tax-gatherers, pilfering as lacquies, and venal, . . . the rabble of the empire," but claimed generously, if inaccurately, that all of them "treated her with respect. Her love never excited disgust, nor her familiarity contempt. She might be deceived, won, seduced, but she would never suffer herself to be governed."[49]

Only rarely did a text consider why the empress tolerated any exploitation of her affection, but *Pansalvin* was an exception, offering an astute depiction of the psychology of denial that affected how the empress perceived her lover's feelings for her. An effective use of free indirect speech in a series of short sentences conveys her infatuated but suddenly slightly worried internal reaction to her lover's excessive demands and her effort to suppress her insight by remembering the comments of one of her generals:

> [The excessive demand Pansalvin made] was just one of those sudden ideas. It could not have been serious. Because Pansalvin loved her so inexpressibly! His words had a persuasive power that required no reasons. He seemed to her to be the wisest, the most excellent person.
>
> General Basta's testimony spoke so favorably of him. He always praised him, spoke about his progress, up to the most recent moment, when a few doubts seemed to arise. Those might just be little attacks of jealousy! (189)

Readers, of course, could suspect, as Albrecht hints, that even the empress's highest-ranking underlings might not provide honest assessments of her favorites.

Failed love affairs of the famous gave readers across borders of geography, rank, and wealth new chances to sort out society's norms for individuals and pairs. Fortia-de-Piles had claimed that some of Catherine's dismissed favorites had imprudently revealed "secret details that a woman does not forgive." He added: "We have to say, in praise of Catherine, that she never showed resentment toward the men who merited reproof, and never deprived any of benefits, even if they wronged her; that she always pardoned, and that this forbearance is great in the soul of a woman and a woman cloaked in supreme power!"[50] In the immediate moment, she might be angry and yet comparatively restrained. According to one termination story that was later much repeated, Catherine found her lover Mamonov and one of her ladies lying together; she promptly dismissed them both from their palace appointments, ordered their marriage, and selected the guard who chanced to be on duty as her next favorite. Noticing moments later that some of Mamonov's powder was still on her sleeve, "she brushed it away coldly and said, 'Now nothing remains of the ingrate!'"[51] After Catherine's death, Helbig, interpreting the parting gifts as payment to a prostitute, sneered: "At the dismissal of a favorite, the empress behaved in a way that we will not specify but which our readers can readily name."[52] A love affair's collapse could bolster celebrity discourse, which thrives on doses of discontent and tales of disintegrating personal and sexual relationships. There was much for readers in taverns and tearooms to dissect and debate.

Venomous Poetry and Further Fiction

Rulhière's scalding text was not the only one that had been cautiously on a shelf for years and was then sped into print after Catherine's death. *Il Poeme Tartaro* was a long mock-heroic work by Giambattista Casti, who presented a bound fair copy of his composition to Joseph II in about 1786 but did not dare to distribute it further.[53] Convinced that Russia was a dangerous force that should be isolated and contained, the Italian poet-diplomat in service to the Habsburgs wrote his venomous verses in an attempt to show readers Catherine's debased and unreliable character and behavior. When the hero, Tommaso Scardassale, after other adventures, arrives in Mogollia/Russia, Toctabei/Potemkin introduces him to Turrachina/Catherine, and he becomes her lover, succeeding "fifteen or sixteen" others (II.7). (The invented names are decoded at the end of the second volume.) Labeled by one scholar as "a bizarre and hysterical denunciation of Catherine" and her court,[54] the poem deprecates all the empress's supposed achievements and depicts her Russian subjects as incapable of improvement. It also denigrates the empress by alluding to her fat and her age, calling her "big and old," and having her say, "It has always been impossible for me to resist my loving inclinations. / Now, since I reign alone, I may love liberally, and choose lovers from among the finest around me."[55] In the end, Tommaso is overthrown by the slanders of the pimping Potemkin figure and is sent to Siberia, where he meets an old courtier and learns contentment and self-sufficiency. It is a grim and misogynist depiction of an autocratic woman who is unconstrained by any feelings of humanity or any emotions of love rather than lust.

Celebrity discourse, whether of the admiring or scolding variety, usually adores stories of sexual affairs for their elements of familiarity regardless of status or rank, their many twists and turns, the gendered power struggles that may be involved, and the purported revelations about the character of the celebrity that both the joys and the strains of such affairs supposedly uncover. Fiction could magnify all these elements, as three post-reign novelists—the Marquis de Sade, Johann Friedrich Ernst Albrecht, and Caroline Auguste Fischer—showed. While de Sade reveled in a namesake vicious version of libertinism, Albrecht and Fischer invoke two contrasting interpretations of passionate attachment, with Albrecht relishing a libertine empress, and Fischer, over a decade later, denouncing any form of sexual relationship that was not exclusive, eternal, and aimed toward marriage.

De Sade's *L'Histoire de Juliette*, published in 1797, the same year as Rulhière's *Histoire, ou Anecdotes sur la Revolution de Russie*, contained episodes depicting the Russian empress eagerly organizing and joining in orgies of extreme lasciviousness and cruelty; in some scenes she inflicts murderous sexual violence.[56] Caring and personal sentiment have no place there. From *Pansalvin* in 1794 to *Staub der Erste* in 1802 about Paul, Albrecht's five anonymously published biographical novels about Catherine, her son, Potemkin, and her most notorious general recycled published sources with elaborate commentary while generally maintaining the secret history's voyeuristically salacious tone. In *Miranda, Queen of the North* (1798), Albrecht rewrote Rulhière to depict Miranda/Catherine's affair with Zadro/Orlov and included a subplot (which also appears in Laveaux) about a deceived officer who falls in love with the princess and believes she has married him incognito. With invented incidents and insinuations, such as that Miranda's sexual license meant Orlov/Zadro was eventually "no longer the only one who was allowed to carouse in the blissful pleasure of the oversized royal charms," Albrecht invited voyeuristic fantasies and offered both the parasocial feeling of intimacy and the opportunity to criticize that celebrity discourse promises.[57] He had trained as a doctor and later composed dozens of pamphlets and books of medical advice, including several—in language he called "simple and decent"—about issues of sexuality.[58] In *Miranda*, he provided a playfully erotic account of a clever and sexually active empress. It was quickly translated into Dutch and published in Amsterdam in 1798.[59]

As the nineteenth century began, other writers joined the discussion of the tsarina now mostly in full-throated condemnation of her alleged promiscuity. Hester Piozzi, for example, whose biography might have made her sympathetic to the empress—she had boldly entered a second marriage with an Italian music teacher—declared the behavior of the "grand Autocratrix" toward her favorites was too kindly judged. In her immense narrative of world history in 1801, Piozzi praised Catherine's accomplishments within her empire but complained that when the empress's former lovers received "gifts of land and money, tenants and cottagers, diamonds and trinkets," Catherine's panegyrists labeled the prodigality as "bounty," but Piozzi found it morally offensive.[60] In a major change from the relaxed attitude of Fortia-de-Piles, a few years earlier, who had written that since Catherine's reign "has lasted much longer than those of other empresses, it is entirely natural that the number of her favorites is also greater,"[61] Piozzi expressed horror at the lovers' numbers. Acknowledging that other monarchs usually had one or two of "these rapacious appendages to greatness," she fumed that "Catherine's biographers enumerate fourteen I think."[62] Any readers previously unacquainted with the empress's reputation had the chance here to be intrigued.

Caroline Auguste Fischer, writing in 1808, deployed the emerging cultural demands on love and marriage to maul a Catherine II figure in the novel *Der Günstling* (The favorite).[63] The eponymous court official of the title acts in close conformity with Luhmann's analysis of what passionate love had come to mean. He tells his libertine empress that because he does not love her, he is not interested in her sexually, and she, infuriated when he plans to marry his chaste ward, turns into a murderess, a variation of the most heinous rumors about Catherine II. With Fischer's and Piozzi's distillation of harsh early nineteenth-century criticisms of Catherine II's sexuality, the terms were set for one strand of Catherine's long-lasting grip on the public imagination, as an icon of female sexual insatiability and depravity. Another more accepting strand, as an example of serial monogamy over a prolonged reign, survived as well. Both could fire celebrity discourse within a public grappling to understand, resist, or promote its own changing customs and conventions.

13

Celebrity after Death

In December 1796 and into January 1797, news of Catherine's death was in every news publication in Europe. Some reports were laconic and laden with procedural detail; a German one reported that on the morning of December 10 the imperial Russian ambassador reported the death of Her Majesty to the king of Prussia at a private audience.[1] Some were agitated; the *Oracle and Public Advertiser* for December 20 proclaimed in London: "The most important news which we have this day to communicate, is the DEATH of the EMPRESS of RUSSIA. This event—great in the eyes of all Europe—happened on the 17th November, about twelve o'clock at noon, when Her Majesty, very unexpectedly dropped down dead, supposed to be by the bursting of a blood vessel." All the articles of course went on to announce Paul's succession and most, either immediately or within a few issues, offered a summary of Catherine II's life. The *Oracle and Public Advertiser* followed its announcement with the promise to publish the next day its "Historical Anecdotes of this wonderful Woman, whose reign forms one of the most interesting periods in Modern Europe."[2] The influential new gazette in revolutionary France, the *Gazette nationale ou le Moniteur Universel*, first printed a one-sentence announcement at the end of its December 15 issue and then added sarcastic detail in the next issue, concluding, "She bore some of the charms of her sex, many of their faults, none of their virtues."[3] With opportunities for sociable discourse about the empress stirred up again, the lively final phase of Catherine's celebrity had begun.

Accounts and Images of Catherine II's Demise for All

Soon papers began printing more details about her dying. One often repeated version was that she was "found lying senseless on the floor of her water-closet," having lain there for almost an hour after being "seized with a fit of apoplexy." Though "medical assistance" soon arrived, her current favorite insisted on waiting for her preferred doctor, but by then "all human relief was in vain."[4] Another account suggested the medicine she had been taking for swollen legs may have caused her illness. Yet another, with a dateline from Petersburg of November 23, claimed she had been "somewhat indisposed" for several days but was "very cheerful" on the morning of her death "and took her coffee, as usual." Afterward she "went to the water-closet, where she had already been twice in the course of the morning." When she did not return, one of her "extremely alarmed" pages listened at the door and, hearing nothing, summoned "one of her principal female attendants, who opened the door, and found the empress extended on her back, with her feet towards the door." When her physician, "Dr. Rogerson (a Scotch Gentleman)" arrived, she was bled and seemed to improve but did not regain her speech, dying the following evening.[5] In the end, the doctors could do nothing.

The new emperor, taking "a very early opportunity of shewing his detestation of his mother's conduct towards his deposed father,"[6] provided new material for distant audiences to discuss and dispute. The broadsheets mentioned two startling orders by Paul I attempting to rehabilitate Peter III"s memory, at Catherine II's expense: "Three pictures of his father [were] to be hung up in the Palace," and Peter III's corpse was to be reinterred "in the family vault of his ancestors."[7] With such actions, media workers making products hostile to the empress knew they need fear no interventions from Russia.

Catherine's death reawakened all the strands of her controversial celebrity and circulated new ones in heaps of articles, pamphlets, and new books. The alluring and tainted story of her rise from obscurity in Germany to stunning wealth and power in Russia was eagerly retold, its tale of social mobility made vivid to any who had forgotten or were too young to know of the long-ago events, dream-inducing for those who could still admire monarchs, repulsive and infuriating for others who could not, and just another good celebrity-making story for the many who were little engaged in political debate. Media workers again packaged the celebrity empress for diverse potential

Figure 13.1 In *Representation of the Russian Empress Catherine II Surprised by Death*, the slender empress is elegantly gowned and wears a huge ring, but the imperial crown is already slipping from her head. A Russian touch to the print is the samovar steaming near the throne. Source: *Vorstellung der vom Tod plötzlich überraschten Rußischen Kaiserinn, Katharina II*, in *Verbesserter und Alter Vollkommener Staats-Calender, Genannt der Hinkende Bott* (Basel: Deckerischen Buchdruckerey, 1798). Public Domain. Courtesy of the Swiss National Museum, Kal BS 12: 1798.

customers. In the vicinity of Basel, for example, where the borders of Switzerland, France, and Germany converge, townspeople, villagers, and peasants had the chance to acquire a large new woodcut of her death (Figure 13.1). They could buy it either as a separate sheet or included in the French and the German printings of the local almanac for 1798, where it appeared along with excerpts from Rulhière about Catherine's climb to power.[8] Whatever their reading skills, the image of Catherine in a dance with death was familiar: cemeteries in Basel and in at least one nearby village contained late medieval warning murals of death striking down everyone from the highest to the lowest members of society. The new *dance macabre* shows an elegant, youthful empress in a sumptuous and spacious palace room staggered by a skeletal figure holding an hourglass up to her. As he points out the window to the graveyard, the empress, dismayed, reaches futilely toward the orb on a nearby table and the throne beyond it.

A different print, by an anonymous artist and with a German caption, was probably intended for an audience less steeped in medieval allegory and more interested in the otherness of Russia (Figure 13.2). The empress's body, slender here too, and clothed yet again in the fur-trimmed dress of so many earlier portraits, lies in state on a catafalque surrounded by rows of candles. Soldiers stand guard at one end, and a priest gestures vigorously at the other while two more priests sit casually at the foot of the bier. In the middle foreground, Russians in boots and long coats prostrate themselves. It is an odd and busy image, made odder by the skewed perspective, with the candles and cross not

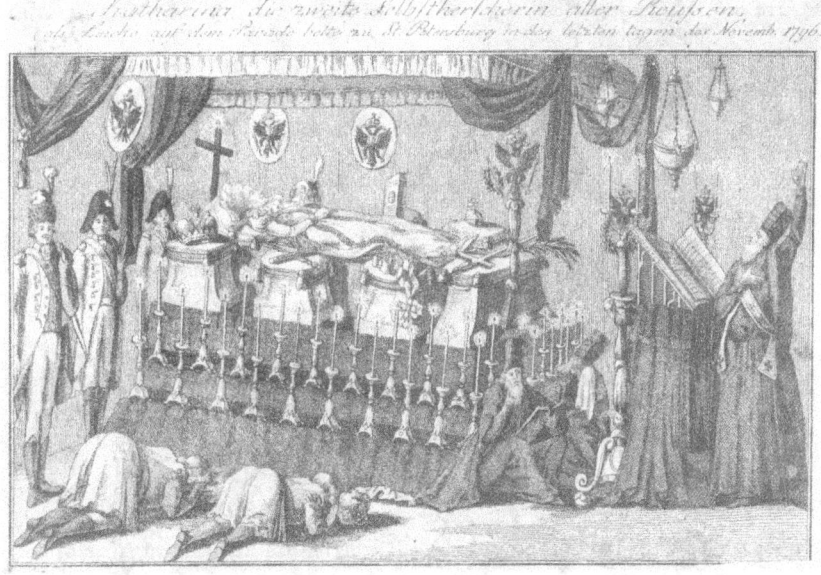

Figure 13.2 An anonymous German artist imagined the Russian setting of Catherine II lying in state, with bearded priests and prostrating mourners. Source: *Katharina die zweite Selbstherscherinn aller Reussen, als Leiche auf dem Parade bette zu St. Petersburg in den letzten tagen des Novemb. 1796*. Inventar-Nr. HB 3544, Kapsel-Nr. 1243a. Courtesy of Graphische Sammlung, Germanisches Nationalmuseum, Nürnberg.

quite vertical and the downward tipping catafalque shown at a slight angle from the plane of the picture. The accessories of mourning, black hangings and a lectern skirted in black, are mixed with a hint of admonition in the priest's raised arm as he addresses the deceased and in the less respectful behavior of his two colleagues, though one at least thoughtfully strokes his chin.

For English viewers, Isaac Cruikshank concocted one final visual satire of the czarina, *The Moment of Reflection or a Tale for Future Times* (Figure 13.3). Like the print for the French- and German-language editions of the Basel almanac, it too personifies death, poised to strike as Catherine, seated on the privy mentioned in the newspapers, confronts a cloud filled with the ghostly victims of her crimes. Some were well known and attested, such as a gesturing king labeled Poland, the shackled Tadeusz Kosciuszko, shown near a scene of slaughter labeled "Warsaw," and Peter III, in a nightshirt, closest to the huge, cowering empress. Among anonymous victims, one hangs by his arms from a gibbet, another looks skyward, and an animated child holds a cup overhead (possibly a reference to the rumor that Catherine had poisoned Paul's first wife so that she and her infant died in childbirth); nearby an old lady in a cap is being stabbed

Figure 13.3 Cruikshank's furious etching of Catherine II's death, hand colored in this instance, is dated December 26, 1796, less than two weeks after news of her demise reached London. The figure of death is the same as in the continental *dance macabre* (Figure 13.1), but the criminal empress is a grotesque and cloven-hooved hybrid, closely resembling Fox, who looks on once again. Source: Isaak Cruikshank, *The Moment of Reflection or a Tale for Future Times!!* (London: Fores, S.W., 1796). https://commons.wikimedia.org/wiki/File:The _moment_of_reflection_or_a_tale_for_future_times_LCCN99404753.jpg.

from behind and a man shows a facial wound, a dagger nearby. A woman's arm in a lace-trimmed sleeve in the middle of the cloud seems to conduct events. Toward the bottom, in an unlabeled reference to the French Revolution, a decapitated man with blood gushing out of his neck holds his guillotined head.

The carefully drawn figure labeled "Empss Russia" is extremely peculiar, a demonized being, not a woman at all but a ghastly imposter to be reviled, part man and part beast, with a dark and clearly delineated moustache, a flat chest, and large, hirsute hands. The lack of any visible curls or long hair peeking out from her strange cap-like crown further defeminizes her, and she more closely resembles the full-faced, hairy portrait of Fox on the wall above her shoulder than other images of the empress, whether serious or satirical. Despite the familiar fur-trimmed dress, this is no glamorous woman but a masculinized and criminal being, Catherine the Great as a man who is cross-dressed as a woman, with strings of beads around his neck and ruffles at his wrists. His eyes start at the vision he beholds, but his pitiless expression is more of indignation than contrition or even horror. Underscoring the demonic character of this brutal monstrous-feminine creature are the two cloven hooves visible beneath the dress. Through the open end of the chest on which she/he sits, against a backdrop of flames, two small black demons grin as they hold up an open box labeled "for Kates Spirit." By the time this print was made, French revolutionaries had declined to give women the vote, and Czar Paul had restored "the old Russian law that Peter II had rescinded whereby women were excluded from the Russian throne."[9] Cruikshank's vitriolic cartoon incarnates Louise de Kéralio's assertion that access to immense power changed a woman's sex and made the mighty woman an object of revulsion "capable of anything."[10]

Further Accusations and Complex Response

Late in Catherine II's reign, writers, printers, engravers, peddlers, and shopkeepers had worked to entice customers by producing new items—rich, storytelling "secret histories" that promised to unmask the famous woman, satirical images that turned her sexuality into allegory or pornography, travel books and biographies, whether steeped enticingly in admiration or invective—all of which fed her celebrity. After her death, the Cruikshank print was an inventory of the appalling rumors that circulated about the czarina. The print accurately foretold what was soon to occur: a flood of new discrediting and demystifying accounts of the Russian empress, but also rounds of adoring tributes, all of them adding to the last phase of her controversial celebrity, the phase occurring among the last group of people whose lifetimes overlapped with hers.

With the empress dead, her record again became the target of scrutiny. The theme, for example, of education and public enlightenment reappeared. An anonymous writer who posited Catherine II facing her last judgment declared that public education in Russia remained "miserable" and that "in religious affairs the most shameful superstition persisted," leaving Russians "almost as wild, unenlightened, and uneducated at the end of the eighteenth century as at the beginning." Outside St. Petersburg, "where an effort was made to give the throne the vacuous shimmer of a protector of the arts and sciences," he declared, "the night of barbarism and the deepest darkness flourished,"[11] a situation that explained Pugachev's success: ignorant people threw themselves in his arms in the desire to be liberated from serfdom. Yet Russian parents who hoped education might provide upward mobility were derided for employing empty-headed runaway domestic servants from France to educate their children in French, or even for mistaking other languages for the high-status one.[12] The Smolny Institute, a school that admitted girls from all classes and trained the non-elite students to become governesses (figure 0.2), was marked for especially misogynist attack; one account proclaimed, in a tone of prurient satisfaction, that institute graduates who did not get governessing positions immediately became "actresses or brothel girls." Eager to further besmirch this "true temple of Venus," the writer asserted that allowing the girls to attend balls with young men from the cadet academy meant "many" had become pregnant and given birth. Almost with regret, the account noted some recent improvement. None of the schools for boys—offering training in the arts, the military, medicine, and the like—stimulated this kind of half-pornographic salaciousness, in which the turn to prostitution is described as "certainly a very natural transition from the mamsell at a convent to strumpet.[13]

The failed codification of Catherine's intended legal reform was another important theme, though gradually the effort regained its sheen, at least in some quarters. One biographer called Catherine's *Grand Instructions* "the most marvelous work through which she earned the just admiration of the whole civilized world." To him, the failure of implementation was less important than the grand ideas, so "extraordinary in Europe at the time."[14]

New documents appeared in print too, such as Catherine's correspondence with two feuding German doctors, Johann Georg Zimmermann in Hannover and his erstwhile friend Melchior Adam Weikard in St. Petersburg; they separately published their own letters and the notes and letters in French and German that they had received from Catherine.[15] The combined exchanges provided glimpses of the empress ignoring the explicit private flattery of Zimmermann's slavish missives and urging the two "Msrs. Scholars" to stop the "scolding and quarreling," which "earns them very little credit."[16] In 1808, a successor to the original publisher of Zimmermann's correspondence, calculating that there was still an audience for the celebrity empress, liberated the hundred pages of Catherine's letters from the turgid scholarly quarrel—though thriftily using the same plates with the old pagination—and marketed them with "très interessante" in the new title.[17]

Fresh inventions about the empress also appeared. In 1799, Luciano Francisco Comella, probably Spain's most popular and prolific dramatist of the late eighteenth century, cranked out yet another play about her, "Catherine the Second at Cronstadt." Loosely related to any actual events, the play, which was performed by the Compañía de Francisco Ramos in Madrid, depicts Catherine as an insightful empress who detects deceit and rectifies its consequences.[18]

Yet exactly the czarina's failure to see through the falsehoods and deceptions of her own court and government was another important theme of posthumous criticism, with her journey to the Crimea as the quintessential example. Spectacle has always been a powerful detour away from intractable real problems; exotic spectacle is potentially even more enthralling and more effective at blinding the viewer, including the empress. As one observer claimed, "nothing was neglected to conceal from the observation of the Empress, wretched realities, under the most brilliant appearances."[19] Criticism of the illusions of prosperity that the trip elicited had already appeared in two biographies of Potemkin published while Catherine was still alive. "Whole districts in the interior of the empire were depopulated," one biography asserted, to create "the deceptive appearance of a busy life" in the new regions of the empire.[20]

After Catherine's death, new books amplified the suggestions of deceit. France's ambassador to Catherine's court, Louis Philippe, comte de Ségur, claimed in his 1801 memoirs that Potemkin manipulated Catherine's impressions, "intoxicat[ing] her by the magnificent illusions, with which he took care she should be continually environed."[21] In this view, Potemkin as the extravagant producer of frauds, the creator of flimsy village mirages, carefully scripted what she saw. The most devastating assertions of deceit, however, had already appeared in 1798, when Georg Adolf Wilhelm von Helbig discussed the Crimea tour in his serialized Potemkin biography. Helbig, newly arrived in Russia at the time of the journey, did not take part in the trip but collected information from others who were there. In his estimation, the "theatrical machinery" was set in motion when Catherine got on the barge to descend the Dnieper and it continued as long as she was in the territory that Potemkin administered:

> From a distance, one believed one was seeing villages, but the houses and church steeples were just painted on boards. Other nearby villages had just been built and seemed to be occupied. The inhabitants had often been corralled there from forty miles away. In the evening they had to leave their dwellings and rush to other villages, which they again inhabited for a few hours, just until the empress had passed by. Of course compensation had been promised to these people, but, hard though it is to believe, none was paid. Many fell victim to despair and physical afflictions. Herds of animals were driven from one place to another at night too, and the empress often admired them five or six times.[22]

These then were the Potemkin villages of lasting fame, traceable to Helbig's vivid account. He added to it by asserting, for example, that bags of grain shown to the empress were actually filled with sand, that palisades were made from painted reeds, and that the houses where Catherine stayed tended to collapse soon after her departure.[23]

Melchior Adam Weikard, as a medical doctor for the expedition's vast staff, corroborated the spirit though not the details of Helbig's account, but he added that the spell over the empress was broken near the end of the journey at a dinner with Aleksey Orlov outside Moscow. An abundance of wine induced her old friend, brother of her longtime lover, to speak "more boldly than is usual at court." Beginning his complaint "in the name of the whole nation," he told her that everything she had seen was staged. When the empress disputed his arguments, he begged one of the governors who was present to "confess the truth to your empress." After Orlov had grabbed him "with his customary fervor," the governor reluctantly cooperated, as did others, until Catherine "was finally convinced that in the country through which she had traveled with so much glory there was nothing but real misery." The empress departed toward Moscow "humbled and full of consternation." She hurried to the Kolomenskoye palace there, where crowds of people lined both sides of the street. "It was touching," Weikard wrote, "to see Russia's majestic empress, who had been so cheerful, and satisfied and of such a sublime spirit during the whole trip, now suddenly so withdrawn, abashed, and discouraged, hastening out of the sight of people's eyes. Everywhere was glum silence."

That was not all. The pomp and jubilation that had been planned in Moscow to celebrate Catherine II's twenty-five years on the Russian throne was canceled, Weikard asserted. Windows with views toward her procession to one of the Kremlin churches had been rented at high prices, but the glamorous parade did not happen, and Catherine, Weikard claimed, avoided opportunities to be seen. The doctor concluded his book about the journey "that created so much excitement in Europe" by estimating not its accomplishments but its immense total cost.[24] Catherine II, according to this admonitory theme, had allowed herself to be deceived and betrayed.

Criminality

Rebukes about her failed policies, undiscerning governance, and wastefulness were joined by old and new accusations of criminality, specifically, various murder charges, both now resumed and freshly formed. One tract claimed sarcastically, for example, that whenever a sudden decease had seemed necessary for her greatness or her security, "nature" came to her aid so that a death occurred and at just the right time. Yet, the unnamed author noted, when one drew any negative conclusions from these events, "a whole army of writers, great and small, obscure and familiar, would arise" to defend the cruel empress.[25]

Cruikshank's satirical cloud of accusers had promptly suggested the list of murders attributed to Catherine II, starting, of course, with Peter III's in 1762 and Ivan VI's in 1764. Ferocious Saldern added Nikita Panin to the list because, as the former minister of foreign affairs and governor for the grand duke, he was allegedly too energetic an advocate for Paul.[26] In addition to including a shadowy illegitimate daughter of Tsarina Elizabeth, who supposedly died in a Russian prison after being kidnapped from Italy,[27] Saldern asserted that "the world" blamed Catherine for the death in childbirth of Paul's first wife, the Grand Duchess Natalia Alexeievna, "this ornament of the female sex."[28] Accusations reappeared elsewhere about powerful Potemkin's demise in 1791 at the age of fifty-two, at a moment when his military role was less valuable to Catherine,[29] and when, at least one writer jubilantly asserted, he was planning to overthrow her.[30]

Shreds of putative evidence were pieced into delectable tales of crimes in high places. According to Laveaux, after the "Agrippine of Anhalt" had a tremendous row with Potemkin, she summoned a woman "especially noted for intrigue" and then had "an air of tranquility and even of gaiety. A short time after that, of course, a courier brought to Petersburg the news that Potemkin had died."[31] Finally, as if such a string of insinuations were not enough, in 1801, the first biography of Paul added another thrillingly wicked death to Catherine's credit, that of her lover Lanskoy, but not, as had been rumored years earlier, because she stabbed him. Instead, this allegation uses the folk motif of a difficult task the suitor must complete to win the bride, claiming that the empress demanded Lanskoy demonstrate "the courage to be worthy of the

Amazon Catherine" by assassinating her son, the grand duke. Unfortunately for the lover, the plot was discovered, and Lanskoy, "covered with wounds," died in her arms.[32] Demeaning and disparaging though the heaping of charges was, for readers with no stake in the lives of distant Russians they could also add relish to the debate about Catherine II as a brazen woman wielding personal and imperial violence.

And Yet Ambivalence

Opinions about the empress remained entangled with her gender. The Swiss Charles François Philibert Masson, one of the foreigners who had been in her presence frequently over many years, struggled with this theme in his popular and much-translated *Secret Memoirs*: "Her crimes were the crimes of her station, not of her heart," he wrote. "The woman whose spirit seemed to preside over the terrible butcheries of Ismail and of Praga appeared to her court to be humanity itself." Arguing that "probably nothing was lacking for her to possess the purest virtues except that she had never known misfortune," he then gave his account a gendered turn: "Vanity, that fatal rock to women, was so to Catharine; and her reign will ever bear the distinguishing characteristic of her sex."[33] Women, he seemed to say, became too arrogant if they were successful. It was the kind of claim, along with the postulate that men were not or less vulnerable to this defect, that was excellent material for the sociable mode of celebrity.

Masson's ambivalent feelings about the Russian empress could give distant fans both the feeling of intimacy and the opportunity to chastise that celebrity fosters:

> O Catharine! dazzled by thy greatness, of which I have had an intimate view; charmed with thy beneficence, which rendered so many individuals happy; seduced by the thousand amiable qualities that have been admired in thee, I would fain have erected a monument to thy glory: but the torrents of blood thou hast shed rush in and overthrow it: the chains of thirty millions of slaves ring in my ears, and deafen me; and the crimes which were perpetrated in thy name call forth my indignation. I throw away my pen, and exclaim, "Let there be henceforth no glory without virtue! Let injustice and depravity be transmitted with no other wreath to posterity than the snakes of Nemesis!" (93)

Yet he earlier begged, "Let not the misfortunes and abuses of her reign give to the private character of this princess too dark and repulsive a shade!" and stated that "all who were admitted to her intimacy were delighted with the good-humored sallies of her wit: all who lived with her were happy." On the one hand, he argued, "Her active and regular life, her moderation, firmness, fortitude, and even her temperance, are moral qualities which it would be highly unjust to ascribe to hypocrisy" (63), and on the other, accepting her within the ethos of the privileged, he blithely links her conviviality and carnality with the reassuring politesse required of an empress, adding, "Her manners were gay and licentious, but she still preserved an exterior decorum." Masson gave his readers opportunities to vacillate with him as they pondered Catherine II's celebrity.

Before and after her death, a matrix of key factors affected how the Russian empress was represented in words and images. Some emanated directly from Catherine II, such as her wealth and rank, which included her great political and military power; her German heritage, which gave her advantages in some regions and invited scorn in others; the official actions she took as empress; and her gender. Some, such as genre choice, geography, technology, distribution networks, skill levels, and materials, came from the assorted media workers who created and disseminated the engravings, wood block prints, ceramic plaques, letters, poems, biographical sketches, book dedications, reviews, street songs, and more. The intended market of fans or possible fans had an impact too, sometimes requiring speed, always driven by desires, the desire, for example, to see Catherine II's presumably fabulous wardrobe or learn something personal about her, anything that might nurture a feeling of connection with the Russian empress.

As saleable texts and images proliferated, the representations sometimes slipped from elite to non-elite media and occasionally rose back up the ladder again. Taken separately, the invitation to see a coach, the porcelain and pottery displays, the invented prints, shop signs, and hasty biographies show little, but in combination and in the context of other indicators traceable in Austria-Germany, France, the Low Countries, England, and Italy, the pictures, cards, displays, books, and other products and events were signs that the empress of Russia was an international celebrity in her day. By attending to her own glory in the eyes of other monarchs and high aristocrats, Catherine had done her part within the troika that produces celebrity. By making and distributing representations of the distant empress, from costly to cheap, from fine to poor, media workers had done their part. Once large numbers of ordinary people, most of whom would never visit any court at all during their lifetimes, began savoring the German Cinderella on the Russian throne and buying the commodities that supposedly represented her, they joined the troika too, as fans and anti-fans.

Invented Libertine Death as Crime and Punishment

Among posthumous representations of Catherine II, a large image in which she appears as a demure and elegant, almost fairy-tale, princess appeared in a book with a title that seemed to promise glowing celebrity discourse, *Vita, e fasti di Caterina II. imperatrice ed autocratrice di tutte le Russie* (Life and Splendor of Catherine II, Empress and Autocrat of all the Russias). It was an Italian multipart history of her reign, featuring a foldout print in the second volume (Figure 13.4). In the picture, spectators lean out the windows of the nearby building to watch her go by. Courtiers lead her horse, along with a mounted guard before and after, and in the background, members of the clergy look on. The French and Italian titles of the print, *Catherine II riconosciuta Imperatrice* (Catherine II recognized as empress) on the Italian side, seems to suggest that this scene depicts the 1762 coup occurring in a version of St. Petersburg imagined in familiar European terms, with the empress wearing her coronation regalia, complete with bulbous crown. It was probably a captivating and affirmative scene to many viewers, despite new accounts of Catherine II as a sexually immodest woman that were burgeoning at the same time. Although unalloyed admiration for

Figure 13.4 In a large foldout print, a beautiful young Catherine sits astride a festively accoutered white horse amid a crowd of glad courtiers and soldiers. The setting is urban and elegant, a paved square bounded by neoclassical buildings. Catherine, confident but prim and glowing in the light, wears an enormous crown and seems to look sideways toward the viewer, inviting a feeling of connection, a last round of imagined relationship with the remarkable woman in distant Russia. Source: Pietro Antonio Novelli, *Caterina II. riconosciuta Imperatrice / di tutte le Russie. / Catherine II. qu'on vient de reconnoitre / Imperatrice de toutes les Russies*, in *Vita e fasti di Caterina II imperatrice ed autocratrice di tutte le Russie*, vol 2 of 6. Lugano: Ant. Zatta, 1797. Getty Images. Catherine II . . . on horseback. Editorial #: 857126600. Credit: DE AGOSTINI PICTURE LIBRARY / Contributor.

her was difficult among the morally and economically anxious early nineteenth-century middling and lower classes, they may have enjoyed reading celebrity-stoking texts nonetheless.

Mary Hays's biography of the empress, for example, vividly written for women and based on an array of the best sources, mixes attention to Catherine's policies and accomplishments with detailed recounting of her love affairs. Hays calls the empress "constant in her ambition" but "fickle in her attachments," and declares: "by those who admire her as a sovereign, she cannot be defended as a woman."[34] The self-righteous bourgeoisie, to which Hays belonged, asserted its moral superiority to the aristocracy by assailing the licentiousness of the upper classes and especially of women like Catherine—but found her fascinating.

Whatever motivations artists, writers, and publishers may have had for producing and disseminating their representations of Catherine II, the results were, aside from private communications, always commodities, objects for sale that could contribute to the maintenance of her celebrity. The satirical prints, travel narratives, biographies, secret histories, and occasionally even political analysis not only fed celebrity discourse by inducing and addressing the desire of a general public of readers and listeners to uncover hidden "truths" about Catherine II's sexuality (always expected to be emphatically heterosexual)[35] but also helped translate their political and sexual-cultural anxieties about the empress into manageable forms. Even long-postponed narratives about the persons of her lovers, the way they were chosen, their role in her life and in the life of the empire, their dismissal, and their price—all could make for voyeuristic pleasures and the riveting gossip and speculation that is the fans' side of celebrity discourse.

For many of them, high and low, the thought of a famous and powerful woman aroused the notion of transgression, which in turn aroused the expectation of something sexual. In 1819, when Byron imagined his Don Juan visiting St. Petersburg, he could still assume his audience would remember stories of Catherine's lovers as he lingered for many satiric stanzas over the empress encountering the newly arrived Spaniard:

> The courtiers stared, the ladies whispered, and
>   The Empress smiled: the reigning favourite frowned--
>   I quite forget which of them was in hand
>   Just then, as they are rather numerous found, [507]
> Who took, by turns, that difficult command
>   Since first her Majesty was singly crowned.[36]

While Byron's tone is more bemused than indignant, part of Catherine's public disagreed. It may have been about this time that an utterly insupportable, castigatory rumor about the sexually active, self-directed woman appeared.

What better punishment than to invent the punitive and derogatory story of her death copulating with a horse?[37] The direct assertion that Catherine's excessive sexuality, carried to the extreme of bestiality, had killed her, demonstrates the neatness and economy of a fable, uses the readily available stuff of eighteenth-century pornographic prints, and gives a vicious twist to glamorous pictures, such as the Italian one, of Catherine II on horseback. Recent scholars argue that the broad oral dissemination of rumors about her sexual life, and the story of the horse in particular, endlessly punish her autonomous, self-defining sexual behavior. Especially after Catherine's death the powerful woman could be excoriated sexually, and the unmotherly, unchaste aristocratic woman vilified. Catherine the "Great" could be transformed from the most powerful woman of her century into the most ignominious. Under the guise of a "joke," the libertine woman celebrity would be crushed to death again and again.

Becoming an Icon: Afterlife

In only a few cases does stardom last until the end of a celebrity's life. At that point, most remaining marks of celebrity decline quickly, both because new, living competitors have arisen—Napoleon nudging aside Catherine II, in this case—and because the simultaneity that is crucial to celebrity cannot persist when the star's lifetime long ceases overlapping with the lifetimes of the fans. With that loss of a shared presence in the world, the nature of the relationship of fan or anti-fan to star gradually changes. In my analysis, the former celebrity who several years posthumously gains the attention of a large new audience becomes an icon, a face, or a name that reverberates out of the past, frequently in a few fixed poses. Queen Victoria, Marilyn Monroe, and Princess Diana are among the icons who populate our imaginations even now. Catherine II of Russia, the only woman widely designated as "the Great," has the status of icon too. The news magazine *Der Spiegel* signaled her continuing resonance by putting one of her elegant portraits on the cover of a 2013 issue with German chancellor Angela Merkel's face superimposed on the empress's and labeled "Angela the Great."[38] From popular biographers, to novelists, to celebrity female stars of stage and screen, twenty-first-century media workers still expect to make money from the long-ago Russian empress who reigns as an icon today. They follow the lead of Mae West, a century earlier, who wrote and starred in a Broadway play, "Catherine was Great," depicting the glamorous and sexy tsarina.

Mocking allusions to the story of bestiality that has been imposed on her continue, though rarely in print. The twenty-first century's popular "Catherine the Great" demonstrates the constructedness and incoherence of both icon and celebrity. The historical figure is famous and notorious for an apocryphal event. Importantly, even in current social media, *story* is still critical to both celebrity and icon status, and a story maintains Catherine II's fame. As is common for women celebrities, it reduces her to her sexuality. Yet it is precisely a story that was meant to destroy her that still enables public discussion, provides entertainment, and shapes opportunities for identification—all the functions of celebrity—and so, in its perverse way, has preserved her icon status for over two centuries.

Notes

Introduction

1 Exactly what to call the region in which I am interested is complicated. The categories "Eastern Europe" and "Western Europe" were not common in the eighteenth century; Larry Wolff, *Inventing Eastern Europe. The Map of Civilization on the Mind of the Enlightenment* (Stanford: Stanford University Press, 1994), 217. Russia was more likely to be identified as part of the "North," along with places like Sweden (which was a larger country then than now) and also, sometimes, Prussia and Poland. The area of Europe outside the North did not have a collective name in the eighteenth century. In effect, even though I mainly (aside from the preface and this introduction) avoid the terminology of Eastern and Western Europe, this study primarily addresses Western Europe.
2 Historisch-genealogischer Kalender auf das gemein-Jahr 1798 (Berlin: Unger 1797).
3 This description is indebted especially to David Giles, *Illusions of Immortality: A Psychology of Fame and Celebrity* (New York: St. Martin's, 2000), 61–3.
4 Robert Darnton, *The Forbidden Best-Sellers of Pre-Revolutionary France* (New York: W.W. Norton, 1995), 217.
5 Antoine Lilti details the use of "celebrity" as a word in French and English and explains its changing meanings in *The Invention of Celebrity, 1750–1850* (Malden, MA: Polity, 2017), 102–8. Heather McPherson traces usage in English starting in 1751. *Art and Celebrity in the Age of Reynolds and Siddons* (University Park, Pennsylvania: The Pennsylvania State University Press, 2017), 9. In eighteenth-century German, my research indicates, the words *Celebrität* or *Zelebrität* went through semantic transitions similar to those that Lilti discussed.
6 For example, the earliest citation with the meaning "A well-known or famous person" in the *Oxford English Dictionary* is dated 1831. "celebrity, n." (Oxford University Press).
7 R.F., "Mr. Editor," *Morning Herald*, January 31, 1784.
8 See, for example, Laura Engel, *Fashioning Celebrity: Eighteenth-Century British Actresses and Strategies for Image Making* (Columbus: Ohio State UP, 2011).
9 For Sacheverell, see Brian Cowan, "Doctor Sacheverell and the Politics of Celebrity in Post-Revolutionary Britain," in *Intimacy and Celebrity in Eighteenth-Century Literary Culture: Public Interiors*, ed. Emrys Jones and Victoria Joule (London: Palgrave Macmillan, 2018). For the others, see Lilti, *Invention*, 62–5, 177–93, and 206–16.
10 *Art and Celebrity*, 8.
11 German scholars, for example, have engaged infrequently with the topic of celebrity (generally using the terms *Prominenz*, *Celebrität*, or *Zelebrität*) and not at all with its manifestations before the twentieth century. Peter Rehberg and Brigitte Weingart, "Celebrity Cultures. Einleitung in den Schwerpunkt," *Zeitschrift für*

Medienwissenschaft 9, no. 16 (2017): 10–20; Birgit Peters, *Prominenz: Eine soziologische Analyse ihrer Entstehung und Wirkung* (VS Verlag für Sozialwissenschaften, 1996); Julia Wippersberg, *Prominenz: Entstehung, Erklärungen, Erwartungen*, Volume 25 of Forschungsfeld Kommunikation (Konstanz: UVK Verlagsgesellschaft, 2007).
12 *Invention*, 8.
13 P. David Marshall, *Celebrity and Power: Fame in Contemporary Culture* (Minneapolis: University of Minnesota Press, 1997), 9, 12.
14 "Celebrity in the Twenty-First Century Imagination," *Cultural and Social History* 8, no. 3 (2011): 407.
15 *Celebrity* (London: Reaktion Books, 2001), 110.
16 The radically different conditions in Russia, such as the size of the middle class, the extremely low rate of literacy overall, and the low availability and isolation of newspapers and other print media within the Russian Empire at the time make the possibility of celebrity there questionable.
17 Tim Blanning, "The Holy Roman Empire of the German Nation Past and Present," *Historical Research* 85, no. 277 (2012): 65–8.
18 Patrick Merziger, "Der öffentliche König? Herrschaft in den Medien während der drei Schlesischen Kriege," in *Friedrich der Grosse in Europa: Geschichte einer wechselvollen Beziehung*, ed. Bernd Sösemann and Gregor Vogt-Spira (Stuttgart: Franz Steiner Verlag, 2012).
19 Barbara Stollberg-Rilinger, *Maria Theresia: die Kaiserin in ihrer Zeit, eine Biographie* (München: C.H. Beck, 2017), 87–8, 123, 48–50. Michael Elia Yonan, *Empress Maria Theresa and the Politics of Habsburg Imperial Art* (University Park, PA: Pennsylvania State University Press, 2011).
20 *Invention*, 9.
21 Marshall, *Celebrity and Power*. 17.
22 I have done almost no research addressing representations made in Sweden or Poland. I think the possibility for Catherine II to become a celebrity there was limited both because they lacked the prerequisite of a flourishing middle-class print culture and because geographical proximity to Russia was so often laden with imminent threats not conducive to celebrity. Also, given the limits of my language skills, my archive and library time, and my knowledge base, the concentration on limited languages was a practical choice.
23 *Sexual/Textual Politics: Feminist Literary Theory, New Accents* (London and New York: Methuen, 1985), 158.

Chapter 1

1 See especially Franz A. J. Szabo, *The Seven Years War in Europe, 1756–1763* (Harlow, England: Pearson/Longman, 2008).
2 Anna Luisa Karsch and Johann Wilhelm Ludwg Gleim, *"Mein Bruder in Apoll." Briefwechsel zwischen Anna Louise Karsch und Johann Wilhelm Ludwig Gleim*, ed. Regina Nörtemann ed. (Göttingen: Wallstein, 1996), I:138.
3 At the time, Europe was still in the transition from the Julian to the Gregorian calendar, with Russia still following the Julian, called "old style," and most of the rest of Europe, probably including all the countries except Russia where newspapers were published, using "new style." Unless otherwise specified, this book, which focuses

mainly on sources produced outside Russia, uses the Gregorian "new" calendar throughout.
4 Szabo, *Seven Years*, 427.
5 Karsch and Gleim, *Mein Bruder*, 1:138.
6 "Brussel, den 27. July," *Gazette van Gendt* 1762. "Yesterday a report was spread," *Gazetteer and London Daily Advertiser*, July 30, 1762. "London," *Lloyd's Evening Post and British Chronicle*, July 28–30, 1762. "Historical Chronicle (July)," *Gentleman's Magazine*, July 1762, 341.
7 "Madrid, 10 de Agosto de 1762," *Gaceta de Madrid*, August 10, 1762.
8 "Hague (in Holland) July 29," *Providence Gazette and Country Journal*, October 20, 1762. "Foreign Affairs," *Providence Gazette and Country Journal*, October 30, 1762; "Tho' the Russian Empire," *Providence Gazette and Country Journal*, November 27, 1762; *Carta, con noticias circunstanciadas de la revolucion acaecida en Petersburgo en los dias 9. y 10 de julio proximo pasado, para destronar al emperador Pedro. III. y declarar soberana de todas las Rusias à la emperatriz Catalina II. su muger* (Lima? 1763).
9 One example is the *Weimarische wöchentliche Anzeigen* available through Universal Multimedia Electronic Library (UrMEL) at the Thüringer Universitäts- und Landesbibliothek Jena. See also Ruth Pritchard Dawson, "Perilous News and Hasty Biography: Representations of Catherine II Immediately after her Seizure of the Throne," *Biography* 27 (2004): 517–34.
10 "Venezia 31. Luglio," *Gazzette Bolognesi*, August 3, 1762. The official newspaper in Vienna published the news on July 28: "Wien den 28. Julii 1762," *Wienerisches Diarium*, July 28, 1762.
11 "Venezia 31. Luglio," 2. Other papers quickly avowed they too had foreseen the change, for example, "Account of the Late Revolution in Russia," *London Magazine*, August 1762, 434.
12 "Die Entthronung des Russischen Kaysers Peter III. und dessen darauf erfolgtes Ende," in *Fortgesetzte neue genealogisch-historische Nachrichten* (n.p.: 1763), 387. For confusion in London, see, for example, "Postscript. London," *Lloyd's Evening Post and British Chronicle*, July 30–August 2, 1762.
13 "Staats-Sachen," *Auszug der neuesten Weltgeschichte*, August 3, 1762.
14 "Staats-Geschichte. Russland," *Auszug der neuesten Weltgeschichte*, August 12, 1762.; "Staats-Geschichte von Russland," *Auszug der neuesten Weltgeschichte*, August 5, 1762.
15 "Staats-Geschichte von Russland," *Auszug der neuesten Weltgeschichte*, August 5.
16 "Petersburg den 10. Jul.," *Auszug der neuesten Weltgeschichte*, August 10, 1762, 776.
17 Robert van Krieken, *Celebrity Society* (New York: Routledge, 2012), 17. David Marshall writes about "sympathetic identification," "identification with the familiar" in *Celebrity and Power*, 190–3.
18 van Krieken, *Celebrity Society*, 56–8; Joshua Gamson, *Claims to Fame: Celebrity in Contemporary America* (Berkeley: University of California Press, 1994), 29–30; Georg Franck, "The Economy of Attention," *Journal of Sociology* 55 (2018): 8–19. Simon Morgan, "Celebrity: Academic 'Pseudo-Event' or a Useful Concept for Historians?," *Cultural and Social History* 8 (2011): 100.
19 Morgan, "Celebrity," 107.
20 "To the Printer," *Gazetteer and London Daily Advertiser*, August 2, 1762.
21 "Holland," *Northampton Mercury*, August 9, 1762.
22 Stella Tillyard, "Celebrity in 18th-Century London," *History Today*, 2005.

23　"De Bruxelles, le 2. Août," *Nouvelles Extraordinaires de Divers Endroits* [*Gazette de Leyde*], August 6, 1762.
24　Richard Wortman, *Scenarios of Power: Myth and Ceremony in Russian Monarchy* (Princeton: Princeton University Press, 1995), 110.
25　"Lettre CLXXVIII A.M. Pictet, à Petersbourg, Septembre," in *Recueil des lettres de M. de Voltaire, Mai 1762 - Octobre 1763*, vol. 7 of *Recueil des lettres de M. de Voltaire, 1715-1778* (1784): 222.
26　Lilti, *Invention*, 79-82; Marshall, *Celebrity and Power*, 86-91; Gamson, *Claims to Fame*, 28-30.
27　"Contenant ce qui s'est passé de plus considérable en Russie, depuis le mois dernier," *La Clef du Cabinet des Princes de l'Europe, ou Recuëil Historique & Politique sur les Matières du Tems* 1762, 229.
28　August von Schlözer, writing in 1767, totally rejected this kind of royal biography. Distinguishing between a monarch and a person, he argued: "The life of a monarch consists of a series of deeds, which he has committed as monarch, that is, which stand in a certain relationship to his approval. Recounting these deeds means describing his life." Schlözer then proceeded to produce a "biography" of Catherine II as monarch, comprising official acts, statistics, and economic facts. August Ludwig Schlözer [Joh. Joseph Haigold, pseud.], *Neuverändertes Russland, oder, Leben Catharina der Zweyten, Kayserinn von Russland aus authentischen Nachrichten beschrieben* (Riga, 1767), 2.
29　"The [Second] Manifesto of the Empress of Russia," *Gentleman's Magazine*, 1762, 437.
30　Ibid.
31　"London, August 5," *Northampton Mercury*, August 9, 1762.
32　Catherine II, "[Second] Manifesto," 438.
33　Ibid., 439.
34　The original painting, by Vigilius Erichsen, is now at Peterhof Palace; copies outside of Russia are known in Copenhagen and Chartres. Susan Tipton, "Die russische Minerva: Katharina die Große und die Ikonographie der Aufklärung," in *Katharina die Grosse* [Catalog of the exhibit of the Staatlichen Museen Kassel, in the Museum Fridericianum Kassel 13. Dezember 1997-1998. März 1998] (Eurasburg: Edition Minerva, 1997), 76. See also Elizaveta Renne, "Catherine II."
35　Marshall, *Celebrity and Power*, 8. For a discussion of the official portraiture of Catherine II in relation to that of Maria Theresa, see Christina Strunck, "The 'Two Bodies' of the Female Sovereign: Awkward Hierarchies in Images of Empress Maria Theresia, Catherine the Great of Russia, and their Male Consorts," in *Queens Consort, Cultural Transfer and European Politics, c. 1500-1800*, ed. Helen Watanabe-O'Kelly and Adam Morton (London: Routledge, 2017).
36　Catherine II, "[Second] Manifesto," 439.
37　Ibid.
38　Neal Gabler makes a similar point in *Toward a New Definition of Celebrity* (Los Angeles: Norman Lear Center, Annenberg School for Communication and Journalism, University of Southern California, 2001), 4-8. In most studies of celebrity, story receives minimal attention.
39　"Zum Staat von Russland," *Auszug der neuesten Weltgeschichte*, August 17, 1762.
40　Sofia Johannson, "'Sometimes You Wanna Hate Celebrities': Tabloid Readers and Celebrity Coverage," in *Framing Celebrity: New Directions in Celebrity Culture*, ed. Su Holmes and Sean Redmond (Routledge, 2006), 345-6.

41 "From the London Gazette. Petersburgh, July 10," *London Evening Post*, August 3–5, 1762.
42 "Das Merkwürdigste aus den Zeitungen. Regenspurg, vom 27. Jul.," *Weimarer Wöchentliche Anzeigen*, August 7, 1762. Also: "Das Merkwürdigste aus den Zeitungen. Dresden, vom 26. Jul.," *Weimarer Wöchentliche Anzeigen*, August 7, 1762.
43 The source seems to have been the *Gazette de la Haye* for August 6. Versions appeared, for example, in Gendt, Belgium, on August 9 ("Moscovien. Petersburg den 12. July," *Gazette van Gendt*, August 9, 1762.), in Hamburg on August 11 ("Nieder-Elbe, vom 2 August," *Staats- und Gelehrte Zeitung des Hamburgischen unpartheyischen Correspondenten*, August 3, 1762.), and in London on 13 August ("Yesterday arrived the Mails from Holland and Flanders," *Public Advertiser*, August 13, 1762. "Friday, August 13," *Lloyd's Evening Post and British Chronicle*, August 11–13, 1762). Magazines reprinted it too, for example, from The Hague, "De Petersbourg," *Mercure historique et politique contenant l'état présent de l'Europe, ce qui se passe dans toutes les cours, les Intérêts des Princes, & généralement tout ce qu'il a de plus curieux*, September 1, 1762, 216–23.
44 "Tuesday, August 17. Yesterday Arrived a Mail from Holland," *London Chronicle*, August 14–17, 1762.
45 "Zum Staat von Russland," *Auszug der neuesten Weltgeschichte*, August 21, 1762, 818.
46 The archbishop's later furious sermon justifying the coup became available in German translation. D.A. Sečenov, *Feyerliche Danckrede des hochwürdigsten Ertz-Bischoffens von Groß-Novogrod, oder Neugard an dem Fluß Wolfowa in West-Rußland zu Gott, und an seine versammelte Cleresey auf die Abthronung Peters des Dritten Czaars in Rußland zu Oranien-Baum in Ingerman-Land bey dem Einfluß des Nieva-Stroms Cronschlott gegenüber den 28. Junius des alten, und 9. Julius des neuen Stils 1762. Gesprochen, und aus dem Griechischen in die teutsche Sprache übersetzt*, trans. C. J. Ivanowiz (Smolensk, Lithuania: Erhard, 1762).
47 "Friday, August 13," *Lloyd's Evening Post and British Chronicle*, August 11–13.
48 "Postscript," *London Chronicle*, August 10–12, 1762.
49 "Yesterday arrived," *Public Advertiser*, August 13.
50 "Yesterday a Report," *Gazetteer and London Daily Advertiser*, July 30.
51 "Nieder-Elbe, vom 2 August," *Staats- und Gelehrte Zeitung des Hamburgischen unpartheyischen Correspondenten*, August 3, The *Gazzette Bolognesi* printed the story on August 17 under the title "Venezia 31. Luglio."
52 "Staats-Geschichte," *Auszug der neuesten Weltgeschichte*, August 5, 1762, 778.

Chapter 2

1 James Lull and Stephen Hinerman, *Media Scandals: Morality and Desire in the Popular Culture Marketplace* (Columbia University Press, 1997), 3. Quoted in Simon Cottle, "Mediatized Rituals: Beyond Manufacturing Consent," *Media, Culture & Society* 28, no. 3 (2006): 421.
2 Lilti, *Invention*, 35–6.
3 "London, August 5," *Northampton Mercury*, August 9.

4 Simon Dixon argues, "there seems no reason to disbelieve ... that Peter was killed in a drunken scuffle." *Catherine the Great* (London: Pearson Education, 2001), 124–5.
5 Italics in original. "An Account of the Chief Circumstances of the Revolution That Has Happened in Russia," *Gentleman's Magazine*, August 1762.
6 Felicity Nussbaum, *Rival Queens: Actresses, Performance, and the Eighteenth-Century British Theater* (Philadelphia: University of Pennsylvania Press, 2010), 45.
7 "Her Imperial Majesty's Declaration, &c. on the Death of the Emperor Her Husband," *The Annual Register: World Events*, 1763.
8 "Mein Lieber Peter, Gute Nacht!," in *Fortgesetzte russische Anekdoten oder Zweyter Theil* (n.p.: 1766), 37.
9 Dixon, *Catherine the Great*, 35.
10 "Russia," *Northampton Mercury*, August 16, 1762, 83.
11 When the English accounts of the coup and its aftermath were transferred to the American colonies, both the political skepticism that was somewhat more emphasized in the British press and the direct and indirect sexual references that were slightly stronger among the German and other sources vanish. The *Providence Gazette* published one reference to Edward II and Peter's death "of a Disorder in his Bowels," but without mentioning the charge of infidelity (italics in the original: "Foreign Affairs," *Providence Gazette and Country Journal*, October 30, [4].)
12 Peter's death quickly precipitated three brief biographies of the tsar. Although all three were published in German territories, one was in French—by D. G*** [Ange Goudar], *Memoires pour servir à l'histoire de Pierre III. Empereur de Russie... Le pour et contre du Pierre III. Empereur de Russie* (Berlin et Dresde, 1763)—and two, both anonymous, were in German, *Denkwürdigkeiten der Lebens- und Staats-Geschichte des ohnlängst verstorbenen unglücklichen Czaars Peter des Dritten, aus glaubwürdigen Nachrichten und richtigen Urkunden in der Kürze verfasst* (Danzig, 1762) and *Merkwürdige Lebensgeschichte Peter des Dritten, Kaisers und Selbsthalters aller Reußen, nebst einer Erläuterung zweyer bereits seltener Münzen, welche dieser Herr hat prägen lassen*, 2d ed. (Frankfurth und Leipzig, 1762).

According to Bilbassoff, this last one, which has been knowledgeably attributed since the eighteenth century to Georg Andreas Will, may have been commissioned by Catherine; see Katharina II, *Kaiserin von Russland, im Urtheile der Weltliteratur*, 2 vols. (Berlin: Räde, 1897), 1:12. It was successful enough to have four editions. To its second edition was appended a "Letter from St Petersburg" that energetically attacked the dead tsar and glorified Catherine, extolling her intelligence, diligence, and dedication, and calling her "a true woman philosopher on the throne." With this endorsement of the new tsarina attached to the narration of Peter's life, Catherine had usurped Peter's biography as well as his throne. The anonymous author, however, asserted his credibility and independence from imperial influence by claiming he was an eyewitness who sent his manuscript out of Russia in a diplomatic pouch.
13 "Extract of a letter from Cologne, Aug. 22," *London Chronicle*, August 26–28, 1762.
14 "Venezia 31. Luglio."
15 Joseph R. Roach, "Public Intimacy: The Prior History of 'It'," in *Theatre and Celebrity in Britain, 1660–2000*, ed. Mary Luckhurst and Jane Moody (New York: Palgrave Macmillan, 2005).
16 Marshall, *Celebrity and Power*, 4.

17 A fictitious example of an illiterate laundry woman who was well informed about the events appears in "An Account of the late Revolution in Russia; collected from authentic Papers never before published," *The Beauties of All Magazines Selected for the Year 1762*, September 1762.
18 "Mein Lieber," 33-37.
19 Rudolf Schenda, *Volk ohne Buch: Studien zur Sozialgeschichte der populären Lesestoffe 1770-1910* (Frankfurt: Vittorio Klostermann, 1970).
20 Corinna Heipcke, "Landgräfin Karoline of Hessen-Darmstadt: Epistolary Politics and the Problems of Consort Biography," *Biography* 27, no. 3 (2004): 535-53.
21 Bilbassoff, *Katharina II*, 1:14-15.
22 "London, August 5." The article did not mention Anna's death the next year.
23 "London, August 12," *Northampton Mercury*, August 16, 1762. 83.
24 *Fortgesetzte russische Anekdoten oder Zweyter Theil* (n.p. 1766), 38.
25 "Translation of Part of an Intercepted Letter from the K. of P— to Count Finkenstein Handed about in Holland," *London Chronicle*, November 11-13, 1762.
26 "London, August 5."
27 Catherine II, "[Second] Manifesto," 438.
28 "De Petersbourg," *Mercurio histórico y político* (1762), 368.
29 "London, August 12," *Northampton Mercury*, August 16.
30 *Wahrhaffte Nachricht von der am 9ten Julii 1762 in Petersburg vorgefallenen Revolution* (1762), 2.
31 I have found no text printed before the coup that contains this allegation, but it may have spread outside Russia through less formal circuits, especially since Peter surrounded himself with foreigners, mostly Germans, who could have conveyed such ideas in their letters.
32 *Friedrich Ludew. Ant. Hörschelmanns pragmatische Geschichte der merkwürdigen Staatsveränderungen im rußischen Reiche von dem Ableben Peters des grossen an bis auf den Regierungs-Antrit der ietzregierenden Kaiserin Catharina II. Aus sichern Quellen und authentischen Nachrichten mit unparteiischer Feder vorgetragen auch mit nötigen Beweisen bestätigt*, (Erfurt: J.J. F. Straube, 1763), 153. *Denkwürdigkeiten*, 70. The same pretext for discussing Catherine's sexual behavior under the guise of criticizing Peter III also occurs in other works; see Ruth Pritchard Dawson, "Eighteenth-Century Libertinism in a Time of Change: Representations of Catherine the Great," *Women in German Yearbook* 18 (2002): 71-2.
33 Each of the multiple French-language editions has an at least slightly different title: *Anecdotes russes, ou lettres d'un officier Allemand à un gentil-homme Livonien, écrites de Pétersburg en 1762, temps du règne et du détronement de Pierre III, empereur de Russie* (London (really den Haag), 1764); *Nouveaux Mémoires, ou anecdotes du règne et du détrônement de Pierre III. Empereur de Russie* (Berlin et Dresde, 1765); *Anecdotes Russes ou Lettres d'un officier allemand, a un gentilhomme livonien, écrites de Petersbourg en 1762; tems du règne & du détrônemement de Pierre III. empereur de Russie* (London: Aux dépons de la compagnie, 1765); *Histoire et anecdotes de la vie, du règne, du détrônement et de la mort de Pierre III. dernier empereur de toutes les Russies, etc. etc. etc.* (London: Aux dépens de la Compagnie, 1766).
34 *Russische Anekdoten von der Regierung und Tod Peters des Dritten; imgleichen von der Erhebung und Regierung Catherinen der Andern* (Petersburg [i.e. Frankfurt], 1764); *Russische Anekdoten; oder Briefe eines deutschen Offiziers an einen livländischen*

Edelmann, worinnen die vornehmsten Lebensumstände des russischen Kaisers, Peter III., nebst dem unglücklichen Ende dieses Monarchen enthalten sind (1765).
35 *Russische Anekdoten* (1765), 18.
36 Karsch and Gleim, *Mein Bruder*, 1:138.
37 Simon Dixon in his careful account of the coup ascribes more advance planning to Dashkova and Panin than to Grigory Orlov, *Catherine the Great* (New York: HarperCollins, 2009), 120–4.
38 "By Many Good Accounts from Russia," *Northampton Mercury*, August 23, 1762, 86.
39 Catherine II, "[Second] Manifesto," 439.
40 *Fortgesetzte*, 41.
41 *Hörschelmanns pragmatische Geschichte*, 154–5.
42 Margaret Homans, *Royal Representations: Queen Victoria and British Culture, 1837–1876* (Chicago: Univeraity of Chicago Press, 1998), xxix.
43 *Gespräch im Reiche derer Todten zwischen Sr. Königlichen Majestät von Pohlen, August dem Dritten, und Sr. Russisch-Kaiserlichen Majestät, Petern dem Dritten* (Frankfurt: Leipzig, 1764), 41.
44 "Entthronung," 409–10. Simon Dixon assesses Peter as neither a coward nor a hero in the choices he made; *Catherine* 123.
45 G*** [Goudar], *Memoires*, 97.
46 *Gespräch*, 39, 42.
47 G*** [Goudar], *Memoires*, 95.
48 Ibid., 96–7.
49 Eventually the likelihood that Peter was not Paul's father was strongly supported by Catherine's own memoirs, published in the middle of the nineteenth century. Catherine II, *The Memoirs of Catherine the Great*, ed. Hilde Hoogenboom, trans. Mark Cruse (New York: Random House, 2006).
50 Emily Lorraine de Montluzin, "Attributions of Authorship in the *Gentleman's Magazine*, 1731–1868; A supplement to Kuist," *Bibliographical Society of the University of Virginia*, 2003.
51 "Historical Chronicle (August & September)," *Gentleman's Magazine*, July 1762.
52 Catherine II, "[Second] Manifesto," 437.
53 "Annual Register," *Annual Register, or a View of the History, Politicks, and Literature of the Year 1762* (1763), 18.
54 "Es ist uns ein Sinngedicht zugeschickt worden," *Auszug der neuesten Weltgeschichte*, August 28, 1762, 838.
55 "Nell Gwyn and Covent Garden Goddesses," in *The First Actresses: Nell Gwyn to Sarah Siddons*, ed. Gillian Perry (Ann Arbor: University of Michigan Press, 2011), 74.
56 "Extract of a Letter from Dantzick," *London Chronicle*, September 18–21, 1762.
57 "Holland," *Northampton Mercury*, August 9.
58 "Foreign Affairs," *Northampton Mercury*, December 13, 1762.
59 Karsch and Gleim, *Mein Bruder*, 238. Karsch had reacted to Peter's death by writing and later publishing a lament for the tsar who had so bravely come to Prussia's aid, "Aufmunterung an den Geheimen Rath Freyherrn von Labes, wegen seiner Betrübniß über Peter den dritten" (Encouragement to Privy Councillor Baron von Labes, on account of his sadness about Peter the third). Omitting mention of Catherine, the poem bewails as irretrievably gone but leaves the how and why unstated. *Auserlesene Gedichte* (Berlin, 1764; repr., Karben, Germany: Petra Wahl, 1996), 294–7.

Chapter 3

1. Lilti, *Invention*, 101.
2. *Geschichte des gegenwärtigen Kriegs zwischen Russland, Polen und der Ottomannischen Pforte* (Franckfurt: Leipzig, 1771), 46.
3. "Account of the Late," 343.
4. "Catherine the Great and the Art of Collecting: Acquiring the Paintings that Founded the Hermitage," in *Word and Image in Russian History: Essays in Honor of Gary Marker*, ed. Maria di Salvo, Daniel H. Kaiser, and Valerie A. Kivelson (Brookline, MA: Academic Studies Press, 2015).
5. The first play appeared in multiple editions in different cities. *Catalina segunda, emperatriz de Rusia* (Valencia, 1795); *Catarina Segunda, emperatriz de Rusia, drama heroyco en tres actos* (Madrid: Antonio Cruzado, 1797); *Catalina segunda, emperatriz de Rusia: drama heroyco en tres actos* (Barcelona: J.F. Piferrer impressor, 1797 or so); *Catarina Segunda en Cronstadt, drama heroyco en dos actos* (Madrid: Fermin Tadeo Villapando, 1799).
6. Frieda Koeninger, "Race at the Intersection of Religion, Aesthetics, and Politics: Comella's 'El Negro Sensible' and the Censors," *Hispanic Enlightenment* 40 Fall (2017): 224.
7. [Pierre Adrien LeBeau], *Catherine Alexiewna II. / Née le 2 Mai 1729, Impératrice et autocratrice de toutes les Russies / le 28 Iuin 1762, Couronnée à Moscou le 3 Octobre 1762* (Paris).
8. The portrait was reproduced in two versions: a fine one by Yefim Grigoryevich Vinogradov and Ivan Alexandrovich Sokolov, *Ihro Kayserliche Hoheit Die Groß-Fürstin Catharina Alexeiewna* (1761), and a much clumsier one of the same title by K. Jahrmargt.
9. At least one of the Rotari copies in the west of Europe, now in the palace museum in Jever, signals Catherine's status as empress by giving her the imperial insignia and also by amplifying the picture from half-length format to three quarters; thus it was devised, or possibly revised, after the coup.
10. Examples include *Catharina Alexiewna | Russorum Imperatrix*, and: I.E. Gericke, *Catharine Alexiewna II. / Imperatrice de Russie /* (Berlin, 1763).
11. Johann Georg Heinzmann, *Historisches Bilderbuch des Edlen und Schönen aus dem Leben würdiger Frauenzimmer* (Bern: Haller, 1790), 178.
12. It appears that the various fur-trimmed-dress-and-braids engravings are based on an original painting, probably by Pietro Rotari, that is now lost. A version with a Cyrillic inscription is apparently the earliest paper example of the type and probably also the parent of the numerous others that were varied by engravers to the West.
13. The same weaving, but in blue and white, is in the Deutsches Historisches Museum in Berlin.
14. *Das Iahr braChte zV Vns ALLen eInen eDLen frIeDen* (Augsburg: Joseph Friedrich Rein, 1763).
15. Thomas Biskup and Peter H. Wilson, "Grossbritanien, Amerika und die atlantische Welt," in *Friederisiko: Friedrich der Grosse*, ed. Stiftung Preussische Schlösser und Gärten Berlin-Brandenburg (Munich: Hirmer, 2012), 154. Tim Blanning, *Frederick the Great: King of Prussia* (New York: Random House, 2016), 375–8.
16. Blanning, *Frederick*, 392–4.
17. An early nineteenth-century short novel for girls includes a visit to a print room where the characters discuss exactly this print by Mosley but identify the empress

as Catherine I and then note, when seeing another print showing Catherine II, "as she was not Catherine the Good, we had better, on the present occasion, pass by her." Maria Edgeworth, *Rosamond: A Sequel to Early Lessons*, 2 vols. (Philadelphia: J. Maxwell, 1821) 2:59–62.

18 *Catalogue of Cameos, Intaglios, Medals, Bas-Reliefs, Busts and Small Statues; with a General Account of Tablets, Vases, Ecritoires, and Other Ornamental and Useful Articles, the Whole Formed in Different Kinds of Porcelain and Terra Cotta, Chiefly after the Antique, and the Finest Models of Modern Artist*, 6th ed. (Etruria, 1787).

19 Marshall, *Celebrity and Power*, 12.

20 Vernon Hyde Minor, *Baroque & Rococo: Art and Culture* (New York: Harry N. Abrams, 1999), 227ff, Gisold Lammel, *Kunst im Aufbruch. Malerei, Graphik und Plastik zur Zeit Goethes* (Stuttgart: Metzler, 1998), 58ff.

21 Andrew Benjamin Bricker, "After the Golden Age: Libel, Caricature, and the Deverbalization of Satire," *Eighteenth-Century Studies* 51, no. 3 (2018): 305–36.

22 *Inventing Exoticism: Geography, Globalism, and Europe's Early Modern World* (Philadelphia: University of Pennsylvania, 2015), 293–4.

23 [LeBeau], *Catherine Alexiewna II*.

24 Since cheap prints were often not preserved over the intervening two centuries, it can be hard to determine today whether they appeared in a series, especially if the items are not numbered.

25 *Catherine II. d'Anhalt-Zerbst, Impératrice de Russie, d'Après un Medaille du temps*, in *Receuil d'estampes, représentant les Grades, les Rangs & les Dignités, suivant le costume de toutes les Nations existantes; avec des Explications historiques, & la Vie abrégée des grands Hommes qui ont illustré les dignités dont ils étoient décorés* (Paris: Duflos, 1784).

26 *Bitte und Erhoerung* ([Germany], 1779).

27 The original wording is *Catharina II. Heutige Czaarin* in the title, followed by *Fürst, Christ. Von Anhalt Zerbst, Tochter, geb. den 2. May 1729*. The color on the print is too dense to be effectively reproduced in black and white.

28 Michel Melot, "Caricature and the Revolution: The Situation in France in 1789," in *French caricature and the French Revolution, 1789–1799* (Los Angeles, Chicago: Grunwald Center for the Graphic Arts; University of Chicago, 1988), 29.

29 "Arts. Gravure," *Affiches, Annonces et Avis Divers ou Journal Général de France*, February 21, 1784, 109.

30 Madeleine Delpierre, *Dress in France in the Eighteenth Century* (New Haven and London: Yale University Press, 1997), 131.

31 Actual color printing using multiple plates, each with a different ink, was being developed in Paris, but it was exceptionally costly. National Gallery of Art (U.S.) and Margaret Morgan Grasselli, *Colorful Impressions: The Printmaking Revolution in Eighteenth-Century France* (Washington, DC: National Gallery of Art, 2003).

32 Seen in the art collection of the Palace Museum, Stadtschloss, Weimar, now part of the Klassik Stiftung Weimar.

33 *Abriss des Lebens und der Regierung Kaiserin Katharina II. von Russland* (Berlin: Nicolai, 1797), viii–ix.

34 Graeme Turner, *Understanding Celebrity*, 2 ed. (London: SAGE Publications, 2013), 17.

35 "Curious French Pyes," *Argus*, January 9, 1790 "Patence's Address to the Nobility and Gentry," *World*, December 6, 1787. "To the Ladies," *Morning Chronicle and London Advertiser*, September 29, 1783. "Advertisements and Notices," *Morning Herald*, April 17, 1781.

36 David Adshead, "Wedgwood, Wimpole and Wrest. The Landscape Drawings of Lady Amabel Polwarth," *Apollo* 143, April (1996): 33.
37 Iakov Karlovitch Grot, ed., *Lettres de Grimm à l'impératrice Catherine II. Lettres de Grimm au prince Galitzine. Lettres d'Ernest-Jean Biron à l'ambassadeur H. Keyserlingk. Lettres de Diderot à l'impératrice Catherine II* (Saint-Pétersbourg: Impr. de l'Académie des sciences, 1881), 20.
38 The image is in the vast and rich picture collection of the Austrian National Library, ONB Pg VIII in Ptf 28: (19). It is attributed there to the portrait engraver Johann Ernst Mansfeld (1738–96), although comparison with another piece, PG VIII in Ptf 28: (37), signed by Mansfeld and showing Catherine in a similar pose but depicting her quite differently, casts doubt on the attribution.
39 Lilti, *Invention*, 42.
40 [Trade card of Hatchett, Coach-Maker] (London: Darling & Thompson, 1790).
41 "Description of Mr. HATCHETT'S Manufactory in Long Acre, London," *The European Magazine, and London Review*, January 3 1783, 18; [Trade card of Hatchett, Coach-Maker] (London: Darling & Thompson, 1783).
42 "Description."
43 "Empress of Russia State Carriage," *British Museum Newspaper Clipping J*, 9.289.

Chapter 4

1 Henry Kamen, *Early Modern European Society* (New York: Routledge, 2000). In some societies, such as the Low Countries, the well-established, powerful, and wealthy hereditary elite were patricians without titles.
2 Maxine Berg and Elizabeth Eger, *Luxury in the Eighteenth-Century: Debates, Desires and Delectable Goods* (New York: Palgrave Macmillan, 2007), 195–219.
3 Daniel L. Purdy, *The Tyranny of Elegance: Consumer Cosmopolitanism in the Era of Goethe* (Baltimore, MD: Johns Hopkins University Press, 1998), 22–50.
4 "Lettres sur la Russie," in *Oeuvres philosophiques et littéraires* (Chez B. G. Hoffmann, 1795), 109. The publication history of this material is tangled. It seems to have appeared swiftly in both French and German: Lettre à Mad. de *** (Paris: chez Desenne, libraire au Palais Royal, 1792). *La merveille du siecle ou observations sur la vie politique es privee de Catharine II l'Incomparable* (1792); "Schreiben des Herrn Senac de Meillan aus Petersburg an Madame de *** in Paris," *Minerva* 1792. In 1796, it was published again in German: "Briefe über Rußland," *Olla Potrida* 1796.

   Sénac sent his epistolary essay about Catherine to her and received a rather detailed and boastful reply, but he made no mention of this correspondence when his epistolary essay went into print. *Catherine the Great: Selected Letters*, trans. Andrew Kahn and Kelsey Rubin-Detlev (Oxford: Oxford University Press, 2018), 309–10.
5 Brian Cowan, "News, Biography, and Eighteenth-Century Celebrity," in *Oxford Handbooks Online* (Oxford: Oxford University Press, 2016), https://www.oxfordhandbooks.com/view/10.1093/oxfordhb/9780199935338.001.0001/oxfordhb-9780199935338-e-132?rskey=Dx3gFY&result=4. PDF p. 4.
6 Sénac, "Lettres," 109.
7 "An Account of the late Revolution in Russia; collected from authentic Papers never before published," *The Beauties of All Magazines Selected for the Year 1762*, September 1762, 343–4.

8 Joh. Lorenz Rügendas, *Catharina Alexiewna / Russorum Imperatrix / Nata Princeps Anhalt: Servest: / nata d. 2. Mai 1729.* I am indebted to Rosie Razzall, Curator of Prints and Drawings, Royal Collection Trust, for investigating the two prints: https://www.rct.uk/collection/614318/catharina-ii-empress-of-russia https://www.rct.uk/collection/613856/josepha

In another instance, a picture of a princess named Bernhardina Christian Sophia was relabeled to be Catherine during her period as grand duchess.

9 Roach, "Nell Gwyn," 67.
10 One example: I.C. Kerstens, "Dass die Ehre und die Wohlfahrt eines Landes eine Folge von der Aufnahme der Wissenschaften sey, wurde in einer Rede erwogen von I. C. Kerstens" (Moskau, 1762).
11 Otto Dann, "Herder und die deutsche Bewegung," in *Johann Gottfried Herder 1744–1803*, ed. Gerhard Sauder (Hamburg: Felix Meiner Verlag, 1987), 317.
12 Cowan, "News."
13 Steven R. Fischer, *A History of Reading* (London: Reaktion, 2003), 256. T.C.W. Blanning, *The Culture of Power and the Power of Culture: Old Regime Europe, 1660–1789* (Oxford: Oxford University Press, 2002), 112–15.
14 "Zeitung," in *Grosses vollständiges Universal-Lexicon aller Wissenschafften und Künste*, ed. Johann Heinrich Zedler (Halle, 1749), col. 900, col. 06.
15 Ibid., col. 906–7.
16 Andrew Pettegree, *Invention of News: How the World Came to Know About Itself*, (New Haven: Yale University Press, 2014), 201–5, 233.
17 Jeremy D. Popkin, *News and Politics in the Age of Revolution: Jean Luzac's Gazette de Leyde* (Ithaca: Cornell University Press, 1989), 2.
18 In 1760 "the total number of copies of newspapers sold yearly in Britain amounted to . . . 9,464,790 and in 1767 to 11,300,980. In 1776 the number of newspapers published in London alone had increased to 53." Kevin Williams, *Read All About It: A History of the British Newspaper* (London: Routledge, 2010), 302.
19 Martin Welke, "Gemeinsame Lektüre und frühe Formen von Gruppenbildungen im 17. und 18. Jahrhundert: Zeitunglesen in Deutschland," in *Lesegesellschaften und europäische Emanzipation: Ein europäischer Vergleich*, ed. Otto Dann (München: Beck, 1981).
20 Popkin, *News*, 2.
21 *Fanny Burney and Her Friends: Select Passages from Her Diary and Other Writings*, ed. L.B. Seeley (Scribner and Welford, 1890).
22 *Amaliens von Lieman, eines eilfjährigen Frauenzimmers, Reisen durch einige Russiche Länder in vertrauten Briefen an ihre Freundin und vormalige Gouvernante Helena Gatterer in Göttingen* (Göttingen: Rosenbusch, 1794), 46–7. Helena Gatterer was the sister of the poet Philippine Engelhard-Gatterer and the daughter of a prolific German history professor.
23 Fischer, *History*, 255.
24 "Versuch über meine Verstandeserziehung," in *"Ich wünschte so gar gelehrt zu werden." Drei Autobiographien von Frauen des 18. Jahrhunderts. Texte und Erläuterungen*, ed. Magdalene Heuser et al. (Göttingen: Wallstein, 1994), 16. Ruth Pritchard Dawson, *The Contested Quill: Literature by Women in Germany*, 1770–1800 (Newark [Del.]: University of Delaware Press, 2002), 46–51; Dawson, "'Lights out! Lights out!' Women and the Enlightenment," *Gender in transition: Discourse and practice in German-Speaking Europe, 1750–1830*, ed. Ulrike Gleixner and Marion W Gray (Ann Arbor: University of Michigan Press, 2006), 218–45.

25 Susanne Greilich and York-Gothart Mix, *Populäre Kalender im vorindustriellen Europa: der "Hinkende Bote" / "Messager boiteux": kulturwissenschaftliche Analysen und bibliographisches Repertorium: ein Handbuch* (Berlin: Walter de Gruyter, 2006).
26 "Abschilderung der Russischen Kayserin Catharina II," in *Alter und neuer grosser Staats-, Kriegs- und Friedens Appenzeller-Calender, oder, Der hinkende Bott* (1773).
27 See the much cited article by Donald Horton and R. Richard Wohl, "Mass Communication and Para-Social Interaction: Observations on Intimacy at a Distance," *Psychiatry* 19, no. 3 (1956): 215–29.
28 Johann Georg Bullmann, *16 geheime verborgene Silhouetten* (Augsburg, 1795); *Fünfzehen geheim verborgene silhouetten, nebst einer Erklärung* / zu haben bey Johann Jacob Müller in Hanau (Hanau, Germany: Müller, 1793 or later); Edward Orme, *A New Puzzle. Portraits of a Great Politician & a Celebrated Duke, a Great Empress & the Grand Turk* (1794).
29 *Understanding Celebrity*, 24.
30 "Lettres," 108,110.
31 "Lettres," 108, 110.
32 John B. Thompson, *The Media and Modernity: A Social Theory of the Media* (Stanford, CA: Stanford University Press, 1995), 82–100.
33 Ewen, quoted in Rosemary J. Coombe, "The Celebrity Image and Cultural Identity: Publicity Rights and the Subaltern Politics of Gender," *Discourse* 14, no. 3 (1992): 66.
34 Ruth Stummann-Bowert, "Philippine Engelhard, geborene Gatterer: Ein bürgerliches Frauenleben zwischen Aufklärung und Empfindsamkeit," in *"Des Kennenlernens werth," Bedeutende Frauen Göttingens*, ed. Traudel Weber-Reich (Göttingen: Wallstein, 1995), 35.
35 *Secret Memoirs of the Court of Petersburg: Particularly towards the End of the Reign of Catharine II and the Commencement of that of Paul I. Serving as a Supplement to The Life of Catharine II.*, 2 ed. (London: T.N. Longman and O. Rees, 1801).
36 *Anecdotes of the Russian Empire. In a Series of Letters, Written, a Few Years Ago, from St. Petersburg* (London: Strahan & Cadell, 1784), 24–5.
37 *Invention*, 84.
38 Chris Barker and Dariusz Galasi´nski, *Cultural Studies and Discourse Analysis: A Dialogue on Language and Identity* (London: Sage, 2001), 125.
39 Biester, *Abriss*, 21.
40 Coombe, "Celebrity Image," 59.
41 *Celebrity*, 177. Marshall, *Celebrity and Power*, 105–10.
42 Caminer, *Geschichte*, 46.
43 Lorraine Gamman and Margaret Marshment, *The Female Gaze: Women as Viewers of Popular Culture* (Seattle: Real Comet Press, 1989), 1.
44 Karsch and Gleim, *Mein Bruder*, I,138.
45 Turner, *Understanding Celebrity*, 20.
46 Johann Joachim Bellermann, "Etwas über Rußland," *Olla Potrida*, 1788, 41.
47 Karl Ludwig Blum, *Ein russischer Staatsmann. Des Grafen Jakob Johann Sievers Denkwürdigkeiten zur Geschichte Rußlands*, 2 vols. (Leipzig: Winter, 1857), 1:379–87.
48 Ibid., 2:220.
49 Ibid., 2:22–3.
50 A similar pattern is evident in Ruth Pritchard Dawson, "Catherine II, Polyxene Büsching, and Johanna Charlotte Unzer: A Literary 'Community of Practice,'" in *Writing the Self, Creating Community: German Women Authors and the Literary*

Sphere, 1750–1850, ed. Elizabeth Krimmer and Lauren Nossett (Rochester, NY: Camden House, 2020), 87–115.
51 *The Letters of Horace Walpole: 1760–1764*, ed. Paget Toynbee, 16 vols. (Oxford: Clarendon Press, 1904), 5:314.
52 Johann Wolfgang von Goethe, *Briefe aus der Schweiz*, ed. Ernst Beutler, 2nd ed., vol. 4, *Gedenkausgabe* (1962), 488–9.
53 *Anekdoten aus dem Privatleben der Kaiserin Catharina, Pauls des Ersten und seiner Familie* (Hamburg, 1797), 26–7.
54 "Lettres," 110.
55 Ann Bermingham and John Brewer, *The Consumption of Culture, 1600–1800: Image, Object, Text* (London: Routledge, 1997).
56 van Krieken, *Celebrity Society*, 68.
57 H.F. Andrä, *Katharina die Zweite, Kaiserin von Russland und Selbstherrscherin aller Reussen. Ein biographisch-karakteristisches Gemälde* (Halle, 1797), 203.
58 Joseph A. Boone and Nancy J. Vickers, "Introduction—Celebrity Rites," *PMLA* 126, no. 4 (2011): 909.

Chapter 5

1 Norbert Elias, *Die höfische Gesellschaft: Untersuchungen zur Soziologie des Königtums und der höfischen Aristokratie* (Frankfurt a.M.: Suhrkamp, 1997). With *gloire* in court society functioning as both demonstration and source of power, formal or informal, it was closely related to another concept, *Repräsentation* (representation). As Jürgen Habermas explained, before European societies began shifting in the late eighteenth century from princely power to emerging bourgeois power, *Repräsentation* referred to an imposing display designed to correspond with an individual's high rank and status. *Repräsentation* suggests the intrinsic superior qualities of social elites and makes those qualities visible. It attaches to concrete persons, giving their authority a legitimizing "aura." *The Structural Transformation of the Public Sphere: An Inquiry into a Category of Bourgeois Society* (Cambridge, MA: MIT Press, 1989), 7–14. Unlike my usage of *gloire*, which is attached to the high-ranking elites, Antoine Lilti uses "glory" as a term for the fame achieved by anyone, regardless of rank, "who is judged to be extraordinary because of his or her achievements, whether these are acts of bravery, or artistic or literary works." Lilti, *Invention*, 5.
2 Abigail Green, *Fatherlands: State-Building and Nationhood in Nineteenth-Century Germany* (Cambridge: Cambridge University Press, 2001). 81). T. C. W. Blanning points out that this form of intimidation was not always effective, *Culture*, 384–8.
3 Her correspondence with Voltaire repeatedly shows this. *Lettres de l'Imperatrice de Russie et de M. de Voltaire*, vol. 67, *Oeuvres complètes* (Kehl, 1785), 13, 17, 32, 41, 53, 64, 70, 85, 154, 213, 326, and more. See also Kelsey Rubin-Detlev, *The Epistolary Art of Catherine the Great* (Liverpool University Press, 2019), passim.
4 *Structural Transformation*, 9–11.
5 John T. Alexander, *Catherine the Great: Life and Legend* (New York: Oxford, 1989), 242–3.
6 Johann Georg Mayer, *Der erhabene Adler in der Maske des Falken, oder Kaiser Joseph II Reise nach Russland unter dem Namen eines Grafen von Falkenstein, nebst einigen*

merkwürdigen Umständen (Augsburg: Johann Georg Bullmann, Buchhändler, 1780), 18–19.
7 Vigilius Erichsen, *Kaiserin Katharina II. von Rußland*, 1762, GK I 1023. In Stiftung Preußische Schlösser und Gärten Berlin-Brandenburg.
8 Lydia Liackhova, "Catherine II Enthroned," in *Treasures of Catherine the Great*, ed. State Hermitage Museum and Hermitage Development Trust (London: Christie's International Media, 2000), 45.
9 "An die Mütter des reisenden Chur- und liefländischen Adels," in *Neue Gedichte* (1772), 91–4.
10 *Reisen durch Brandenburg, Pommern, Preußen, Curland, Rußland und Pohlen, in den Jahren 1777 und 1778*, vol. 4 Aufenthalt zu St. Petersburg, nebst dem Verzeichniss der kaiserl. Gemäldesammlung, (Leipzig: Fritsch, 1780), 95.
11 Joachim Grafen von Sternberg, *Bemerkungen über Russland, auf einer Reise gemacht im Jahre 1792 und 1793* (n.p. 1794), 163.
12 *Fortgesetzte*, 21.
13 *Bemerkungen über Russland in Rücksicht auf Wissenschaft, Kunst, Religion und andere merkwürdige Verhältnisse* (Erfurt, 1788), 307.
14 *Cursory Remarks Made in a Tour through Some of the Northern Parts of Europe, Particularly Copenhagen, Stockholm and Petersburgh* (London: T. Cadell, 1775), 207.
15 *Secret Memoirs of the Court of Petersburg: Particularly towards the End of the Reign of Catharine II and the Commencement of that of Paul I*, 2 vols. (London: Printed by C. Whittingham for T.N. Longman and O. Rees, 1800), 1:46.
16 *Bemerkungen über Russland*, 307.
17 *Bemerkungen über Esthland, Liefland und Russland nebst einigen Beiträgen zur Empörungs-Geschichte Pugatschews, während eines achtjährigen Aufenthalts gesamlet von einem Augenzeugen* (Prag u. Leipzig: Meissner, 1792), 112–13.
18 *Bemerkungen . . . auf einer Reise*, 162.
19 *Secret Memoirs*, 1:45.
20 Patricia Meyer Spacks, *Gossip* (New York: Knopf, 1985), 87.
21 Casper von Saldern, *Biographie Peters des Dritten, Kaiser aller Reussen; zur unpartheyischen Ansicht der Wirkung der damaligen Revolution, und zur Berichtigung der Beurtheilung des Charakters Catharinens II* (Petersburg 1800), 236.
22 *Reisen durch Brandenburg, Pommern, Preußen, Curland, Rußland und Pohlen, in den Jahren 1777 und 1778*, vol. 5 Fortsetzung des Aufenthalts zu St. Petersburg (1780), 61–2.
23 *A History, Or Anecdotes, of the Revolution in Russia, in the Year 1762* (London: M. Beauvalet, 1797), 167–8.
24 *Catharina die zweite, die einzige Kaiserinn der Erde, Selbstherrscherinn aller Reussen, Tauriens würdigste Königinn, mächtigste Erretterinn und großmüthigste Beglückerinn. Ein unterthänigstes Opfer tiefster Bewunderung und reinster Ehrfurcht zum feierlichsten Glückwunsch unzählbar frohlockender Völker, am unsterblichsten Ihrer wohlthätigen Tage, am herrlichsten wonnevollen Krönungstag der Allgütigen und Allgeliebten Huldgöttin zu Tauriens urerster Alleinherrscherinn* (Frankfurt am Mein: Eichenberg, 1787), 49–50.
25 Joan B. Landes, *Visualizing the Nation: Gender, Representation, and Revolution in Eighteenth-Century France* (Cornell University Press, 2001), 17.
26 "Lettre sur la Russie," 108–9.
27 *Fortgesetzte*, 21.
28 *Bemerkungen über Russland*, 317.

29. Perhaps the foreign men who wrote about the empress did not understand the code. In one of her several memoir fragments, number II as assigned by the St. Petersburg Imperial Academy of Science in its 1907 publication of the pieces, Catherine mentioned notifying the Empress Elizabeth that ritual prohibitions about menstruation would prevent her from attending a particular mass; Elizabeth, according to the memoir, responded that she was in the same situation. Whether Catherine wrote this passage because her expected readership would find the information familiar or unsurprising or because she was simply comfortable with this aspect of her female body, is unclear. This and other menstrual references do not appear in her memoirs in English, which translate only the largest fragment of them; see *Memoirs*, lxxi. A German translation of all the fragment pieces includes the brief menstrual references; *Katharina die Grosse: Memoiren*, trans. Erich Boehme (1913; reprint, Frankfurt a. M.: Insel, 1996), 154–6, 229.
30. In addition to all the doubts about Paul's paternity that were raised during the coup, Helbig, writing after Catherine's death, insinuated that Poniatowski was Anna's father, adding that Peter received news of her imminent arrival with "apparent wonderment and visible revulsion." *Biographie Peter des Dritten*, 2 vols. (Tübingen: Cotta, 1808), 1:107.
31. *Reisen durch Brandenburg, Pommern, Preußen, Curland, Rußland und Pohlen, in den Jahren 1777 und 1778*, vol. 4 *Aufenthalt zu St. Petersburg* (1780), 110.
32. *Summer amusement at Farmer G-'s near Windsor*, British Museum, satirical print, asset number 80718001. https://www.britishmuseum.org/collection/object/P_1868-0808-6091.
33. These numbers are based on the collection at the British Museum, the best source of eighteenth-century visual satires.
34. Available online, for example: *The Queen of Hungary Stript* (1741) https://www.britishmuseum.org/collection/object/P_1868-0808-3719, *The Qu_n of Hungary stript* (1742) https://www.britishmuseum.org/collection/object/P_1868-0808-3685, *The Consultation of Physicians, on the case of the Queen of Hungary* (1742), https://www.britishmuseum.org/collection/object/P_1868-0808-3684 and *The Queen of Hungary's Whetstone* (1744) https://www.britishmuseum.org/collection/object/P_1868-0808-3769.
35. Hans van Koningsbrugge, "A Dutch Disaster: Russia and the Netherlands and the Fourth Anglo-Dutch War," in *"A Century Mad and Wise": Russia in the Age of the Enlightenment*, ed. Emmanuel Waegemans et al. (Groningen: 2015).
36. *Bemerkungen über Russland*, 315.
37. "Lettre sur la Russie," 112–13.
38. *Bemerkungen über Russland*, 315.
39. *Bemerkungen . . . auf einer Reise*, 162.
40. *Cursory Remarks Made in a Tour through Some of the Northern Parts of Europe, Particularly Copenhagen, Stockholm and Petersburgh* (London: T. Cadell, 1775), 207.
41. *Bemerkungen über Russland*, 315.
42. *Bemerkungen . . . auf einer Reise*, 162.
43. *Secret Memoirs*, 1:76.
44. Ibid., 1:53.
45. Ibid., 1:54. Or as the original text put it: "un air un peu sinister." *Mémoires secrets sur la Russie et particulièrement sur la fin du règne de Catherine II et le commencement de celui de Paul I.*, 3 vols. (Paris: C. Pougens, 1800), 1:87.

II

1 Van Krieken, *Celebrity Society*, 56

Chapter 6

1 Johann Gottfried Herder, "Die unsre Mutter ist," *Rigische Anzeigen von allerhand Sachen, deren Bekanntmachung dem gemeinen Wesen nöthig und nützlich ist*, July 4, 1765.
2 *Merkwürdige Lebensgeschichte*, 64.
3 Nina Rattner Gelbart, *Feminine and Opposition Journalism in Old Regime France: "Le Journal des Dames"* (Berkeley: University of California Press, 1987), 151.
4 In February the letter began to appear in French and English in magazines: "Lettre de l'Impératrice de Russie à M. d'Alembert au sujet de l'invitation qu'elle lui avoit fait fair de venir en Russie pour l'éducation du grand Prince son fils," *Journal encyclopédique* 1763. Catherine II, "Translation of a Letter from the Empress of Russia to M. d'Alembert, at Paris, whom she had invited into Russia to educate her Son," *The London magazine; or, Gentleman's monthly intelligencer*, February 1763.
5 "Translation of a Letter."
6 For example, Bachaumont, *Mémoire secrets pour servir a l'histoire de la republique des lettres en France, depuis MDCCLXII jusqu'a nos jours; ou Journal d'un observateur* (Londres: John Adamsohn, 1777), 217.
7 *From Peter the Great to the death of Nicholas I*, 2 vols., vol. 1, *Scenarios of Power: Myth and Ceremony in Russian Monarchy* (Princeton, NJ, 1995), 111–2. Wortman calls his chapter about Catherine II "Minerva Triumphant." For a satirical print of Catherine in a helmet, see Isaac Cruikshank's *The Genius of France extirpating Despotism, Tyranny & Oppression from the face of the Earth or the royal warriors defeated* (London: Fores, 1792).
8 "Schreiben aus Petersburg bey Gelegenheit der letztern Revolution," in *Merkwürdige Lebensgeschichte Peter des Dritten, Kaisers und Selbsthalters aller Reußen*, 2nd ed. (Frankfurth und Leipzig: 1762). Whether Catherine II was actually displeased by the letter's publication remains doubtful; Petr Romanovic Zaborov, "Katharina II. und Madame Geoffrin," in *Katharina II., Russland und Europa. Beiträge zur internationalen Forschung*, ed. Claus Scharf (Mainz: Philipp von Zabern, 2001), 322.
9 George Seymour, *The Instructive Letter-Writer, and Entertaining Companion: Containing Letters on the Most Interesting Subjects . . . Most of Which Are Wrote by . . . Royal and Eminent Personages, and the Best Authors* (London, 1763).
10 Dawson, "Catherine."
11 Ostensibly knowledge-based national academies had clear political elements, as is evident in the invitation Catherine received to join the Berlin academy in 1767 (L. Schiebinger, *The Mind Has No Sex?: Women in the Origins of Modern Science* (Cambridge, MA: Harvard University Press, 1991), 299.
12 "Monsieur Diderot," *The Gentleman's Magazine, and Historical Chronicle*, May 1765, 242.
13 As a few examples: "Gran-Russia," *Gazzetta universale: o sieno notizie istoriche, politiche, di scienze, arti agricoltura, ec*, April 1, 1780; *Authentic Memoirs of the Life and Reign of Catherine II. Empress of all the Russias* (London, 1797), 42–9; Biester, *Abriss*, 198.

14 "Nouvelles Politiques. Pétersbourg (le 12 Décembre)," *Journal encyclopédique ou universel*, January 1767.
15 Bachaumont, *Mémoires Secrets*, 218–19.
16 Some scholars attribute the break to Geoffrin's failure to continue to St. Petersburg despite visiting Warsaw; Andrew Kahn and Kelsey Rubin-Detlev, "Introduction," in *Catherine the Great: Selected Letters* (Oxford: Oxford University Press, 2018).
17 [Johann Georg Heinzmann], "Madam de Geoffrin," in *Historisches Bilderbuch des Edlen und Schönen aus dem Leben würdiger Frauenzimmer* (Bern: Haller, 1790). 95.
18 "Supplement a la Gazette de Vienne 97," *Gazette de Vienne*, December 8, 1763.
19 *Catharina die Zweite. Darstellungen aus der Geschichte ihrer Regierung, und Anekdoten von ihr und einigen Personen, die um sie waren* (Altona: Hammerich, 1797).
20 "On peut se rappeller les instances," *Gazette des gazettes ou Journal politique: pour l'année*, November, first fortnight 1764. Albert Lortholary, *Le Mirage russe en France au XVIIIe siècle* (Paris, 1951), 92.
21 Pierre Ricaud de Tiregale, *Medailles sur les principaux evenements de l'Empire de Russie depuis le Regne de Pierre le Grand jusqu'à celui de Catherine II, avec des explications historiques* (Potsdam: Sommer, 1772).
22 *Account of the Prisons and Hospitals in Russia, Sweden, and Denmark. With Occasional Remarks on the Different Modes of Punishments in Those Countries* (London: T. Cadell, 1781), 16–17.
23 *Travels in Poland, Russia, Sweden, and Denmark: Illustrated with Charts and Engravings*, 5 vols. (Printed for T. Cadell, jun. and W. Davies, 1802), 1:389.
24 August Ludwig Schlözer (Joh. Joseph Haigold, pseud.), *Neuverändertes Russland, oder, Leben Catharina der Zweyten, Kayserinn von Russland aus authentischen Nachrichten beschrieben* (Riga und Mietau: Bey Johann Friedrich Hartknoch, 1771), 20 of unnumbered introduction. Especially in Protestant areas of Europe, foundling hospitals met with criticism. See Otto Ulbricht, "The Debate about Foundling Hospitals in Enlightenment Germany: Infanticide, Illegitimacy, and Infant Mortality Rates," *Central European History* 18, Sep/Dec, no. 3/4 (1985).
25 "Gran-Russia," *Gazzetta universale: o sieno notizie istorice, politiche, di scienze, arti agricoltura, ec*, April 1.
26 Adam Friedrich Geisler, *Gallerie edler deutscher Frauenzimmer, mit getroffenen Schattenrissen* (Dessau und Leipzig: Buchhandlung der Gelehrten, 1784).
27 "Beytrag zur Geschichte der Menschheit," *Deutsche Chronik* (Deutsche Neudrucke. Reihe Goethezeit, 1774; reprint, Heidelberg: Schneider, [1975]), 379.
28 *Forbidden*, 115.
29 Louis-Sébastien Mercier, *Memoirs of the Year Two Thousand Five Hundred*, 2 vols., vol. 1 (Dublin: Wilson, 1772), 77–8.
30 Voltaire, *Œuvres de Voltaire: Lettres de l'imperatrice de Russie et de M. de Voltaire*, ed. C.P. de Montenoy (Chez Stoupe: Imprimeur, 1802), 53. Voltaire and Catherine II, *Voltaire and Catherine the Great: Selected Correspondence*, ed. A. Lentin (Cambridge: Oriental Research Partners, 1974), 69.
31 "Russia," *The Scots Magazine*, March 30, 1768: 156. That Catherine took most of her ideas from other writers was immediately recognized.
32 *On Marriage*, trans. Timothy F. Sellner (Detroit: Wayne State UP, 1994), 103; Theodor Gottlieb von Hippel, *Über die Ehe*, 3rd. enlarged ed. (Berlin: Voss, 1792); Ruth Pritchard Dawson, "The Feminist Manifesto of Theodor Gottlieb von Hippel (1741–1796)," in *Gestaltet und Gestaltend: Frauen in der deutschen Literatur*, ed. Marianne Burkhard, Amsterdamer Beiträge zur neueren Germanistik (Amsterdam: Rodopi, 1980).

33 Pieter van Woensel, *Der gegenwärtige Staat von Russland* (St. Petersburg, Leipzig 1783), 48.
34 [Bellermann], *Bemerkungen über Russland*, 1:164–6.
35 "General Aspect of Affairs at the Beginning of the Year," in *The Annual Register, or a View of the History, Politicks and Literature of the Year, for the Year 1766* (London: Dodsley, 1767), 6.
36 M[elchior] A[dam] Weikard, *Denkwürdigkeiten aus der Lebensgeschichte des kaiserl. Russischen Staatsraths M.A. Weikard* (Leipzig, 1802), 351.
37 J.H. Merck et al., *Briefwechsel*, vol. 2 (Wallstein, 2007), 489.
38 Voltaire, *Lettres* 67, 67, 75–6.
39 Weikard, *Denkwürdigkeiten*, 351.
40 Grot, quoted in H. L. C. Bacmeister, review of Grot, "Kanzelrede von der Rechtmäßigkelt der Blattern-Einimpfung," *Russische Bibliothek, zur Kenntniss des gegenwärtigen zustandes der Literatur in Russland* 1772, 511.
41 "Mittau. 16. November," *Gazette van Gendt*, December 5, 1768; "Petersburgo 15 de Noviembre de 1768," *Gazeta de Madrid*, December 27, 1768.
42 "Etats du Nord," *Suite de la clef ou journal historique sur les matieres du tems*, February 1769. "De St. Petersbourg," *Mercure historique et politique: contenant l'état présent de l'Europe, ce qui se passe dans toutes les cours, les intérêts des princes et généralement tout ce qu'il y a de plus curieux*, December 1768.
43 Voltaire and Catherine, *Selected*, 52–4.
44 "Curious Anecdotes of Dr. Dimsdale's Inoculation of the Empress of Russia," *The Town and Country Magazine, or Universal Repository of Knowledge, Instruction, and Entertainment* 1769. Dimsdale's compensation was itemized, for example, in I. Kimber and E. Kimber, *The London Magazine, or, Gentleman's Monthly Intelligencer* (London, 1768), 707.
45 A review of Roman's *L'Inoculation*, for example, appeared in the *Journal des Beaux-Arts* and was reprinted in *L'Esprit des journaux, françois et étrangers*, January, 1774, 107. An Italian poem about inoculation appeared in "Notizie Letterarie," *Gazzetta universale: o sieno notizie istorice, politiche, di scienze, arti agricoltura, ec* , April 25, 1775.
46 Richardson, *Anecdotes*, 33; *Authentic*, 92–3; Biester, *Abriss*, 210–11; [James Walker], *Paramythia; or, Mental Pastimes: Being Original Anecdotes, Historical, Descritive, Humourous, and Witty* (London: Lawler, 1821), 104.
47 John Joseph Therese Roman, *L'inoculation, poëme en quatre chants* (Lacombe, 1773), viii. The poetic account of Catherine's inoculation on pp. 164–6 and the accompanying note on p. 203 closely resembles the account cited above in *Suite de les Clefs*, which may have been in turn either a copy or a much-copied original.
48 Ibid., xviii–xix.
49 F. Zacchiroli, *L'inoculazione. Poemetto* (1775). [Johann Gottlieb Willamow], "Auf die Inoculation der Kaiserinn von Rußland," in *Almanach der deutschen Musen: auf das Jahr 1771*, ed. C. H. Schmid and F. T. Hase (Weygand, 1771), 67–8.
50 *Observations on the Present State of Denmark, Russia and Switzerland. In a Series of Letters* (London: T. Cadell, 1784), 159–60.
51 Catherine's colonization project is thoroughly discussed in Roger P. Bartlett, *Human Capital: The Settlement of Foreigners in Russia 1762–1804* (Cambridge: Cambridge University Press, 1979).
52 "Die Regierungs-Geschichte der Rußischen Kaiserinn im Jahr 1766," *Fortgesetzte neue genealogisch-historische Nachrichten*, 1767, 635–8.

53 "Philosophers Despise Etiquette," *General Advertiser*, September 14, 1786.
54 "Kurze Nachrichten," *Gothaische gelehrte Zeitungen* 1774, 200.
55 Johann Bernhard Basedow, *Des Elementarwerks Dritter Band: Ein geordneter Vorrath aller nöthigen Erkenntniß*, vol. 3 of *Elementarwerk* (Dessau, 1774), 143–4.
56 *Am Geburtsfest der Großen Kayserin Katharina der Zweyten den 21 April 1781* (St. Petersburg, 1781), [3, 8].
57 "A Genuine Anecdote of the Empress of Russia," *General Evening Post*, July 27–29, 1773.
58 Robert Zaretsky, *Catherine & Diderot: The Empress, the Philosopher, and the Fate of the Enlightenment* (Cambridge, MA: Harvard University Press, 2019).
59 *Denkwürdigkeiten*, 246.
60 "Petersburg, vom 12 April," *Frankfurter Kayserl. Reichs-Ober-Post-Amts-Zeitung*, May 9, 1774.
61 "A Gentleman Just Arrived from Holland," *General Evening Post*, Nov. 3–5, 1774, 4.
62 Christian Friedrich Daniel Schubart, "Russland," *Deutsche Chronik*, no. 54 (1774). Lortholary, *Mirage*, 222–42. Zaretsky discusses Diderot's long unpublished accounts of his experience with the empress; *Catherine & Diderot*, 198–224.
63 *Aechte Nachrichten von dem Grafen Cagliostro: Aus der Handschrift seines entflohenen Kammerdieners* (Berlin, 1786), 39–40, 66.
64 *Nachricht von des berüchtigten Cagliostro Aufenthalte in Mittau, im Jahre 1779, und von dessen dortigen magischen Operationen* (Berlin: Nicolai 1787). Elisa von der Recke, *Tagebücher und Selbstzeugnisse*, ed. C. Träger (C.H. Beck, 1984), 356.
65 Catherine II, "Schreiben der Kaiserinn von Rußland an Frau von der Recke," *Berlinische Monatsschrift* (1788): 194. In 1794, the poet visited St. Petersburg and was granted financial assistance by the empress; Recke, *Tagebücher*, 298. See also Rubin-Detlev, *Epistolary*, passim.
66 Since it appeared anonymously, the bad-tempered *Antidote* (1770), an attack in French on a visiting astronomer's account of her empire, could have no impact on Catherine's image (and her role in its authorship is still disputed) [Catherine II], *Antidote ou examen du mauvais libre intitulé: Voyage en Sibiré faut en 1761*, 2 vols. (1770).
67 "Note de l'éditeur," in *Théâtre de l'Hermitage de Catherine II, impératrice de Russie composé par cette princesse, par plusieurs personnes de sa société intime, et par quelques ministres etrangers* (Paris: Gide, 1799), 1. Catherine II and L.P. de Ségur, "Imitation de Schakespear, scene historique, sans observation d'aucune règle du theatre, tirée de la vie de Rurick," in *Théâtre de l'Hermitage de Catherine II, impératrice de Russie* (F. Buisson, 1799).
68 "Review of *Acta Academia*," *Appendix to the Monthly Review* 69 (1783): 585.
69 Anton Friderich Büsching, "S. Petersburg," *Wöchentliche Nachrichten von neuen Landcharten, geographiscen, statistichen und historischen Büchern und Schriften* (1783).
70 Saldern, *Biographie*, 110.
71 Sophie von La Roche, *Fanny und Julia, oder die Freundinnen*, 2 vols., vol. 2 (Leipzig: Gräff, 1802), 132.
72 The new German friend of most importance to Catherine was Friedrich Melchior Grimm, recognized in the periodical press of the time as Catherine's agent and occasional public intermediary. "Il circule," *Journal historique et politique des principaux événements des différentes cours de l'Europe*, December 10, 1778; "Berichtigung," *Allgemeine Literatur-Zeitung*, October 26, 1786. Because he moved mostly in elite circles, not the sphere of celebrity fans, and kept his friendship with

Catherine II out of the public eye, he did not contribute significantly to her popular fame, but see Zaretsky, *Catherine & Diderot*, passim.
73 For example, "Vermischte Nachrichten," *Münchner Zeitung*, February 11, 1785, 104.
74 This is the title as it was published in translation in 1791. In German it is: *Über Friedrich den Grossen und meine Unterredungen mit Ihm kurz vor seinem Tode* (Vienna: Diepold, 1788).
75 The German Enlightenment figure Georg Christoph Lichtenberg probably refers to Catherine's relationship with Zimmermann in a letter from February 3, 1785, begging, "Do write me the anecdote about the empress and the trumpeter. Call her Cousin Meichel and the other one . . . Mouthpiece; then no one will understand it but you and I, but, in any case, also use a separate large sheet of paper and I will burn it up. Please, please." Georg Christoph Lichtenberg, *Briefwechsel 1785–1792*, ed. Ulrich Joost and Albrecht Schöne, vol. 3 of 5, *Georg Christoph Lichtenberg Briefwechsel* (München: C.H. Beck, 1990).
76 [Theodor Gottlieb von Hippel], *Zimmermann der I. und Friedrich II.* (Lagarde, 1790).
77 J. G. B. Büschel, *Ueber die Charlatanerie der Gelehrten seit Menken* (Leipzig: bey J.G.Büschels Wittwe, 1791), 171.
78 [August Friedrich Ferdinand von Kotzebue], *Doctor Bahrdt mit der eisernen Stirn, oder die deutsche Union gegen Zimmermann; ein Schauspiel in 4 Aufz*, 1791.
79 J. G. Zimmermann, *Fragmente über Friedrich den Grossen zur Geschichte seines Lebens, seiner Regierung, und seines Charakters*. 3 vols. (Leipzig: Weidmann, 1790), 3:329–36.

Chapter 7

1 "Revolution in Denmark. Counts Struensee and Brandt Are Confined in the Citadel . . . Magnificence of the Empress of Russia," in *Annual Register, or a View of the History, Politicks, and Literature of the Year 1772* (London: Dodsley, 1773), 80.
2 Ibid.
3 The poem appeared in the *Poetische Blumenlese auf das Jahr 1777* (Poetic Flower Bouquet for the Year 1777) and is quoted in the "Poetische Blumenlese auf das Jahr 1777," *Neueste critische Nachrichten* 3, no. 27 (1777), which names some of the contributors, including Klopstock, Gleim, Ramler, and Karsch, and says this is one of the prettiest "flowers" in the collection.
4 "Amsterdam 10. Agosto," *Notizie del Mondo* 1772.
5 "Revolution."
6 Marcia Pointon, "Intrigue, Jewellery, and Economics: Court Culture and Display in England and France in the 1780s," in *Markets for Art, 1400–1800*, ed. C.E. Núñez, M. North, and D. Ormrod (Seville: Secretariado de Publicaciones de la Universidad de Sevilla, 1998), 201.
7 *Des pierres précieuses et des pierres fines, avec les moyens de les connoître & de les évaluer* (Paris: Didot & DeBure, 1776). 19–20.
8 For example, Guillaume-Thomas-François Raynal, abbé, *Histoire philosophique et politique des établissemens et du commerce des Européens dans les deux Indes*, vol. 5 (Geneva: chez J.-L. Pellet, 1781), 251. Catherine's own correspondence asserts that she organized the purchase. Whittaker, "Catherine," 159.

9. Nathaniel William Wraxall, *A tour "round the Baltic: Thro" the Northern Countries of Europe, Particularly Denmark, Sweden, Finland, Russia and Prussia*, 4 ed. (London: T. Cadell, 1807). Helbig later repeated Pallas's claims about the stone; *Russische Günstlinge* (Tübingen, 1809), 277, 409.
10. Elias, *Höfische Gesellschaft*, 102–13, 235–8.
11. Pointon, "Intrigue," 209.
12. John Lind, *Letters Concerning the Present State of Poland. With an Appendix, Containing the Manifestoes of the Courts of Vienna, Petersburg, and Berlin* (London: T. Payne, 1773), 11–12.
13. "Lettre sur la Russie," in *Oeuvres philosophiques et littéraires* (Chez: B. G. Hoffmann, 1795), 115–16. For more on the party, see George E. Munro, "Catherine Discovers St. Petersburg," *Jahrbücher für Geschichte Osteuropas* 56 (2008): 337–8.
14. *Ways of Seeing* (London: Penguin, 1972), 131–3.
15. This list draws on the work of Stephen Gundle, although I disagree with his rejection of glamour at courts. *Glamour: A History* (Oxford: Oxford University Press, 2008), 5–6.
16. Friedrich Carl Moser, "Catherina die Zweyte, Kaiserin von Rußland. Ein Gemäld ohne Schatten, 1773," *Deutsches Museum* 5 (1776): 384.
17. Mayer, *Erhabene*, 34–5.
18. Theodor Josephides von Tomanskiy, *Kurzer Entwurf der Lebensbeschreibung Ihro Majestät, Katharinen der Zweiten, Kaiserin und Selbstherrscherin von ganz Rußland* (n.p. 1774), 53.
19. Sternberg, *Bemerkungen ... auf einer Reise*, 162–3.
20. [Bellermann], *Bemerkungen über Russland*, 317.
21. Elizaveta Renne, "Catherine II through the Eyes of Vigilius Eriksen and Alexander Roslin," *Catherine the Great and Gustav III*, ed. Nationalmuseum (Sweden) and the State Hermitage Museum (St. Petersburg), Exhibition catalog (Helsingborg: Boktryck AB, 1999), 104–5, 7.
22. Rosalind Savill, "'Cameo Fever': Six Pieces from the Sèvres Porcelain Dinner Service Made for Catherine II of Russia," *Apollo* CXVI, no. 249 (1982).
23. [Christoph von Schmidt-Phiseldek], *Briefe über Russland. Erste Sammlung*, 2 vols. (Braunschweig: Schrödersche Buchhandlung, 1770). 70.
24. Ulrich Wyrwa, "Luxus und Konsum: Begriffsgeschichtliche Aspekte," in *Luxus und Konsum - eine historische Annäherung*, ed. Reinhold Reith and Torsten Meyer (Münster: Waxmann, 2003); Dena Goodman, "Furnishing Discourses: Readings of a Writing Desk in Eighteenth-Century France," in *Luxury in the Eighteenth Century: Debates, Desires, and Delectable Goods*, ed. Maxine Berg and Elizabeth Eger (New York: Palgrave Macmillan, 2007); John Sekora, *Luxury: The Concept in Western Thought, Eden to Smollett* (Baltimore: Johns Hopkins University Press, 1977).
25. "For the Inspection of the Curious," *Morning Post*, April 18, 1785.
26. *Ways of Seeing*, 131.
27. Marshall, *Celebrity and Power*, 118.
28. Maxine Berg, *Luxury and Pleasure in Eighteenth-Century Britain* (Oxford: Oxford University Press, 2007), 11–45. Purdy, *The Tyranny of Elegance*, 22–50.
29. "For the Inspection," *Morning Post*, April 18, 1785; "This and Every Evening This Week," *Morning Herald and Daily Advertiser*, April 17, 1781; "Patence's Operations, and Extraordinary Gift in Curing Diseases," *World and Fashionable Advertiser*, June 6, 1787; "Patence's Address to the Nobility and Gentry," *World*, December 6, 1787.

30 Johann Heinrich Christian Meyer, *Briefe über Russland*, 2 vols. (Göttingen: Rosenbusch, 1778–1779), 2:11–12.
31 Nina Kosareva, "Masterpieces of Eighteenth-Century French Sculpture," *Apollo* 101, June (1975): 447. A young sculptor in Paris who tried to help with the Russian recruitment of artists was sent to the Bastille for his efforts.
32 "Russie," *Courier de l'Europe*, March 7, 1777, 295.
33 Dixon, *Catherine*, 234–5.
34 Wraxall, *Cursory*, 211. Repeated in Brydone and Wraxall, "Anecdotes of Signiora Gabrieli, the Celebrated Opera Singer," *Annual Register, or a View of the History, Politicks, and Literature of the Year 1775* (1776).
35 Moser, "Catherina," 384.
36 Mayer, *Erhabene*.
37 *Beurlaubung Josephs II röm. Kais. und Cathar. II russische Kaiser*, In Mayer, *Der erhabene Adler* (Augsburg u. Kauffbeiren, 1780).
38 Berg, *Luxury*, 162–8, 310–11.
39 [F. Sastres], "12 Agosto. / 12th August," *Il Mercurio italico, o sia, Ragguaglio generale intorno alla letteratura, belle arti, utili scoperte, ec. di tutta l'Italia - The Italian Mercury: or, a General Account Concerning the Literature, Fine Arts, Useful Discoveries, &c. of All Italy*, August 1789, 127–8.
40 Michael Schneider, "The Nature, History, and Significance of the Concept of Positional Goods," *History of Economics Review* 45, Winter (2007): 60–81.
41 *An Inquiry into the Nature and Causes of the Wealth of Nations*, 1776, Bk.1, ch.11.
42 Whittaker, "Catherine," 148–54.
43 *Collecting in a Consumer Society* (London: Routledge, 1995), 66–7.
44 "Hamburgh, Aug. 16," *Annual Register, or a View of the History, Politicks, and Literature of the Year 1771* (1772).
45 Moira Vincentelli, *Women and Ceramics: Gendered Vessels* (Manchester: Manchester University Press, 2000). 115.
46 Whittaker, "Catherine," 163–6.
47 For an example of payment problems, see "Deaths. 10. At London," *Edinburgh Magazine, or Literary Miscellany* 1787; "The Late Lyde Browne," *Gazetteer & New Daily Advertiser* (1787). For the disastrous loss of an art collection at sea, see Christian Ahlström, "The Empress of Russia and the Dutch Snow the Vrouw Maria," National Board of Antiquities, Finnland, http://www.nba.fi/en/cultural_environment/archaeological_heritage/research/wreck_finds/vmuw/articles/empress. Oscar Gelderblom, "Coping with the Perils of the Sea: The Last Voyage of Vrouw Maria in 1771," *International Journal of Maritime History* 15, no. 2 (2003): 95–115.
48 "Progress of the Arts," *English Chronicle*, January 26, 1786, 4.
49 Grigorieva, Irina, and Madeleine Pinault Sorensen, "L'Acquisition du cabinet Hoüel par Catherine II," *Gazette des Beaux-Arts*, November 1995, 171–86.
50 Pierre Descargues, *The Hermitage Museum Leningrad* (New York: Harry N. Abrams, 1961), 46–7.
51 "Berlin," *Berlinische Nachrichten von Staats- und gelehrten Sachen*, September 3, 1774.
52 Ludwig Heinrich Nicolay and Friedrich Nicolai, eds., *Die beiden Nicolai: Briefwechsel zwischen Ludwig Heinrich Nicolay in St. Petersburg und Friedrich Nicolai in Berlin (1776–1811)* (Lüneburg: Verlag Nordostdeutsches Kulturwerk, 1989), 54–6, 128. Near the end of Catherine's life, when the much admired Elizabeth Louise Vigée le Brun came to St. Petersburg, the aging empress was not interested. D. Sutton, "Russian Francophiles of the Dix-huitième," *Apollo* 101 (1975): 420.

53 Inna Gorbatov, *Catherine the Great and the French Philosophers of the Enlightenment: Montesquieu, Voltaire, Rousseau, Diderot, and Grimm* (Bethesda, MD: Academica, 2006).
54 Merck et al., *Briefwechsel*, 2, 472–3., 472–3.
55 Ibid., 476–7.
56 Cited in Brian Grosskurth, "Shifting Monuments: Falconet's Peter the Great between Diderot and Eisenstein," *Oxford Art Journal* 23, no. 2 (2000): 43.
57 Marin Carburi, calling himself Chevalier de Lascary, *Monument élevé à la gloire de Pierre-le-Grand, ou relation des travaux et de moyens méchaniques pour transporter à Petersbourg un rocher destiné à servir de base à la statue équestre de cet empereur; avec un examen physique et chymique du même rocher* (Paris: chez Nyon, Stoupe, 1777); Richardson, *Anecdotes*, 179.
58 *Reisen*, 89–90, 47; Richardson, *Anecdotes*, 179; Woensel, *Der gegenwärtige Staat von Russland*, 140; [Bellermann], *Bemerkungen über Russland*, 218.
59 I.C. Krüger, [Medal illustration for] "Nachricht von der Bearbeitung und Fortschaffung des Felsen, auf welchem Catherina II. die Statüe Peter I. errichtete; mit dem Kupferstich derselben," *Historisches Portefeuille* September (1783).
60 Basile Baudez, "The Monument to Peter the Great by Falconet: A Place Royale by the Neva?," in *Reading the Royal Monument in Eighteenth-Century Europe*, ed. Charlotte Chastel-Rousseau (Farnham, UK: Ashgate Pub., 2011).
61 [William Thomson], *Letters from Scandinavia: On the Past and Present State of the Northern Nations of Europe* (Printed for G.G. and J. Robinson, 1796), 233, 196.
62 Moser, "Catherina," 387–8.
63 Edmund Heier, *L. H. Nicolay (1737–1820) and His Contemporaries* (The Hague,: M. Nijhoff, 1965), 134–5.
64 "Accounts from Petersburgh," *Public Advertiser*, October 14, 1784.
65 Joachim Berger, *Anna Amalia von Sachsen-Weimar-Eisenach (1739–1807): Denk- und Handlungsräume einer "aufgeklärten" Herzogin* (Heidelberg: Universitätsverlag Winter, 2003), 436.
66 *Stettiner Zeitung*, January 9, 1797. He sent more music at the beginning of November 1796, hoping for another reward, but it arrived in the hands of a different ruler. Fortunately for Benda, Paul responded with a golden snuffbox and handwritten note.
67 "Lettre adressée aux Editeurs de la Gazette Littéraire de l'Europe," *Gazette littéraire de l'Europe: augm. de plus. articles, qui ne se trouvert pas dans l'éd. de Paris*, v. 75 (1776). Juliane Cornelia de Lannoy, "A Sa Majesté l'Imperatrice de Russie," *Gazette Littéraire de l'Europe* 75 (1776).
68 Sophie von La Roche, "Zwey schöne Erscheinungen des letzten Jahres," *Pomona für Teutschlands Töchter* 2, no. 1 (1784): 132–3.
69 "Über Teutschland," *Pomona für Teutschlands Töchter* 1, no. 8 (1783): 732.
70 Nicolay and Nicolai, *Die beiden Nicolai*, 188. Sophie von La Roche, *Briefe an Lina* (Speier: Enderesischen Schriften, 1785). She dedicated the third edition, published the year after Catherine's death, to the next Russian empress.
71 *Catharina II dargestellt in ihren Werken zur Beherzigung der Völker Europens* (Berlin, 1794), 24. Bilbassoff, *Katharina II*, 1:641.
72 William Dent, *The Italian Poet*, 1783. Etched satire.
73 "Excerpts from A Sketch of the Secret History of Europe, since the Peace of Paris," *London Chronicle*, September 26–29, 1772.
74 *Catherine the Great: Selected Letters*, 29–30, 40.

75 Joseph Bourdillon, "Essai Historique & Critique sur les Dissentions des Eglises de Pologne," *L'Evangile du Jour* 1769, 103–7, 12–22; Voltaire, *Nouveaux mélanges philosophiques, historiques, critiques, etc. etc* (1768), 29, 304, 67.
76 "Geneve," *Journal historique et politique des principaux événements des différentes cours de l'Europe*, December 10, 1778, 443.
77 "Ces armes du ridicule," *Journal politique, ou Gazette des gazettes*, December 5, 1791, 57–8; translated in "Correspondence of Volney and Baron de Grimm," *The Gentleman's Magazine, and Historical Chronicle*, November 1830, 387–90.

Chapter 8

1 After Elizabeth's death, Catherine immediately put on the voluminous robes of mourning, which concealed the fact that she was pregnant again, and not by Peter.
2 La Roche, "Über Teutschland," 741.
3 Andrä, *Katharina die Zweite*, 165.
4 Strunck, "Two Bodies."
5 A print of Catherine in coronation garb with a framed picture of Paul on the table beside her was devised by an engraver in Venice, but, because even this exception was large, fine, and undoubtedly expensive, it did not become widely known. Josef/Giuseppe Lante, *Catherina.II. Magna Felix Augusta*, double portrait. See also Strunck, "Two Bodies," 70–1.
6 Ruth Pritchard Dawson, "Katharina II. Kaiserin von Russland: Das Märchen vom Zarewitsch Chlor (1782)," in *Lexikon deutschsprachiger Epik und Dramatik von Autorinnen (1730–1900)*, ed. Gabriele Pailer and Gudrun Loster-Schneider (Tübingen: Narr Francke Attempto Verlag, 2006), 237–9.
7 [Johann Friedrich Ernst Albrecht], *Miranda, Königinn im Norden. Geliebte Pansalvins* (Germanien (Erfurt): Hennings, 1798); *Pansalvin, Fürst der Finsterniss, und seine Geliebte. So gut wie geschehen* (Germanien, 1794); *Kakodämon der Schreckliche. Pansalvins und Mirandas Donnerkeil, Revisor des Codex der Menschen-Rechte* (Pyropolis, 1800); *Staub der Erste, Kayser der Unterwelt, als Beschluß des Pansalvin und der Miranda* (Persepolis, 1802); *Turbans Turbandus der grossen Miranda kleiner Sohn. Von einer diplomatischen Feder* (1802).
8 Albrecht, *Staub*, 23–4.
9 Ibid. 34–5.
10 Strunck, "Two Bodies," 68–70.
11 "Foreign Affairs," *The London Magazine, Or, Gentleman's Monthly Intelligencer*, August 1764.
12 Marie Daniel Bourrée Corberon, *Edition électronique du Journal du baron Marie Daniel Bourrée de Corberon, Paris-Saint Pétersbourg-Paris 1775-1785*, ed. Dominique Taurisson and Pierre-Yves Beaurepaire (Used, June 2007), 202.
13 *Letters written by the late Right Honourable Philip Dormer Stanhope, Earl of Chesterfield, to his son, Philip Stanhope*, ESTC T092045 ed., 4 vols. (London: P. Dodsley, 1797), 4:160.
14 *Anecdoten zur Lebensgeschichte des Ritters und Reichs-Fürsten Potemkin. Nebst einer kurzen Beschreibung der ehemaligen Krimm . . . desgleichen der Reise der Kaiserin Katharina der Zweiten nach der Krimm* (Freistadt am Rhein: Brockhaus, 1792), 231.

15 Robert K. Massie, *Catherine the Great: Portrait of a Woman*, 1st ed. (New York: Random House, 2011), 429–30; Sebag Montefiore, *Prince of Princes: The Life of Potemkin* (New York: St. Martin's, 2000), 136–50.
16 [Charles François Philibert Masson], *Secret Memoirs of the Court of Petersburg: Particularly towards the End of the Reign of Catharine II and the Commencement of that of Paul I. Serving as a Supplement to the Life of Catherine II* (London: T.N. Longman and O. Rees, 1802), 305–6.
17 For example, [Schmidt-Phiseldek], *Briefe über Russland*. Erste Sammlung, 113–14. Linguet, *Annales politiques, civiles, et littéraire du dix-huitieme siècle* (1777): 8–9.
18 Masson, *Secret*, 305–6.
19 Halem, "Arion, An Katharina die Zweite," *Deutsches Museum*, no. 1 (1786): 1–9.
20 *Lasting peace to Europe. The Dream of an Cosmopolite. Dedicated to her Imperial Majesty the Empress of Russia* (London, 1781), iii.
21 Quoted in Sarah Maza, "The Diamond Necklace Affair Revisited (1785-1786): The Case of the Missing Queen," in *Eroticism and the Body Politic*, ed. Lynn Hunt (Baltimore: Johns Hopkins UP, 1991), 82.
22 *Essays on physiognomy; For the Promotion of the Knowledge and Love of Mankind*, trans. Holcroft, abridged ed. (London: Vernor & Hood, 1806).
23 *Congres Politique, ou Entretiens Libres des Puissances de l'Europe; sur le bal géenéral prochain* (London, 1772).
24 Voltaire, *Oeuvres*, v. 67, *Lettres* XV, November 15, 1768.
25 Noël Lemire, *Le Gâteau des Rois. The troelfth cake* (London: Printed for Rob. Sayer, 1773); *Abgelegte Beantwortung verschiedener Gesandten an dem König von Pohlen über die weltbekannte Theilung des Königreichs Pohlen mit unpartheyischer Feder eröfnet* (Warsaw, 1773); *Picture of Europe for July 1772* (1773–); J. Lodge, *The Polish Plumb-Cake* (1774).
26 Lemire, *Gâteau*. He signed the work with an anagram of his name, Erimeln. Herbert Gaisbauer, ed., *Maria Theresia und ihre Zeit* (Vienna: Bundesministerium für Wissenschaft und Forschung, 1980), 192.
27 For example, G. Pansmouzer [alias for John Lind], "The Polish Partition, Illustrated; in Seven Dramatic Dialogues or Conversation Pieces, between Remarkable Personages, Published from the Mouths and Actions of the Interlocutors," *London Chronicle*, February 24 to 26, 1774.
28 *The Polish Partition, Illustrated in Seven Dramatick Dialogues or Conversation Pieces Between Remarkable Personages Published from the Mouths and Actions of the Interlocutors* (London, 1773). Frederick II thought he had identified the author, as evident in his correspondence with Voltaire (*Lettres du Roi de Prusse et de M. de Voltaire*, vol. 54, *Oeuvres complètes* (Basel: Tourneisen, 1788), Letter 82 p. 191). For the many English readers who would never own Voltaire's correspondence, comments in the *Monthly Review* provided a detailed treatment of what the philosopher and the king had written about the pamphlet. The king, reporting that he had investigated the pamphlet's author, claimed he was "an Englishman, whose name is Lindsic (written so by mistake for Lind)." Why such a mistake would happen is unclear, but attribution of authorship in libraries and books of pseudonyms has wavered ever since between Theophilus Lindsey and John Lind, even though Lindsey, a Unitarian theologian, had no particular interest in Poland (Personal communication from Grayson Ditchfield, editor of the letters of Theophilus Lindsey, July 23, 2006), whereas John Lind (1737–81) is generally considered the author of the anonymous *Letters Concerning the Present State of*

Poland. With an Appendix, Containing the Manifestoes of the Courts of Vienna, Petersburg, and Berlin (London: T. Payne, 1773). The king further asserted that the author was "an ecclesiastic, and preceptor to the young prince Poniatowski, nephew to the king of Poland," which fit John Lind. The English reviewer, however, who claimed to be "one of the very small number of persons" who knew the truth about the authorship, acknowledged that John Lind wrote the *Letters concerning the Present State of Poland* but categorically denied that Lind had written the dialogues (*Monthly Review*'s Addendum, 633). Perhaps this was a strategy of obfuscation to protect Mr. Lind from royal charges of libel despite the obvious reliance of the Pansmouser pamphlet on the analysis in the *Letters*.

29 Similar allegations about being dupes and maintaining the appearance of virtue occur in the *Letters Concerning the Present State of Poland* in similar language.
30 Rojek, *Celebrity*, 177. Marshall, *Celebrity and Power*, 105-10.
31 Voltaire, *Lettres* 67, 113-4.
32 C. L. Römpler, "Ode," in *Kurzer Entwurf der Lebensbeschreibung Ihro Majestät, Katharinen der Zweiten, Kaiserin und Selbstherrscherin von ganz Rußland*, ed. Theodor Josephides von Tomanskiy (1774).
33 Johann Wolfgang von Goethe, *Dichtung und Wahrheit*, 2nd ed., vol. 10, *Gedenkausgabe* (1962), 770-1. My translation.
34 "After p. 684."
35 *Vorstellung und Abbildung von Catharina Alexiewna, Keiserin von Rusland, und Achmeth der Vierte, türkische Keiser oder Großsultan, als vorhin in viele Jahren krigführende Potentaten* (Copenhagen: Johan Rudolph Thiele, 1774).
36 *De Edelmoedige Hollander of de Verbontbreekende Kyser* (1784); *De Nederlandsche Leeuw* (1787); *De Ontwaakte Leeuw / Verklaaring van de Plaat*, 1780; *De Tyd geeft verandering* (1780); *De verloste Hollander, of de gedwongen dog* (1780); *Dees Nederlandsche Koe*; *Den Britsen Leopard tot Reden gebracht*; *Joseph II ou L'Empereur Mistifie* (c. 1784); *Loon na. werk 1780* (1780). A German cartoon (in two variations) that also addresses the Dutch situation is *Politische Käß Collation oder die gedemüthigte Myn Heers* (1787).
37 Ian Haywood, *Romanticism and Caricature* (Cambridge: Cambridge University Press, 2013), 2.
38 *Forestilling og Afbilding af Den Russiske Keiserinde Catharina den Anden, og den Tyrkiske Keiser eller Stor-Soltanen Achmeth den Fierde: som har i dette Aar 1787 erklæret Rusland Krig* . . . (Haderslev: Trykt og at bekomme paa Bogtrykkeriet i Haderslev, 1787).
39 J.M. Will, *Wenn Achmet noch so stolz auch wäre* (Augsburg: Will, 1788-1789). This print was probably made in 1789 (since Joseph died in 1790), which places it after a string of successes by Russia's armies.
40 Birmingham, *Politische Spazierfahrt* (London, 1788). Despite the claim of London as place of production, the title in German and the odd phrasing of its production information, "in the Newport Street," seem to affirm the print's German origin. The print is undated, but Joseph's death early in 1790 provides a *terminus ante quem*. It is unclear whether the version described in a French magazine article—Guillaume Imbert, "La guerre actuelle des deux cours impériale," *La chronique scandaleuse, ou mémoires pour servir à l'histoire des moeurs de la génération présente* (1791)—had its dialog in French. The only copy I have found is titled in German, lacks the words that Imbert quotes, and leaves the small figures unidentified.
41 Boluzion, *Kriegs Theater* (1789).

42 The writer, Luise Mejer, seemed to consider newspaper accounts of Catherine's generosity to the lover's family as part of the confirmation. Although Mejer gets the name completely wrong, she evidently heard this rumor about the death of Alexander Lanskoy (Chapter 12). Ulrich Joost, *Nachträge, Besserungen, Personenregister*, ed. Ulrich Joost and Albrecht Schöne, 5 vols., *Georg Christoph Lichtenberg Briefwechsel* (München: C.H. Beck, 1990), 5.1:188.

43 Viewers knowledgeable in Latin (as all educated German men of the time were) might read Nic. as a punning abbreviation for *nicto*, Latin, to wink, a confirmation of the gag.

44 Quoted in Vincent Carretta, "'Petticoats in Power': Catherine the Great in British Political Cartoons," *1650–1850: Ideas, Aesthetics, and Inquiries in the Early Modern Era* 1 (1994): 39.

45 *Vested Interests: Cross-Dressing and Cultural Anxiety* (New York: Routledge, 1992), 147–52, and throughout.

46 Carretta, "Petticoats," 38–43.

Chapter 9

1 William Coxe, *Travels into Poland, Russia, Sweden and Denmark*, 3 vols. (London: T. Cadell, 1784), 1:492.

2 Benjamin Schmidt includes notions that I categorize as barbaric within his account of exoticism as that concept was emerging in the sixteenth through early eighteenth centuries. *Inventing*.

3 Wolff, *Inventing*, 6–13.

4 "Lettres sur la Russie," 111–12.

5 Schmidt, *Inventing*, 18.

6 Monarchomachus [Johann Friedrich Ernst Albrecht], *Des politischen Thierkreises oder der Zeichen unsrer Zeit Zweyter Theil. / Neuestes graues Ungeheuer* (Bagdad, 1798), 2:355.

7 *A Journey into Siberia: Made by Order of the King of France* (London: T. Jefferys, 1770), 57, 315.

8 *The Rise, Progress, and Present State of the Northern Governments; viz. the United Provinces, Denmark, Sweden, Russia, and Poland*, 2 v. (London: T. Becket, 1777), 2:308–9.

9 *Travels through Holland, Flanders, Germany, Denmark, Sweden, Lapland, Russia, the Ukraine and Poland (France and Spain) in the years 1768, 1769, 1770 (and 1771)*, 4 vols., vol. 3 (1772), 140.

10 Chappe d'Auteroche, *Journey*, 331.

11 "Rev. of Chappe d'Auteroche, Voyage en Siberie," *The Monthly Review*, 1769.

12 Marche, *Russische Anekdoten*, 93–8.

13 Marcus Levitt, "An Antidote to Nervous Juice: Catherine the Great's Debate with Chappe D'Auteroche over Russian Culture," *Eighteenth-Century Studies* 32, no. 1 (1998).

14 Guzel Ibneyeva, "Catherine Discovers the Volga Region," *Jahrbücher für Geschichte Osteuropas* 56 (2008).

15 Magnus Alopäus, *Rede Ihrer Majestät der Glorwürdigst regierenden Kaiserin von Russland Catherinen der Zweyten bey seiner Aufnahme als Beysitzer in die königliche Deutsche Gesellschaft zu Göttingen den 24. September 1768* (Göttingen, 1768), 13–14.

16 *The Antidote, or, An Enquiry into the Merits of a Book, entitled A Journey into Siberia, made in 1761 in obedience to an order of the French king, and published, with approbation, by the Abbé Chappe d'Auteroche; in Which Many Essential Errors and Misrepresentations are Pointed out and Confuted . . . By a Lover of Truth* (London: S. Leacroft, 1772).
17 "De Hambourg, le 13 Décembre 1773," *Gazette de France*, January 3, 1774. Also see Peter Hoffmann and Horst Schützler, "Der Pugacev-Aufstand in zeitgenössischen deutschen Berichten," *Jahrbuch für Geschichte der sozialistischen Länder Europas* 6 (1962): 341.
18 "London. Extract of a Letter from the Hague, Feb. 4," *London Chronicle*, February 10–12, 1774.
19 It was summarized in English dailies but appeared in full elsewhere, such as in a newspaper from Danish Altona, just outside Hamburg: "Von Gottes Gnaden Wir Catharina die Zweyte," *Reichs Post Reuter*, February 12, 1774.
20 "Italia, Venezia 5. Novembre," *Gazzetta universale*, November 12, 1774.
21 "Warschau den 5. Jänner," *Wienerisches Diarium [Wiener Zeitung]*, January 22, 1774, 3.
22 *Instruction donnée par Catherine II., impératrice et législatrice de toutes les Russies, a la commission établie par cette souveraine, pour travailler à la rédaction d'un nouveau code de loix*, augm. ed. (A Lausanne: François Grasset & Comp., 1769), §92.
23 Michael Khodarkovsky, *Where Two Worlds Met: The Russian State and the Kalmyk Nomads, 1600-1771* (Ithaca: Cornell University Press, 1992), 207–35.
24 Ibid. 262.
25 "Foreign Affairs. Cologne, Jan 28," *General Evening Post*, February 12–15, 1774. Philip Longworth, "The Last Great Cossack-Peasant Rising," *Journal of European Studies* 3 (1973).
26 Hoffmann and Schützler, "Pugacev-Aufstand," 349.
27 "Auszug einer Schreibens aus Petersburg an ein Comtoir in Hamburg vom 22. Hornung," *Wienerisches Diarium [Wiener Zeitung]* Anhang, 1774.
28 Thomas Tickell, *A Poem to His Excellency the Lord Privy-Seal, on the Prospect of Peace* 4ed. (London: J. Tonson, 1713), 6.
29 "De Casan, le 7 Février 1774," *Gazette de France*, April 11, 1774.
30 "Kaminick, vom 28 Febr.," *Frankfurter Kayserl. Reichs-Ober-Post-Amts-Zeitung*, March 28, 1774, 2.
31 "Duytsland," *Wekelijks nieuws uit Loven*, May 29, 1774. "London," *London Chronicle*, February 10–12.
32 "Kaminick, vom 28 Febr."
33 Wraxall, *Cursory*, 264.
34 "Warschau, vom 5 März," *Frankfurter Kayserl. Reichs-Ober-Post-Amts-Zeitung*, March 21, 1774.
35 "Noticias de Rusia. Petersbourgo," *Mercurio histórico y político*, July 1774; "De las Fronteras de Rusia," *Mercurio histórico y político*, July 1774.
36 "Articles of Intelligence from the Other Daily Papers of Yesterday," *Gazetteer and New Daily Advertiser*, April 7, 1774, 149.
37 "From the Upper Rhine, Feb. 18," *General Evening Post*, March 5–8, 1774.
38 For example, "Kaminick, vom 28 Febr.," *Frankfurter Kayserl. Reichs-Ober-Post-Amts-Zeitung*, March 28, 1774, and "De las Fronteras de Rusia," *Mercurio histórico y político*, July 1774, 224–5.
39 "Vermischte Neuigkeiten," *Frankfurter Kayserl. Reichs-Ober-Post-Amts-Zeitung*, February 15, 1774.

40 "Petersburg, vom 10 Febr.," *Frankfurter Kayserl. Reichs-Ober-Post-Amts-Zeitung*, March 14, 1774.
41 "Maynstrom, vom 21 März," *Frankfurter Kayserl. Reichs-Ober-Post-Amts-Zeitung*, March 22, 1774.
42 "Vermischte Neuigkeiten," *Frankfurter Kayserl. Reichs-Ober-Post-Amts-Zeitung* 1774, May 13, 1774, 1–2. Also: Hoffmann and Schützler, "Pugacev-Aufstand," 343–4.
43 "Königsberg, vom 19 May," *Frankfurter Kayserl. Reichs-Ober-Post-Amts-Zeitung*, June 3, 1774.
44 "De Leipsig, le 4. Mai," *L'Esprit des journaux, françois et étrangers*, June 15, 1774.
45 "Warsaw, Aug 31," *General Evening Post*, September 15–17, 1774.
46 "De Petersbourg, le 7 Octobre 1774," *Gazette de France*, November 11, 1774.
47 "Vermischte Neuigkeiten," *Frankfurter Kayserl. Reichs-Ober-Post-Amts-Zeitung*, November 4, 1774.
48 *London Chronicle* March 26, 1774, cited in John T. Alexander, "Western Views of the Pugachov Rebellion," *Slavonic and East European Review* 113 (1970): 530.
49 "St. Petersburg den 14. Jänner," *Wienerisches Diarium* [*Wiener Zeitung*], February 23, 1774.
50 "Warsaw, August 31," *Gazetteer & New Daily Advertiser*, April 22, 1774.
51 "According to the Latest Advices from Petersburgh," *General Evening Post*, January 27–29, 1774.
52 "Extract of a Letter from Hambourg, Feb. 1," *London Chronicle*, February 10–12, 1774.
53 "Vermischte Nachrichten," *Frankfurter Kayserl. Reichs-Ober-Post-Amts-Zeitung*, March 4, 1774, 2–3.
54 "Petersburg, vom 10 Febr.," *Frankfurter Kayserl. Reichs-Ober-Post-Amts-Zeitung*, March 14.
55 "Vermischte," *Frankfurter*, February 15. Even months after his capture, a periodical that claimed to be published in Brussels, but was actually in Paris, speculated about an indirect association between Pugachev and the alleged daughter of Empress Elizabeth. "De Livourne, le 10 Avril," *Journal de politique et de littérature* (1775).
56 "London," *Gazetteer & New Daily Advertiser* (1774).
57 "A Letter from the Lower Elbe, Dated Jan. 13," *General Evening Post*, January 25–27, 1774.
58 "London," *General Evening Post*, January 29–February 1, 1774.
59 "This Day Arrived Two Mails from Flanders," *General Evening Post*, March 3–5, 1774.
60 "Our letters from Petersburgh." *Gazetteer & New Daily Advertiser* (1774). Several years later, a report by a Frenchman, Francois Auguste Thesby de Belcour, who had been in the mutinous region as a prisoner of war, included the claim that Pugachev had intercepted a group of Polish prisoners returning from Siberia, hoping to find French officers among them whom he could add to his army. *Tagebuch eines französischen Officiers in Diensten der Pohlnischen Konföderation, welcher von den Russen gefangen und nach Sibirien verwiesen worden* (Amsterdam, 1776), 202–3.
61 "Petersburg, vom 10 Febr.," *Frankfurter Kayserl. Reichs-Ober-Post-Amts-Zeitung*, March 14.
62 "Petersburg den 31 Jänner." *Wienerisches Diarium,* March 4, 1775, 2.
63 See, for example, *Scots Magazine* vol. xxxvii, March 1775, 115.
64 Christian Friedrich Daniel Schubart, *Deutsche Chronik* 17 (1775), 132.
65 "Petersburg den 31 Jänner"; "Authentic History of the Famous Rebel Pugatschew," *London Magazine,* March 1775, 103–5.

66 Pierre Nicolas Chantreau, *Philosophical, Political, and Literary Travels in Russia, during the Years 1788 & 1789*, 2 vols. (Perth: R. Morison Junior, 1794) 2: 190. Chantreau had relied in part on Dietrich Heinrich Stöver (1767–1822), a correspondent for the *Hamburgischer Correspondent*, who wrote the "Lebens- und Empörungsgeschichte des Kosaken Pugatschew" (History of the Life and Rebellion of Pugachev) in *Unser Jahrhundert: oder Darstellung der interessantesten Merkwürdigkeiten und Begebenheiten und der grössten Männer desselben* (Altona, 1791), 295–342. Stöver subscribed to the theory that the executioner had incorrectly hacked off Pugachev's head before inflicting the intended pain of first chopping off his hands and feet. Catherine's most widely distributed later biography suggested a political explanation for this leniency: apprehension "lest the declarations of the culprit might oblige her to multiply punishments, and plunge the empire into new calamities"; Jean-Henri Castéra and William Tooke, *The life of Catherine II, Empress of Russia*. 3rd ed. 3 vols. (London: T. N. Longman and O. Rees, 1799), 2: 243.
67 "Russland," *Historisches portefeuille*, April 1787, 520.
68 *Anecdotes of the Russian Empire. In a Series of Letters, Written, a Few Years Ago, from St. Petersburg* (London: Strahan & Cadell, 1784), 92–4. He takes up the same theme at greater length in a later chapter again (454–74).
69 [Schmidt-Phiseldek], *Briefe über Russland, Erste Sammlung*, 174.
70 "London," *St. James's Chronicle or the British Evening Post*, November 5, 1774, 1.
71 *Travels into Poland, Russia, Sweden and Denmark. Interspersed with Historical Relations and Political Inquiries*, 2 vols. (London, 1784), 1:226.
72 *Erhabene*, 17.
73 Ibid., 26–7.
74 *Freudengesang der Judenschaft zu Sclow beym Durchzuge ihrer Kaiserlichen Majestät* (1780).
75 *Lob- und Danklied der Judengemeine zu Mohilow beym Einzuge Ihrer Kayserlichen Majestät Katharina II. Selbstbeherrscherinn aller Reussen* (Mohilow, 1780).
76 David M. Griffiths, "Catherine Discovers the Crimea," *Jahrbücher für Geschichte Osteuropas* 56 (2008). "Russia," *The English Review, Or, An Abstract of English and Foreign Literature*, March 1787.
77 "L'empereur aura-t-il une entre vue avec l'impératrice de Russie?," *Journal politique, ou Gazette des gazettes*, February 1787.
78 "Noticias de Turquía y Africa: Constantinopla," *Mercurio histórico y político* 1787, 277–9. Ruth Hill, Hierarchy, *Commerce and Fraud in Bourbon Spanish America: a Postal Inspector's Exposé* (Vanderbilt University Press, 2005), 28.
79 "Russia," *The English Review*, March 1787, 238.
80 "Lemberg, vom 21. May," *Bayreuther Zeitung*, July 14, 1787.
81 "Frankreich," *Auszug aller Europäischen Zeitungen*, January 19, 1787.
82 *Taurische Reise der Kaiserin von Russland Katharina II* (Koblenz, 1799).
83 "Russland. Ankunft und Aufenthalt der Kaiserin zu Kaniew," *Schwäbischer Merkur*, June 4, 1787, 233–4.
84 For example, "Russland," *Historisches Portefeuille*, June 1787, 766–8.
85 Kevin Sharpe, *Selling the Tudor Monarchy: Authority and Image in Sixteenth-Century England* (New Haven, CT: Yale University Press, 2009), 169.
86 *Anecdoten zur Lebensgeschichte des Ritters und Reichs-Fürsten Potemkin* (Freistadt am Rhein, 1792), 196.
87 Thomas Hubmayer, *Hieronymus Löschenkohl im Kontext der Kultur- und Sozialgeschichte des Josephinismus* (Diplomarbeit: Universität Wien, 2012).

88 Johann Hieronymus Löschenkohl, *Zusammenkunft Joseph II Römischen Kaisers mit Catharina II Kaiserin von Russland bei Koudak d. 18ten May 1787* (1787),
89 One print, *Catherine II. voyageant dans ses états*, attempted to include the diverse ethnic peoples whom the empress visited on the journey. J. J. Avril based his 1790 engraving on a painting by Ferdinand de Meys, who had not been on the trip but created a flattering allegorical representation of it nonetheless. The empress is depicted as a goddess spreading prosperity and enlightenment to the various grateful peoples of her realm.
90 "Wien, vom 11. Dec.," *Allgemeine Zeitgeschichte in einem Auszug aller Europäischen Zeitungen*, January 3, 1787.
91 *Anecdoten zur Lebensgeschichte des Ritters und Reichs-Fürsten Potemkin. Nebst einer kurzen Beschreibung der ehemaligen Krimm . . . desgleichen der Reise der Kaiserin Katharina der Zweiten nach der Krimm (Freistadt am Rhein: Brockhaus, 1792)*, 197–8.
92 "Warsaw. March 28," *Morning Chronicle and London Advertiser*, April 27, 1787.
93 *Anecdoten . . . Potemkin*, 196, 200.
94 Ibid., 196, 200–4, 211–12. Classical references such as Tauride were inevitable in discussions of the trip since the Russians had reverted in most cases to old Greek names for the places they had seized, including Tauris for the Crimean peninsula. Sara Dickinson, "Russia's First 'Orient': Characterizing the Crimea in 1787," *Kritika: Explorations in Russian and Eurasian History* 3, no. 1 (2002); "Allemagne. De Hambourg, le 3 Août," *Journal Politique de Bruxelles*, 1787.
95 "Kiew (Capital of the Ukraine) Feb. 12," *The European Magazine, and London Review*, 1787.
96 "Russland," *Allgemeine Zeitgeschichte in einem Auszug aller europäischen Zeitungen*, January 29, 1787, 443.
97 Wolff stresses the presence of this theme in the journey accounts of two ambassador participants. *Inventing*, 126–41.
98 "Russland," *Schwäbischer Merkur*, June 8, 1787.
99 "Pologne. De Varsovie le 16 Mai," *Gazette d'Amsterdam*, June 1.
100 "Foreign Affairs," *St. James's Chronicle or the British Evening Post*, June 7–9, 1787. "Pologne, de Varsovie le 16 Mai," *Gazette d'Amsterdam*, June 1, 1787.
101 "Petersburg, Feb. 27," *Gentleman's Magazine*, April 1787, 355.
102 *Anecdoten . . . Potemkin*, 198.
103 "De Sèbastopolis, en Crimée, le 3 Juin 1787," *Journal Politique de Bruxelles*, July 7, 1787. English in "Extract of a Letter from Sebastopolis, in the Crimea, June 4," *Whitehall Evening Post*, July 26–28, 1787.
104 "Russland," *Allgemeine Zeitgeschichte in einem Auszuge aller europäischen Zeitungen*, February 2, 519–20.

Chapter 10

1 Chappe d'Auteroche, *Journey*, 278.
2 [Schmidt-Phiseldek], *Briefe über Russland*, 73.
3 Guillaume Francois Le-Trosne, *Reflexions politiques sur la guerre actuelle de l'Angleterre avec ses colonies & sur l'etat de la Russie* (n.p. 1777), 11,14–15.

4 After her death, biographers sometimes argued Catherine had been frightened away from liberating the serfs by anxieties about the huge peasant rebellion that had convulsed her empire. Andrä, *Katharina die Zweite*, 149; [Johann Gottfried Seume], *Ueber das Leben und den Charakter der Kaiserin von Rusland Katharina II* (Altona [probably Leipzig], 1797), 96–8. Isabel de Madariaga, agrees with this hypothesis; *Catherine the Great: A Short History* (New Haven: Yale University Press, 1990), 126–30.
5 *Anekdoten zur Lebensgeschichte*, 44–5, 62–8.
6 A.C. Strenge, "Begebenheiten eines Deutschen Predigers an den Ufern der Wolga," *Deutsche Monatsschrift* (1792): 55–6.
7 F. Frensdorff, "Katharina II von Rußland und ein Göttingscher Zeitungsschreiber," *Nachrichten von der Königlichen Gesellschaft der Wissenschaften zu Göttingen. Philologisch-historische Klasse* (1905): 311.
8 The rarity today of Swedish political cartoons outside Scandinavia suggests that the caricatures produced there that seem to be of Catherine had little impact elsewhere. For a rich and well-illustrated analysis of British satirical images of Catherine, see Carretta, "Petticoats."
9 Haywood, *Romanticism*, 6.
10 Jonathan Bate, "Shakespearean Allusion in English Caricature in the Age of Gillray," *Journal of the Warburg and Courtauld Institutes* 49 (1986): 196.
11 "Lettres sur la Russie," 109.
12 Richard Sheridan, dramatist and orator, he said he "pictured the Empress as a female Colossus, standing with one foot on the banks of the Black sea, and the other on the coast of the Baltic." "Mr. Sheridan [April 12, 1791]," *The Parliamentary Register; Or, History of the Proceedings and Debates of the House of Commons* 1791, 143.
13 The knowledgeable Russian specialist Dimitrii Aleksandrovitch Rovinskii thought that the first version of the print was the one in French, which he dates to 1787. *Podrobny Slovar' Russkikh Gravirovannykh Portretov* (1889). It is clear that the French version quickly became known also in Britain, because a different political cartoon, *An Amusing State of Uncertainty* published in London on June 15, 1791, uses a visual citation of the breast-displaying French print; see Figure 11.6.
14 The Beineke Rare Book and Manuscript Library at Yale University, for example, identifies Rowlandson as the print's creator. http://brbl-dl.library.yale.edu/vufind/Record/3954915 Used on October 23, 2016.
15 https://www.britishmuseum.org/collection/object/P_1876-0510-764
16 Among the prints that cite the *Stride/L'Enjambée* image, one entitled *Ainsi va la Monde*, published in at least three versions, puts a striding Catherine II at the center and apex of the print, atop a coach in which French royals, aristocrats, and clergy flee the revolution. Yet another allusion, entitled *ah! ca va Mal | Les puissance étrangères faisant dansér*, shows Catherine, identified in the key and highly recognizable with crown and stance, with an array of other similarly posed male rulers beside her, all poking a huge bonfire beneath the French National Assembly.
17 Sylvain Maréchal, *Le jugement dernier des rois: prophétie en un acte, en prose* (Paris: C.F. Patris, 1793); Hyacinthe Pellet-Desbarreaux, *Les Potentats foudroyés par la Montagne et la Raison, ou, la Déportation des Rois de l'Europe, pièce prophétique et révolutionnaire, en un acte* (Toulouse: Citoyen P. Francés, 1793).
18 De Roo, *La coalition des rois ou des brigands couronnes contre la republique francoise* (1794). *A Grand Battle between the famous English Cock and Russian Hen!* (1791). The

Russian Bear and her invincible rider encountering the British legion (London: Holland, 1791).
19 For the term "monstrous-feminine," see Barbara Creed, "Horror and the Monstrous-Feminine: An Imaginary Abjection," *Screen* 27, no. 1 (1986).
20 Quoted in Maza, "Diamond Necklace," 82.
21 *The Prussian Prize fighter and his Allies attempting to tame Imperial Kate* 1791 (1791).
22 *La mascarade* (1791); Frederic George Stephens, "A.D. 1761- c. A.D. 1770," in *Political and personal satires*, ed. British Museum. *Catalogue of Prints and Drawings* (London: British Museum, 1883). Also *Les Pelerins de St. Jacques* (1792–4).
23 *The Ladies Church Yard* (London: Pownall, 1783).
24 *Amsterdam in a Dam'd Predicament, or, the Last Scene of the Republican Pantomime*, November 1, 1787 (London, 1787).
25 The emperor's line, "To the devil with the project and those who designed it," is probably a reference to the unfulfilled plan to exchange the distant Austrian Low Countries for Bavaria, a district that would have been contiguous with the rest of his Hapsburg lands.
26 https://www.britishmuseum.org/research/collection_online/collection_object_details.aspx?assetId=357225001&objectId=3074046&partId=1
27 Fox appears under a chair or throne in the print at the British Museum: https://www.britishmuseum.org/collection/object/P_1948-0214-468. He reclines under a curtained bed in a print at Yale's Lewis Walpole Library: http://hdl.handle.net/10079/digcoll/551037. While eighteenth-century viewers would have recognized Catherine immediately in these prints, twentieth-century curators have not, identifying the figure instead as Britannia.
28 "The Great Empress," *The World*, November 4, 1791.
29 "Countess of Friskiwowsky," *The World*, September 27, 1791.
30 Carretta, "Petticoats," 63.
31 "Voyeurism, Pornography and "La Regenta,'" *Modern Language Studies* 19, no. 4 (1989): 94.
32 "Celebrity," 406.
33 "Jacques-Louis David, Scatological Discourse in the French Revolution, and the Art of Caricature," *Arts Magazine*, February 1988, 72.
34 *Imperial Salute, or invitation to Peace Rejected* (London: S. Aitkin, 1792).
35 *Bobadill Disgraced or Kate in a rage* (London: Fores, 1792). The reversed map in the French rendition is a result of direct copying from a printed image and thus shows that the English print came first. *Catherine II donnant conge a François et a Brunswick le foireux* (London (i.e. Paris?), 1792).
36 The cap resembles the small, pointed kokoshnik that Catherine wears in an engraving by James Walker, *Catharine II. Empress of Russia* (1783), which was included in the August issue of the *British Magazine* for 1783.
37 *Catherine II donnant congé à François et à Brunswick le foireux*
38 *Oxford English Dictionary Online*.
39 *The Northen Bugga Bo* (London: Aitken no 14 Castle Street Leicester Fields, 1791).
40 Isabel de Madariaga, the great British Catherinist, calls it "one of the bloodiest and most savage assaults on an unfortified town which Europe had seen for a long time." *Catherine*, 171.
41 "Nell Gwyn," 74.
42 *Royal Recreation* (London: Fores, S.W., 1795).
43 *Poems. The Tears of Poland* (Edinburgh, 1795), 9.

44 Charles François Philibert Masson, *Mémoires secrets et particulièrement sur la fin du règne de Catherine II et le commencement de celui de Paul I* (Paris: Charles Pougens, 1800) 1:124. The description of this image is not included in the English translation of Masson, which was explicitly sanitized to preserve "decency and propriety" (*Secret Memoirs* v).
45 Lynn Hunt, ed., *The Invention of Pornography: Obscenity and the Origins of Modernity, 1500–1800* (New York: Zone Books, 1993), 329–30.
46 *Poems*, 9–11.
47 Marshall, *Celebrity and Power*, 12.

Chapter 11

1 In original: "die Russisch Kaethel ... die enk jetzt ist so heilig." Franz Hebenstreit, "Eipeldauerlied."
2 Alphonse Fortia-de-Piles, *Voyage de deux Francais en Allemagne, Danemarck, Suede, Russie et Pologne* 5 vols. (Paris, 1796), 4:180.
3 A. G. Cross, *Cambridge, Some Russian Connections: An Inaugural Lecture Delivered before the University of Cambridge on 26 February 1987* (Cambridge: Cambridge University Press, 1987), 12.
4 *Travels into Poland, Russia, Sweden and Denmark. Interspersed with Historical Relations and Political Inquiries.* 2 vols. (London, 1784). And further, especially: *Travels in Poland, Russia, Sweden, and Denmark: illustrated with charts and engravings.* 5 vols. (Printed for T. Cadell, jun. and W. Davies, 1802).
5 William Coxe, *Reise durch Polen, Russland, Schweden und Dänemark*, trans. J. Pezzl, 3 vols. (Zürich, 1792); William Coxe and Jacques Mallet du Pan, *Voyage en Pologne, Russie, suede et Danemark ... enrici de notes ... et augmente d'un voyage en Norvege*, 4 vols. (Geneve, 1786).
6 Coxe, *Travels* (1802), 3:43. Unless otherwise stated, citations from Coxe refer to the 1784 edition.
7 Coxe's influential account of the coup was based on an impressive mix of evidence. In the 1802 edition he named among several printed sources as well as "several British merchants, who witnessed the revolution," and "several Russian nobles and officers, some of whom were with Peter at Oranienbaum, and others who espoused the party of the empress." Coxe added intriguingly, "I was principally indebted to count Solms, the Prussian envoy, who had resided at Petersburgh since 1763," noting that Victor Friedrich, Count Solms-Sonnenwalde, "collected various anecdotes relative to the life and accession of the empress" and used them to write "an interesting narrative, which he read to me, during my continuance at Petersburgh." To these individuals he added "Sir Thomas Wroughton, who long resided at Petersburgh [and] was the intimate friend of the king of Poland, when [he was still] count Poniatowski, and possessed the implicit confidence of the empress" along with "two curious dispatches from Mr. Keith, the English minister at St. Petersburgh, to the secretary of state, and a private note from the earl of Buckinghamshire, who succeeded Mr. Keith" (3:44). That volume contained some of the actual documents on which he had previously based his account, especially a letter by the British minister at St. Petersburg written during the first days of the coup that has all the freshness and some of the confusion of an immediate first-hand report and that raised most of the canonical themes and motifs.

8 Though Hordt claimed that Catherine years later had "the goodness to tell me one evening the history of the last revolution," and though she spoke with "candor, good faith, truth, simplicity during the whole recital" (*Mémoires* 1789, 315–16), he did not repeat her account. His book was published first in French and then translated into German; in 1794 it was massively quoted (without attribution) and slightly rewritten in a French book by Pierre Nicolas Chantreau that in turn was translated into English even before the formal English version of Hordt appeared in 1806.

9 *Du péril de la balance politique, ou Expose des causes qui l'ont alteree dans le nord, debuis l'avenement de Catherine II au trone de Russie* (London, 1789). *The Danger of the Political Balance of Europe* (Dublin: Printed by Graisberry & Campbell, 1790), 16–67.

10 Rev. of *Du péril de la balance politique de l'Europe*, in *Annalen der Geographie und Statistic* 1 (1790): 507.

11 *Danger*. The Library of Congress takes no stand on the matter, listing Gustav III, king of Sweden (1746–92), Claude Charles de Peyssonnel (1727–1790), and Jacques Mallet du Pan (1749–1800) as possible authors. The Berlin State Library lists both Peyssonnel and Mallet du Pan, while the Bibliotheque Nationale de France lists only Mallet du Pan, the choice that seems most probable to me. The usually judicious German scholar Helbig accepted the attribution to Gustav III, *Biographie*, 1:viii.

12 *Histoire ou Anecdotes sur la Revolution de Russie; en l'Année 1762* (Paris: Desenne, 1797). *History*, 1.

13 Heinrich Storch, *Gemälde von St Petersburg*, 2 vols. (Riga: Hartknoch, 1794), 1:157–8.

14 "This Day was Published," *Morning Post and Fashionable World*, June 5, 1797.

15 The semiannual "limping messenger" published in Basel, Switzerland, for example, provided its minimally literate readers in the area, including nearby parts of France and Germany, with an extended passage from Rulhière without naming him. "Tod der russischen Kaiserinn Katharina II," *Verbesserter und Alter Vollkommener Staats-Calender, genannt der Hinkende Bott . . . auf das Gnadenreiche Christ-Jahr MDCCXCVIII 1797*.

16 "Articles of Intelligence from the Other Daily Papers of Yesterday," *Gazetteer and New Daily Advertiser*, April 7, 1774. One of Catherine's best informed current biographers gives more detail about "unscrupulous Saldern." Dixon, *Catherine the Great*, 219.

17 Saldern, *Biographie*. For example, on p. 172.

18 Ibid., xvi.

19 *Russische Günstlinge*; *Biographie*; *Potemkin: ein interessanter Beitrag zur Regierungsgeschichte Katharina's der Zweiten* (1804).

20 The installments appeared in the journal *Minerva*, published in Hamburg, starting in 1797.

21 *Potemkin de Taurier* (Deventer, 1806). *Vie du prince Potemkin, feld-maréchal au service de Russie sous le règne de Catherine II* (Paris: Chez H. Nicolle, 1808). *Memoirs of the Life of Prince Potemkin* (London: H. Colburn, 1812). A second edition of this English version appeared in 1813.

22 Carol S. Leonard, *Reform and Regicide: The Reign of Peter III of Russia* (Bloomington: Indiana University Press, 1993), 13.

23 *Histoire secrète des amours et des principaux amans de Catherine II., impératrice de Russie* (Paris: LaBriffe, 1799); *Geschichte Peters des Dritten, Kaisers von Rußland. Mit hinzugefügten wichtigen Aufschlüssen; und begleitet von der geheimen Geschichte der vornehmsten Liebschaften Katharinen II.* (1799); *Minnarijen van Catharina II.*

Keizerin van Rusland, en Geschiedenis van haare voornaamste Minnaars (J. Allart, 1800).
24 Eve Tavor Bannet, "'Secret History': Or, Talebearing Inside and Outside the Secretorie," *Huntington Library Quarterly* 68, no. 1/2 (2005).
25 Michael McKeon, *The Secret History of Domesticity: Public, Private, and the Division of Knowledge* (Baltimore: Johns Hopkins University Press, 2005), 455.
26 *D. Anton Friderich Büschings, königl. Preußisch. Oberconsistorialraths, Directors des vereinigten berlinischen und cölnischen Gymnasiums, und der beyden Schulen desselben, eigene Lebensgeschichte* (Halle: Johann Jacob Curts Witwe, 1789), 465.
27 Coxe, *Travels* (1802), 3:31.
28 Paul Cobley, *Narrative* (New York: Routledge, 2013), 64.
29 *Eigene Lebensgeschichte* (Halle: Johann Jacob Curts Witwe, 1789), 464–6.
30 [Helbig], *Biographie Peter*, 112.
31 Cobley, *Narrative*, 63–4.
32 Büsching, *Eigene Lebensgeschichte*, 468.
33 Saldern, *Biographie*, 71. But in Kraft's *Peter de Terde*, Voronzova is creatively interpreted as intelligent and a wise adviser to the good-hearted tsar.
34 Anton Friderich Büsching, "Burchard Christophs M Münnich," *Magazin für die neue Historie und Geographie*, 1769. Gerh. Ant. Halem, *Lebensbeschreibung des Russisch-Kaiserlichen General-Feldmarschalls, B.C. Grafen von Münnich* (Oldenburg: Schulze, 1803).
35 Richardson, *Anecdotes*, 87.
36 *Travels*, 3:20.
37 Unacknowledged use and English translation of Hordt in: Pierre Nicolas Chantreau, *Philosophical, Political, and Literary Travels in Russia, during the years 1788 & 1789*. (Perth: R. Morison Junior, 1794), 2:114–5.
38 Johann Ludwig Hordt, *The Military, Historical and Political Memoirs of the Count de Hordt, a Swedish Nobleman, and Lieutenant General in the Service of His Majesty the King of Prussia*, 2 vols. (London: Egerton, 1806), 2:120. The same story of humiliation, without attribution, appears in [Jean-Benoît Schérer], *Anecdotes intéressantes et secrètes de la cour de Russie: tirées de ses archives* (London and Paris: Buisson, 1792), 211.
39 *Des Elementarwerkes erster bis vierter Band. Ein geordneter Vorrath aller nöthigen Erkenntniß. Zum Unterrichte der Jugend von Anfang, bis ins academische Alter*, 5 vols. (Dessau, 1774), 1:142.
40 *Travels*, 2:14.
41 *Danger*, 26–7, 35.
42 Ibid., 23–4.
43 *Travels*, 3:5, 15.
44 Ibid., 3:15.
45 Wraxall, *Cursory*, 240.
46 *Katharine II. vor dem Richterstuhle der Menschheit. Grösstentheils Geschichte* (Leipzig, 1797), 5–6.
47 Rulhière, *History*, 46–7.
48 Ibid., 22.
49 Büsching, *Eigene Lebensgeschichte*, 468.
50 Coxe, *Travels*, 3:31.
51 Rulhière, *History*, 118–19.
52 *Travels* (1802), 2:208.
53 *Cursory*, 206.

54 *Bemerkungen über Russland*, 253.
55 J.B. Fosseyeux, *Catherine II. Imperatrice de toutes les Russies* (Kehl, 1788). It is the frontispiece in Voltaire, *Lettres de L'Imperatrice de Russie et de M. de Voltaire*, vol. 67, *Oeuvres Completes de Voltaire* (Kehl, 1784). Also apparently sold separately.
56 *History*, 7–8.
57 Ibid., 17.
58 Nancy K. Miller, "Female Sexuality and Narrative Structure in *La Nouvelle Héloïse* and *Les Liaisons dangereuses*," *Signs* 1 (1976): 612.
59 Rulhière, *History*, 10.
60 *Vie de Catherine II, impératrice de Russie* (Paris: F. Buisson, 1797), 194.
61 Jean-Henri Castéra and William Tooke, *The life of Catharine II. Empress of Russia*, 2 ed. (London, 1798), 1:216.
62 *Biographie Peter*, 2:176.
63 *Histoire secrète* 55.
64 *Histoire de Pierre III. Empereur de Russie: Avec plusieurs anecdotes singulieres / dignes de curiosité* (London, 1774), unnumbered ii-iii.
65 *Danger*, 46–7.
66 *Freundschaftliche Briefe über den gegenwärtigen Zustand des Russischen Reichs* (1769), 109–10.
67 Caminer, *Geschichte*, 57.
68 Beauclair, *Histoire*, 117.
69 Bouffonidor, *Les fastes de Louis XV, de ses ministres, maîtresses, généraux, et autres personnages de son regne: pour servir de suite à la vie privée* (Chez la veuve Liberté, 1783), 56.
70 *Universal history, ancient and modern; in a series of letters to a youth at school* (London, 1787), 201.
71 *Design for the new gallery of busts and pictures* (London: Humphrey, 1792).
72 Coxe, *Travels* (1802), 3:38.
73 John Sinclair, *General Observations Regarding the Present State of the Russian Empire* (London 1787), 37-38. Coxe, *Travels* (1802), 3:38.
74 *Histoire de Pierre III, empereur de Russie, imprimée sur un manuscript trouvé dans les papiers de Montmorin* (Paris: Maison La Briffe, 1799), 1:237.
75 *The memoirs of Jacques Casanova de Seingalt in London and Moscow.*, trans. Arthur Machen (New York: Putnam). 9.
76 Voltaire, *The Works of Mr. de Voltaire*, vol. 38 *The Age of Louis XV* (London, 1774), 130.
77 *Danger*, 46.
78 *Biographie*, 84.
79 Ibid. 83.
80 *L'ultima confession generale fatta da Catterina 2. imperatrice delle Russie al Gran Patriarca di Pietroburgo prima della sua morte seguita li 6 novembre 1796. Dialogo storico-critico tra gli attori dissopra espressi* (1797), 4.
81 *Biographie Peter*, 2:159–63.
82 *Travels* (1802), 3:38.
83 Roger P. Bartlett, "'Ropsha, Where Peter III Was Murdered . . .': Faces and Facades of an Imperial Estate," in *Personality and Place in Russian Culture: Essays in Memory of Lindsey Hughes*, ed. Simon Dixon (London: Modern Humanities Research Association, 2010), 156–9.

84 *Voyage de deux Francais en Allemagne, Danemarck, Suede, Russie et Pologne*, 5 vols. (Paris: Chez Desenne, 1796), 4:183.
85 *Eigene Lebensgeschichte* 469.
86 [Goebel], *Fragmens historiques sur Pierre III et Catherine II* (Paris: Libraire du Cercle-Social, 1797), 24.
87 *Czaar Peter de Derde. Treuerspel* (Amsterdam, 1801).
88 *Catherine II, impéritrice de Russie Tragédie en cinq actes* (Paris: Cellot, 1807).
89 *Biographie*, 154.

Chapter 12

1 Emrys D. Jones, "'A Man in Love': Intimacy and Political Celebrity in the Early Eighteenth Century," in *Intimacy and Celebrity in Eighteenth-Century Literary Culture: Public Interiors*, ed. Emrys D. Jones and Victoria Joule (London: Palgrave Macmillan, 2018).
2 [Rudolf Erich Raspe?], *Gulliver Revived; Containing Singular Travels, Campaigns, Voyages, and Adventures . . . By Baron Munchausen*, Fifth Edition (G. Kearsley, 1787), 126–7.
3 Johann Georg Röllig, *Als die erfreuliche Botschaft von der Vermählung des Herrn Peters Feodorowiz wie auch der Frau Catharina Alexiena bekannt und Derselben hohe Feyer an dem Hochfürstlichen Anhalt-Zerbstischen Hofe begangen wurde, wolte seine Pflicht in Drama und Musica an den Tag legen J. G. Röllig* (Zerbst, 1746). Unnumbered p. 7.
4 [Bellermann], *Bemerkungen über Russland*, 1:41.
5 Friedrich II of Prussia, for example, was recorded as sneering at Catherine and Orlov: "It is a terrible business when the prick and the cunt decide the interests of Europe" (qtd. in Alexander, *Catherine*, 137).
6 M. de Vichy Chamrond du Deffand, *The Unpublished Correspondence of Madame Du Deffand with D'Alembert, Montesquieu, the President Hénault, the Duchess Du Maine, Mesdames de Staal, de Choiseul, the Marquis D'Argens, the Chevalier D'Aydie, &c: Followed by the Letters of Voltaire to Madame Du Deffand*, trans. Meeke, 2 vols. (For A.K. Newman & Company, 1810), 1:350.
7 *Le Procès des trois Rois, Louis XVI. de France-Bourbon, Charles III. d'Espagne-Bourbon, et George III. d'Hanovre, fabricant de bouton, plaide au tribunal des puissances-Europeennes. Par appendix, l'appel au Pape* (London: George Carenaught, 1780), 141.
8 Dawson, "Eighteenth-Century Libertinism."
9 While many scholars suggest Lanskoy died of diphtheria (e.g., Dixon, *Catherine the Great*, 266), a medical historian argues for anthrax poisoning. Marwart Michler, *Melchior Adam Weikard (1742–1803) und sein Weg in den Brownianismus: Medizin zwischen Aufklärung und Romantik, Eine medizinhistorische Biographie*, ed. Christoph Scriba, vol. 24, Acta Historica Leopoldina (Halle: Deutsche Akademie der Naturforscher Leopoldina, 1995), 33.
10 *Katharine II. vor dem Richterstuhle.*
11 Simon Burrows, *A King's Ransom: The Life of Charles Théveneau de Morande, Blackmailer, Scandalmonger & Master-Spy* (London: Bloomsbury Publishing, 2010), 163.
12 "Lord George Gordon," *Morning Herald*, June 7, 1787.

13 *Anecdoten . . . Potemkin*, 129. The other early book about Potemkin contains such an abundance of apparently closely observed detail of Potemkin's daily life that the author might well have been a member of his household: S., *Privatleben des berühmten Russisch-Kaiserlichen Feldmarschalls Fürsten von Potemkin Tawrotschewskoy* (Leipzig und Grätz: bei Franz Ferstl in Kommission, 1793).
14 *Ueber das Leben*, 141–2.
15 Faramerz Dabhoiwala, *The Origins of Sex: A History of the First Sexual Revolution* (London: Penguin, 2013), 282–348.
16 *Love as Passion: The Codification of intimacy* (Stanford, CA: Stanford University Press, 1998).
17 *Art and Celebrity*, 179.
18 *Voyage*, 4:132–3.
19 Lichtenberg, *Nachträge, Besserungen, Personenregister*, 5,1:188.
20 For a good discussion of favoritism, especially as Catherine II practiced it, see Smith, Douglas. "Introduction. Catherine the Great, Prince Grigory Potemkin, and Their Correspondence," in *Love and Conquest: Personal Correspondence of Catherine the Great and Prince Grigory Potemkin*, ed. Douglas Smith (DeKalb, IL: Northern Illinois University, 2004), xxxii–xliii.
21 *Anekdoten zur Lebensgeschichte*, 151–3, 64.
22 *Anecdoten . . . Potemkin*, 4–5. Overall, the unexcited tone and the speedy publication of so much accurate information about Catherine's liaisons within a year of Potemkin's death suggest that much of the content, specifically the sexual content, was already in circulation in some levels or pockets of German society, though I have found no direct evidence of this.
23 Ibid., 231; Dixon, *Catherine the Great*, 233–4; Madariaga, *Catherine*, 209; Smith, *Love*, xxxvii–xxxix.
24 S., *Privatleben des berühmten . . . Potemkin*.
25 *Pansalvin*, 389.
26 "Bücherverbot," *Intelligenzblatt der Neuen allgemeinen deutschen Bibliothek*, no. 44 (1795).
27 "Potemkin der Taurier. Einleitung," *Minerva* (April 1797): 3–4. But see Walter Grab, *Demokratische Strömungen in Hamburg und Schleswig-Holstein zur Zeit der ersten französischen Republik* (Hamburg: Christians, 1966), 179.
28 *Pansalvin, Fürst der Finsterniss, und seine Geliebte. So gut wie geschehen. Geheime Lebensgeschichte eines Günstlings* (Germanien, 1795).
29 "Schöne Künste," *Allgemeine Literatur-Zeitung*, no. 9 (1795): 69–70. The serious and well-qualified early nineteenth-century biographer of Potemkin, Helbig, several times praised Pansalvin's accuracy ("Potemkin der Taurier. Einleitung" 3–4), and Sebag Montefiore, author of the most recent major biography of the man, refers to Pansalvin too, although he dislikes Albrecht's harsh criticism (*Prince*, 94–105, 463).
30 Ruth P. Dawson, "The Internet, the Eighteenth Century, and a Forgotten Novel," *Friends Newsletter*, Friends of Germanic Studies, Institute of Germanic and Romance Studies, University of London (2012).
31 *Origins*, 342–8.
32 *Bemerkungen über Russland*, 319–21.
33 *Voyage*, 136–7.
34 Ibid., 137.
35 Zb., Rev. of [Laveaux] *Geschichte Peters des Dritten*, in *Neue allgemeine deutsche Bibliothek* 53, no. 1 (1800).

36 Catherine perhaps wrote her memoirs in part as a reply to what informants had told her of Rulhière's manuscript. The effort to compose an antidote to rumors she heard about Rulhière might explain the odd fact that Catherine II repeatedly drafted autobiographies, but none of them extended further into her reign than the short period he covered.
37 *Life*, 154–61.
38 *A Sketch of the Secret History of Europe, since the Peace of Paris, with Observations on the Present Critical State of Great Britain* (London: J. Murray, 1772), 15. Also in 'Excerpts,' London Chronicle, September 26–29.
39 *History*, 24–6. The political dimensions of the affair meant that Coxe, with his excellent connections, explained in his 1802 edition that the British ambassador wrote about it "in several dispatches" (*Travels* 1802, 1:22.). Supposedly Poniatowski "facilitated his intercourse with his mistress" by obtaining a Polish diplomatic appointment that gave him better status at the Russian court (*History*, 17). But, as Coxe continued, he also became "the channel of communication between the Grand duchess and the British ministry."
40 *Biographie Peter*, 1:131.
41 *History*, 63–4.
42 *Russische Günstlinge*, 267.
43 [Goebel], *Fragmens*, 87–90. The text also does not specify which of the several Orlov brothers was meant.
44 "Histoire ou Anecdotes sur le Revolution de Russie, &c. i.e. a History of, or Anecdotes respecting, the Revolution in Russia," *The Monthly Review* 1797, 567.
45 Saldern, *Biographie*, for example, 133, 259–60.
46 *Biographie Peter*, 25.
47 *Biographie*, xiii.
48 *Histoire de Pierre III, empereur de Russie: imprimée sur un manuscrit trouvé dans les papiers de Montmorin*, 3 vols. (Paris: Maison La Briffe, 1799), 1:iii–iv.
49 *Secret Memoirs*, 84, 63.
50 *Voyage*, 133.
51 Ibid., 133–5.
52 *Russische Günstlinge*, 383.
53 *Il Poema Tartaro*, 2 ed. (1796). A blog posting by Simon Beattie shows the cover page and adds further detail; http://simonbeattie.co.uk/blog/archives/1547/
54 Peter Vassallo, "Don Juan, Il Poema Tartaro and the Italian Burlesque Tradition," in *Byron: The Italian Literary Influence* (London: Macmillan, 1984).
55 *Poema*. IV, 71, and IV, 76–7. Translation by Peter Cochran in Peter Cochran, "Casti's 'Il Poema Tartaro' and Byron's 'Don Juan,' Cantos V–X," *The Keats-Shelley Review* 17 (2003): 71. Casti's poem, according to Cochran's arguments of Peter Cochran, influenced Byron's depiction of Russia in *Don Juan*.
56 Larry Wolff, "The Fantasy of Catherine in the Fiction of the Enlightenment: From Baron Munchausen to the Marquis de Sade," in *Eros and Pornography in Russian Culture*, ed. Marcus C. Levitt and A. Toporkov (Moscow: Ladomir, 1999), 256–60.
57 For example, *Miranda*, 82–3, 306. Dawson, "Eighteenth-Century Libertinism," 78–80.
58 *Die Heimlichkeiten der Frauenzimmer: ein Lesebuch für Mütter, Erzieherinnen und mannbare Mädchen* (1809), iii.
59 *Miranda, Koningin van Noorden, beminde van Pansalvinus, Vorst der Duisternis* (1798).

60 *Retrospection: or: A Review of the Most Striking and Important Events, Characters, Situations, and Their Consequences, Which the Last Eighteen Hundred Years Have Presented to the View of Mankind* (Printed for J. Stockdale, 1801), 492.
61 *Voyage*, 132–3.
62 *Retrospection*, 474.
63 Dawson, "Eighteenth-Century Libertinism," 80–4.

Chapter 13

1 For example in a provincial newspaper in Germany: "Vermischte Nachrichten. Berlin von 10. Dec.," *Langensalzisches Wochen-Blat*, December 17, 1796.
2 "London, Dec. 20," *The Oracle and Public Advertiser*, December 20, 1796.
3 "En annonçant," *Gazette Nationale ou Le Moniteur Universel*, December 17, 1796.
4 "The Circumstances of the Death of the late Empress of Russia," *Evening Mail*, December 23–26, 1796.
5 "Private Correspondence: Death of the Empress of Russia, Petersburgh, Nov. 23," *True Briton*, Tuesday, December 20, 1796.
6 "The New Emperour of Russia Has Taken," *St. James's Chronicle or the British Evening Post*, December 24–27, 1796.
7 "Circumstances," *Evening Mail*, December 23–26.
8 Rulhière, "Tod der russischen Kaiserinn Katharina II," *Verbesserter und Alter Vollkommener Staats-Calender, genannt der Hinkende Bott . . . auf das Gnadenreiche Christ-Jahr MDCCXCVIII*, 1797.
9 "Russland," *Wiener Zeitung*, 1796.
10 Quoted in Maza, "Diamond Necklace," 82.
11 *Katharine II. vor dem Richterstuhle*, 54.
12 [August Ludwig von Schlözer], *Russische Schul-Projecte* (Göttingen, 1783), 258–9. *Catharina die Zweite. Darstellungen aus der Geschichte ihrer Regierung, und Anekdoten von ihr und einigen Personen, die um sie waren* (Altona: Hammerich, 1797). 239. Schubart wrote an item about a monolingual Finn who got a job in the interior of Russia pretending to be a French tutor, duping the unwitting parents. "Eine russische Anecdote," *Deutsche Chronik*, September 1, 1774.
13 *Catharina die Zweite*, 240–1.
14 Johann Erich Biester, *Abriss des Lebens und der Regierung Kaiserin Katharina II. von Russland* (Berlin: Nicolai, 1797), 213–24.
15 Weikard, *Denkwürdigkeiten*; Heinrich Matthias Marcard, *Zimmermanns Verhältnisse mit der Kayserin Catharina II und dem Herrn Weikard* (Bremen: C. Seyffert, 1803).
16 Weikard, *Denkwürdigkeiten*, 337.
17 H.M. Marcard, *Correspondance originelle et très interessante de l'Imperatrice de Russie Catharina II. avec le chevalier de Zimmermann* (Bremen: Joh. Heinr. Müller, 1808).
18 Comella, *Catarina Segunda en Cronstadt*, (Madrid: Fermin Tadeo Villapando, 1799).
19 Louis Philippe de Segur, *History of the Principal Events of the Reign of Frederic William II. King of Prussia; and a political picture of Europe, from 1786 to 1796*, 3 vols. (London: Longman and Rees, 1801), 1:52.
20 Georg Forster, "Gregor Potemkin," in *Erinnerungen aus dem Jahr 1790, in historischen Gemälden und Bildnissen*, ed. von D. Chodowiecki, d. Berger, Cl. Kohl, J.F. Bolt und J.S. Ringck (Berlin: Voss, 1793), 157.

21 *History*, 1:51–2.
22 [Gustav Adolf Wilhelm von Helbig], "Potemkin der Taurier," in *Minerva* (Hamburg, 1798), 300–1.
23 Ibid., 301, 314, 315, 317.
24 [Melchior Adam Weikard], *Taurische Reise der Kaiserin von Russland Katharina II* (Koblenz, 1799), 193–5, 211.
25 *Bruchstücke aus den Ruinen der Menschheit* (Kopenhagen, 1797), 80.
26 *Biographie*, 181–2.
27 Ibid., 194–202.
28 Ibid.; *Paul der Erste, Kaiser und Selbstherrscher aller Reußen, Eine historische Skizze* (Leipzig: Müller, 1802); Albrecht, *Staub*.
29 *Bruchstücke*, 79–80.
30 Unsigned introduction to the German edition of [Thieboult de Laveaux], *Geschichte Peters des Dritten, Kaisers von Russland. Aus der Handschrift eines geheimen Agenten Ludwigs XV. am Hofe zu Petersburg. Begleitet von der geheimen Geschichte Katharinen II* (1799), vii–viii.
31 *Histoire secrète*, 311.
32 *Paul der Erste, Kayser von Russland. Von einem unbefangenen Beobachter* (Leipzig: Sommersche Buchhandlung, 1801), 27–9. The copy in the British Library was originally in the library of King George III.
33 *Secret Memoirs*, 65.
34 *Female Biography; or, Memoirs of Illustrious and Celebrated Women, of All Ages and Countries*, 6 vols. (London, 1803), 3:129.
35 The expectation that a powerful, famous woman would be heterosexual had probably been shaken in the late eighteenth century by the accusations of lesbianism against Marie Antoinette. But by the time those angry allegations were being made, Catherine already had a well-established and contentious heterosexual reputation.
36 George Gordon Byron, *Don Juan* (1819 or later), Canto 9 stanza XLVI.
37 Although the communities where this degrading tale exists today are all societies of the written word, it is still circulated mostly orally, a situation that makes tracing its origin difficult. The story and some speculation about how it started are in Alexander, *Catherine*, 332–5; "Catherine the Great as Porn Queen," in *Eros and Pornography in Russian Culture*, ed. Marcus C. Levitt and A. Toporkov (Moscow: Ladomir, 1999), 240–2.
38 "Die Neue Selbst-Gefälligkeit der Angela M.: Angela die Grosse," *Der Spiegel*, September 9, 2013.

Bibliography

List of Works Cited, in Two Sections

I Primary literature, omitting newspaper articles, which are included only in the notes and index. Also omitting images, which are listed in the index under *political cartoons, prints*, and printed portraits. When both originals and translations are referenced, the originals come first.
II Secondary literature

I Primary Literature

"An Account of the Chief Circumstances of the Revolution that has Happened in Russia." *Gentleman's Magazine*, August 1762, 361–2.
"Account of the Late Revolution in Russia." *London Magazine*, August 1762, 434–6.
"An Account of the Late Revolution in Russia; Collected from Authentic Papers Never Before Published." *The Beauties of All Magazines Selected for the Year 1762*, September 1762, 343–50.
Aechte Nachrichten von dem Grafen Cagliostro: Aus der Handschrift seines entflohenen Kammerdieners. Berlin, 1786.
[Albrecht, Johann Friedrich Ernst]. *Pansalvin, Fürst der Finsterniss, und seine Geliebte. So gut wie geschehen*. Germanien, 1794.
[Albrecht, Johann Friedrich Ernst]. *Pansalvin, Fürst der Finsterniss, und seine Geliebte. So gut wie geschehen. Geheime Lebensgeschichte eines Günstlings*. Germanien, 1795.
[Albrecht, Johann Friedrich Ernst]. *Miranda, Königinn im Norden. Geliebte Pansalvins*. Germanien (Erfurt): Hennings, 1798.
[Albrecht, Johann Friedrich Ernst]. Dutch: *Miranda, Koningin van Noorden, Beminde van Pansalvinus, Vorst der Duisternis*. 1798.
[Albrecht, Johann Friedrich Ernst]. *Kakodämon der Schreckliche. Pansalvins und Mirandas Donnerkeil, Revisor des Codex der Menschen-Rechte*. 1 vols. Pyropolis, 1800.
[Albrecht, Johann Friedrich Ernst]. *Staub der Erste, Kayser der Unterwelt, als Beschluß des Pansalvin und der Miranda, von demselben Verfasser*. Persepolis, 1802.
[Albrecht, Johann Friedrich Ernst]. *Turbans Turbandus der grossen Miranda kleiner Sohn. Von einer diplomatischen Feder*. 1802.
[Albrecht, Johann Friedrich Ernst]. *Die Heimlichkeiten der Frauenzimmer: ein Lesebuch für Mütter, Erzieherinnen und mannbare*. Mädchen, 1809.
[Albrecht, Johann Friedrich Ernst], Monarchomachus, pseud. *Des politischen Thierkreises oder der Zeichen unsrer Zeit Zweyter Theil. / Neuestes graues Ungeheuer. Hrsg. von einem Freunde der Menschheit*. vol. 2, Bagdad, 1798.

"Allemagne. De Hambourg, le 3 Août." *Journal Politique de Bruxelles*, 1787.

Alopäus, Magnus. *Rede Ihrer Majestät der Glorwürdigst regierenden Kaiserin von Russland Catherinen der Zweyten bey seiner Aufnahme als Beysitzer in die königliche Deutsche Gesellschaft zu Göttingen den 24. September 1768*. Göttingen, 1768.

Andrä, H.F. (pseud.). *Katharina die Zweite, Kaiserin von Russland und Selbstherrscherin aller Reussen. Ein biographisch-karakteristisches Gemälde*. Halle, 1797.

Anecdoten zur Lebensgeschichte des Ritters und Reichs-Fürsten Potemkin. Nebst einer kurzen Beschreibung der ehemaligen Krimm...desgleichen der Reise der Kaiserin Katharina der Zweiten nach der Krimm. Freistadt am Rhein: Brockhaus, 1792.

Anekdoten zur Lebensgeschichte des Fürsten Gregorius Gregoriewitsch Orlow. Frankfurt u. Leipzig, 1791.

Anekdoten aus dem Privatleben der Kaiserin Catharina, Pauls des Ersten und seiner Familie. Hamburg, 1797.

"Annual Register." *Annual Register, or a View of the History, Politicks, and Literature of the Year 1762* (1763): 11–23, 222–8.

"Authentic History of the Famous Rebel Pugatschew." *London Magazine*, March 1775, 103–5.

Authentic Memoirs of the Life and Reign of Catherine II. Empress of all the Russias. Collected from authentic MS'S, translations, &c. of the King of Sweden, Right Hon. Lord Mountmorres, Lord Malmesbury, M. De Volney, and other indisputable authorities. London: printed for the author and sold by B. Crosby, 1797.

Bachaumont, Louis Petit de. *Mémoire secrets pour servir a l'histoire de la republique des lettres en France, depuis MDCCLXII jusqu'à nos jours; ou Journal d'un observateur*. Londres: John Adamsohn, 1777.

Bacmeister, H.L.C. Review of Grot, "Kanzelrede von der Rechtmäßigkelt der Blattern-Einimpfung." In *Russische Bibliothek, zur Kenntniss des gegenwärtigen zustandes der Literatur in Russland*, 1772, 500–14.

Baldinger, Friderika. "Versuch über meine Verstandeserziehung." In *'Ich wünschte so gar gelehrt zu werden.' Drei Autobiographien von Frauen des 18. Jahrhunderts. Texte und Erläuterungen*, edited by Magdalene Heuser, Ortrun Niethammer, Marion Roitzheim-Eisfeld, and Petra Wulbusch, 7–24. Göttingen: Wallstein, 1994.

Basedow, Johann Bernhard. *Des Elementarwerkes erster bis vierter Band. Ein geordneter Vorrath aller nöthigen Erkenntniß. Zum Unterrichte der Jugend von Anfang, bis ins academische Alter. Zur Belehrung der Eltern, Schullehrer und Hofmeister. Zum Nutzen eines jeden Lesers, die Erkenntniß zu vervollkommnen*. 5 vols. Dessau, 1774.

[Beauclair, Pierre Louis]. *Histoire de Pierre III. Empereur de Russie: Avec plusieurs anecdotes singulieres / dignes de curiosité*. London, 1774.

Bellermann, Johann Joachim. *Bemerkungen über Russland in Rücksicht auf Wissenschaft, Kunst, Religion und andere merkwürdige Verhältnisse*. Erfurt, 1788.

Bellermann, Johann Joachim. "Etwas über Rußland." *Olla Potrida*, 1788, 11–27.

Bemerkungen über Esthland, Liefland und Russland nebst einigen Beiträgen zur Empörungs-Geschichte Pugatschews, während eines achtjährigen Aufenthalts gesamlet von einem Augenzeugen. Prag u. Leipzig: Meissner, 1792.

Bernoulli, Johann. *Reisen durch Brandenburg, Pommern, Preußen, Curland, Rußland und Pohlen, in den Jahren 1777 und 1778*. 6 vols., 1779–1780.

Bernoulli, Johann. *Aufenthalt zu St. Petersburg, nebst dem Verzeichniss der kaiserl. Gemäldesammlung. Reisen durch Brandenburg, Pommern, Preußen, Curland, Rußland und Pohlen, in den Jahren 1777 und 1778*. 6 vols., Leipzig: Fritsch, 1780.

Biester, Johann Erich. *Abriss des Lebens und der Regierung Kaiserin Katharina II. von Russland*. Berlin: Nicolai, 1797.

Bouffonidor. *Les fastes de Louis XV, de ses ministres, maîtresses, généraux, et autres personnages de son regne: pour servir de suite à la vie privée.* Chez la veuve Liberté, 1783.
Bourdillon, Joseph. "Essai Historique & Critique sur les Dissentions des Eglises de Pologne." *L'Evangile du Jour*, 1769, 83–107.
Bruchstücke aus den Ruinen der Menschheit. *Eine Darstellung der wichtigsten Begebenheiten seit 1789 nebst einigen Blicken in die Zukunft.* Kopenhagen, 1797.
Brydone, and Wraxall. "Anecdotes of Signiora Gabrieli, the Celebrated Opera Singer." *Annual Register, or a View of the History, Politicks, and Literature of the Year 1775* (1776): 63–7.
"Bücherverbot." *Intelligenzblatt der Neuen allgemeinen deutschen Bibliothek*, no. 44 (1795): 397.
Burney, Fanny. *Fanny Burney and Her Friends: Select Passages from Her Diary and Other Writings.* Edited by L.B. Seeley. Scribner and Welford, 1890.
Büsching, Anton Friderich. "Lebensgeschichte Burchard Christophs von Münnich." *Magazin für die neue Historie und Geographie*, 1769, 3:387–536.
Büsching, Anton Friderich. "S. Petersburg." *Wöchentliche Nachrichten von neuen Landcharten, geographiscen, statistichen und historischen Büchern und Schriften*, March 24, 1783, 96.
Büsching, Anton Friderich. *D. Anton Friderich Büschings. königl. Preußisch. Oberconsistorialraths, Directors des vereinigten berlinischen und cölnischen Gymnasiums, und der beyden Schulen desselben, eigene Lebensgeschichte.* Halle: Johann Jacob Curts Witwe, 1789.
Byron, George Gordon. *Don Juan.* 1819.
Caminer, Domenico. *Geschichte des gegenwärtigen Kriegs zwischen Russland, Polen und der Ottomannischen Pforte.* Franckfurt: Leipzig, 1771.
Carburi, Marin, calling himself Chevalier de Lascary. *Monument élevé à la gloire de Pierre-le-Grand, ou relation des travaux et de moyens méchaniques pour transporter à Petersbourg un rocher destiné à servir de base à la statue équestre de cet empereur; avec un examen physique et chymique du même rocher.* Paris: chez Nyon, Stoupe, 1777.
Carta, con noticias circunstanciadas de la revolucion acaecida en Petersburgo en los dias 9. y 10 de julio proximo pasado, para destronar al emperador Pedro. III. y declarar soberana de todas las Rusias à la emperatriz Catalina II. su muger. Lima?, 1763.
Castéra, Jean-Henri. *Vie de Catherine II, impératrice de Russie.* Paris: F. Buisson, 1797.
Castéra, Jean-Henri, and William Tooke. English: *The life of Catharine II. Empress of Russia.* Translated by Tooke. 2 ed. London, 1798.
Casti, G.B. *Il poema Tartaro.* 2 ed., 1796.
Catharina die Zweite. Darstellungen aus der Geschichte ihrer Regierung, und Anekdoten von ihr und einigen Personen, die um sie waren. Altona: Hammerich, 1797.
Catharina die zweite, die einzige Kaiserinn der Erde, Selbstherrscherinn aller Reussen, Tauriens würdigste Königinn, mächtigste Erretterinn und großmüthigste Beglückerinn. Ein unterthänigstes Opfer tiefster Bewunderung und reinster Ehrfurcht zum feierlichsten Glückwunsch unzählbar frohlockender Völker, am unsterblichsten Ihrer wohlthätigen Tage, am herrlichsten wonnevollen Krönungstag der Allgütigen und Allgeliebten Huldgöttin zu Tauriens urerster Alleinherrscherinn. Frankfurt am Mein: Eichenberg, 1787.
[Catherine II]. *Antidote ou examen du mauvais libre intitulé: Voyage en Sibiré faut en 1761.* 2 vols., 1770.

[Catherine II]. English: *The Antidote, or, An Enquiry into the Merits of a Book, entitled A Journey into Siberia, made in 1761 in obedience to an order of the French king, and published, with approbation, by the Abbé Chappe d'Auteroche; in Which Many Essential Errors and Misrepresentations are Pointed out and Confuted ... By a Lover of Truth.* London: S. Leacroft, 1772.

Catherine II. "The [Second] Manifesto of the Empress of Russia." *Gentleman's Magazine*, September 1762, 437–9.

Catherine II. "Lettre de l'Impératrice de Russie à M. d'Alembert au sujet de l'invitation qu'elle lui avoit fait fair de venir en Russie pour l'éducation du grand Prince son fils." *Journal encyclopédique*, 1763, 131–3.

Catherine II. English: "Translation of a Letter from the Empress of Russia to M. d'Alembert, at Paris, whom she had invited into Russia to educate her Son." *The London Magazine; or, Gentleman's Monthly Intelligencer*, February 1763, 92.

Catherine II. *Instruction donnée par Catherine II., impératrice et législatrice de toutes les Russies, a la commission établie par cette souveraine, pour travailler à la rédaction d'un nouveau code de loix*. Nouvelle éd., augm. ed. A Lausanne. François Grasset & Comp, 1769.

Catherine II. "Schreiben der Kaiserinn von Rußland an Frau von der Recke." *Berlinische Monatsschrift* (1788): 129–30.

Catherine II, and L.P. de Ségur. "Imitation de Schakespear, scene historique, sans observation d'aucune règle du theatre, tirée de la vie de Rurick." In *Théâtre de l'Hermitage de Catherine II, impératrice de Russie*, Paris: F. Buisson, 1799, 2:369–430.

Catherine II. *Correspondance originelle et très interessante de l'Imperatrice de Russie Catharina II. avec le chevalier de Zimmermann*. Bremen: Joh. Heinr. Müller, 1808.

Catherine II. *Katharina die Grosse: Memoiren*. Translated by Erich Boehme. 1913. Reprint, Frankfurt a. M.: Insel, 1996.

Catherine II. *The Memoirs of Catherine the Great*. Translated by Mark Cruse. Edited by Hilde Hoogenboom. New York: Random House, 2006.

Catherine II. *Catherine the Great: Selected Letters*. Translated by Andrew Kahn and Kelsey Rubin-Detlev. Oxford: Oxford University Press, 2018.

Chantreau, Pierre Nicolas. *Voyage philosophique, politique et litteraire, fait en Russie pendant le années 1788 et 1789*. 2 vols. Hamburg: Fauche, 1794.

Chantreau, Pierre Nicolas. English: *Philosophical, Political, and Literary Travels in Russia, during the Years 1788 & 1789*. 2 vols. Perth: R. Morison Junior, 1794.

Chappe d'Auteroche, Jean. *A Journey into Siberia: Made by Order of the King of France*. London: T. Jefferys, 1770.

Chesterfield, Philip Dormer Stanhope, Earl of. *Letters Written by the Late Right Honourable Philip Dormer Stanhope, Earl of Chesterfield, to his son, Philip Stanhope*. ESTC T092045 ed. 4 vols. Vol. 4, London: P. Dodsley, 1797.

Comella, Luciano Francisco. *Catalina segunda, emperatriz de Rusia*. Valencia, 1795.

Comella, Luciano Francisco. *Catarina Segunda, emperatriz de Rusia, drama heroyco en tres actos*. Madrid: Antonio Cruzado, 1797.

Comella, Luciano Francisco. *Catalina segunda, emperatriz de Rusia : drama heroyco en tres actos*. Barcelona: J.F. Piferrer impressor (1797?).

Comella, Luciano Francisco. *Catarina Segunda en Cronstadt, drama heroyco en dos actos*. Madrid: Fermin Tadeo Villapando, 1799.

Congres Politique, ou Entretiens Libres des Puissances de l'Europe; sur le bal géenéral prochain. , 1772.

"Contenant ce qui s'est passé de plus considérable en Russie, depuis le mois dernier." *La Clef du Cabinet des Princes de l'Europe, ou Recuëil Historique & Politique sur les Matières du Tems*, 1762, 220–36.

Corberon, Marie Daniel Bourrée. *Edition électronique du Journal du baron Marie Daniel Bourrée de Corberon, Paris--Saint- Pétersbourg--Paris 1775--1785*. Edited by Dominique Taurisson and Pierre-Yves Beaurepaire. Used, June 2007.

Coxe, William. *Account of the Prisons and Hospitals in Russia, Sweden, and Denmark. With Occasional Remarks on the Different Modes of Punishments in Those Countries*. London: T. Cadell, 1781.

Coxe, William. *Travels into Poland, Russia, Sweden and Denmark. Interspersed with historical relations and political inquiries*. 2 vols. London, 1784.

Coxe, William. *Travels into Poland, Russia, Sweden and Denmark*. 3rd ed. 4 vols. London: T. Cadell, 1787.

Coxe, William. *Travels in Poland, Russia, Sweden, and Denmark: Illustrated with Charts and Engravings*. 5 vols. London: T. Cadell, jun. and W. Davies, 1802.

Coxe, William. German: *Reise durch Polen, Russland, Schweden und Dänemark*. Translated by J. Pezzl. 3 vols. Zürich, 1792.

Coxe, William, and Jacques Mallet du Pan. French: *Voyage en Pologne, Russie, suede et Danemark...enrici de notes ...et augmente d'un voyage en Norvege par P. Mallet*. 4 vols. Geneve, 1786.

"Curious Anecdotes of Dr. Dimsdale's Inoculation of the Empress of Russia." *The Town and Country Magazine, or Universal Repository of Knowledge, Instruction, and Entertainment*, 1769, 309.

"De las Fronteras de Rusia." *Mercurio histórico y político*, July 1774, 224–5.

"De Petersbourg." *Mercurio histórico y político*, August 1762, 359–78.

"De St. Petersbourg." *Mercure historique et politique: contenant l'état présent de l'Europe, ce qui se passe dans toutes les cours, les intérêts des princes et généralement tout ce qu'il y a de plus curieux*, December 1768, 683–4.

"Deaths. 10. At London." *Edinburgh Magazine, or Literary Miscellany*, 1787, 486.

Deffand, M. de Vichy Chamrond du. *The Unpublished Correspondence of Madame du Deffand with D'Alembert, Montesquieu, the President Hénault, the Duchess du Maine, Mesdames de Staal, de Choiseul, the Marquis D'Argens, the Chevalier D'Aydie, &c: Followed by the Letters of Voltaire to Madame du Deffand*. Translated by Mrs. Meeke. 2 vols. London: A.K. Newman & Company, 1810.

Denkwürdigkeiten der Lebens- und Staats-Geschichte des ohnlängst verstorbenen unglücklichen Czaars Peter des Dritten, aus glaubwürdigen Nachrichten und richtigen Urkunden in der Kürze verfasst. Danzig, 1762.

Dutens, Louis. *Des pierres précieuses et des pierres fines, avec les moyens de les connoître & de les évaluer*. Paris: Didot & DeBure, 1776.

Edgeworth, Maria. *Rosamond: A Sequel to Early Lessons*. 2 vols. Philadelphia: J. Maxwell, 1821.

Engelhard, Philippine. *Neujahrs-Geschenk für liebe Kinder*. Göttingen: Johann Christian Dieterich, 1787.

"Die Entthronung des Russischen Kaysers Peter III. und dessen darauf erfolgtes Ende." In *Fortgesetzte neue genealogisch-historische Nachrichten*, Parts 7 and 8 (1763): 387–415.

"Etats du Nord." *Suite de la clef ou journal historique sur les matieres du tems*, February 1769, 104.

"Foreign Affairs." *The London Magazine, Or, Gentleman's Monthly Intelligencer*, August 1764, 430–2.

Forster, Georg. "Gregor Potemkin." In *Erinnerungen aus dem Jahr 1790, in historischen Gemälden und Bildnissen*. Edited by D. Chodowiecki, d. Berger, Cl. Kohl, J.F. Bolt and J.S. Ringck, 147–66. Berlin: Voss, 1793.

Fortgesetzte russische Anekdoten oder Zweyter Theil. Aus dem Englischen übersetzt. n.p., 1766.

Fortia-de-Piles, Alphonse. *Voyage de deux Francais en Allemagne, Danemarck, Suede, Russie et Pologne*. 5 vols. Paris: Chez Desenne, 1796.

Freudengesang der Judenschaft zu Sclow beym Durchzuge ihrer Kaiserlichen Majestät. 1780.

Freundschaftliche Briefe über den gegenwärtigen Zustand des Russischen Reichs, mit richtigen und denkwürdigen Nachrichten von den gesammten europäischen und asiatischen Provinzen, verschiedenen Völkerschaften, Lebensart, Handel und überhaupt von der Macht dieses grossen Staats, bey Gelegenheit der itzigen Weltbegebenheiten in Norden, zu dessen näherer Kenntnis herausgegeben. 1769.

Galloway, George. *Poems. The Tears of Poland*. Edinburgh, 1795.

Geisler, Adam Friedrich *Gallerie edler deutscher Frauenzimmer, mit getroffenen Schattenrissen*. Dessau und Leipzig: Buchhandlung der Gelehrten, 1784.

"General Aspect of Affairs at the Beginning of the Year." *The Annual Register, or a View of the History, Politicks and Literature of the Year, for the Year 1766*, 1–7. London: Dodsley, 1767.

"Genève." *Journal historique et politique des principaux événements des différentes cours de l'Europe*, December 10, 1778, 441–4.

Gespräch im Reiche derer Todten zwischen Sr. Königlichen Majestät von Pohlen, August dem Dritten, und Sr. Russisch-Kaiserlichen Majestät, Petern dem Dritten, worin beider hoher Monarchen merkwürdige Lebensgeschichte aus zuverlässigen Nachrichten erzälet wird. Frankfurt: Leipzig, 1764.

G[odineau]. *Catherine II, impéritrice de Russie. Tragédie en cinq actes*. Paris: Cellot, 1807.

G*** [Ange Goudar], D. *Memoires pour servir à l'histoire de Pierre III. Empereur de Russie. Avec un detail historique des differends de la Maison de Holstein avec la cour de Dannemarc. Le pour et contre du Pierre III. Empereur de Russie*. Berlin et Dresde, 1763.

[Goebel]. *Fragmens historiques sur Pierre III et Catherine II*. Paris: Libraire du Cercle-Social, 1797.

Goethe, Johann Wolfgang von. *Briefe aus der Schweiz. Gedenkausgabe*. Edited by Ernst Beutler. 2nd ed. Vol. 4, 1962.

Goethe, Johann Wolfgang von. *Dichtung und Wahrheit. Gedenkausgabe*. 2nd ed. Vol. 10, 1962.

Grimm, Friedrich Melchior. [Lettres de Grimm à l'impératrice Catherine II. Lettres de Grimm au Prince Galitzine. Lettres d'Ernest-Jean Biron à l'ambassadeur H. Keyserlingk. Lettres de Diderot à l'impératrice Catherine II.] *Sbornik Imperatorskago russkago istoricheskago obshchestva*. Edited by J. Grot. Saint-Pétersbourg: Impr. de l'Académie des sciences, 1881.

Halem, Gerh. Ant. "Arion, An Katharina die Zweite." *Deutsches Museum*, no. 1 (1786): 1–9.

Halem, Gerh. Ant. *Lebensbeschreibung des Russisch-Kaiserlichen General-Feldmarschalls, B.C. Grafen von Münnich*. Oldenburg: Schulze, 1803.

"Hamburgh, Aug. 16." *Annual Register, or a View of the History, Politicks, and Literature of the Year 1771* (1772): 137.

Hays, Mary. *Female Biography; or, Memoirs of Illustrious and Celebrated Women, of All Ages and Countries*. 6 vols. London, 1803.

[Heinzmann, Johann Georg]. *Historisches Bilderbuch des Edlen und Schönen aus dem Leben würdiger Frauenzimmer*. Bern: Haller, 1790.

[Helbig, Gustav Adolph Wilhelm von] *Biographie Peter des Dritten*. 2 vols. Tübingen: Cotta, 1808.

[Helbig, Gustav Adolph Wilhelm von]. "Potemkin der Taurier." In *Minerva, ein Journal historischen und politischen Inhalts*, Hamburg, 1797–1800.

[Helbig, Gustav Adolph Wilhelm von.]. *Potemkin: ein interessanter Beitrag zur Regierungsgeschichte Katharina's der Zweiten*. Halle und Leipzig, 1804.

[Helbig, Gustav Adolph Wilhelm von]. Dutch: *Potemkin de Taurier*. Deventer, 1806.

[Helbig, Gustav Adolph Wilhelm von]. French: *Vie du Prince Potemkin, feld-maréchal au service de Russie sous le règne de Catherine II, rédigée d'après les meilleurs ouvrages allemands et français qui ont paru sur la Russie à cette époque*. Paris: Chez H. Nicolle, 1808.

[Helbig, Gustav Adolph Wilhelm von]. English: *Memoirs of the Life of Prince Potemkin*. London: H. Colburn, 1812.

[Helbig, Gustav Adolph Wilhelm von]. *Russische Günstlinge*. Tübingen: Cotta, 1809.

"Her imperial majesty's declaration, &c. on the Death of the Emperor Her Husband." *The Annual Register: World Events*, 1763.

Hippel, Theodor Gottlieb von. *Zimmermann der I. und Friedrich II*. n.p., 1790.

Hippel, Theodor Gottlieb von. *Über die Ehe*. 3rd. enlarged ed. Berlin: Voss, 1792.

Hippel, Theodor Gottlieb von. *On Marriage*. Translated by Timothy F. Sellner. Detroit: Wayne State University Press, 1994.

"Historical Chronicle (August & September)." *Gentleman's Magazine*, July 1762, 361–2, 86, 437–9, 43.

"Historical Chronicle (July)." *Gentleman's Magazine*, July 1762, 341.

Hordt, Johann Ludwig. *The Military, Historical and Political Memoirs of the Count de Hordt, a Swedish Nobleman, and Lieutenant General in the Service of his Majesty the King of Prussia*. 2 vols. London: Egerton, 1806.

Hörschelmann, Friedrich Ludewig Anton. *Friedrich Ludew. Ant. Hörschelmanns pragmatische Geschichte der merkwürdigen Staatsveränderungen im rußischen Reiche von dem Ableben Peters des grossen an bis auf den Regierungs-Antrit der ietzregierenden Kaiserin Catharina II. Aus sichern Quellen und authentischen Nachrichten mit unparteiischer Feder vorgetragen auch mit nötigen Beweisen bestätigt*. Erfurt: J.J. F. Straube, 1763.

Imbert, Guillaume. "La guerre actuelle des deux cours impériale." *La chronique scandaleuse, ou mémoires pour servir à l'histoire des moeurs de la génération présente* (1791): 84.

Karsch, Anna Luisa. "An die Mütter des reisenden Chur- und liefländischen Adels." In *Neue Gedichte*, 1772.

Karsch, Anna Luisa. *Auserlesene Gedichte*. 1764. Reprint, Karben, Germany: Petra Wahl, 1996.

Karsch, Anna Luisa, and Johann Wilhelm Ludwg Gleim. "Mein Bruder in Apoll." *Briefwechsel zwischen Anna Louise Karsch und Johann Wilhelm Ludwig Gleim*. Edited by Regina Nörtemann. Göttingen: Wallstein, 1996.

Katharine II. vor dem Richterstuhle der Menschheit. Grösstentheils Geschichte. Leipzig, 1797.

Kerstens, Johann Christian. *Dass die Ehre und die Wohlfahrt eines Landes eine Folge von der Aufnahme der Wissenschaften sey, wurde in einer Rede erwogen von I. C. Kerstens*. Moskau, 1762.

"Kiew (Capital of the Ukraine) Feb. 12." *The European Magazine, and London Review,* 1787, 210.

Kraft, Andries. *Czaar Peter de Derde. Treuerspel.* Amsterdam, 1801.

"L'empereur aura-t-il une entre vue avec l'impératrice de Russie?" *Journal politique, ou Gazette des gazettes,* February 1787, 18–19.

La Roche, Sophie von. "Über Teutschland." *Pomona für Teutschlands Töchter,* no. 8 (August 1783): 725–64.

La Roche, Sophie von. "Zwey schöne Erscheinungen des letzten Jahres." *Pomona für Teutschlands Töchter* 2, no. 1 (1784): 131–4.

La Roche, Sophie von. *Briefe an Lina.* Speier: Enderesischen Schriften, 1785.

La Roche, Sophie von. *Fanny und Julia, oder die Freundinnen.* 2 vols. Vol. 2, Leipzig: Gräff, 1802.

Lannoy, Juliane Cornelia de. "A Sa Majesté l'Imperatrice de Russie." *Gazette Littéraire de l'Europe* 75 (1776): 145–9.

Lannoy, Juliane Cornelia de. "Lettre adressée aux Editeurs de la Gazette Littéraire de l'Europe." *Gazette littéraire de l'Europe: augm. de plus. articles, qui ne se trouvert pas dans l'éd. de Paris* 75 (1776): 142–4.

Lasting peace to Europe. The Dream of a Cosmopolite. Dedicated to her Imperial Majesty the Empress of Russia. London, 1781.

Lavater, J.C. *Essays on Physiognomy; For the Promotion of the Knowledge and Love of Mankind.* Translated by Holcroft. abridged ed. London: Vernor & Hood, 1806.

[Laveaux, Jean Charles Thibault de.] *Histoire de Pierre III, empereur de Russie: imprimée sur un manuscrit trouvé dans les papiers de Montmorin.* 3 vols. Paris: Maison La Briffe, 1799.

[Laveaux, Jean Charles Thibault de.]. *Histoire secrète des amours et des principaux amans de Catherine II., impératrice de Russie.* Paris: LaBriffe, 1799.

[Laveaux, Jean Charles Thibault de.]. German: *Geschichte Peters des Dritten, Kaisers von Rußland : Aus der Handschrift eines geheimen Agenten Ludewigs XV. am Hofe zu Petersburg, die sich unter den Papieren des vormaligen Ministers der auswärtigen Angelegenheiten Montmorin vorgefunden hat : Mit hinzugefügten wichtigen Aufschlüssen; und begleitet von der geheimen Geschichte der vornehmsten Liebschaften Katharinen II.* 1799.

[Laveaux, Jean Charles Thibault de, and J. Linden]. Dutch: *Minnarijen van Catharina II. Keizerin van Rusland, en Geschiedenis van haare voornaamste Minnaars.* J. Allart, 1800.

Lichtenberg, Georg Christoph. *Briefwechsel.* Edited by Ulrich Joost and Albrecht Schöne. 5 vols. München: C.H. Beck, 1990.

Lieman, Amalie von. *Amaliens von Lieman, eines eilfjährigen Frauenzimmers, Reisen durch einige Russiche Länder in vertrauten Briefen an ihre Freundin und vormalige Gouvernante Helena Gatterer in Göttingen.* Göttingen: Rosenbusch, 1794.

Lind, John. *Letters Concerning the Present State of Poland. With an Appendix, Containing the Manifestoes of the Courts of Vienna, Petersburg, and Berlin. And the Letters Patent of the King of Prussia.* London: T. Payne, 1773.

Linguet, Simon-Nicholas Henri. *Annales politiques, civiles, et littéraire du dix-huitieme siècle.* The Hague: Pierre Frederic Gosse, Libraire de S.A.S., 1777.

Lob- und Danklied der Judengemeine zu Mohilow beym Einzuge Ihrer Kayserlichen Majestät Katharina II. Selbstbeherrscherinn aller Reussen. Mohilow, 1780.

Marcard, Heinrich Matthias, ed. *Zimmermanns Verhältnisse mit der Kayserin Catharina II und dem Herrn Weikard. Nebst einer Anzahl Original-Briefe der Kayserin.* Bremen: C. Seyffert, 1803.

Marche, C. F. S. de la. *Anecdotes Russes, ou Lettres d'un officier Allemand à un gentilhomme Livonien, écrites de Pétersburg en 1762, Tems du Règne et du Détronement de Pierre III, Empereur de Russie.* London (really den Haag), 1764.

Marche, C. F. S. de la. German: *Russische Anekdoten von der Regierung und Tod Peters des Dritten; imgleichen von der Erhebung und Regierung Catherinen der Andern. Ferner von dem Tode des Kaisers Iwan, welchem zum Anhange beygefügt die Lebens-Geschichte Catherinen der Ersten.* Petersburg [i.e. Frankfurt]: [Heinrich Remigius Brönner, Johann Karl Brönner], 1764.

Marche, C. F. S. de la. *Anecdotes Russes ou Lettres d'un officier allemand, a un gentilhomme livonien, écrites de Petersbourg en 1762; tems du règne & du détrônemement de Pierre III. empereur de Russie.* London: Aux dépons de la compagnie, 1765.

Marche, C. F. S. de la. *Nouveaux Mémoires, ou anecdotes du règne et du détrônement de Pierre III. Empereur de Russie.* Berlin et Dresde, 1765.

Marche, C. F. S. de la. German: *Russische Anekdoten; Oder Briefe eines deutschen Offiziers an einen livländischen Edelmann, worinnen die vornehmsten Lebensumstände des russischen Kaisers, Peter III., nebst dem unglücklichen Ende dieses Monarchen enthalten sind.* 1765.

Marche, C. F. S. de la. *Histoire et anecdotes de la vie, du règne, du détrônement et de la mort de Pierre III. dernier empereur de toutes les Russies, etc. etc. etc. ecrites en forme de lettres.* London: Aux dépens de la Compagnie, 1766.

Maréchal, Sylvain. *Le jugement dernier des rois: prophétie en un acte, en prose.* Paris: C.F. Patris, 1793.

[Masson, Charles François Philibert]. *Mémoires secrets sur la Russie et particulièrement sur la fin du règne de Catherine II et le commencement de celui de Paul I. Formant un tableau des moeurs de St. Pétersbourg à la fin du 18e siècle.* 3 vols. Paris,: C. Pougens, 1800.

[Masson, Charles François Philibert]. English: *Secret Memoirs of the Court of Petersburg: Particularly Towards the End of the Reign of Catharine II and the Commencement of That of Paul I.* 2 vols. London: Printed by C. Whittingham for T.N. Longman and O. Rees, 1800.

[Masson, Charles François Philibert]. *Secret Memoirs of the Court of Petersburg: Particularly Towards the End of the Reign of Catharine II and the Commencement of That of Paul I. Serving as a Supplement to The Life of Catharine II.* 2 ed. London: T.N. Longman and O. Rees, 1801.

[Masson, Charles François Philibert]. *Secret Memoirs of the Court of Petersburg: Particularly Towards the End of the Reign of Catharine II and the Commencement of That of Paul I. Serving as a Supplement to the Life of Catherine II.* London: T.N. Longman and O. Rees, 1802.

Mayer, Johann Georg. *Der erhabene Adler in der Maske des Falken, oder Kaiser Joseph II Reise nach Russland unter dem Namen eines Grafen von Falkenstein, nebst einigen merkwürdigen Umständen.* Augsburg: Johann Georg Bullmann, Buchhändler, 1780.

"Mein lieber Peter, gute Nacht!" In *Fortgesetzte russische Anekdoten oder Zweyter Theil.* Aus dem Englischen übersetzt, 30–7. n.p., 1766.

Mercier, Louis-Sébastien. *Memoirs of the Year Two Thousand Five Hundred.* 2 vols. Dublin: Wilson, 1772.

Merck, Johann Heinrich. *Briefwechsel.* Edited by U. Leuschner, J. Bohnengel, Y. Hoffmann, and A. Krebs. Göttingen: Wallstein, 2007.

Merkwürdige Lebensgeschichte Peter des Dritten, Kaisers und Selbsthalters aller Reußen, nebst einer Erläuterung zweyer bereits seltener Münzen, welche dieser Herr hat prägen lassen. 2nd ed. Frankfurth und Leipzig, 1762.

Meyer, Johann Heinrich Christian. *Briefe über Russland*. 2 vols. Göttingen: Rosenbusch, 1778–1779.
"Monsieur Diderot." *The Gentleman's Magazine, and Historical Chronicle*, May 1765, 242.
Moser, Friedrich Carl. "Catherina die Zweyte, Kaiserin von Rußland. Ein Gemäld ohne Schatten, 1773." *Deutsches Museum*, no. 5 (May 1776): 383–9.
"Mr. Sheridan [April 12, 1791]." *The Parliamentary Register; Or, History of the Proceedings and Debates of the House of Commons*, 1791, 143.
Müller, Carl Ernst Christian. *Catharina II dargestellt in ihren Werken zur Beherzigung der Völker Europens*. Berlin, 1794.
Nicolay, Ludwig Heinrich, and Friedrich Nicolai, eds. *Die beiden Nicolai : Briefwechsel zwischen Ludwig Heinrich Nicolay in St. Petersburg und Friedrich Nicolai in Berlin (1776–1811)*. Edited by Heinz Ishreyt. Lüneburg: Verlag Nordostdeutsches Kulturwerk, 1989.
"Note de l'éditeur." In *Théâtre de l'Hermitage de Catherine II, impératrice de Russie composé par cette princesse, par plusieurs personnes de sa société intime, et par quelques ministres etrangers*. Paris: Gide, 1799.
"Noticias de Rusia. Petersbourgo." *Mercurio histórico y político*, July 1774, 220–2.
"Noticias de Turquía y Africa: Constantinopla." *Mercurio histórico y político*, 1787, 275–8.
"Notizie Letterarie." *Gazzetta universale: o sieno notizie istorice, politiche, di scienze, arti agricoltura*, ec, 1775.
"Nouvelles Politiques. Pétersbourg (le 12 Décembre)." *Journal encyclopédique ou universel*, January 1767, 150–65.
Observations on the present state of Denmark, Russia and Switzerland. In a series of letters. London: T. Cadell, 1784.
"On peut se rappeller les instances." *Gazette des gazettes ou Journal politique: pour l'année*, November, first fortnight 1764, 40.
Pansmouzer [alias for John Lind], Gotlieb. *The Polish Partition, Illustrated in Seven Dramatick Dialogues or Conversation Pieces Between Remarkable Personages Published from the Mouths and Actions of the Interlocutors*. London, 1773.
Pansmouzer [alias for John Lind], Gotlieb. French: *Le partage de la Pologne: en sept dialogues en forme de drame ou conversation entre des personnages distingués, dans laquelle on fait parler les interlocuteurs conformément a leurs principes et a leur conduite*. Translated by J.M.G. de Rayneval. De l'imprimerie de P. Elms[l]y, 1775.
Pansmouzer [alias for John Lind], G. German: *Die Theilung von Pohlen in sieben Gesprächen, oder: Unterredung zwischen hohen Personen, worinn sich diesselben ihren Grundsätzen und Betragen gemäss ausdrücken*. Hanau, 1775.
Pansmouzer [alias for John Lind], G. Italian: *Divisione della Polonia in sette dialoghi a guisa di dramma conversazione tra potenze Distinte, in cui si fanno parlare gli interlocutori second I loro principi, e la loro condotta. Opera di G. Pansmouser. Tradotta dall'inglese*. The Hague, 1775.
Pansmouzer [alias for John Lind], G. Polish: *Podział Polski w siedmiu rozmowach, z Francuskiego (The division of Poland in seven interviews, from the French)*. Leipzig, 1775.
Pansmouzer [alias for John Lind], G. Dutch: *De Verdeeling van Pohlen, in VII somenspraken, tusschen hooge standspersonen, tooneelswijze voorgedragen. Door den Herr Gotlieb Pansmouser, uit he Engelsch vertaeld door eine leefsche Mevrouw*. Keulen (Cologne): Johan Kreitzer, 1775.
Paul der Erste Kaiser und Selbstherrscher aller Reußen, Eine historische Skizze. Leipzig: Müller, 1802.

Paul der Erste, Kayser von Russland. Von einem unbefangenen Beobachter. Leipzig: Sommersche Buchhandlung, 1801.

Pellet-Desbarreaux, Hyacinthe. *Les Potentats foudroyés par la Montagne et la Raison, ou, la Déportation des Rois de l'Europe, pièce prophétique et révolutionnaire, en un acte [and in prose], etc.* Toulouse: Citoyen P. Francés, 1793.

Du péril de la balance politique, ou Expose des causes qui l'ont alteree dans le nord, debuis l'avenement de Catherine II au trone de Russie. London, 1789.

Du péril de la balance politique de l'Europe, ou Exposé des causes qui l'on altérée das le Nord depui l'avénement de Catherine II au trône de Russie. 1790.

English: *The Danger of the Political Balance of Europe.* Dublin: Printed by Graisberry & Campbell, 1790.

"Petersburgh, Nov. 19." *The London Magazine, or, Gentleman's Monthly Intelligencer,* December 1768, 707.

Piozzi, Hester L. *Retrospection, or: A Review of the Most Striking and Important Events, Characters, Situations, and Their Consequences, Which the Last Eighteen Hundred Years Have Presented to the View of Mankind.* London: Stockdale, 1801.

"Poetische Blumenlese auf das Jahr 1777." *Neueste Critische Nachrichten* 3, no. 27 (1777): 214–15.

Le Procès des trois Rois, Louis XVI. de France-Bourbon, Charles III. d'Espagne-Bourbon, et George III. d'Hanovre, fabricant de bouton, plaide au tribunal des puissances-Europeennes. Par appendix, l'appel au Pape. London: George Carenaught, 1780.

[Raspe?, Rudolf Erich]. *Gulliver Revived; Containing Singular Travels, Campaigns, Voyages, and Adventures. ... By Baron Munchausen.* Fifth Edition, considerably enlarged, and ornamented with a variety of explanatory Views, engraved from Original Designs ed. G. Kearsley, 1787.

Raynal, Guillaume-Thomas-François, abbé. *Histoire philosophique et politique des établissemens et du commerce des Européens dans les deux Indes.* Vol. 5, Geneva: chez J.-L. Pellet, 1781.

Recke, Elisa von der. *Nachricht von des berüchtigten Cagliostro Aufenthalte in Mittau, im Jahre 1779, und von dessen dortigen magischen Operationen.* Berlin: Nicolai, 1787.

Recke, Elisa von der. *Tagebücher und Selbstzeugnisse.* Edited by C. Träger. C.H. Beck, 1984.

Reflexions politiques sur la guerre actuelle de l'Angleterre avec ses colonies & sur l'etat de la Russie. n.p., 1777.

"Die Regierungs-Geschichte der Rußischen Kaiserinn im Jahr 1766." *Fortgesetzte neue genealogisch-historische Nachrichten,* 1767, 635–50.

Review of Acta Academia. *Appendix to the Monthly Review* 69 (1783): 585–8.

Review of Du péril de la balance politique de l'Europe. *Annalen der Geographie und Statistic* 1 (1790): 504–9.

Review of Histoire ou anecdotes sur le Revolution de Russie, &c. i.e. A History of, or Anecdotes respecting, the Revolution in Russia, by Rulhière. *The Monthly Review,* 1797, 557–67.

Review of L'Inoculation [by Roman]. *L'Esprit des journaux, françois et étrangers,* 1774, 107–12.

Review of Voyage en Siberie by Chappe d'Auteroche. *The Monthly Review,* 1769, 586–99.

"Revolution in Denmark. Counts Struensee and Brandt are confined in the Citadel ... Magnificence of the Empress of Russia." Chap. VI In *Annual Register, or a View of the History, Politicks, and Literature of the Year 1772,* 70–80. London: Dodsley, 1773.

Richardson, William. *Anecdotes of the Russian Empire. In a Series of Letters, Written, a Few Years Ago, from St. Petersburg.* London: Strahan & Cadell, 1784.

Röllig, Johann Georg. *Als die erfreuliche Botschaft von der Vermählung des Herrn Peters Feodorowiz wie auch der Frau Catharina Alexiena bekannt und Derselben hohe Feyer an dem Hochfürstlichen Anhalt-Zerbstischen Hofe begangen wurde, wolte seine Pflicht in Drama und Musica an den Tag legen J. G. Röllig.* Zerbst, 1746.
[Roman, John Joseph Therese]. *L'inoculation, poëme en quatre chants.* Lacombe, 1773.
Römpler, C. L. "Ode." In *Kurzer Entwurf der Lebensbeschreibung Ihro Majestät, Katharinen der Zweiten, Kaiserin und Selbstherrscherin von ganz Rußland*, edited by Theodor Josephides von Tomanskiy, unnumbered pages 57-59, 1774.
Rulhière, Claude Carloman de. *Histoire ou Anecdotes sur la Revolution de Russie; en l'Année 1762.* Paris: Desenne, 1797.
Rulhière, Claude Carloman de. English: *A History, Or Anecdotes, of the Revolution in Russia, in the Year 1762.* London: M. Beauvalet, 1797.
Rulhière, Claude Carloman de. German: *Geschichte der russischen Revolution im Jahr 1762.* Germanien, 1797.
Rulhière, Claude Carloman de. Danish: *Anekdoter om Statsforandringen i Rusland.* Kopenhagen, 1797.
Rulhière, Claude Carloman de. Dutch: *Geschiedenis of Anecdotes der Russische Omwenteling, in den Jaare 1762.* Translated by Ernst Zeydelaar. In den Haag: J. Plaat, 1797.
Rulhière, Claude Carloman de. Excerpt: "Tod der russischen Kaiserinn Katharina II." *Verbesserter und Alter Vollkommener Staats-Calender, genannt der Hinkende Bott … auf das Gnadenreiche Christ-Jahr MDCCXCVIII*, 1797, 7 unnumbered pages.
"Russia." *The Scots Magazine* 30, March 1768, 156.
"Russia." *The English Review, Or, An Abstract of English and Foreign Literature*, March 1787.
"Russland." *Historisches Portefeuille*, May 1787, 520.
Saldern, Casper von. *Biographie Peters des Dritten, Kaiser aller Reussen; zur unpartheyischen Ansicht der Wirkung der damaligen Revolution, und zur Berichtigung der Beurtheilung des Charakters Catharinens II.* Petersburg, 1800.
Saldern, Casper von. *Histoire de la vie de Pierre III, empereur de toutes les Russies, présentant, sous un aspect impartial, les causes de la révolution arrivée en 1762.* Metz: Collignon, 1802.
[Schérer, Jean-Benoît]. *Anecdotes intéressantes et secrètes de la cour de Russie: tirées de ses archives.* London and Paris: Buisson, 1792.
Schlözer, August Ludwig (Joh. Joseph Haigold, pseud.). *Neuverändertes Russland, oder, Leben Catharina der Zweyten, Kayserinn von Russland aus authentischen Nachrichten beschrieben.* Riga und Leipzig: Bey Johann Friedrich Hartknoch, 1767.
Schlözer, August Ludwig (Joh. Joseph Haigold, pseud.). *Neuverändertes Russland, oder, Leben Catharina der Zweyten, Kayserinn von Russland aus authentischen Nachrichten beschrieben.* Riga und Mietau: Bey Johann Friedrich Hartknoch, 1771.
[Schlözer, August Ludwig von]. *Russische Schul-Projecte.* Göttingen, 1783.
[Schmidt-Phiseldek, Christoph von]. *Briefe über Russland. Erste Sammlung.* 2 vols. Braunschweig: Schrödersche Buchhandlung, 1770.
"Schreiben aus Petersburg bey Gelegenheit der letztern Revolution." In *Merkwürdige Lebensgeschichte Peter des Dritten, Kaisers und Selbsthalters aller Reußen.* 2nd ed., 55–64. Frankfurth und Leipzig, 1762.
Sečenov, D.A. *Feyerliche Danckrede des hochwürdigsten Ertz-Bischoffens von Groß-Novogrod, oder Neugard an dem Fluß Wolfowa in West-Rußland zu Gott, und an seine versammelte Cleresey auf die Abthronung Peters des Dritten Czaars in Rußland zu Oranien-Baum in Ingerman-Land bey dem Einfluß des Nieva-Stroms Cronschlott gegenüber den 28. Junius des alten, und 9. Julius des neuen Stils 1762. Gesprochen, und*

aus dem Griechischen in die teutsche Sprache übersetzt. Translated by C.J. Ivanowiz. Smolensk, Lithuania: Erhard, 1762.

Segur, Louis-Philippe de. *History of the Principal Events of the Reign of Frederic William II. King of Prussia; and a Political Picture of Europe, from 1786 to 1796. Containing a Summary of the Revolutions of Brabant, Holland, Poland, and France*. 3 vols. London: Longman and Rees, 1801.

Sénac de Meilhan, Gabriel. *La merveille du siecle ou observations sur la vie politique es privee de Catharine II l'Incomparable*. 1792.

Sénac de Meilhan, Gabriel. *Lettre à Mad. de ****. Paris: chez Desenne, libraire au Palais Royal, 1792.

Sénac de Meilhan, Gabriel. German: "Schreiben des Herrn Senac de Meillan aus Petersburg an Madame de *** in Paris." *Minerva*, 1792, 36–56.

Sénac de Meilhan, Gabriel. "Lettres sur la Russie." In *Oeuvres philosophiques et littéraires*, 107–51. Chez B. G. Hoffmann, 1795.

Sénac de Meilhan, Gabriel. German: "Briefe über Rußland." *Olla Potrida*, 1796, 61–88.

[Seume, Johann Gottfried]. *Ueber das Leben und den Charakter der Kaiserin von Rusland Katharina II. Mit Freymüthigkeit und Unpartheylichkeit*. Altona [vielm. Leipzig]: [Göschen], 1797.

Seymour, George. *The Instructive Letter-Writer, and Entertaining Companion: Containing Letters on the Most Interesting Subjects... Most of Which Are Wrote by ...Royal and Eminent Personages, and the Best Authors*. London, 1763.

Sievers, Johann Jakob. *Ein russischer Staatsmann. Des Grafen Jakob Johann Sievers Denkwürdigkeiten zur Geschichte Rußlands*. Edited by Karl Ludwig Blum. 2 vols. Leipzig: Winter, 1857.

A Sketch of the Secret History of Europe, since the Peace of Paris, with Observations on the Present Critical State of Great Britain. London: J. Murray, 1772.

S. *Privatleben des berühmten Russisch-Kaiserlichen Feldmarschalls Fürsten von Potemkin Tawrotschewskoy*. Leipzig und Grätz: bei Franz Ferstl in Kommission, 1793.

Sternberg, Joachim Graf von. *Bemerkungen über Russland, auf einer Reise gemacht im Jahre 1792 und 1793; Mit statistischen und meteorologischen Tabellen*. n.p., 1794.

Storch, Heinrich. *Gemälde von St Petersburg*. 2 vols. Riga: Hartknoch, 1794.

Strenge, A.C. "Begebenheiten eines Deutschen Predigers an den Ufern der Wolga." *Deutsche Monatsschrift*, 1792, v. 1:137–43, v. 2: 53–61, 67–73.

Thesby de Belcour, François Alphonse. *Tagebuch eines französischen Officiers in Diensten der Pohlnischen Konföderation, welcher von den Russen gefangen und nach Sibirien verwiesen worden*. Amsterdam, 1776.

[Thomson, William]. *Letters from Scandinavia: On the Past and Present State of the Northern Nations of Europe*. Printed for G.G. and J. Robinson, 1796.

Tickell, Thomas. *A Poem to His Excellency the Lord Privy-Seal, on the Prospect of Peace* 4 ed. London: J. Tonson, 1713.

de Tiregale, Pierre Ricaud. *Medailles sur les principaux evenements de l'Empire de Russie depuis le Regne de Pierre le Grand jusqu'a celui de Catherine II, avec des explications historiques*. Potsdam: Sommer, 1772.

Tomanskiy, Theodor Josephides von. *Kurzer Entwurf der Lebensbeschreibung Ihro Majestät, Katharinen der Zweiten, Kaiserin und Selbstherrscherin von ganz Rußland*. n.p., 1774.

"[Trade Card of Hatchett, Coach-Maker]." *British Museum D,2,679*. London: Darling & Thompson, 1783.

"[Trade Card of Hatchett, Coach-Maker]." *British Museum D,2,1496*. London: Darling & Thompson, 1790.

Turner, Richard. *Universal History, Ancient and Modern; in a Series of Letters to a Youth at School*. London, 1787.

L'ultima confession generale fatta da Catterina 2. imperatrice delle Russie al Gran Patriarca di Pietroburgo prima della sua morte seguita li 6 novembre 1796. Dialogo storico-critico tra gli attori dissopra espressi. 1797.

Voltaire. *Nouveaux mélanges philosophiques, historiques, critiques, etc. etc.* s.n., 1768.

Voltaire. *The Age of Louis XV*. In: *The Works of Mr. de Voltaire*. Vol. 38, London, 1774.

Voltaire. *Lettres de L'Imperatrice de Russie et de M. de Voltaire. Oeuvres Complètes de Voltaire*. Vol. 67, Kehl, 1784.

Voltaire. *Lettres de l'Imperatrice de Russie et de M. de Voltaire. Oeuvres Complètes de Voltaire*. Vol. 67, Kehl, 1785.

Voltaire. *Lettres du Roi de Prusse et de M. de Voltaire. Oeuvres Complètes de Voltaire*. Vol. 54, Basel: Tourneisen, 1788.

Voltaire. *Mémoires. Frédéric le Grand*. Vol. 70, Oeuvres complètes, 1789.

Voltaire. "Lettre CLXXVIII A.M. Pictet, à Petersbourg, Septembre." In *Recueil des lettres de M. de Voltaire, Mai 1762 - Octobre 1763*. Vol. 10, *Recueil des lettres de M. de Voltaire, 1715-1778*. Hamburg: Fauche, 1792.

Voltaire. *Œuvres de Voltaire: Lettres de l'imperatrice de Russie et de M. de Voltaire*. Edited by C.P. de Montenoy. Chez Stoupe, Imprimeur, 1802.

Voltaire and Catherine II. *Voltaire and Catherine the Great: Selected Correspondence*. Edited by A. Lentin. Cambridge: Oriental Research Partners, 1974.

Wahrhaffte Nachricht von der am 9ten Julii 1762 in Petersburg vorgefallenen Revolution. 1762.

[Walker, James]. *Paramythia; or, Mental Pastimes: Being Original Anecdotes, Historical, Descritive, Humourous, and Witty: Collected Chiefly During a Long Residence at the Court of Russia*. London: Lawler, 1821.

Walpole, Horace. *The Letters of Horace Walpole: 1760-1764*. Edited by Paget Toynbee. 16 vols. Vol. 5, Oxford: Clarendon Press, 1904.

Wedgwood, Josiah. *Catalogue of Cameos, Intaglios, Medals, Bas-Reliefs, Busts and Small Statues; with a General Account of Tablets, Vases, Ecritoires, and Other Ornamental and Useful Articles, the Whole Formed in Different Kinds of Porcelain and Terra Cotta, Chiefly after the Antique, and the Finest Models of Modern Artist*. 6th ed. Etruria, 1787.

[Weikardt, Melchior Adam]. *Taurische Reise der Kaiserin von Russland Katharina II*. Koblenz, 1799.

Weikard, M[elchior] A[dam]. *Denkwürdigkeiten aus der Lebensgeschichte des kaiserl. Russischen Staatsraths M.A. Weikard*. Leipzig, 1802.

Willamow, [Johann Gottlieb]. "Auf die Inoculation der Kaiserinn von Rußland." In *Almanach der deutschen Musen: auf das Jahr 1771*, edited by C.H. Schmid and F.T. Hase, 64-9. Weygand, 1771.

Williams, John. *The Rise, Progress, and Present State of the Northern Governments; viz. the United Provinces, Denmark, Sweden, Russia, and Poland*. 2 v. 4o vols. London: T. Becket, 1777.

Woensel, Pieter van. *Der gegenwärtige Staat von Russland*. 8 vols. St. Petersburg: Leipzig, 1783.

Wraxall, Nathaniel William. *Cursory Remarks Made in a Tour Through Some of the Northern Parts of Europe, Particularly Copenhagen, Stockholm and Petersburgh*. London: T. Cadell, 1775.

Wraxall, Nathaniel William. *A Tour 'round the Baltic: Thro' the Northern Countries of Europe, Particularly Denmark, Sweden, Finland, Russia and Prussia*. 4 ed. London: T. Cadell, 1807.

Zacchiroli, F. *L'inoculazione*. Poemetto, 1775.
Zb. "Rev. of Laveaux Geschichte Peters des Dritten." *Neue allgemeine deutsche Bibliothek* 53, no. 1 (1800): 161–4.
"Zeitung." In *Grosses vollständiges Universal-Lexicon aller Wissenschafften und Künste*, edited by Johann Heinrich Zedler, col. 899 (misnumbered 799)–911. Halle, 1749.
Zimmermann, J.G. *Über Friedrich den Grossen und meine Unterredungen mit Ihm kurz vor seinem Tode*. Vienna: Diepold, 1788.

II Secondary Literature

Adshead, David. "Wedgwood, Wimpole and Wrest. The Landscape Drawings of Lady Amabel Polwarth." *Apollo* 143 (April 1996): 31–6.
Ahlström, Christian "The Empress of Russia and the Dutch Snow the Vrouw Maria." *National Board of Antiquities, Finnland*, http://www.nba.fi/en/cultural_environment/archaeological_heritage/research/wreck_finds/vmuw/articles/empress.
Alexander, John T. "Western Views of the Pugachov Rebellion." *Slavonic and East European Review* 113 (1970): 520–36.
Alexander, John T. *Catherine the Great: Life and Legend*. New York: Oxford, 1989.
Alexander, John T. "Catherine the Great as Porn Queen." In *Eros and Pornography in Russian Culture*, edited by Marcus C. Levitt and A. Toporkov, 237–47. Moscow: Ladomir, 1999.
Bannet, Eve Tavor. "'Secret History': Or, Talebearing Inside and Outside the Secretorie." *Huntington Library Quarterly* 68, no. 1/2 (2005): 275–96.
Barker, Chris, and Dariusz Galasi´nski. *Cultural Studies and Discourse Analysis: A Dialogue on Language and Identity*. London: Sage, 2001.
Bartlett, Roger P. *Human Capital: The Settlement of Foreigners in Russia 1762–1804*. Cambridge: Cambridge University Press, 1979.
Bartlett, Roger P. "'Ropsha, Where Peter III Was Murdered...': Faces and Facades of an Imperial Estate." In *Personality and Place in Russian Culture: Essays in Memory of Lindsey Hughes*, edited by Simon Dixon, 156–79. London: Modern Humanities Research Association, 2010.
Bate, Jonathan. "Shakespearean Allusion in English Caricature in the Age of Gillray." *Journal of the Warburg and Courtauld Institutes* 49 (1986): 196–210.
Baudez, Basile. "The Monument to Peter the Great by Falconet: A Place Royale by the Neva?" In *Reading the Royal Monument in Eighteenth-Century Europe*, edited by Charlotte Chastel-Rousseau, 93–106. Ashgate Pub., 2011.
Belk, Russell W. *Collecting in a Consumer Society*. London: Routledge, 1995.
Berg, Maxine. *Luxury and Pleasure in Eighteenth-Century Britain*. Oxford: Oxford University Press, 2007.
Berg, Maxine, and Elizabeth Eger. *Luxury in the Eighteenth-Century: Debates, Desires and Delectable Goods*. New York: Palgrave Macmillan, 2007.
Berger, Joachim. *Anna Amalia von Sachsen-Weimar-Eisenach (1739–1807): Denk- und Handlungsräume einer 'aufgeklärten' Herzogin*. Heidelberg: Universitätsverlag Winter, 2003.
Berger, John. *Ways of Seeing*. London: Penguin, 1972.
Bermingham, Ann, and John Brewer. *The Consumption of Culture, 1600–1800: Image, Object, Text*. London: Routledge, 1997.

Bilbassoff, B. von. *Katharina II., Kaiserin von Russland, im Urtheile der Weltliteratur.* 2 vols. Berlin: Räde, 1897.
Biskup, Thomas, and Peter H. Wilson. "Grossbritanien, Amerika und die atlantische Welt." In *Friederisiko: Friedrich der Grosse*, 146–60. Munich: Hirmer, 2012.
Blanning, T. C. W. *The Culture of Power and the Power of Culture: Old Regime Europe, 1660–1789*. Oxford: Oxford University Press, 2002.
Blanning, Tim. "The Holy Roman Empire of the German Nation Past and Present." *Historical Research* 85, no. 277 (2012): 57–70.
Blanning, Tim. *Frederick the Great: King of Prussia*. New York: Random House, 2016.
Boime, Albert. "Jacques-Louis David, Scatological Discourse in the French Revolution, and the Art of Caricature." *Arts Magazine*, February 1988, 72–81.
Boone, Joseph A., and Nancy J. Vickers. "Introduction—Celebrity Rites." *PMLA* 126, no. 4 (2011): 900–11.
Bricker, Andrew Benjamin. "After the Golden Age: Libel, Caricature, and the Deverbalization of Satire." *Eighteenth-Century Studies* 51, no. 3 (2018): 305–36.
Carretta, Vincent. "'Petticoats in Power': Catherine the Great in British Political Cartoons." *1650–1850: Ideas, Aesthetics, and Inquiries in the Early Modern Era* 1 (1994): 23–81.
Cashmore, Ellis. "Celebrity in the Twenty-First Century Imagination." *Cultural and Social History* 8, no. 3 (2011): 405–13.
"Celebrity, n." *Oxford English Dictionary*. Oxford University Press.
Charnon-Deutsch, Lou "Voyeurism, Pornography and 'La Regenta'". *Modern Language Studies* 19, no. 4 (1989): 93–101.
Cobley, Paul. *Narrative*. New York: Routledge, 2013.
Cochran, Peter. "Casti's Il *Poema Tartaro* and Byron's *Don Juan*, Cantos V–X." *The Keats-Shelley Review* 17 (2003): 61–85.
Coombe, Rosemary J. "The Celebrity Image and Cultural Identity: Publicity Rights and the Subaltern Politics of Gender." *Discourse* 14, no. 3 (1992): 59–88.
Cottle, Simon. "Mediatized Rituals: Beyond Manufacturing Consent." *Media, Culture & Society* 28, no. 3 (2006): 411–32.
Cowan, Brian. "News, Biography, and Eighteenth-Century Celebrity." In *Oxford Handbooks Online*. Oxford: Oxford University Press, 2016. https://www.oxfordhandbooks.com/view/10.1093/oxfordhb/9780199935338.001.0001/oxfordhb-9780199935338-e-132?rskey=Dx3gFY&result=4.
Cowan, Brian. "Doctor Sacheverell and the Politics of Celebrity in Post-Revolutionary Britain." In *Intimacy and Celebrity in Eighteenth-Century Literary Culture: Public Interiors*, edited by Emrys Jones and Victoria Joule, 111–37. London: Palgrave Macmillan, 2018.
Creed, Barbara. "Horror and the Monstrous-Feminine: An Imaginary Abjection." *Screen* 27, no. 1 (1986): 44–71.
Cross, A.G. *Some Russian Connections: An Inaugural Lecture Delivered before the University of Cambridge on 26 February 1987*. Cambridge: Cambridge University Press, 1987.
Dann, Otto. "Herder und die deutsche Bewegung." In *Johann Gottfried Herder 1744–1803*, edited by Gerhard Sauder. Studien zum Achtzehnten Jahrhundert, 308–40. Hamburg: Felix Meiner Verlag, 1987.
Darnton, Robert. *The Forbidden Best-Sellers of Pre-Revolutionary France*. New York: W.W. Norton, 1995.
Dawson, Ruth Pritchard. "The Feminist Manifesto of Theodor Gottlieb von Hippel (1741–1796)". In *Gestaltet und Gestaltend: Frauen in der deutschen Literatur*, edited

by Marianne Burkhard. Amsterdamer Beiträge zur neueren Germanistik, 13–32 Amsterdam: Rodopi, 1980.

Dawson, Ruth Pritchard. *The Contested Quill: Literature by Women in Germany, 1770-1800*. Newark [Del.]: University of Delaware Press, 2002.

Dawson, Ruth Pritchard. "Eighteenth-Century Libertinism in a Time of Change: Representations of Catherine the Great." *Women in German Yearbook* 18 (2002): 67–88.

Dawson, Ruth Pritchard. "Perilous News and Hasty Biography: Representations of Catherine II Immediately after her Seizure of the Throne." *Biography* 27 (2004): 517–34.

Dawson, Ruth Pritchard. "Katharina II. Kaiserin von Russland: Das Märchen vom Zarewitsch Chlor (1782)." In *Lexikon deutschsprachiger Epik und Dramatik von Autorinnen (1730-1900)*, edited by Gabriele Pailer and Gudrun Loster-Schneider. Tübingen: Narr Francke Attempto Verlag, 2006.

Dawson, Ruth Pritchard. ""Lights out! Lights out!" Women and the Enlightenment." In *Gender in transition: Discourse and practice in German-speaking Europe, 1750-1830*, edited by Ulrike Gleixner and Marion W Gray, 218–45. Ann Arbor: University of Michigan Press, 2006.

Dawson, Ruth Pritchard. "The Internet, the Eighteenth Century, and a Forgotten Novel." *Friends Newsletter*, Friends of Germanic Studies, Institute of Germanic and Romance Studies, University of London (2012): 9–11.

Dawson, Ruth Pritchard. "Catherine II, Polyxene Büsching, and Johanna Charlotte Unzer: A Literary 'Community of Practice'." In *Writing the Self, Creating Community: German Women Authors and the Literary Sphere, 1750–1850*, edited by Elizabeth Krimmer and Lauren Nossett, 87–115. Rochester, NY: Camden House, 2020.

Delpierre, Madeleine. *Dress in France in the Eighteenth Century*. New Haven: Yale University Press, 1997.

Descargues, Pierre. *The Hermitage Museum Leningrad*. New York: Harry N. Abrams, 1961.

Dickinson, Sara. "Russia's First "Orient": Characterizing the Crimea in 1787." *Kritika: Explorations in Russian and Eurasian History* 3, no. 1 (2002): 3–25.

Dixon, Simon. *Catherine the Great*. London: Pearson Education, 2001.

Dixon, Simon. *Catherine the Great*. New York: HarperCollins, 2009.

Elias, Norbert. *Die höfische Gesellschaft: Untersuchungen zur Soziologie des Königtums und der höfischen Aristokratie*. Frankfurt a.M.: Suhrkamp, 1997.

Engel, Laura. *Fashioning Celebrity: Eighteenth-Century British Actresses and Strategies for Image Making*. Columbus: Ohio State University Press, 2011.

Fischer, Steven R. *A History of Reading*. London: Reaktion, 2003.

Franck, Georg. "The Economy of Attention." *Journal of Sociology* 55 (2018): 8–19.

Frensdorff, F. "Katharina II von Rußland und ein Göttingscher Zeitungsschreiber." *Nachrichten von der Königlichen gesellschaft der wissenschaften zu Göttingen. Philologisch-historische Klasse* (1905): 305–20.

Gabler, Neal. *Toward a New Definition of Celebrity*. Los Angeles: Norman Lear Center, Annenberg School for Communication and Journalism, University of Southern California, 2001.

Gaisbauer, Herbert, ed. *Maria Theresia und ihre Zeit*. Vienna: Bundesministerium für Wissenschaft und Forschung, 1980.

Gamman, Lorraine, and Margaret Marshment. *The Female Gaze: Women as Viewers of Popular Culture*. Seattle: Real Comet Press, 1989.

Gamson, Joshua. *Claims to Fame: Celebrity in Contemporary America*. Berkeley: University of California Press, 1994.
Garber, Marjorie. *Vested Interests: Cross-Dressing and Cultural Anxiety*. New York: Routledge, 1992.
Gelbart, Nina Rattner. *Feminine and Opposition Journalism in Old Regime France: "Le Journal des Dames."* Berkeley: University of California Press, 1987.
Gelderblom, Oscar. "Coping with the Perils of the Sea: The Last Voyage of Vrouw Maria in 1771". *International Journal of Maritime History* 15, no. 2 (2003): 95–115.
Giles, David. *Illusions of Immortality: A Psychology of Fame and Celebrity*. New York: St. Martin's, 2000.
Goodman, Dena. "Furnishing Discourses: Readings of a Writing Desk in Eighteenth-Century France." In *Luxury in the Eighteenth Century: Debates, Desires, and Delectable Goods*, edited by Maxine Berg and Elizabeth Eger, 71–88. New York: Palgrave Macmillan, 2007.
Gorbatov, Inna. *Catherine the Great and the French Philosophers of the Enlightenment: Montesquieu, Voltaire, Rousseau, Diderot, and Grimm*. Bethesda, MD: Academica, 2006.
Grab, Walter. *Demokratische Strömungen in Hamburg und Schleswig-Holstein zur Zeit der ersten französischen Republik*. Hamburg: Christians, 1966.
Green, Abigail. *Fatherlands: State-Building and Nationhood in Nineteenth-Century Germany*. Cambridge: Cambridge University Press, 2001.
Greilich, S., and Y.G. Mix. *Populäre Kalender im vorindustriellen Europa: der 'Hinkende Bote' / 'Messager boiteux': kulturwissenschaftliche Analysen und bibliographisches Repertorium: ein Handbuch*. Berlin: Walter de Gruyter, 2006.
Griffiths, David M. "Catherine Discovers the Crimea." *Jahrbücher für Geschichte Osteuropas* 56 (2008): 339–48.
Grigorieva, Irina, and Madeleine Pinault Sorensen. "L'Acquisition du Cabinet Hoüel par Catherine II." *Gazette des Beaux-Arts* 126, November (1995): 171–86.
Grosskurth, Brian. "Shifting Monuments: Falconet's Peter the Great between Diderot and Eisenstein." *Oxford Art Journal* 23, no. 2 (2000): 29–48.
Gundle, Stephen. *Glamour: A History*. Oxford: Oxford University Press, 2008.
Habermas, Jürgen. *The Structural Transformation of the Public Sphere: An Inquiry into a Category of Bourgeois Society*. Cambridge, MA: MIT Press, 1989.
Haywood, Ian. *Romanticism and Caricature*. Cambridge: Cambridge University Press, 2013.
Heier, Edmund. *L. H. Nicolay (1737–1820) and His Contemporaries*. The Hague,: M. Nijhoff, 1965.
Heipcke, Corinna. "Landgräfin Karoline of Hessen-Darmstadt: Epistolary Politics and the Problems of Consort Biography." *Biography* 27.3 (2004): 535–53.
Hill, Ruth. *Hierarchy, Commerce and Fraud in Bourbon Spanish America: A Postal Inspector's Exposé*. Nashville, TN: Vanderbilt University Press, 2005.
Hoffmann, Peter, and Horst Schützler. "Der Pugacev-Aufstand in zeitgenössischen deutschen Berichten." *Jahrbuch für Geschichte der sozialistischen Länder Europas* 6 (1962): 337–65.
Homans, Margaret. *Royal Representations: Queen Victoria and British Culture, 1837–1876*. Chicago: Univeraity of Chicago Press, 1998.
Horton, Donald, and R. Richard Wohl. "Mass Communication and Para-Social Interaction: Observations on Intimacy at a Distance." *Psychiatry* 19, no. 3 (1956): 215–29.

Hunt, Lynn, ed. *The Invention of Pornography: Obscenity and the Origins of Modernity, 1500–1800*. New York: Zone Books, 1993.
Ibneyeva, Guzel. "Catherine Discovers the Volga Region." *Jahrbücher für Geschichte Osteuropas* 56 (2008): 349–57.
Johannson, Sofia. "'Sometimes You Wanna Hate Celebrities': Tabloid Readers And Celebrity Coverage." In *Framing Celebrity: New Directions in Celebrity Culture*, edited by Su Holmes and Sean Redmond, 343. London: Routledge, 2006.
Kahn, Andrew, and Kelsey Rubin-Detlev. "Introduction." In *Catherine the Great: Selected Letters*, vii–xxix. Oxford: Oxford University Press, 2018.
Kamen, Henry. *Early Modern European Society*. New York: Routledge, 2000.
Khodarkovsky, Michael. *Where Two Worlds Met: The Russian State and the Kalmyk Nomads, 1600–1771*. Ithaca: Cornell University Press, 1992.
Koeninger, Frieda. "Race at the Intersection of Religion, Aesthetics, and Politics: Comella's "El Negro Sensible" and the Censors." *Hispanic Enlightenment* 40 (Fall 2017): 217–32.
Koningsbrugge, Hans van. "A Dutch Disaster: Russia and the Netherlands and the Fourth Anglo-Dutch War." In *'A Century Mad and Wise': Russia in the Age of the Enlightenment*, edited by Emmanuel Waegemans, Hans van Koningsbrugge, Marcus C. Levitt, and Mikhail Ljustrov, 181–5. Groningen: Netherlands Russia Centre, 2015.
Kosareva, Nina. "Masterpieces of Eighteenth-Century French Sculpture." *Apollo* 101 (June 1975): 443–51.
van Krieken, Robert. *Celebrity Society*. New York: Routledge, 2012.
Lammel, Gisold. *Kunst im Aufbruch. Malerei, Graphik und Plastik zur Zeit Goethes*. Stuttgart: Metzler, 1998.
Landes, Joan B. *Visualizing the Nation: Gender, Representation, and Revolution in Eighteenth-Century France*. Ithaca: Cornell University Press, 2001.
Leonard, Carol S. *Reform and Regicide: The Reign of Peter III of Russia*. Bloomington: Indiana University Press, 1993.
Levitt, Marcus. "An Antidote to Nervous Juice: Catherine the Great's Debate with Chappe D'Auteroche over Russian Culture." *Eighteenth-Century Studies* 32, no. 1 (1998): 49–63.
Liackhova, Lydia "Catherine II Enthroned." In *Treasures of Catherine the Great*, edited by State Hermitage Museum and Hermitage Development Trust, 45. London: Christie's International Media, 2000.
Lilti, Antoine. *The Invention of Celebrity, 1750–1850*. Malden, MA: Polity, 2017.
Longworth, Philip. "The Last Great Cossack-Peasant Rising." *Journal of European Studies* 3 (1973): 1–34.
Lortholary, Albert. *Le Mirage russe en au XVIIIe siècle*. Paris: Boivin, 1951.
Luhmann, Niklas. *Love as Passion: The Codification of Intimacy*. Stanford, CA: Stanford University Press, 1998.
Lull, James, and Stephen Hinerman. *Media Scandals: Morality and Desire in the Popular Culture Marketplace*. Columbia University Press, 1997.
McKeon, Michael. *The Secret History of Domesticity: Public, Private, and the Division of Knowledge*. Baltimore: Johns Hopkins University Press, 2005.
McPherson, Heather. *Art and Celebrity in the Age of Reynolds and Siddons*. University Park, Pennsylvania: The Pennsylvania State University Press, 2017.
Madariaga, Isabel de. *Catherine the Great: A Short History*. New Haven: Yale University Press, 1990.
Marshall, P. David. *Celebrity and Power: Fame in Contemporary Culture*. Minneapolis: University of Minnesota Press, 1997.

Massie, Robert K. *Catherine the Great: Portrait of a Woman*. 1st ed. New York: Random House, 2011.
Maza, Sarah. "The Diamond Necklace Affair Revisited (1785–1786): The Case of the Missing Queen." In *Eroticism and the Body Politic*, edited by Lynn Hunt, 63–89. Baltimore: Johns Hopkins UP, 1991.
Melot, Michel. "Caricature and the Revolution: The Situation in France in 1789." In *French Caricature and the French Revolution, 1789–1799*. Los Angeles: Grunwald Center for the Graphic Arts, 1988.
Merziger, Patrick. "Der öffentliche König? Herrschaft in den Medien während der drei Schlesischen Kriege." In *Friedrich der Grosse in Europa: Geschichte einer wechselvollen Beziehung*, edited by Bernd Sösemann and Gregor Vogt-Spira, 209–23. Stuttgart: Franz Steiner Verlag, 2012.
Michler, Marwart. *Melchior Adam Weikard (1742–1803) und sein Weg in den Brownianismus: Medizin zwischen Aufklärung und Romantik, Eine medizinhistorische Biographie. Acta Historica Leopoldina*. Edited by Christoph Scriba. Vol. 24, Halle: Deutsche Akademie der Naturforscher Leopoldina, 1995.
Miller, Nancy K. "Female Sexuality and Narrative Structure in 'La Nouvelle Héloïse' and 'Les Liaisons dangereuses.'" *Signs* 1 (1976): 609–38.
Minor, Vernon Hyde. *Baroque & Rococo: Art and Culture*. New York: Harry N. Abrams, 1999.
Moi, Toril. *Sexual/Textual Politics: Feminist Literary Theory*. New Accents. London and New York: Methuen, 1985.
Montefiore, Sebag. *Prince of Princes: The Life of Potemkin*. New York: St. Martin's, 2000.
Montluzin, Emily Lorraine de. "Attributions of Authorship in the *Gentleman's Magazine*, 1731–1868; A Supplement to Kuist." *Bibliographical Society of the University of Virginia*, 2003.
Morgan, Simon. "Celebrity: Academic 'Pseudo-Event' or a Useful Concept for Historians?" *Cultural and Social History* 8 (2011): 95–114.
Munro, George E. "Catherine Discovers St. Petersburg." *Jahrbücher für Geschichte Osteuropas* 56 (2008): 330–8.
National Gallery of Art (U.S.), and Margaret Morgan Grasselli. *Colorful Impressions: The Printmaking Revolution in Eighteenth-Century France*. Washington, DC: National Gallery of Art, 2003.
"Die Neue Selbst-Gefälligkeit der Angela M.: Angela die Grosse." *Der Spiegel*, September 9, 2013.
Nussbaum, Felicity. *Rival Queens: Actresses, Performance, and the Eighteenth-Century British Theater*. Philadelphia: University of Pennsylvania Press, 2010.
Peters, Birgit. *Prominenz: Eine soziologische Analyse ihrer Entstehung und Wirkung*. Wiesbaden: VS Verlag für Sozialwissenschaften, 1996.
Pointon, Marcia. "Intriguing Jewellery: Royal Bodies and Luxurious Consumption." *Textual Practice* 11, no. 3 (1997): 493–516.
Pointon, Marcia. "Intrigue, Jewellery, and Economics: Court Culture and Display in England and France in the 1780s." In *Markets for Art, 1400–1800*, edited by C.E. Núñez, M. North, and D. Ormrod, 155–216. Seville: Secretariado de Publicaciones de la Universidad de Sevilla, 1998.
Popkin, Jeremy D. *News and Politics in the Age of Revolution: Jean Luzac's Gazette de Leyde*. Ithaca: Cornell University Press, 1989.
Purdy, Daniel L. *The Tyranny of Elegance: Consumer Cosmopolitanism in the Era of Goethe*. Baltimore, MD: Johns Hopkins University Press, 1998.

Rehberg, Peter, and Brigitte Weingart. "Celebrity Cultures. Einleitung in den Schwerpunkt." *Zeitschrift für Medienwissenschaft* 9, no. 16 (2017): 10–20.
Renne, Elizaveta. "Catherine II through the Eyes of Vigilius Eriksen and Alexander Roslin." In *Catherine the Great and Gustav III*, edited by Nationalmuseum (Sweden) and the State Hermitage Museum (St. Petersburg). Exhibition catalog, 97–107. Helsingborg: Boktryck AB, 1999.
Roach, Joseph R. "Public Intimacy: The Prior History of 'It.'" In *Theatre and Celebrity in Britain, 1660–2000*, edited by Mary Luckhurst and Jane Moody, 15–30. New York: Palgrave Macmillan, 2005.
Roach, Joseph R. "Nell Gwyn and Covent Garden Goddesses." In *The First Actresses: Nell Gwyn to Sarah Siddons*, edited by Gillian Perry, 63–75. Ann Arbor: University of Michigan Press, 2011.
Rojek, Chris. *Celebrity*. London: Reaktion Books, 2001.
Rovinskii, Dimitrii Aleksandrovitch. Подробный словарь русских гравированных портретов. Санктпетербург: Tip. Imp. akademii nauk, 1889.
Rubin-Detlev, Kelsey. *The Epistolary Art of Catherine the Great*. Oxford University Studies in the Enlightenment. Liverpool: Liverpool University Press, 2019.
Savill, Rosalind. ""Cameo Fever": Six Pieces from the Sèvres Porcelain Dinner Service Made for Catherine II of Russia." *Apollo* CXVI, no. 249 (1982): 304–11.
Schenda, Rudolf. *Volk ohne Buch: Studien zur Sozialgeschichte der populären Lesestoffe 1770-1910*. Studien zur Philosophie und Literatur des neuzehnten Jahrhunderts 5. Frankfurt: Vittorio Klostermann, 1970.
Schiebinger, L. *The Mind Has No Sex?: Women in the Origins of Modern Science*. Cambridge, MA: Harvard University Press, 1991.
Schmidt, Benjamin. *Inventing Exoticism: Geography, Globalism, and Europe's Early Modern World*. Philadelphia: University of Pennsylvania, 2015.
Schneider, Michael. "The Nature, History, and Significance of the Concept of Positional Goods." *History of Economics Review* 45 (Winter 2007): 60–81.
Sekora, John. *Luxury: The Concept in Western Thought, Eden to Smollett*. Baltimore: Johns Hopkins University Press, 1977.
Sharpe, Kevin. *Selling the Tudor Monarchy: Authority and Image in Sixteenth-Century England*. New Haven: Yale University Press, 2009.
Smith, Douglas. "Introduction. Catherine the Great, Prince Grigory Potemkin, and Their Correspondence." In *Love and Conquest: Personal Correspondence of Catherine the Great and Prince Grigory Potemkin*, edited by Douglas Smith. DeKalb, IL: Northern Illinois University, 2004.
Spacks, Patricia Meyer. *Gossip*. New York: Knopf, 1985.
Stollberg-Rilinger, Barbara. *Maria Theresia: die Kaiserin in ihrer Zeit, eine Biographie*. München: C.H. Beck, 2017.
Strunck, Christina. "The 'Two Bodies' of the Female Sovereign: Awkward Hierarchies in Images of Empress Maria Theresa, Catherine the Great of Russia, and Their Male Consorts." In *Queens Consort, Cultural Transfer and European Politics, c. 1500–1800*, edited by Helen Watanabe-O'Kelly and Adam Morton, 64–83. London: Routledge, 2017.
Stummann-Bowert, Ruth. "Philippine Engelhard, geborene Gatterer: Ein bürgerliches Frauenleben zwischen Aufklärung und Empfindsamkeit." In *'Des Kennenlernens werth,' Bedeutende Frauen Göttingens*, edited by Traudel Weber-Reich, 27–52. Göttingen: Wallstein, 1995.
Sutton, D. "Russian Francophiles of the Dix-huitième." *Apollo* 101 (1975): 420–7.

Szabo, Franz A. J. *The Seven Years War in* Europe, *1756-1763. Modern Wars in Perspective*. 1st ed. Harlow, England: Pearson/Longman, 2008.
Thompson, John B. *The Media and Modernity: A Social Theory of the Media*. Stanford, CA: Stanford University Press, 1995.
Tillyard, Stella. "Celebrity in 18th-Century London." *History Today*, 2005, 20-7.
Tipton, Susan. "Die russische Minerva: Katharina die Große und die Ikonographie der Aufklärung." In *Katharina die Grosse: [Catalog of the Exhibit of the Staatlichen Museen Kassel, in the Museum Fridericianum Kassel 13. Dezember 1997-8. März 1998]*, 73-80. Eurasburg: Edition Minerva, 1997.
Turner, Graeme. *Understanding Celebrity*. 2 ed. London: SAGE Publications, 2013.
Ulbricht, Otto. "The Debate about Foundling Hospitals in Enlightenment Germany: Infanticide, Illegitimacy, and Infant Mortality Rates." *Central European History* 18, no 3/4 (1985): 211-57.
Vassallo, Peter. "*Don Juan, Il Poema Tartaro* and the Italian Burlesque Tradition." Chap. 82-106 In *Byron: The Italian Literary Influence*. London: Macmillan, 1984.
Vincentelli, Moira. *Women and Ceramics: Gendered Vessels*. Manchester: Manchester University Press, 2000.
Welke, Martin. "Gemeinsame Lektüre und frühe Formen von Gruppenbildungen im 17. und 18. Jahrhundert: Zeitunglesen in Deutschland." In *Lesegesellschaften und europäische Emanzipation: Ein europäischer Vergleich*, edited by Otto Dann, 29-53. München: Beck, 1981.
Whittaker, Cynthia Hyla. "Catherine the Great and the Art of Collecting: Acquiring the Paintings That Founded the Hermitage." In *Word and Image in Russian History: Essays in Honor of Gary Marker*, edited by Maria di Salvo, Daniel H. Kaiser and Valerie A. Kivelson, 147-71. Brookline, MA: Academic Studies Press, 2015.
Williams, Kevin. *Read All About It: A History of the British Newspaper*. London: Routledge, 2010.
Wippersberg, Julia. *Prominenz: Entstehung, Erklärungen, Erwartungen*. Volume 25 of Forschungsfeld Kommunikation. Konstanz: UVK Verlagsgesellschaft, 2007.
Wolff, Larry. *Inventing Eastern Europe. The Map of Civilization on the Mind of the Enlightenment*. Stanford, CA: Stanford University Press, 1994.
Wolff, Larry. "The Fantasy of Catherine in the Fiction of the Enlightenment: From Baron Munchausen to the Marquis de Sade." In *Eros and Pornography in Russian Culture*, edited by Marcus C. Levitt and A. Toporkov, 249-61. Moscow: Ladomir, 1999.
Wortman, Richard. *Scenarios of Power: Myth and Ceremony in Russian Monarchy*. Vol. 1: *From Peter the Great to the Death of Nicholas I*. Princeton: Princeton University Press, 1995.
Wyrwa, Ulrich. "Luxus und Konsum: Begriffsgeschichtliche Aspekte." In *Luxus und Konsum - eine historische Annäherung*, edited by Reinhold Reith and Torsten Meyer. Cottbuser Studien zur Geschichte von Technik, Arbeit und Umwelt, 47-60. Münster: Waxmann, 2003.
Yonan, Michael Elia. *Empress Maria Theresa and the Politics of Habsburg Imperial Art*. University Park, PA: Pennsylvania State University Press, 2011.
Zaborov, Petr Romanovic. "Katharina II. und Madame Geoffrin." In *Katharina II., Russland und Europa. Beiträge zur internationalen Forschung*, edited by Claus Scharf. Veröffentlichen des Instituts für europäische Geschichte Mainz. Abteilung für Universalgeschichte. Mainz: Philipp von Zabern, 2001.
Zaretsky, Robert. *Catherine & Diderot: The Empress, the Philosopher, and the Fate of the Enlightenment*. Cambridge, MA: Harvard University Press, 2019.

Index

Adshead, David 223 n.36
Aechte Nachrichten von dem Grafen Cagliostro 232 n.63
Africans, enslaved 60, 109, 132
Albrecht, Johann Friedrich Ernst (1752–1814), writer 117, 188, 191, 195, 197, 252 n.29
Alexander, John T. 226 n.5, 242 n.48, 251 n.5, 255 n.37
Alexander I (1777–1825) 5, 117
Allgemeine Zeitgeschichte, see Gross, J.G.
Alopäus, Magnus Maximilian (1748–1822), diplomat 240 n.15
Alter und neuer grosser Staats-, Kriegs- und Friedens Appenzeller-Calender 225 n.26
Andrä, Heinrich Friedrich, probably pseud, *see* Geisler
Anecdoten zur Lebensgeschichte ... Potemkin 188, 190–1
Anecdotes russes (Marche) 219 nn.33, 34, 220 n.35, *see also* Marche; *Russische Anekdoten*
Anekdoten aus dem Privatleben der Kaiserin Catharina 226 n.53
Anekdoten zur Lebensgeschichte des Fürsten Gregorius Gregoriewitsch Orlow 245 n.5, 252 n.21
Anhalt-Zerbst 5, 20, 151
Anna Petrovna (1757–1759), daughter of Catherine II 35
Annual Register 39, 98, 104, 111, 218 n.7, 220 n.53
Anti-fans, *see* fans
Anting, Johann Friedrich (1753–1805), artist 49
Argus 222 n.35
aristocracy 1, 57, 60, 71, 74, 76, 108, 114, 144, 157, 168, 189, 209
art collecting and commissioning 104, 111–12

prices 111–12
artists, visual 30, 42, 61–2, 80, 114, 130, 208, *see also individual artist names*
  amateur 56
  engravers of images 7, 41, 49, 53–4, 85, 108, 202
  engravers of text 43, 61, 156
  painters 44, 49, 76
  sculptors 112
Asia, Asiatic 132–41, 143–8
audience, of celebrity discourse about Catherine II 1–3, 8, 19–20, 34, 42, 60–1, 70–2, 91
  enlarged by varied genres 99
  non-elite 3, 30–4
  outside Russia 1–2, 64, 104, 187, 214 nn.16, 22
  partly illiterate 29–34
  signs of intended inclusiveness 42
Auszug der neuesten Weltgeschichte, see Gross, J.G.
"Authentic History of the Famous Rebel Pugatschew" 242 n.65
Authentic Memoirs of the Life and Reign of Catherine II 229 n.13
Avril, Jean Jacques the Elder (1744–1831), engraver 244 n.89

Bachaumont, Louis Petit de (1690–1771), writer 229 n.6, 230 n.15
Bacmeister, Hartwig Ludwig Christian (1730–1806), historian 231 n.40
Baldinger, Friderike (1739–1786), writer 65
Bannet, Eve 249 n.24
barbaric, barbarism 10–11, 240 n.2
  Russia as 132, 134–5
Bariatinsky, Fedor (1742–1814) 181–2
Barker, Chris 225 n.38

Bartlett, Roger   231 n.51, 250 n.83
Basedow, Johann Bernhard (1724–1790), educator   100, 177
Bate, Jonathan   245 n.10
Baudez, Basile   236 n.60
Bause, Johann Friedrich (1738–1814), printmaker   53, 118–19
Beattie, Simon   253 n.53
Beauclair, Pierre Louis (1735–1804), writer   181
The Beauties of all the Magazines Selected   41, 218–19 n.17
Behr, Isachar Falkensohn (1746–1817), poet   100
Belgium, Belgian, *see* Low Countries
Belk, Russell W.   111
Bellermann, Johann Jacob (1754–1842), travel writer   78–9, 81, 84–5, 179, 192, 225 n.41
Bemerkungen über Esthland, Liefland und Russland   227 n.17
Benda, Friedrich (1745–1814), musician   114, 236 n.66
Berg, Maxine   223 n.2
Berger, Daniel, (1744–1825), Berlin engraver   44–5, 50, 52, 56
Berger, Joachim   236 n.65
Berger, John   107, 109
Bermingham, Ann   226 n.55
Bernigeroth, Johann Martin (1713–1767), printmaker   49, 51
Bernoulli, Johann, III (1744–1807), travel writer   78, 80, 112
Berthault, Jean-Pierre (1779–1850), printmaker   86–7
Biester, Johann Erich (1749–1816), biographer   56–7, 225 n.39
Bil'basov, V. A.   218 n.12, 219 n.21
biographers of Catherine II, *see* Andrä; Biester; Castéra; Masson, Seume; Tooke
Biskup, Thomas   221 n.15
Bitte und Erhoerung   53, 55, 222 n.26
Black Sea   143–4, 147, 161, 164–5
Blanning, Tim   214 n.17, 221 nn.15, 16
Blum, Karl Ludwig   225 n.47–9
Bobrinsky, Aleksey (1762–1813), son of Catherine II and Orlov   83
Boim, Albert   162

Boluzion, ficitious engraver   129
booksellers   41–2, 48, 56, 113
Boone, Joseph A.   226 n.58
Bouffonidor, pseudonym for unknown author   250 n.69
Bourdillon, Joseph, *nom de plume* of Voltaire   257 n.75
Bourrée de Corberon, Marie Daniel (1748–1810), diplomat and letter writer   117
Braamcamp, Gerrit (1699–1771), art collector   111
Bricker, Andrew Benjamin   222 n.21
British political cartoons, *see* political cartoons, British
Broglie, Charles-François de (1719–1781), diplomat   187
Bruchstücke aus den Ruinen der Menschheit   255 nn.25, 29
Bruel, Count Heinrich (1700–1763), art collector   111
Buchwald, Juliane Franziska von (1707–1789), aristocrat   114
Bullmann, Johann Georg (1740–1811), printer   225 n.28
Burney, Fanny (1752–1840), writer   64
Büschel, Johann Gabriel Bernhard (1758–1813), writer   233 n.77
Büsching, Anton Friedrich (1724–1793), geographer   102, 174–6, 183
Büsching, Polyxene Christiane Auguste née Dilthey (1728–1777), poet   93–4, 174, 183, 226 n.50
Byron, George Gordon "Lord" (1788–1824), poet   210

Cagliostro, Alessandro di (1743–1795), occultist adventurer   101–2
calendar, Julian to Gregorian   214 n.3
Callot, Jaques (c. 1592–635), printmaker   157
Caminer, Dominico (1721–1795), journalist   41, 181, 225 n.42
capitalism   3, 109, *see also under* celebrity
Caravaque, Louis (1684–1754), Italian portraitist   49, 51
Carburi, Marin (1729–1782), engineer   112

Caretta, Vincent 161
caricatures, *see* cartooning, political
Carta, con noticias circunstanciadas de la revolucion acaecida en Petersburgo 215 n.8
Casanova, Giacomo (1725–1798), writer 181
Cashmore, Ellis 3, 162
Castéra, Jean-Henri (1749–1838), biographer 171–2, 180, 188, 194
Casti, Giambattista/Giovanni Battista (1724–1803), poet 196, 253 n.55
Catharina die Zweite, die einzige Kaiserinn der Erde 80, 227 n.24
Catharina die Zweite. Darstellungen 230 n.19
Catherine II (1729–1796), Empress of Russia 5, 175
  adultery charge 36, 180, 194, 228 n.30
  appearance, descriptions 81–8
    aging 84–8, 196
    stout 81, 85, 99, 196
  autonomy 10, 33, 69, 72–3, 125–6, 189–90, 210
  body 8–9, 78, 155
    menstruation and menopause 82–3, 129–30, 228 n.29
    pregnancies 35, 83, 179–80, 194–5
  character and emotions 29–30, 80, 87, 94, 151, 177, 209
    anger 80, 196
    desiring to please 125, 175
    friendliness and good humor 68–9, 79, 81, 83, 85, 87, 207
    vindictiveness 151
    weeping and tears 39, 80
  conspiracies against 40 (*see also* Pugachev rebellion)
  Crimean journey 11, 137, 143–8, 204–6, 244 n.94
    transportation 146–7
  criminality and murderess rumors and claims 13, 128–30, 190, 202, 206–7

death 5, 13, 199–203, 210
decorum and demeanor 79–81, 83–5, 155, 207
drinking 80
dress, clothes, and fashion 8, 48–50, 56, 58, 78, 107, 118–19, 145 (*see also* crossdressing *and under* prints)
  Amazonian dress 99, 107, 131
  coiffure 46, 81–2
  cross-dressing 6–7, 23, 26, 48, 78, 129, 178–9
  fur trim 46, 53–4, 78, 127–8, 154, 158, 165, 172, 201, 203, 221 n.12
  makeup 81, 85
  in Russian style 78, 81, 107, 162, 246 n.36
and Enlightenment (*see* Enlightenment)
feminizing attributes 23, 39, 48, 125, 175
and French *philosophes* 41, 89, 92, 100, 102
gender 8–13, 39, 83, 97, 120–1, 130
generosity 92, 94–5, 99–100, 104, 113–15, 190, 240 n.42
German origin 5, 22, 28, 68, 200
gifts from 95, 99, 100, 104, 110, 115, 146
and *gloire* 3, 8, 9, 74–7, 208
horseback riding 23, 26, 78, 148, 178
letters from 91–5, 100, 113, 115, 223 n.4
masculinity and masculine performance 23, 26, 37–9, 176, 178
as Minerva 93
motherhood and tropes of maternality 10, 20–3, 39, 91, 96, 99, 112–17, 139, 142–3
  children (*see* Anna Petrowna, Bobrinski, Paul)
  treatment of grandchildren 117
  treatment of son 117, 139
object of gaze 49, 74, 76, 78–88
patronage by 104–5, 111–15
in political cartoons (*see* political cartoons)
public image, concern about 124–5

self-display 23, 78, 88
self-legitimizing efforts 21–4, 28–9, 35, 37, 74
sexuality, including allegations 7, 12, 39, 71, 154, 157, 179–80, 186–98, 210, 255 n.35
Volga journey 135–6
and war 116, 120, 152
wealth, expenditures, and consumption 1, 104–15, 144, 146, 158, 206 (*see also* consumption)
widow role 116
wife role 23, 116, 177
   marriage to Peter III 12, 34–6, 169–85 (*see also* Peter III)
   not attending Peter III's funeral 28, 30
   remarriage 10, 116–18
writer 102, 225 n.50, 253 n.36 (*see also* manifestos)
   Antidote 136, 232 n.66
   Grand Instruction 96–8, 204
celebrity and celebrity culture 1–3, 15, 17, 19, 40–1, 64, 89, 207–8, *see also* commodification; consumption; glamour; media; scandal; star; women celebrities
   criticism of 3
   cultural, economic, and social conditions necessary for 1–3, 214 nn.16, 22
   central figure (*see* star)
   individualism, agency, and autonomy valued 23, 30, 50, 109, 125
   lives of fans and star overlapping 5, 84, 194, 211
   media (*see* media)
   non-elite audience (*see* audience)
   publicity 4, 6, 74–5, 102
   visibility and seeing 49, 61–2, 69, 74, 80, 82
   definition 3
   discourse 30, 64, 91–2, 107, 118, 123, 134, 190, 197
      contradictions and inconsistencies accepted 21, 39, 49, 69, 73
      documents of 42, 54, 62–3, 174–5, 192
      idealization in 69
      "revelations" emphasized 21, 30, 61, 70–1, 169–70, 191, 197, 210
      savoring sexuality, love affairs, and failed marriage 36, 40, 149, 155, 158–62, 169–74, 186, 196, 198
      story 6, 24–5, 40, 63, 75, 99, 136, 139, 147, 168–70, 186, 197, 211
      trivia and gossip valued 30, 64, 175
   effects and functions 8, 66, 104
      alternative to political discourse 64, 72
      consumption and capitalism promoted 3, 109, 144
      entertainment 20, 24, 155
      fantasy and imagination 25, 66, 73, 186
      feeling of familiarity and parasocial relationship to star 40, 67, 110, 175, 190, 197, 207–8
      identification 20, 30, 40, 66–7, 96, 104, 170
      negotiating norms 25, 97, 102, 155, 196–8
      notion of "being someone" 67–8, 109
      notion of social mobility 20, 25, 40, 66–8, 70, 105, 200
      sociable discussion 25, 35, 39, 64, 115, 131, 155, 181, 207
      transgressiveness explored 28, 39, 70, 73, 125, 189, 210
   eighteenth-century usage of the word celebrity 2, 213 nn.5, 6
   endorsements and advertising 42, 57-, 76–8
   monarchical 2–4
   political type 2, 13, 123–31
   products 3, 5, 19, 24, 30, 41, 45, 49, 56, 61, 72, 203, 208
      intended for non-elite audience 6, 42, 45
      speedy production 56–7, 208
   as troika 19, 41, 74, 208
censorship and libel 92, 165, 187–8, 191

central figure, *see* star
Chantreau, Pierre Nicolas (1741–1808), writer 243 n.66, 248 n.8
Chappe d'Auteroche, Jean (1728–1769), astronomer 134–6
Charlotte (1744–1818), Queen of England 57
Charnon-Deutsch, Lou 162
Chesterfield, (Lord, Philip Dormer Stanhope, 1694–1773) 117
Chodowiecki, Daniel Niklaus (1726–1801), engraver 1, 6
 illustrations of Catherine's life 7–12, 48
Christian August, Prince of Anhalt-Zerbst, (1690–1747), father of Catherine II 56
Christina (1626–1689), Queen of Sweden 37
La chronique scandaleuse, *see* Imbert
Claessens, Lambert Antoine (1763–1834), engraver 193
class and rank 1, 10, 26, 34, 51, 53, 56–8, 60, 64, 68, 71–2, 75–6, 91, 94, 96, 107–10, 114–15, 128, 132, 137, 144, 162, 172, 177, 189, 191–2, 208–10, 214 n.16, 226 n.1
Clef du Cabinet des Princes de l'Europe 216 n.27
Cobley, Paul 249 nn.28, 31
Cochran, Peter 253 n.55
coffee houses 20, 64
Collot, Marie-Anne (1748–1821), sculptor 112
colonies, *see* settlers
Comella, Luciano Francisco (1751–1812) playwright 42, 204, 221 n.5
commodification and commodities 1–7, 19, 41–59, 72, 75–6, 171, 186, 208, 210
 selling and renting printed images 56, 152
communication, eighteenth-century 6, 18, *see also* letters *and* newspapers
Congres Politique (1772) 122
consumption and celebrity 104–15 (*see also* celebrity products; luxury)
 and self-transformation 109

Coombe, Rosemary 69, 225 nn.33, 40
Corberon, *see* Bourrée de Coberon
Cossacks 79, 133, 138–40, 147
Cottle, Simon 217 n.1
coup of 1762 1, 6–7, 12, 17–27, 42, 169–77, 186, 208; *see also gloire*
 non-violent 24, 26, 39
 protecting Catherine from divorce or death 23, 35, 37
courts, imperial and royal 3, 70, 74–80, 104, 115, 132, 190–1
 arranging marriages 34
 display 104, 109–10
 publicity 3–5, 75, 110
Cowan, Brian 213 n.9, 223 n.5, 224 n.12
Coxe, William (1748–1828), travel writer 96, 142, 170, 174–6, 178, 181–2, 247 n.7, 253 n.39
Creed, Barbara 246 n.19
Crimean journey, *see under* Catherine II
Cronstadt, naval fortress 26, 37–8, 42, 176, 178, 204
Cross, A.G. 247 n.3
cross-dressing 6, 131, 203, *see also under* Catherine II
Crozat, Louis Antoine (baron de Thiers, 1699–1770), art collector 111
Cruikshank, Isaac (1764–1811), political cartoonist 162, 166–7, 202–3, 206
 Bobadil Disgraced or Kate in a Rage 162–3, 246 n.35
 The Moment of Reflection or A Tale for Future Times 202–3
 Royal Recreation 166–8
cultural studies 21, 70
culture of celebrity, *see* celebrity
"Curious Anecdotes of Dr. Dimsdale's Inoculation of the Empress of Russia" 231 n.44

Dabhoiwala, Faramerz 191
d'Alembert, Jean-Baptiste le Rond (1717–1783), encyclopedist 29, 92, 94, 132, 229 n.4
The Danger of the Political Balance of Europe, 1790 (disputed authorship) 170, 181–2, 248 n.11

Dann, Otto 224 n.11
Darnton, Robert 2, 97
Dashkova, Yekaterina Romanovna née
	Vorontsova (1743–1810) 140
	coup participant 26, 176, 220 n.37
	Director, Academy of Sciences 102
Dawson, Ruth P. 215 n.9, 219 n.32,
	224 n.24, 225 n.50, 229 n.10,
	230 n.32, 237 n.6, 251 n.8,
	252 n.30, 253 n.57, 254 n.63
dedications to Catherine II 99, 114–15, 120
Deffand, Marie Anne de Vichy-
	Chamrond, marquise du
	(1696–1780) 251 n.6
Delpierre, Madeleine 222 n.30
Denis, Marie Louise Mignot (1712–1790),
	niece of Voltaire 115
Denkwürdigkeiten ... des ohnlängst
	verstorbenen unglücklichen
	Czaars Peter des
	Dritten 218 n.12, 219 n.32
Dent, William (active 1783–1800),
	engraver 236 n.72
Descargues, Pierre 235 n.50
*Design for the new gallery of busts and
	pictures* 181
diamonds 10, 81, 101, 104–7, 109–10,
	135, 146
Diana, Princess (1961–1997) 6, 73, 211
Dickinson, Sara 244
Diderot, Denis (1713–1784),
	philosopher 93–4, 100–1
diffusion 20
Dimsdale, Thomas (1712–1800), smallpox
	inoculator 98–9
Dixon, Simon 218 nn.4, 9, 220 nn.37,
	44, 235 n.33, 248 n.18, 250 n.83,
	251 n.9, 252
dress, clothes, and fashion, *see under*
	Catherine II
Duflos, Claude Augustin (1700–1786),
	publisher 53–4, 56
Dutch political cartoons, *see* Low
	Countries; political cartoons
Dutch Republic, *see* Low Countries
Dutens, Louis (1730–1812), writer 105

education projects, *see under*
	Enlightenment

Edgeworth, Maria (1768–1849),
	writer 221–2 n.17
Edward II (1284–1327), king of
	England 28–9
Elias, Norbert 74, 226 n.1, 234 n.1
Elizabeth (1709–1762), tsarina of
	Russia 20, 22, 25, 31, 35,
	117–18, 180, 187, 194
	daughter 206, 242 n.55
	death 20, 237 n.1
	sexual promiscuity 35
Elizabeth I (1533–1603), queen of
	England 111, 118
Engel, Laura 213 n.8
Engelhard, Philippine née Gatterer
	(1756–1831), poet 67–8, 81,
	224 n.22
engravings, *see* political cartoons; printed
	portraits
Enlightenment and Catherine II 91–103,
	122, 151
	marked as gender exception 97–8
	offsetting the coup 91
	patronage 2, 100, 105, 114
	projects
		education 92–3, 99, 151, 203–4
		Foundling Hospital 95–6,
			230 n.24
		inoculation (*see* inoculation
			against smallpox)
		law code reform 96–8, 125, 204
	raising audience hopes 91, 124
	softening social boundaries 91, 96
	validating fans' preferences 91
Erichsen, Vigilius (1722–1782),
	painter 46, 53, 76, 178–9,
	216 n.34
Ethnic groups in Russian Empire 10–11,
	79, 133–8, 143–8, 244 n.89, *see
	also* Cossacks; Kalmyks; Kyrgyz;
	Pugachev rebellion
*The European Magazine, and London
	Review* 59, 223 n.41
exotic, exoticism 11, 134, *see also*
	barbaric
	Russia as 25, 132, 143–8, 204

Facius, Georg Siegmund (1750–1813),
	engraver 45–6, 50

Falconet, Étienne Maurice (1716–1791), sculptor   112
fans and fandom   1–3, 6–8, 19, 28, 60–73, 209, 210, *see also* celebrity
  ambivalence   3, 69–72, 80, 134, 135, 149
  anti-fans   8, 69–70, 72, 125, 169, 177, 189, 194, 208–10
  benefits from celebrity   1, 8 (*see also* effects and functions *under* celebrity)
  conditions for   60–1 (*see also* cultural *under* celebrity)
  definition   60–1
  evidence of   6, 42, 54, 62
  fantasizing about being Catherine's lover   71–2, 192
  feeling of personal insight and connection   40, 106–7, 125, 171
  fictitious examples (*see* Goody Grogg; Madame de)
  identification   70–1, 104–5, 125 (*see also* effects and functions *under* celebrity)
  impact of fans' wishes on prints   54, 110, 208
  lives overlapping with stars   5, 74, 84, 203, 211
  pleasure of being lifted out of the quotidian   104, 107, 143
  social and material distance from stars   40, 74, 104, 154–5
fashion, *see* dress, clothes, and fashion *under* Catherine II
favorites, *see* lovers and favorites
female celebrity, *see* woman celebrity
Fischer, Caroline Auguste (1764–1842), novelist   197–8
Fischer, Steven R.   224 nn.13, 23
Forster, Georg (1754–1794)   254 n.20
Fortgesetzte neue genealogisch-historische Nachrichten (1763)   215 n.12
Fortgesetzte russische Anekdoten, 1766   218 n.8
Fortia-de-Piles, Alphonse (1758–1826), travel writer   182–3, 190, 192, 196–8
Fosseyeux, Jean-Baptiste (1752–1824), engraver   179, 250 n.55

Foundling Hospital, *see under* Enlightenment
Fox, Charles James (1749–1806), statesman   160–1, 166, 202–3
Fragmens historiques sur Pierre III et Catherine II (perhaps Goebel)   171, 183, 195
Franck, Georg   215 n.18
Franklin, Benjamin (1706–1790), statesman   2, 132
Frederick II (1712–1786), king of Prussia   3–5, 17, 38, 42, 78, 177–8
  about Catherine II   35, 97, 251 n.5
  Polish partition   124–5
  porcelain gift   76–8, 133, 137
  printed portraits and cartoons   45, 47, 83, 121–3
Frederick William II (1744–1797) king of Prussia   128
French political cartoons, *see* political cartoons, French
French Revolution   11, 13, 70, 84–8, 104, 120, 152–64, 189, 199, 203, *see also* French political cartoons
Frensdorff, F.   245 n.7
Freudengesang der Judenschaft zu Sclow   243 n.74
Freundschaftliche Briefe über den gegenwärtigen Zustand des Russischen Reichs   181, 250 n.66

Gabler, Neal   216 n.38
Gabrielli, Caterina (1730–1796), singer   110, 235 n.34
Gaisbauer, Herbert   238 n.26
Galloway, George (1755), poet   167–8
Gamman, Lorraine   225 n.43
Gamson, Joshua   21, 215 n.18, 216 n.26
Garber, Marjorie   131
Gatterer, Helena (1754–1805), governess   64–5, 67–8, 224 n.22
gaze   74, 81, 155
Geisler, Adam Friedrich (1757–c.1800), writer, occasional pseud. Heinrich Friedrich Andrä   171, 226 n.57

Gelbart, Nina Rattner   229 n.3
Gelderblom, Oscar   235
gender   9-13, 17, 22, 37, 97, 106-7, 112,
    see also women
  and celebrity   80
  and power   106-7, 113, 116-17,
    156-9, 167, 176
  and rule   22, 178
  and sexuality   71-2, 154-5, 159
  in state portraiture   118-19, 127
  transgressions of (*see under* political
    cartoons)
  war fighting and   130-1
Gentleman's Magazine   29, 38, 220 n.51
Geoffrin, Marie Thérèse Rodet (1699-
    1777), correspondent   94-5,
    229 n.8, 230 n.16
George Ludwig (1719-1763), Prince of
    Holstein-Gottorp   25, 32, 38
George III (1738-1820), king of
    England   102, 154, 161
Gericke, Johann Ernst (active 1744-69)
    engraver   221 n.10
German political cartoons, *see* political
    cartoons, German
*Gespräch im Reiche derer
    Todten*   220 n.43
Gessner, Solomon (1730-1788),
    poet   113
gifts and gift giving   49, 76-7, 95, 106,
    113-15, 137, 186, 187, 189,
    196-7
  and dedications   114-15, 208
Giles, David   213 n.3
Gilray, James (1756-1815), political
    cartoonist   158, 181
  *Amsterdam in a Dam'd
    Predicament*   158
glamour   105, 107-9, 115
Gleim, Johann Wilhelm Ludwig 1719-
    1803), poet   105, 233 n.3
gloire   3-5, 8-9, 63, 74-6, 88, 94,
    104-15, 124, 144, 205, 207-8,
    226 n.1
  as legitimizing strategy   74-5, 104,
    208
Godineau (active 1790s-1800s),
    dramatist   184
Goebel, Jean (active 1790s), writer   183

Goethe, Johann Wolfgang von (1749-
    1832), poet   56, 71, 126-7
Goodman, Dena   234 n.24
Gorbatov, Inna   236 n.53
Gordon, George (1751-1793),
    politician   188
Goudar, Ange (1720-1791), writer   38,
    218 n.12, 220 nn.45, 47-8
Grab, Walter   252 n.27
Grasselli, Margaret Morgan   222 n.31
Greece   120, 143
Green, Abigail   226 n.2
Greilich, Susanne   225 n.25
Griffiths, David M.   243 n.76
Grigorieva, Irina   235 n.49
Grimm, Friedrich Melchior (1723-
    18807), journalist   223 n.37,
    232 n.72
Grogg, Goody, invented lower-class
    fan   61, 219 n.17
Gross, Johann Gottfried (1703-1768),
    editor of *Allgemeine
    Zeitgeschichte in einem
    Auszuge der neuesten
    Weltgeschichte*   18-19, 25-7, 39
Grosskurth, Brian   236 n.56
Gundle, Stephen   234 n.15
Gustav III (1746-1792), king of
    Sweden   170, 248 n.11

Habermas, Jürgen   60, 75, 226 n.1
Haigold, *see* Schlözer
Halem, Gerhard Anton von (1752-1819),
    poet   238 n.19
Hamilton, Emma (1765-1815), famous
    beauty   112
Hatchett, John, London coach maker   59,
    223 n.40-3
Hays, Mary (1759-1843), writer   209
Haywood, Ian   239 n.37, 245 n.9
Hebenstreit, Franz (1747-1795)   169,
    247 n.1
Heier, Edmund   236 n.63
Heinzmann, Johann Georg (1757-1802),
    bookseller   221 n.11
Heipcke, Corinna   219 n.20
Helbig, Gustav Adolf Wilhelm (1757-
    1813), historian   173-5, 182,
    188, 191, 194-6, 205

Herder, Johann Gottfried (1744–1803), philosopher 63, 101
Hill, Ruth 234 n.78
Hinkender Bott, see Verbesserter
Hippel, Theodor Gottlieb von (1741–1796), writer 97, 103
Historical-Genealogical Calendar, see Historisch-genealogischer
Historisches Portefeuille 236 n.59
Historisch-genealogischer Calender auf das Gemein-Jahr 1798 1, 7–12
Hoffmann, Peter 241 nn.17, 26, 242 n.42
Holland (William) printshop 153
Homans, Margaret 220 n.42
Hoogenbaum, Hilde 220 n.49
Hordt, Johann Ludwig (1719–1798), autobiographer 170–1, 174, 177
Hörschelmann, Friedrich Ludwig Anton 36, 219 n.32, 220 n.41
Hörschelmann, Friedrich Ludwig Anton (1740–1792 or later), biographer 36
Horton, Donald 225 n.27
Houel, Jean (1735–1813), painter 111
Hubertusburg Treaty (1763) 46–7
Hunt, Lynn 168, 238 n.21, 247 n.45

Ibneyeva, Guzel 240 n.14
Icon, as post-celebrity fame 5, 13, 211
identification, *see under* celebrity, effects; fans
Imbert, Guillaume (1744–1803), writer 239 n.40
An Imperial Stride!/L'Enjambée Imperiale (probably by Rowlandson) 86, 152–6, 159–60, 162–4, 167, 245 n.12–16
individualism, *see under* celebrity
inoculation against smallpox 95, 98–9
intimacy 63, 69, 106, 189–90, 194, 197
  "intimacy at a distance" (Horton) 66, 102
  "public intimacy" (Roach) 30, 61
Ivan VI (1740–1764), tsar of Russia as infant, often called John in English news accounts 25, 40, 117–18, 128, 184, 206

Jahrmargt, K. (active 1760's), engraver 221 n.8
Jews 100–1, 106, 132, 141–3
Johannson, Sofia 216 n.40
Johnson, Samuel (1709–1784), writer, lexicographer 130–1
Jones, E. D. 186, 213 n.9, 251 n.1
Joseph II (1741–1790), Habsburg ruler and Holy Roman Emperor 75, 107, 110, 128, 143–5, 147–8, 196
  in cartoons and prints with Catherine II 122–3, 127–8, 130, 148, 158

Kahn, Andrew 223 n.4, 230 n.16
Kalmyk exodus from Russian empire 11, 137–8
Kamen, Henry 223 n.1
Karsch, Anna Luise (1722–1791), poet 17, 36, 40, 70, 77–8, 220 n.59, 233 n.3
Katharine II. vor dem Richterstuhle der Menschheit 249 n.46, 251 n.10, 254 n.11
Kaufmann, Angelika (1741–1807), painter 111
Kazan, Russia 135–6
Kepler, Johannes (1571–1630), astronomer 100
Kéralio, Louise de (1758–1821), writer 120, 156
Kerstens, Johann Christian (1713–1802), professor 224 n.10
Khodarkovsky, Michael 241 n.23
Klassik Stiftung Weimar 222 n.32
knout 135
Koeninger, Frieda 221 n.6
Koningsbrugge, Hans van 228 n.35
Kosareva, Nina 235 n.31
Kosciuszko, Tadeuz (1746–1817), Polish hero 152, 202
Kotzebue, August Friedrich Ferdinand von (1761–1819), playwright 233 n.78
Kraft, Andries (1810), playwright 183–4
Krieken, Robert van 89, 215 nn.17, 18, 226 n.56, 229 n.1
Krüger, I.C. or Krüger, Christian Joseph (1759–1814), medal maker 113

Kyrgyz   10, 135, 147, 151

Lammel, Gisold   222 n.20
Landes, Joan B.   227 n.25
language choice and audience   44
Lannoy, Juliana Cornelia de (1738–1782), poet   114
Lanskoy, Alexander (1758–1784), lover of Catherine II   187–8, 190, 192, 206–7, 251 n.9
Lante, Josef/Giuseppe (b. 1726), printmaker   237 n.5
La Roche, Sophie von (1730–1807), writer   102, 114, 236 n.70
Lasting peace to Europe. The Dream of an Cosmopolite   120
Lavater, Johann Kasper (1741–1801), physiognomist   120–1, 156
Laveaux, *see* Thieboult de Laveaux
law code reform, *see under* Enlightenment
LeBeau, Pierre Adrien (1744/48–1817 c.), printmaker   42–4, 50–2, 56
legitimacy of a ruler   39–40, 104, 112, 141
    based on competence or intellectual qualification   24, 95
    based on dynasty   24
    based on gender   38–9, 116
Lemire, Nicolas Noël (1724–1800), engraver   122–3, 238 n.26
Leonard, Carol S.   248 n.22
Le-Trosne, Guillaume Francois (1728–1780), jurist   244 n.3
letters, of contemporaries   2, 18, 25, 30, 35–6, 61, 65, 71, 91, 94, 139–40, 181, 204
Leuthner, Ferdinand, Vienna shopkeeper   57–8, 108
Levitt, Marcus   240 n.13, 253 n.56, 255 n.37
Liackhova, Lydia   227 n.8
libertinism   12, 158–68, 188–9, 195, 197–8, 210
Lichtenberg, Georg Christoph (1742–1799), physicist and satirist   233 n.75
Liemann, Amalie von, child writer   64–5
Lilti, Antoine   2–3, 5, 21, 28, 69, 213 n.5, 216 n.26, 217 n.2, 221 n.1, 223 n.39, 226 n.1

limping messenger, Hinkender Bote, Messager boiteux   65-5, 248 n.15, *see also* Alter und Neuer; Verbesserter
Lind, John (1737–1781), pamphleteer   124–5, 238 n.28, *see also* Pansmouzer; *Polish Partition*
Lindsey, Theophilus (1723–1808), theologian   238 n.28
Linguet, Simon-Nicholas Henri (1736–1794)   238 n.17
literacy, illiteracy, and reading practices   7, 34, 42, 61, 63, 65, 72, 76, 91
Livia   35, 40, 70
Lob-und Danklied der Judengemeine zu Mohilow   143
Longworth, Philip   241 n.25
Lortholary, Albert   230 n.20, 230 n.62
Löschenkohl, Johann Hieronymus (1753–1807), artist and art dealer   144–5
Louis XIV (1638–1715), king of France   3, 104
Louis XV (1710–1774), king of France   61, 98
Louis XVI (1754–1793), king of France   5, 101, 157, 162
love, concept changing   189, 198
lovers and favorites   13, 71–2, 144, 252 nn.20, 22, *see also* Lanskoy; libertinism; Mamonov; Orlov; Poniatowski; Potemkin; Saltykov
    costs   71, 189, 192, 197–8
    trajectories   190, 192, 194
Low Countries   63, 127, 158–9, 208, 223 n.1, 246 n.25
Luhmann, Niklas   189, 198
Lull, James   217 n.1
luxury   41, 61, 73, 104–11, 115, 143, 223 n.2
    meaning changing   108–9

McKeon, Michael   249 n.25
McPherson, Heather   2, 189, 213 n.5
Madame de ***, *see under* Sénac de Meilhan

Madariaga Isabel de   245 n.4, 246 n.40, 252 n.23
Mallet du Pan, Jacques (1749–1800), journalist   170, 248 n.11
Mamonov, Alexander Dmitriev- (1758–1803), lover of Catherine II   144
manifestos of Catherine   21, 92, 116, 122, 141–2
  explaining first Polish Partition   122
  first, about coup   21
  inviting colonists to Russia   100
  Pugachev rebellion   137, 139
  related to Jews   141–2
  second, about coup and abdication   21–4, 35, 37
  third, about death of Peter III   27–30
Mansfeld, Johann Ernst (1738–96), engraver   223 n.38
Marcard, Heinrich Matthias (1747–1817)   254 n.15
Marche, C. F. S. de la, pseud. of Christian Friedrich Schwan (1733–1815), publisher   240 n.12, see also Anecdotes russes; Russische Anekdoten
Maréchal, Sylvain (1750–1803), playwright   245 n.17
Maria Theresa (1717–1780), ruler of Habsburg domains   3–5, 18, 24, 37, 42, 116, 124–5
  as mother   116–17, 187
  political cartoons   83–4, 122, 158–9
  portraits   47, 216 n.35
  rival to Catherine II   106
  as widow   187
Marie Antoinette (1755–1793), queen of France   5, 155, 162, 188, 255 n.35
market crier or singer   31, 34
Maron, Theresia Concordia née Mengs (1725–1806), painter   111
Marshall, Joseph (active 1760's–1770), writer   135
Marshall, P. David   21, 69, 214 nn.13, 21, 215 n.17, 216 nn.26, 35, 218 n.16, 222 n.19, 225 n.41, 234 n.27, 239 n.30, 247 n.47

Mary Stuart (1542–1587), queen of Scots   36, 40, 70
masculinity, see under Catherine II; Peter III
Massie, Robert K.   238 n.15
Masson, Charles François Philibert, (1761–1807) writer   68–9, 78–9, 85, 87, 120, 188, 195, 207, 247 n.44
Mayer, Johann Georg, writer   75, 110, 142
Maza, Sarah   238 n.21, 246 n.20, 254 n.10
medals and coins issued by Catherine II   92–3, 96
  engravings of   53, 93, 96, 112–13
  as gifts   96, 113, 115
  inexpensive casts of   56, 112
media and mediation   2–3, 19, 36, 41–59, 89, 169, 192
  distributors   3, 6, 19, 23, 34, 42, 49, 56–7, 152, 203 (see also market crier)
  large-scale/mass   1, 6, 17–19, 58, 63, 72
  workers   1, 3, 7–8, 19, 30, 41–59, 74, 84, 112, 122, 145, 152 (see also artists; writers)
    outside Russia   7, 72, 75
"Mein lieber Peter, gute Nacht!"   29–34, 218 n.8
Mejer, Luise (married Boie, 1746–1786), letter writer   128–9, 190, 192, 240 n.42
Melot, Michel   222 n.28
Mercier, Louis-Sébastien (1740–1814), writer   97
Mercure historique et politique   217 n.43
Mercurio Histórico y Político   35, 138, 143, 219 n.28
Merkel, Angela (1954-), German chancellor   211
Merkwürdige Lebensgeschichte Peter des Dritten, 1762   218 n.12
Merziger, Patrick   214 n.18
Mexico   42
Meyer, Johann Heinrich Christian (active 1778–1779), writer   235 n.30
Meys, Ferdinand de (active 1790–1805)   244 n.89

Michler, Marwart 251 n.9
Miller, Nancy K. 180
Minerva (magazine) 248 n.20
Minor, Vernon Hyde 222 n.20
modern international female
　　celebrity 1–3, 5, 13, 15, 17, 40,
　　42, 54, 56, 73, 75, 94, 208, *see
　　also* women celebrities
Mogilev/Mohilow, present-day
　　Belarus 75, 110, 143
Moi, Toril 6
Momonov, *see* Mamonov
Monroe, Marilyn (1926–1962), film
　　star 211
"monstrous-feminine" (Creed) 12, 156,
　　164–8, 203
Montefiore, Sebag 238 n.15, 252 n.29
Montesquieu, Charles-Louis de Secondat,
　　Baron de (1689–1755),
　　philosopher 135
Monthly Review 102, 135, 195
Montluzin, Emily Lorraine de 220 n.50
Moreau, Jean-Michel (1741–1814),
　　artist 122–3
Morgan, Simon 215 nn.18, 19
Moser, Friedrich Carl (1723–1798),
　　jurist 234 n.16, 235 n.35,
　　236 n.62
Mosley, Charles (1744–1770 c.),
　　engraver 48–9, 51, 56, 69,
　　221 n.17
motherhood, *see under* Catherine II
Müller, Johann Jacob (1743),
　　engraver 225 n.28
Müller, Karl Ernst Christian (1813),
　　writer 114–15
Munchausen Tales 186
Münnich, Burkhard Christoph (1683–1767),
　　field marshall 27, 37–8, 176
Munro, George E. 234 n.13
"My dear Peter, good night!", *see* "Mein
　　lieber Peter, gute Nacht"

Nadir/Nader Shah (1688–1747), shah of
　　Iran 105
Napoleon Bonaparte (1769–1821) 5, 70,
　　188, 210
narrative 12, 22–4, 50, 80, 170, 174, 176,
　　190

anecdote 171
dialogue 176
larger forms 169–70, 186 (*see also*
　　secret history)
scene 175
narrator 22–3, 174–6, 183
Netherlands, *see* Low Countries
Das neueste graue Ungeheuer 134
news 1, 4, 20, 24–5, 60, 72, 89, 95,
　　223 n.5
geographical dissemination 18
spread of 20, 31, 36, 38
newspapers 1–2, 5, 17–19, 21–3, 26–30,
　　35, 48, 56–7, 59–60, 63, 72, 76,
　　91, 94, 98, 101–2, 114, 136–40,
　　143, 151, 214 n.3, *see also
　　newspapers by country below*
and celebrity 63–6
geographical reach 18–19, 63–4
non-elite readers and auditors 63–5,
　　72
newspapers, American 18
Providence Gazette 215 n.8, 218 n.11
newspapers, British 224 n.18
Evening Mail 254 n.4
Gazetteer and … Daily Advertiser
　　20, 26, 140, 215 nn.6, 20,
　　217 n.50
General Evening Post (London) 101
*Lloyd's Evening Post and British
　　Chronicle* 215 n.6, 215 n.12,
　　217 n.43, 217 n.47
London Chronicle 30, 38, 39,
　　217 nn.44, 47, 219 n.25,
　　220 n.56
London Evening Post 25, 217 n.41
The London Magazine 117
Morning Chronicle 222 n.35
Morning Herald 213 n.7, 222–3 n.35
Northampton Mercury 18,
　　37, 215 n.21, 216 n.31,
　　217 n.3, 218 n.10, 219 nn.23, 29,
　　220 nn.38, 57
Oracle and Public Advertiser 199
Public Advertiser 114, 217 nn.43, 49
St. James's Chronicle (London) 26–7
*The World and Fashionable
　　Advertiser* 111, 160
newspapers, French

Affiches, annonces et Avis Divers ou Journal Général de France 222 n.29
Courier de l'Europe 110
Courrier d'Avignon 25
Gazette de France 18, 26, 28, 136
Gazette des gazettes ou Journal politique 230 n.20
Gazette littéraire de l'Europe 236 n.67
Gazette Nationale ou le Moniteur Universel 199
newspapers, German
  Allgemeine Zeitgeschichte in einem Auszuge aller europäischen Zeitungen 18–19, 215 n.13, 216 n.39, 217 nn.45, 52 (*see also* Gross)
  Langensaalzisches Wochen-Blat 254 n.1
  Staats- und Gelehrte Zeitung des Hamburgischen unpartheyischen Correspondenten 27, 217 n.43
  Weimarische wöchentliche Anzeigen 215 n.9, 217 n.42
newspapers, Italian
  Gazzetta Bolognesi 215 n.10, 217 n.51
  Gazzetta Universale, Florence 96, 137
  Italian Mercury 111
  Notizie del Mondo, Florence 105
newspapers, Low Countries
  Gazette de la Haye 217 n.43
  Gazette van Gendt 215 n.6, 216 n.23, 217 n.43
  Nouvelles Extraordinaires de Divers Endroits [Gazette de Leyde] 20, 216 n.23
newspapers, Spanish
  Gaceta de Madrid 18, 215 n.7
Newton, Richard (1777–1798), artist 153
Nicolay, Ludwig Heinrich (1737–1820), official 235 n.52, 236 n.63
Nilson, Johannes Esaias (1721–1788), printmaker 123
Nini, Giovanni Battista (1717–1786), artist 49
Noorde, Cornelis van (1731–1795), printmaker 82

Novelli, Pietro Antonio (1729–1804), engraver 209
Nussbaum, Felicity 218 n.6

Observations on the present state of Denmark, Russia and Switzerland 231 n.50
Ochakov battle 129
Oranienbaum, palace 23, 26, 33, 177, 194
Orlov, Alexei Grigoryevich (1737–1808) 205
Orlov, Grigory (1734–1783) 36, 71, 83, 188, 190, 194–5, 220 n.37
  colonists and 151
  diamond gift 106
  fall from favor 71, 190
  rumor of marrying Catherine II 117
Orme, Edward (1775–1848), engraver 225 n.28
other, otherness 132, 134
  stigma and 141
Ottoman Empire 11, 75–8
  Russian wars with 84, 104, 120, 143, 147, 152, 154, 164

Paesiello, Giovanni (1740–1816), composer 110
Pallas, Peter Simon (1741–1811), explorer 105
Panin, Nikita Ivanovich (1718–1783), statesman 21, 206, 220 n.37
Pansalvin, Prince of Darkness (Albrecht) 191, 195
Pansmouzer, Gotlieb pseud., *see* Lind
parasocial relationship, celebrity as 2–3, 72, 91, 102, 162
patronage, *see under* Catherine II; Enlightenment
Paul der Erste, Kayser von Russland 256 n.28
Paul der Erste Kaiser und Selbstherrscher aller Reußen 256 n.28
Paul I (1754–1801), tsar of Russia 5, 18–19, 30, 83, 87, 99, 111, 117, 171, 173, 192, 197, 199–200, 202, 206–7
  absence from Catherine's portraits 117

depicted in *Staub der Erste* by
    Albrecht   117
first wife   202, 206
paternity of Peter III equivocated   33,
    36, 174, 180, 183, 220 n.49
and Pugachev   139–40
Pauquet, Jean Louis Charles (1759–1824),
    engraver   93
peddlers   1, 56, 202
Pellet-Desbarreaux, Hyacinthe (1756)
    playwright   245 n.17
Du péril de la balance politique de l'Europe,
    see *Danger*
Peru   18
Peter I, the Great (1672–1725)   9–10,
    20, 22, 32–3, 112, 132, 142, 171,
    176, *see also* statue
Peter II (1715–1730), tsar of Russia   98
Peter III (1728–1762), tsar of Russia   1,
    6–7, 12, 22, 115, 118–19, 128,
    178–85
    abdication   24, 181
    during coup   23–7, 33–4
    death   26–30, 91, 116, 162, 169, 175,
        181–5, 202, 206, 218 n.12
    demasculinization of   26, 29–30, 35,
        37–9, 177–80
    denies Paul's legitimacy   36, 219 n.31
        (*see also* Paul I)
    drunkenness   32, 181
    dysfunctional marriage   30–6, 169,
        177–80
    as grand duke   20, 68, 194
    hemorrhoidal colic   29, 181
    impersonated by Pugachev   137–9,
        141, 148
    infertility treatment   171, 174,
        180
    lack of military skill   26, 178
    lack of valor at Cronstadt   26
    mistress (*see* Vorontsova)
    planning to reject Catherine   23
    posthumous rehabilitation   200 (*see
        also* Hordt; Saldern)
    sexuality   38, 171, 180
    wearing Prussian uniform   178
Peterhof palace   26, 176, 216 n.34
Peters, Birgit   214 n.11
Pettegree, Andrew   224 n.16

Peyssonnel, Claude Charles de (1727–
    1790)   248 n.11
Pictet, François-Pierre (1728–1798),
    secretary to Catherine
    II   216 n.25
Piozzi, Hester Thrale (1740–1821),
    diarist   197–8
Pitt, William, the Younger (1759–1806),
    prime minister of Great
    Britain   83, 160
plays about Catherine II   42, 155,
    183–4, 186, 204, 221 n.5, *see
    also* Comella; Godineau; Kraft;
    Maréchal; Pellet-Desbarreaux
Pointon, Marcia   106, 233 n.6, 234 n.11
Poland   11–12, 152, 202, 213 n.1,
    214 n.22
    partitions of   101, 137, 142, 152,
        166–8
*The Polish Partition, Illustrated in Seven
    Dramatic Dialogues* ([Lind]/
    Pansmouzer)   123–5, *see also*
    Lind
political cartooning   12, 70, 83–4, 92,
    118, 121–3, 130, 155, 188
    England's Golden Age of   70, 162
political cartoons   12, 245 n.8, *see also*
    political cartoons by country/
    language *below*
    multiple renditions of   155–6, 158,
        160, 162–3, 239 n.36
        mirror-image copies   153–4, 158,
            162–3
    versions in different
        languages   122, 153, 246 n.35
    topoi
        cross-dressing   128–31, 156, 203
            (*see also under* Catherine II)
        defecation   163–4
        farting   163, 165
        femininity transgressed   128–30,
            156–7
        fighting   128–31
        illicit sexual behavior   157–62
        playing games   86
political cartoons, British, *see also*
    Cruikshank; Dent; Gilray
    *An Amusing State of
        Uncertainty*   159–60, 246 n.27

Christian Amazon 130–1, 156–8
Imperial Salute, or invitation to Peace Rejected 162
An Imperial Stride (see *An Imperial Stride!*)
The Ladies Church Yard 158
Merlin: or, A Picture of Europe for 1773 127, 164
The Northen Bugga Bo 164–6
The Prussian Prizefighter 156
Saint Catherine and St. George 161
Summer Amusement at Farmer G-'s 83, 228 n.32
political cartoons, French, *see also* Berthault; Lemire
Bombardement de tous les trônes de l'Europe 163
Congres Politique 122
Jeu de quilles républicain 86–7, 164
La Mascarade 157–8
L'Enjambeé Impériale (see *An imperial Stride!*)
political cartoons, German, *see also* Will
Kriegs Theater 128–9, 156–7, 240 n. 43
Politische Spazierfahrt 128, 239 n.40
political cartoons, Low Countries 50, 127, 158–9, 239 n.36
political cartoons, Polish
Catherine's Mealtime 167–8
Poniatowski, Stanislaw II August (1732–1798) king of Poland 122–3, 144, 146, 162, 187, 194, 253 n.39
Popkin, Jeremy D. 224 nn.17, 20
pornography 152, 158–9, 167–8, 188, 204, 210
portraits, *see also* printed portraits; *individual artists*
celebrity discourse's impact on 49, 53–5
gender in 83, 118–19
state portraits of rulers 76, 83, 118–19, 127
drapes and 48, 51, 55, 68
insignia in 44, 46, 51–5, 58, 76, 86
monarchical gifts 76, 108
subgenres xv, 49–50 (*see also under* printed portraits)
frontal 43–4, 46, 49, 58, 65, 82, 108, 119, 179
full-length 48–9, 53, 62, 77
profile 49–50, 54, 67, 85, 93, 113, 121, 172 (*see also* profile-in-braids)
scene with a group 7–12, 32, 47, 49, 126, 133, 145, 148, 193, 209
types, explained 45
positional goods 10, 110–1
Potemkin, Grigory (1739–1791) 13, 42, 64–5, 71, 143–7, 161, 165, 173, 181, 188, 195–6, 206, 252 nn.20, 22
lavish party 12–13, 106
"Potemkin villages" 13, 205
rise to power 71, 190, 193
secret marriage to Catherine 118, 191
Praga (near Warsaw, Poland)
massacre 11, 166–7, 202, 207, 246 n.40
printed portraits, intaglio and relief
backgrounds 51, 86, 118
captions 31–2, 43, 53, 55, 68
language of 44, 46, 51
cheap 222 n.24
on cloth 47
color 51, 53–4, 126–7, 222 n.31
distribution 56, 107
fashion plates 48, 53, 77
frames, printed 51–3
genres
blends 49, 51
cartooning, political (*see* political cartooning)
invented images (non-satirical) 49, 62, 68
narrative prints
portraits (*see* portraits)
puzzles 66–7, 225 n.28
series 53, 222 n.24
intaglio 43
by language/country
British, of Catherine II 48, 113, 121, 172, 213 n.2 (*see also* Mosley, Warren, Watson)
Dutch, of Catherine II (*see* Noorde)

French, of Catherine II   46, 53, 93, 133 (*see also* Avril; Fosseyeux; LeBeau; Pauquet; Radigues; Saint-Aubin; de Tiregale)
German, of Catherine II   54–55, 58, 62, 110, 126, 128, 148, 222 n.27, 239 n., 40, (*see also* Bause; Berger; Bernigeroth; Chodowiecki; Facius; Gericke; Krüger; Löschenkohl; Rein; Rügendas; Will)
Italian (*see* Lante; Novelli)
Spanish, of Catherine II   51–2
mirror image (reversed)   45, 154
paper choice   49, 51, 53–5
pricing   49, 53, 56
relief, woodcuts   43
reworked old plates   61, 127, 224 n.8
series   53–54, 222 n.24
signs of intended audience   42, 45, 49, 54–6
size   1, 31, 48–51, 53–5, 68, 76, 85, 208–9
skill markers   34, 45
speed of production   51, 56–7
printmakers, *see* artists
Le Procès des trois Rois   251 n.7
profile-in-braids   45–6, 51–2, 55, 77–8
public, *see* audience
publicity about Catherine II   57, 94, 96, 98, 110–1, 113, 115, 137, 141, 144, 186–8, *see also under* celebrity, cultural *and under* courts
Pugachev, Yemelyan (1742–1775), rebellion leader   136–7, 139, 204, *see also* Pugachev rebellion
execution   140, 243 n.66
Pugachev rebellion   11, 136–41, 147
alleged foreign involvement   134–40, 242 n.60
geography of   137–8
Purdy, Daniel L.   223 n.3, 234 n.28

Radigue, Antoine (1721–1809), engraver   46
Raspe, Rudolf Erich (1736–1794), writer   251 n.2

Raynal, Guillaume Thomas, Abbé (1713–1796), *philosophe*   100
Razzall, Rosie   224 n.8
reading   3, 64–6, *see also* literacy
rebellion, *see* Pugachev rebellion
Recke, Elise von der (1754–1833), writer   102
Rehberg, Peter   213 n.11
Rein, Joseph Friedrich (1720–1785), engraver   221 n.14
religion   21, 35, 37, 47, 64, 75, 82, 101, 122, 126–7, 130–1, 136, 141–2, 147, 168, 189, 203
Renne, Elizaveta   216 n.34, 234 n.21
representations and celebrity   2, 6–7, 19, 62–3, 72, 75
Reynolds, Joshua (1723–1792), painter   111
Richardson, Samuel (1789–1761), novelist   61
Richardson, William (1743–1814), travel writer   141
Roach, Joseph R.   30, 39, 167, 218 n.15, 224 n.9
Rogerson, John (1741–1823), Catherine's doctor   200
Rojek, Chris   3, 69, 239
Röllig, Johann Georg (1710–1790), composer   251 n.1
Roman, Jean-Joseph-Thérèse (1726–1787), poet   99
Roslin, Alexander (1718–1793), painter   107–8
Rotari, Pietro (1707–1762), painter   44–6, 221 nn.9, 12
Rovinskiĭ, Dmitriĭ Aleksandrovich (1824–1895), art historian   245 n.13
Rowlandson, Thomas (1756–1827), artist   153
Rubin-Detlev, Kelsey   223 n.4, 226, n.3, 230 n.16, 232 n.65
Rügendas, Johann Lorenz (1730–1799), engraver   61, 232 n.65, 224 n.8
Rulhière, Claude-Carloman de (1735–1791), historian   80, 94–5, 172–4, 178–80, 187, 194–7, 201, 248 n.15, 253 n.36

Russische Anekdoten 219 n.34, 220 n.35, 240 n.12, *see also* Marche (pseud.)

Sade, Donatien Alphonse François, Marquis de (1740–1814), writer 12, 188, 197
Saint-Aubin, Augustin de (1736–1807), printmaker 85–6
Saldern, Caspar von (1711–1786), diplomat and writer 102, 172, 182, 184, 188, 194–5, 206, 248 n.16
Saltykov, Sergei (1726–1765), Catherine's first lover 180, 194
satires
    textual 30, 38, 75, 103, 121–5, 139, 187
    visual (*see* political cartooning)
Savill, Rosalind 234 n.22
scandal 6, 30, 33, 173, 180–1, 193–4
    definition 28
Schenda, Rudolf 219 n.19
Schérer, Jean-Benoît (1741–1824) writer 249 n.38
Schiebinger, L. 229 n.11
Schlözer, August Ludwig von (1735–1809), writer 96, 216 n.28
Schmidt, Benjamin ii, 51, 134, 240
Schmidt-Phiseldek, Christoph von (1740–1801), writer 234, 238, 243 n.69, 244 n.2
Schneider, Michael 235 n.40
Schubart, Christian Friedrich Daniel (1739–1791), journalist 97, 140, 254 n.12
Schwan, *see* Marche (pseud.)
Sečenov, D.A. (active 1757–1767) archbishop of Novgorod 217 n.46
secret history genre 173–4, 192, 203
Ségur, Louis-Philippe, comte de (1753–1830), diplomat and historian 205
Sekora, John 234 n.24
Semiramis 79
Sénac de Meilhan, Gabriel (1736–1803), writer 61, 66–7, 69–73, 79, 81, 106, 133, 223 n.4

description of a fan, Madame de *** 61–2, 66, 152
serfs and serfdom 97, 135, 138, 151, 204, 245 n.4
Settlers for colonizing Russia 100, 151
Seume, Johann Gottfried (1763–1810), biographer 171, 189
Seven Years' War 17, 46–7, 70, 120, 170, 178
Sevres 108
sexuality 124, *see also under* Catherine II; celebrity discourse; gender
Seymour, George (active 1763) 229 n.9
Shakespeare 156
Sharpe, Kevin 243 n.85
Siberia 33, 40, 99, 176, 196
Sievers, Elisabeth von (later Putyatin, 1746–1818), letter writer 71
Sinclair, John (1754–1835), writer 181
A Sketch of the secret history of Europe 236 n.73, 253 n.38
Smith, Adam (1723–1790), economist 111
Smith, Douglas 252 n.20
Smolny Institute 8, 204
Souffras, seller of Orlov diamond 105–6
Spacks, Patricia 79
"spectatorial pleasure" (Marshall, 12) 3, 12, 50, 168, 204–5
spectators 28, 75, 79, 144, 208
Der Spiegel 211
S. Privatleben des ... Potemkin 252 n.13
star and stars 8, 19, 74–88
    agent of publicity 74
    death 5, 211
    object of the gaze 74
    self-display 19, 23, 88
    simultaneously fabulous and ordinary 170, 190
    visibility 8, 19
statue of Peter the Great 9, 112–13, 153–4, *see also* Carburi; Collot; Falconet
    engravings 9, 112–13, 154
    stone chip souvenirs 112
Staub der Erste (Albrecht) 117, 197
Sternberg, Joachim von (1755–1808), travel writer 79, 84–5
Stollberg-Rilinger, Barbara 214 n.19

Storch, Heinrich Friedrich (1766–1835)   248 n.13
story, as component of celebrity, *see under* celebrity discourse
Stöver, Dietrich Heinrich (1767–1822), writer   243 n.66
Strenge, A.C. (active 1792), preacher   245 n.6
Stride, see Imperial Stride!
Strunck Christina   216 n.35, 237 n.4
Stummann-Bowert, Ruth   225 n.34
Sultans, Ottoman Empire   122, 126–8, 130–1, 154, 158, 165
Sutton, D.   235 n.52
Sweden   37, 98, 161, 167–8, 170, 213 n.1, 214 n.22, *see also* Gustav III
Szabo, Franz   214 n.1, 215 n.4

Tartar, Tatar   136, 138, 147
taste   107, 109
Teplov, Grigory Nikolayevich (1717–1779), philosopher   21, 181–2
termagant   162
Théâtre de l'Hermitage (Catherine II et al.)   232 n.67
Therbusch, Anna Dorothea née Liszewska (1721–1782), painter   111–12
Thesby (or Thisbé) de Belcour, François Alphonse (1793 or later)   242 n.60
Thieboult de Laveaux, Jean Charles (1749–1827), writer   173, 181, 188, 193, 197, 206
Thiele, Johan Rudolph (1736–1815), printer   126
Thompson, John B.   225 n.32
Thomson, William (1746–1817), writer   236 n.61
Tickell, Thomas (1685–1740), poet   241 n.28
Tillyard, Stella   215 n.22
Tipton, Susan   216 n.34
de Tiregale, Pierre Ricaud (c. 1725– after 1772), architect and printmaker   230 n.21
Tischbein, Johann Heinrich Wilhelm (1751–1829), painter   112
Tomanskiy, Theodor Josephides von (1746–1810)   234 n.18

Tooke, William (1744–1820), writer   171–2, 188, 194
Torelli, Stefano (1712–1784), painter   76
Truthful News, see Wahrhaffte
Turkey, *see* Ottoman Empire
Turner, Graeme   57, 66, 222 n.34, 225 n.45
Turner, Richard (1753–1788), writer   181

ukase, *see* manifesto
Ulbricht, Otto   230 n.24
Ulrika, queen of Sweden (1720–1782)   98
L'ultima Confession Generale Fatta da Catterina   2
Unzer, Johanna Charlotte (1725–1782), poet   94, 225 n.50

Vasilchikov, Alexander (1744–1813), lover of Catherine II   190
Vassallo, Peter   253 n.53
Verbesserter und Alter Vollkommener Staats-Calender, genannt der Hinkende Bott   200, 248 n.15, 254 n.8
verse and doggerel, anonymous, *see also* "Mein Lieber Peter"
   in newspapers and magazines   20, 29, 160
   on prints   31–2, 127–8, 130
Victoria (1819–1901), queen of Great Britain   211, 220 n.42
Vigée le Brun, Elizabeth Louise   235 n.52
Vincentelli, Moira   235 n.45
Vinogradov, Yefim Grigoryevich (1725/28–1769) engraver   221 n.8
virago   130–1, 156
visual satires, *see* political cartoons
Vita, e Fasti   208
Volney, Constantin François de (1757–1820), writer   115
Voltaire François-Marie Arouet (1694–1778), writer   97, 99, 115, 120, 126, 132, 135, 157, 181
   Catherine II's purchase of his library   115

his publicity for Catherine   115
published correspondence with
    Catherine   179, 238 n.28
Vorontsova, Elizaveta (1739–1792),
    mistress of Peter III   37–8,
    176–7, 184, 194, 248 n.33
Vorstellung der vom Tod (engraving)   200,
    213 n.2
Vorstellung und Abbildung
    (engraving)   126, 213 n.2
voyeurism   38, 70, 162, 169, 210, *see also*
    celebrity discourse

*Wahrhaffte Nachricht von der am 9ten Julii
    1762 in Petersburg vorgefallenen
    Revolution*   36
Walker, James (1760–1823), artist and
    writer   146, 246 n.36
Walpole, Horace (1717–1797), writer   71,
    95
Walpole, Robert (1676–1745), prime
    minister and art collector   111
Warren, Charles Turner (1762–1823),
    engraver   77
wars   126, *see also* Ottoman Empire;
    Seven Years War
    Bavarian War of Succession   120
    Brabant Revolution   158–9
    Russo-Turkish wars against
        Ottomans   10, 104, 126
Watson, Caroline (1761–1814),
    engraver   108
waxworks   109
wealth and celebrity   9–10, 73, 101,
    143
Wedgwood, Josiah (1730–1795),
    entrepreneur   49, 110
    Green Frog service publicity   57
Weikard, Melchior Adam (1742–1803),
    doctor   101, 144, 204–6
Welke, Martin   224 n.19
West, Mae (1893–1980), film star   211
Whittaker, Cynthia Hyla   41, 233 n.8,
    235 nn.42, 46
whore   157–8, 188
Will, F. M. (active 1787–88)
    engraver   147–8
Will, Georg Andreas (1744–1798),
    historian   218 n.12

Will, Johann Martin (1727–1806),
    engraver and publisher   31–2,
    34, 50, 128, 239 n.39
Willamov, [Johann Gottlieb] (1736–1777),
    poet   231 n.49
Williams, John, writer (active 1777)   135
Williams, Kevin   224 n.18
Wippersberg, Julia   214 n.11
Woensel, Pieter van (1747–1808), travel
    writer   97
Wolff, Larry   213 n.1, 240 n.3, 244 n.97,
    253 n.56
Wollf, J. P. (active 1760s), print
    maker   68
women
    celebrities   13, 70–1, 103, 211
        focus on bodies   80
        glamour   107
        and transgressiveness   70–2, 103,
            126
    and Enlightenment   97–8, 102
    rulers   11, 89, 113, 116–31, 139, 161,
        210
        ambition and   23, 124, 184
        androgynous   155–6
        destabilizing gender   37, 120
        Enlightenment as justifying   95
        monstrous-feminine   164–68,
            203
        as peaceable   120, 129
        power-hungry   33, 70
        regency   116–17
        in Russia   39, 118–20
        sexually transgressive   36, 70
        sons   116
        war-making   120, 128–31, 157,
            168
woodcut images   65–6, 126–7, 200–1
Wortman, Richard S.   92, 216 n.24,
    229 n.7
Wraxall, Nathaniel William (1751–1831),
    travel writer   78, 85, 138, 178
Wright, Joseph, of Derby (1734–1797),
    painter   111
Writers, as mediators of celebrity   41–2,
    56, 81
Wyrwa, Ulrich   234 n.24

Yonan, Michael Elia   214 n.19

Zaborov, Petr Romanovic   229 n.8
Zacchiroli, Francesco (1750–1826), poet   231 n.49
Zaretsky, Robert   232 n.58, 233 n.72
Zedler, Johann Heinrich (1706–1751), encyclopedist   63–64
Zimmermann, Johann Georg (1725–1795), doctor   101–3, 151, 204, 233 n.75
Zubov, Platon (1767–1822), Catherine's final lover   188